Basic Concepts of
LabVIEW™ 4

Leonard Sokoloff

DeVry Technical Institute
North Brunswick, New Jersey

Prentice Hall
Upper Saddle River, New Jersey   Columbus, Ohio

Library of Congress Cataloging-in-Publication Data
Sokoloff, Leonard.
    Basic concepts of LabVIEW 4 / Leonard Sokoloff.
        p.   cm.
    Includes index.
    ISBN 0-13-254939-5
    1. Laboratories—Computer programs. 2. LabVIEW. I. Title.
Q183.A1S65 1998
006—DC21   97-20011
                                             CIP

Cover art: Wassily Kandinsky/SuperStock
Editor: Charles E. Stewart, Jr.
Production Editor: Stephen C. Robb
Design Coordinator: Julia Zonneveld Van Hook
Text Designer: Leonard Sokoloff
Cover Designer: Russ Maselli
Production Manager: Laura Messerly
Marketing Manager: Debbie Yarnell

This book was printed and bound by Banta Company. The cover was printed by Phoenix Color Corp.

Printed in the United States of America

10 9 8 7 6 5 4 3 2 1

ISBN: 0-13-254939-5

Prentice-Hall International (UK) Limited, *London*
Prentice-Hall of Australia Pty. Limited, *Sydney*
Prentice-Hall Canada, Inc., *Toronto*
Prentice-Hall Hispanoamericana, S. A., *Mexico*
Simon & Schuster Asia Pte. Ltd., *Singapore*
Prentice-Hall of India Private Limited, *New Delhi*
Prentice-Hall of Japan, Inc., *Tokyo*
Editora Prentice-Hall do Brasil, Ltda., *Rio de Janeiro*

PREFACE

Over the past two decades, the emergence of personal computers as tools for processing data has created challenges and opportunities for software designers. Today, the computer is used routinely to process complex tasks at very high speeds. This trend will undoubtedly continue into the next century, promising faster computers with greater processing capabilities.

High-performance computation and display capabilities offered by the modern personal computer (PC) have dramatically changed the field of instrumentation. Over nearly a century, traditional analog instruments have evolved by borrowing from the emerging technology. For example, when the vacuum but became available, it was used to design an instrument for electronic measurement. Then the transistor became an integral component of instrument design. Similarly, television technology provided the basis for oscilloscope design.

Today, the personal computer finds important applications in the field of instrumentation. A modern instrument uses a general-purpose computer, such as a PC, and a graphical software capability with various interfaces to communicate with and to control the hardware. This type of instrument uses the computer's extensive processing power to offer a very high level of performance.

Virtual instrumentation (VI) is a relatively new term that describes the instrument configured by a user through the application of the graphical programming language. This instrument can be easily reconfigured to meet the requirements of a new specification. The ability to alter the instrument's functionality is an important advantage that was not previously available to the user. (In the past, an instrument's functionality was controlled solely by the instrument's manufacturer.)

Over the years, graphical programming language has gained ground as a programming tool. It has not displaced the C language and other traditional programming languages. On the contrary, these languages are still being used. Graphical programming language offers an environment that is fast and simple to use. In applying this language, the user does not have to remember or write the code. He or she simply manipulates the objects or icons on the computer's screen.

LabVIEW™, a product of National Instruments Corporation, uses the graphical language in creating a VI. A VI is a program that can be used to perform data acquisition, control another instrument, do a simulation, and many other tasks. Because a VI is a software file, it can be modified easily or deleted altogether.

Basic Concepts of LabVIEW™ 4 is a workbook concerned with the fundamental aspects of LabVIEW. Anyone who wants to learn how LabVIEW works will find this book useful. Numerous exercises throughout the book will help the user to understand the important concepts. Although this workbook is based on LabVIEW version 4, Appendixes A, B, and C provide an introduction to version 3 of LabVIEW.

Acknowledgments

The author especially thanks the following at DeVry Technical Institute for their encouragement and support: Amin Karim, Curriculum Manager, Electronics Program, Chicago, Illinois; President Robert Bochino; Richard Ruch, Dean of Academic Affairs; Jim Stewart, Dean of Technology; and Professor Bill Lin, New Brunswick, New Jersey.

The author gratefully acknowledges the insightful suggestions from the following reviewers: A. Kisha, DeVry Technical Institute, Columbus, Ohio; Salomon Oldak, DeVry Technical Institute, Pomona, California; Predrag Pesikan, DeVry Technical Institute, Scarborough, Ontario, Canada; John Slough, DeVry Technical Institute, Dallas, Texas.

Most of all, the author thanks his wife, Helen, and daughter, Larissa, for their patience in the course of the preparation of this book.

Leonard Sokoloff

CONTENTS

Chapter 1

Introduction

Fifty years ago, before the transistor and when the vacuum tube was the *only* amplifying device available, an instrument was designed by a vendor to perform a specific measurement task. The vendor used components available at that time, components such as resistors, capacitors, inductors, and vacuum tubes to design a dedicated instrument. Indeed, the instrument was dedicated to perform one or possibly several specific measurements.

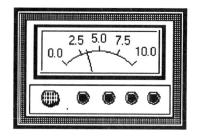

If a meter such as the one shown in this illustration was intended to perform only the DC voltage measurement, the user had to use it for that purpose only and could not modify it in order to accommodate any other specific need. The only alternative he had was to purchase another meter. Needless to say, this meter had no computing or data storage capabilities. The measurement readings had to be taken and recorded manually.

Fifty years ago commercial television was another emerging technology that gave a significant boost to instrumentation. Displaying an image on the face of a cathode ray tube (CRT) by scanning 525 lines applied to instrumentation applications. Video monitors for computers thus

became a reality. At first, video monitors were used in television studios and special industrial applications. But later they made their way into our homes as video monitors for personal computers. This is another instance of commercial technology providing opportunities for advancing the state of the art and the quality of instrumentation.

By the mid-1950s, the transistor was introduced. It replaced the vacuum tube because of its many advantages, such as small size, modest power consumption, and reliability. The transistor allows circuit designers to design circuits with greater complexity yet smaller size.

The new technology, once again, was responsible for the advancement in instrument sophistication. The instruments of the 1960s and 1970s were generally smaller in size because they used transistorized circuits with inherent sophistication and greater measurement capability. However, they were still dedicated to the specific measurement task as dictated by the instrument vendor. The user could not modify or alter the measuring instrument's function to serve his specific needs.

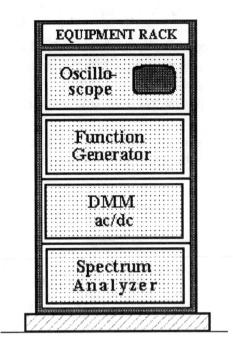

In order to accommodate many measurement needs, the user had to purchase many instruments, each to serve a specific measurement, and rack mount them as shown in this illustration.

The availability of the integrated circuit, commonly referred to as the chip, several decades after the transistor provided the means for circuit miniaturization as well as added circuit complexity. The space on the circuit board formerly occupied by a transistor is now occupied by a semiconductor chip that contains hundreds of transistors. The integrated circuit design approach made it possible to fit many complex circuits into the small area of the chip, setting the stage for

the rather inexpensive design of a computer that we know today as the personal computer. Up to this point the computer was viewed by most people as a mysterious device that only large corporations could afford.

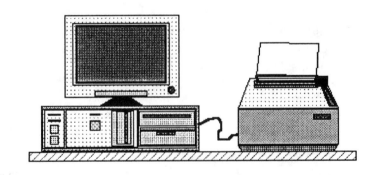

The personal computer, known to most of us as a PC, made its debut around 1980. Small companies that could not afford a mainframe before could now buy a PC. The reasonable pricing of a PC made it available to the average household as well.

This new technology completely revolutionized the world of instrumentation. It offered new opportunities in computer based instrumentation design where the user had options in modifying instrument configuration. In a relatively short time PCs were designed with greater speed and processing capabilities, which offered new opportunities for instrumentation design sophistication.

In order for the computer to be effective in controlling other black boxes or in acquiring data, an interface was necessary. A serial interface such as RS-232 is a relatively slow interface that may be adequate in a computer mouse application but much too slow to transfer blocks of data to a printer, for example. For that, a parallel interface would be a much better choice.

Hewlett Packard was one of the first companies to design a parallel interface. They called it HP-IB 488 (Hewlett Packard Interface Bus). Many companies started designing their equipment to be HP-IB 488 compatible. Before long it became an unofficial industry standard renamed GPIB-488 (General Purpose Interface Bus). Because of GPIB-488s extensive use in the industry, the IEEE standards committee made its use official. The former GPIB-488 became an industrywide standard known as IEEE-488. It is used to this day.

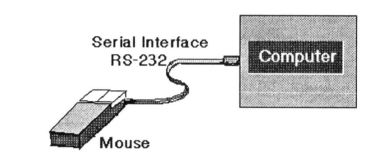

For an instrument to be controlled by the computer, it must have the GPIB interface. As shown in this illustration, if an oscilloscope has a GPIB connector, then it was designed to be controlled by the computer. The instrument and the computer are linked by the GPIB cable, which plugs into the GPIB-488 interface card on the computer side. To control the instrument functions, the driver software designed for that particular instrument must reside inside the computer.

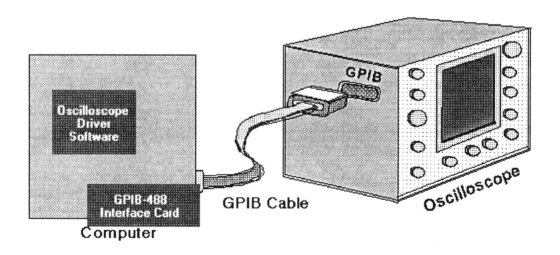

Once under computer control, special command messages and data are sent back and forth over the GPIB cable. Data representing oscilloscope screen images can be stored in the computer's memory for further processing.

Data acquisition under computer control is another area of great activity. With proper data acquisition soft- ware and an interface board, data can be acquired by the computer, stored in memory, or processed. This illustration shows how temperature data is acquired from an external source. The analog temperature data is applied to the analog input port on the data acquisition board, where the data is digitized and then transferred to the computer's memory. The data acquisition board also has an analog output port, which provides an option for the user to control an external device by the computer.

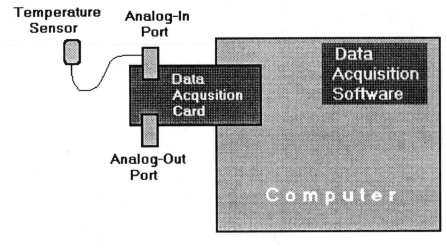

During the last decade or so, object oriented programming has been making its way into the mainstream of various high-level programming language. Graphical programming language, which relieves the user of the responsibility of writing code, offers interesting and exciting programming possibilities. Its major advantage is simplicity because the user manipulates and wires icons in configuring his program. The major drawback of graphical programming is probably the software overhead. In fast-moving data acquisition applications the computer may be unable to keep up with the acquired data. There are still many applications wherein software overhead is not a problem. There are also advanced techniques, such as using onboard timers in place of software generated waveforms and processing acquired data in a quasi real time, that help surmount the software overhead problem.

The graphical programming concept introduced the possibility of creating a new type of instrumentation, not in hardware but rather in software. This new instrument was called the Virtual Instrument (VI). For the first time in instrumentation history, the user will no longer be dependent on the instrumentation vendor, who gave the user no options in modifying the instrument's functionality. The instrument is now simply a file that can be modified to or deleted altogether.

National Instruments Company created exactly this type of software and called it LabVIEW. In the illustration shown below, the image on the screen of the oscilloscope is moved as blocks of data via the GPIB interface into the computer's memory. A LabVIEW program can then display this data or store it in spreadsheet format to a text file. On the other hand, the LabVIEW program that we will be referring to in this book as a VI, can also process the data. For instance, it can use a Fourier Transform on the data and display its spectrum in the frequency domain.

The virtual instrument in this case imports the data from an external device, displays it, processes it, and stores it to a file. The data can be retrieved from the file at a later time and processed again. The instrument that does all this is in software and can be easily reconfigured or modified by the user to give it special features.

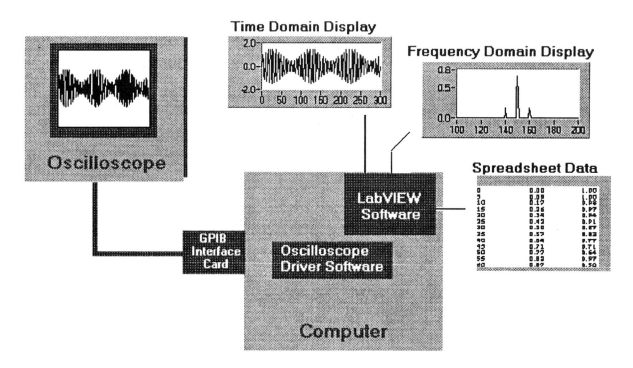

This illustration uses GPIB as an example. However, if we used a DAQ board instead of the GPIB board, LabVIEW can acquire data, then process it, display it, or store it in spreadsheet format.

LabVIEW's versatility can be seen from a variety of applications:

1. **Simulation**
   Physical processes can be simulated in the LabVIEW environment. The ProjMotn.vi in Chapter 3 is an example.
2. **Data Acquisition**
   LabVIEW can acquire and bring inside its environment electronic data from an outside transducer or device. Some of the most recent additions include optically scanned data.
3. **Data Processing**
   LabVIEW can make use of a rich resource center of the Analysis library that includes:
   Signal Generation
   DSP

6

> *Measurement*
> *Filters*
> *Windows*
> *Curve Fitting*
> *Probability and Statistics*
> *Linear Algebra*
> *Numerical Methods*

to process the incoming data. The data may also be *displayed* on a graph or stored to a file.

4. **Instrument Control**

   Using the GPIB interface, LabVIEW can communicate with and control the operation of an instrument. For example, if this instrument is an oscilloscope, the data associated with the oscilloscope's display can be transferred to LabVIEW for processing, storage, or display.

   For data acquisition and instrument control, LabVIEW supports IEEE 488 and RS-232/422 protocols as well as the VXI.

   ATE Application is an extension of instrument control to *Automated Test Equipment*. You can create a GUI (graphical user interface) that closely resembles the control panel of the actual instrument in terms of buttons, switches, controls, and indicators. The ATE application would typically use an instrument driver that you can pick from an extensive collection in the LabVIEW Instrument Driver Library and the Test Executive Toolkit in creating an automated test configuration. ATE provides a highly interactive environment during testing, debugging, verification, or system characterization.

The intent of this book is to introduce the user to the various features of LabVIEW. The user can be a person in a technical school or in industry. It is assumed that the user knows nothing about LabVIEW and wants to find out how it works. In this respect the approach taken to writing this book is very fundamental. The user, however, is expected to be familiar with the Windows environment, the use of files and directories, and so on.

The wide range of exercises expose the user to many features of LabVIEW. The exercises have all been tested thoroughly. They have also been structured in a detailed, step-by-step manner so that the user should have no difficulty in re-creating them. Although more than half the exercises are electronically oriented, there are also some that are non-electronic. Most exercises have also been created with a practical purpose in mind.

Chapter 2 describes the LabVIEW environment. Menu bars, floating palettes, and editing techniques and wiring are discussed in this chapter.

Chapter 3 turns the reader's attention to creating and troubleshooting a VI. Syntax errors are generally easier to pick up, but run-time errors are very often much harder to detect. A single-stepping troubleshooting technique described in this chapter can be used to detect run-time errors.

Creating a VI and then using it as a subVI is in step with the current trend of creating software in modular form. Modularization makes it easier to modify and debug software.

Chapter 4 devotes attention to structures. Repetitive operation and conditional and unconditional branching are powerful tools in high-level programming languages. These tools are just as important in the LabVIEW environment. Although sequential operation is taken for granted in C or other high-level language, because program execution will proceed in the order in which instructions are written, this is not the case in LabVIEW, where program execution is data driven and not program sequence driven. In LabVIEW a particular node will execute only if data is available at all of its inputs. For this reason LabVIEW offers a sequence structure to guarantee that the execution order will be carried out in the desired manner. LabVIEW also offers a Formula Node that allows the user to execute equations. Executing equations is not as routine in a graphical language as it might be in C language, for example.

Chapter 5 discusses arrays and how to create and use one-dimensional and two- dimensional arrays. Use of array functions provided by LabVIEW libraries for operating on and manipulating arrays is also discussed. The spreadsheet or any other data sheet is in the form of a two-dimensional array. It is often necessary as part of data processing to extract a column, a row, and an element, to search for an element, and so on. The techniques described in this chapter can help the user with these operations and more.

Chapter 6 explores graphical features offered by LabVIEW. Considerable attention is given in this chapter to the explanation of creating and using charts, waveform graphs, and X-Y graphs. Many exercises offered in this chapter illustrate with practical applications the use of charts and graphs.

Chapter 7 is dedicated to strings. Strings play an important role in instrument control via the GPIB arrangement, where instrument control messages use the string format. Strings are also used for text messages and for storing numeric data to disk. Detailed explanation about creating and using string controls and indicators and using numerous string functions from the LabVIEW library are provided.

Chapter 8 is concerned with the files. Files provide the user with the means of saving data to the disk. The procedure of writing data to the file or reading data from the file has a specific syntax that is explained in this chapter and illustrated with practical examples. Utilities that simplify the syntax of writing data to a spreadsheet or reading data from a spreadsheet are also explained and illustrated with specific exercises. Saving data to a spreadsheet has a particular advantage because the spreadsheet can be opened by another spreadsheet or word processor software.

Chapter 9 introduces the reader to the basic theory of data acquisition, data acquisition components, data acquisition VIs, and the analog input data acquisition options: immediate single point input, hardware timed single point input, or waveform input.

Appendix A introduces the environment for LabVIEW version 3.

Appendix B deals with creating and troubleshooting a VI for LabVIEW version 3.

Appendix C discusses Structures for LabVIEW version 3.

Workbook.LLB will be the library where you will save all VIs that you will be building in the forthcoming chapters. The path to this library is A:\Workbook.LLB. The library in the LabVIEW environment is a file containing other files with names up to 32 characters long. All files saved to a library are compressed when saved and decompressed when called. This saves memory space and makes file portability an easy task.

The Workbook.LLB has been created for you on the disk supplied with this book. If you want more information on creating a library, refer to Experiment 9 in Chapter 2.

Chapter 2

LabVIEW™ Environment

In this chapter you will learn about:
Menu Bar Options
Floating Palettes: Controls, Functions, and Tools
Editing Techniques
Wiring
VI Library
Documentation

LabVIEW Program Development Environment

Front Panel and Block Diagram

In LabVIEW, programs are developed using the graphical programming language. The user does not have to know the syntax like he would when writing a program in C language, for example. The syntax, although inherent in the structure of LabVIEW, is transparent to the user. The user, however, still has to be familiar with the rules of LabVIEW to be able to construct programs using the many tools that LabVIEW has to offer.

All programs developed in LabVIEW have an extension .vi. *VI stands for Virtual Instrument*, implying that it has something to do with an instrument. Any real instrument that the user might have encountered has two main components: the front panel, which includes controls and indicators, and the various devices inside the case of the instrument. The electronic devices inside the instrument are electrically interconnected and are also connected to the front panel, receiving control signals from the panel and passing measured results to the front panel for display.

A VI is not a real life instrument but can be made to act as a real instrument, and that's why it is called a virtual instrument. It too has a *front panel* and a *block diagram*. The front panel contains controls and indicators, and the block diagram contains various functions that are interconnected by wires. The front panel and the block diagram are shown in Fig. 2-1.

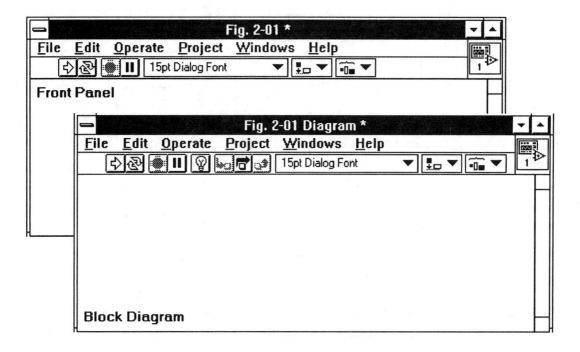

Fig. 2-1 Front Panel and Block Diagram of a VI

11

Toolbars and the Tools Palette

Front Panel Toolbar

The Toolbars located at the top of the front panel and the block diagram serve as the user interface. They provide tools for editing and executing the LabVIEW graphical program, which we will call simply a VI.

The toolbar at the top of the front panel is shown in Fig. 2-2. As you move the mouse cursor over a particular tool icon, a yellow banner appears, informing you of the function of the tool icon. To choose a tool, simply click with the left mouse button on that icon.

Front Panel Toolbar

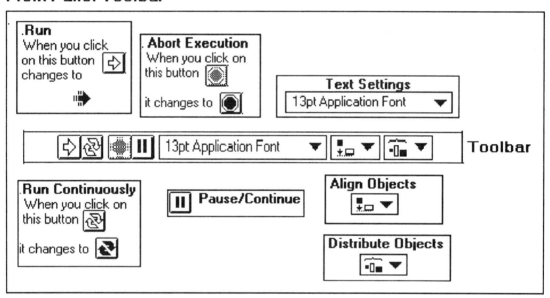

Fig. 2-2 Front Panel Toolbar

Run	By clicking on this button you will execute your VI. When the VI is running, the Run icon changes, as shown in Fig. 2-2.
Run Continuously	Execute VI repeatedly without stopping. Once activated, the icon changes to that shown in Fig. 2-2.
Abort Execution	Stop VI execution. This icon assumes a hexagonal shape with a red center during VI execution. Execution is terminated when you click on this icon.
Pause	Two **black** bars – **Pause** Two **yellow** bars – **Do Not Pause** (not available when VI is running) Two **red** bars – **Continue**

Text Settings When you click on this icon, a pull-down menu appears, as shown in Fig. 2-3. The top section of this menu includes standard LabVIEW fonts such as Application, System, or Dialog. Note that each of these fonts has a shortcut key. This means that you can choose these fonts from the keyboard. You can select the Dialog Font with *Ctrl+3* from the keyboard. The center section of the Text Settings menu has submenus, as shown in Fig. 2-3, that allow you to choose the font size and style. And the bottom part of the menu includes many other fonts that are part of windows. Notice that the Text Settings icon displays the current font and its size. *The Text Settings icon is not available when VI is running.*

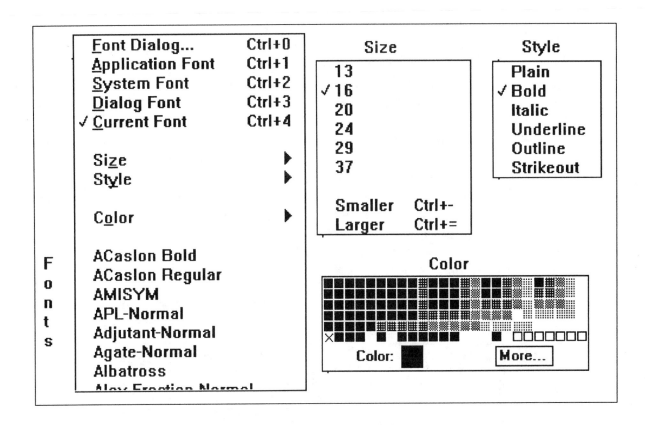

Fig. 2-3 Text Settings Menu

Align Objects *The Align Objects tool is concerned with positioning objects either in the front panel or in the block diagram windows. Objects in the window can be aligned along their top edges, bottom edges, or centers. This can be done in the horizontal or vertical direction.*

When you click on the Align Objects icon, a menu opens with various options on aligning selected objects in the window, as shown in Fig. 2-4a. As you move the mouse cursor over the alignment icons in the menu, a brief functional description appears at the top of the menu. The selected alignment tool is enclosed by a dark outline, as shown in the figure. Its name in this illustration is *Top Edges,* meaning that the selected objects in the window will be aligned along their top edges. This menu offers five other alignment tools. *The Align Objects icon is not available when VI is running.*

Distribute Objects　　*The Distribute Objects tool provides the ability to insert the desired spacing between the selected objects in the front panel or the block diagram windows. The spacing can be measured between the top edges, bottom edges, or centers of the object in the vertical direction. The menu also offers five more distributing options where spacing is measured between the right edges, left edges, or centers in the horizontal direction. A total of ten distributing options are available.*

A pull-down menu appears as soon as you click on the Distributing Objects icon. As you move the mouse cursor over choices in this menu, a helpful text describing the function of each choice appears at the top of the menu. Shown in the illustration of Fig. 2-4b is the selection that will insert equal spaces between the objects in the horizontal direction. *The Distribute Objects icon is not available when VI is running.*

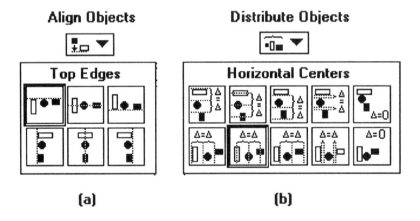

Fig. 2-4 Align/Distribute Menus (a) Align Objects (b) Distribute Objects

Block Diagram Toolbar

The Block Diagram toolbar shares most of the icons with the Front Panel toolbar, as can be seen in Fig. 2-5, except for three of them: Step Into, Step Over, and Step Out. These are troubleshooting tools and are discussed in greater detail in the debugging section.

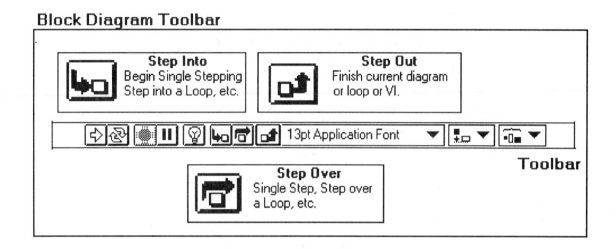

Fig. 2-5 Block Diagram Toolbar

Tools Palette

The Tools Palette shown in Fig. 2-6 contains useful tools for editing text, color, wiring, and operating and positioning objects, as well as tools for troubleshooting a VI. The tools palette is a floating graphical palette that can be moved easily anywhere inside the Panel/Diagram windows or it can be placed outside the windows. In short, the Tools Palette can be placed for easy access by the user.

A brief description of each tool's function in Fig. 2-6 is accompanied by the shape of the cursor assigned to that particular tool. You will note that once you select a tool, the usual arrow-shaped cursor assumes another shape.

As you move the mouse cursor over the tool choices inside the Tool palette and hold the mouse cursor on a tool icon for several seconds, a yellow banner with the tool's name appears. The tool's name alone gives you a hint of its function.

To Open the Tools Palette... Choose **Windows>Show Tools Palette** from the Windows menu. The Tools Palette opens automatically when you launch LabVIEW.
To Move the Tools Palette... Click with the left mouse button on the "Tools" title bar and drag
the   palette to a new location.

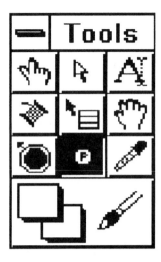

To move this Floating Tools Palette, click with the left mouse button on the "Tools" title bar and drag the palette to a new location.

TOOL/Cursor Shape	TOOL FUNCTION
Operate Value Tool	**Operating Tool** to change values on Front Panel controls and indicators.
Position/Size/Select	**Positioning Tool** to move, select, or resize objects in the Front Panel or the Block Diagram.
Edit Text Tool	**Labeling Tool** to type text in free and owned labels. **Cursor:**
Connect Wire Tool	**Wiring Tool** to connect objects by means of a wire in the Block Diagram.
Object Popup Tool	**Popup Tool** to open Controls/Functions popup menus.
Scroll Window Tool	**Scroll Tool** to scroll window in any direction.

Fig. 2-6 Tools Palette and Its Options

16

TOOL/Cursor Shape	TOOL FUNCTION
Set/Clear Breakpoints	**Breakpoint Tool** to set breakpoints on VIs, functions, loops, sequences, and cases in debugging a VI.
Probe Data Tool	**Probe Tool** to place a probe on a wire between objects for data monitoring or measurement purposes.
Get Color Tool	**Copy Color Tool** to duplicate a color from your VI and paste it with Set Color Tool.
Set Color Tool	**Set Color Tool** to set the background and foreground colors. The colors of your choice appear in the two rectangles of the icon.

Fig. 2-6 Tools Palette and Its Options (continued)

Controls Palette

The Controls palette contains objects of various types such as controls and indicators exclusively for the front panel; it cannot be accessed from the block diagram. In the previous versions of LabVIEW, the Controls menu was a list type menu in the menu bar. In the current 4.0 version, the Controls menu was moved to a floating graphical palette and is similar to the palettes that you may encounter in other graphical programs.

To Open Controls menu...   When you launch LabVIEW, the Controls palette opens automatically. It can be opened also by choosing **Windows>Show Controls Palette**.

To Close the Controls menu...   Double click in the upper lefthand corner of the palette.

To Move the Controls Palette...   Click on the "Controls" title bar and drag the palette to a new location.

Subpalettes

The Controls palette contains nine categories of various types of objects that you can use only in the front panel in constructing your VI. When you click on one of the icons in the Controls palette, *Graph*, for example, as illustrated in Fig. 2-7, a subpalette containing various graph options opens.

Note the *thumb tack* lying on its side at the top of the subpalette. At this time you may move the cursor to the subpalette and select an object of your choice. Should you click outside the subpalette, it will disappear. However, if you click with the left mouse button on the thumb tack,

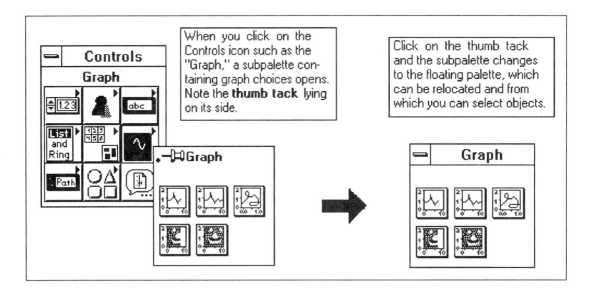

Fig. 2-7 Controls Menu Subpalettes

the subpalette turns into the floating palette, which can be moved around the window and from which you can select objects for your VI. This is illustrated in Fig. 2-7.

Fig. 2-8 includes a brief description of the content for each option in the Controls palette. As you can see, the Controls palette provides the user with a variety of objects to be placed in the front panel of your VI. Many of these will be used throughout the workbook in hands-on exercises, thus giving you ample opportunity to become familiar with them.

Functions Palette

Just like the Controls menu, the Functions menu was moved in version 4.0 of LabVIEW from the pull-down list menu to the graphical floating palette.

To Open the Functions menu...   When you launch LabVIEW and then switch to the Block Diagram window (**Ctrl+e**), the Functions palette opens automatically,
or
Access the Popup Functions palette by clicking with the right mouse button anywhere in the Block Diagram window,
or
Select **Windows>Show Functions Palette**.

Subpalettes of Subpalettes

The top level Functions graphical floating palette has 16 choices for building your VI. Some of the options in the Functions palette have their own subpalettes. The Functions menu can be used only in the block diagram. Examine the illustration shown in Fig. 2-9. When you move the mouse cursor over various options in the Functions menu, the option name appears at the top of the palette.

Should you click with the left mouse button on the Numeric option, for example, the Numeric subpalette opens. At this time you can select objects from the Numeric subpalette or click on the thumb tack lying on its side in the upper left corner of the subpalette. By clicking on the thumb tack you will convert the Numeric subpalette, which is attached to the Functions palette, to a floating palette that can be moved around the window. You may even close the Function palette, but the Numeric palette will remain open. This is illustrated in Fig. 2-9.

Note that along the right edge of the Numeric palette there are five subpalette options. In addition to the numeric tools for your VI in the Numeric palette, these five subpalettes provide additional resources or an additional gamut of numeric tools for the block diagram of your VI. Fig. 2-9 you can access trigonometric functions by clicking on the second subpalette icon from the top. Note once again the thumb tack at the top of the trigonometric subpalette. You can convert the subpalette to the floating palette, as shown in Fig. 2-9, by clicking on the thumb tack.

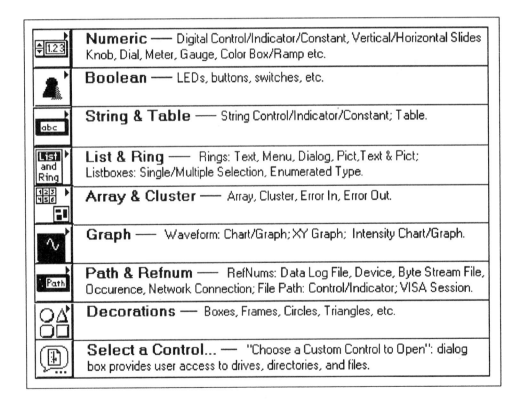

Fig. 2-8 Controls Palette and Its Options

20

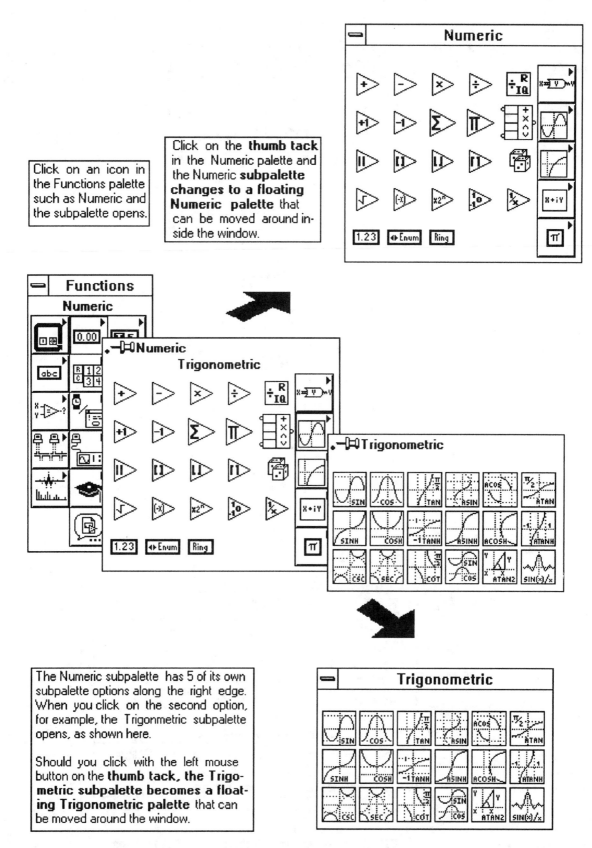

Click on an icon in the Functions palette such as Numeric and the subpalette opens.

Click on the **thumb tack** in the Numeric palette and the Numeric **subpalette changes to a floating Numeric palette** that can be moved around inside the window.

The Numeric subpalette has 5 of its own subpalette options along the right edge. When you click on the second option, for example, the Trigonmetric subpalette opens, as shown here.

Should you click with the left mouse button on the **thumb tack, the Trigometric subpalette becomes a floating Trigonometric palette** that can be moved around the window.

Fig. 2-9 Functions Floating Palette and its Subpalettes

21

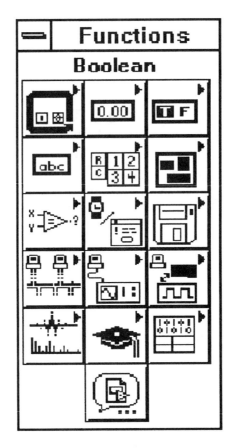

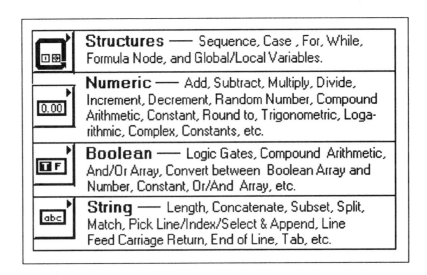

Fig. 2-10 Functions Palette and Its Options

Array —— Size, Index, Subset, Build, Transpose, Sort, Search, Min/Max, Convert Array/Cluster, etc.
Cluster —— Bundle/Unbundle and by Name, Build Cluster Array, Cluster/Array Conversions, Constant, Index & Bundle Cluster Array.
Comparison —— Compare two values, compare one value to zero, Select, Decim/Hex/Octal, Digit?, Min/Max?, etc.
Time & Dialog —— Wait Until Next ms Multiple, Tick Count, Wait, Get Date/Time, Convert between Date/Time and sec, One/Two Button Dialog, Find First Error, Simple/General Error Handler.
File I/O —— R/W: From/To Spreadsheet; R/W Character From/To File; File: Open/Create/Replace, R/W, Close; Constant; Advanced File Functions.
Communication —— TCP, UDP, DDE, System Exec.
Instrument I/O —— VISA, GPIB, GPIB 488.2, Serial.
Data Acquisition —— Analog I/O, Digital I/O, Counter, Signal Conditioning, Calibration and Configuration.
Analysis —— Signal Generation, DSP, Filters, Curve Fitting, Linear Algebra, Array Operations, Array Operations, Probability and Statistics, Windows, Additional Numerical Methods.
Tutorial —— Demo Voltage Read, Digital Thermometer, Generate Waveform.
Advanced —— VI Control, Data Manipulation, Beep, Memory, Occurences, Beep, Code Interface Node, Stop, Call Library Function, Call Chain, Quit LabVIEW.
Select a VI... —— "Choose the VI to Open": dialog box provides user access to drives, directories, and files.

Fig. 2-10 Functions Palette and Its Options (continued)

The Functions floating palette has 18 options, providing you with a wide array of resources for building your block diagram. Many of these are advanced and are beyond the scope of this workbook. Others such as Numeric, Boolean, String, Array, and perhaps few more will be used often in this book. Fig. 2-10 shows all the Functions palette options and provides a brief description of the block diagram tools that the options offer.

Pull-Down Menus

The pull-down menu bar is shown Fig. 2-11. While some of the menus and their options are common to most of the word processors and other software written for windows, others are specific to the LabVIEW programming environment. The pull-down menus provide a host of valuable and useful tools for VI development. Many of the menu options are seldom if ever used, which is why the pull-down menu description that follows is limited to some of the more frequently used items. As the reader becomes familiar with the LabVIEW environment, he will probably prefer the use of the shortcut keys. They offer speedy execution of many tasks.

| File   Edit   Operate   Project   Windows   Help |

Fig. 2-11 Pull-Down Menu Bar

Note the <u>underlined letters</u> in the pull-down menu bar as well as within the pull-down menu. These allow you to use the keyboard to navigate through the menus. For instance, the File menu is brought up by depressing the **Alt+F** keys (F is underlined in File). After releasing the Alt+F keys, depress the **S** key if you wish to save the active VI file to disk (note that S is underlined in the Save option).

File Menu

The File menu, shown in Fig. 2-12, provides the user with the ability to open, close, save, and print VI files.

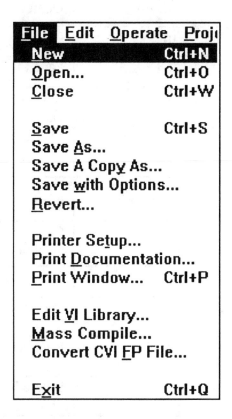

Fig. 2-12 File menu

The description of each File menu option and shortcut keys is given in Fig. 2-13. The **shortcut keys** for some of the options within the menu are shown on the righthand side of the menu. For example, to perform the same Save operation using the shortcut keys, depress **Ctrl+S**. Shortcut keys are generally faster than using the mouse.

If you forgot the shortcut key, open the File menu **Alt+F** (note that every option in the menu bar has an underlined letter) and then press just one more key. For example, by pressing the **A** key while you are in the File menu, you will invoke the **Save As** option.

File Menu Options	Shortcut Key	Description
<u>N</u>ew	Ctrl+N	Open new VI file.
<u>O</u>pen	Ctrl+O	Open existing VI file.
<u>C</u>lose	Ctrl+W	Close the active VI file.
<u>S</u>ave	Ctrl+S	Save the active VI file.
Save <u>A</u>s...		Save the active VI file under a new name.
Save A Cop<u>y</u> As...		Save a copy of the active VI file under a new name.
Save <u>w</u>ith Options...		Options for saving VI without the block diagram.
<u>R</u>evert...		Change active VI to last saved version.
Page Se<u>t</u>up...		Configuration Options for printer.
Print <u>D</u>ocumentation...		Set VI format and layout options.
<u>P</u>rint Window...	Ctrl+P	Print active VI window.
Edit <u>V</u>I Library...		Delete VIs in VI library or rearrange order of VIs in palette.
<u>M</u>ass Compile...		Compile all VIs in library.
Convert CVI <u>F</u>P File...		Provides access to CVI files to be converted.
E<u>x</u>it	Ctrl+Q	Close LabVIEW.

Fig. 2-13 File Menu Options

Edit Menu

The Edit menu, shown in Fig. 2-14, provides you with tools such as cut, copy, paste, remove bad wires, and many others to edit your VI. Fig. 2-15 provides a brief description for each editing tool. Once again note the shortcut keys and also those within the Edit menu (underlined letter).

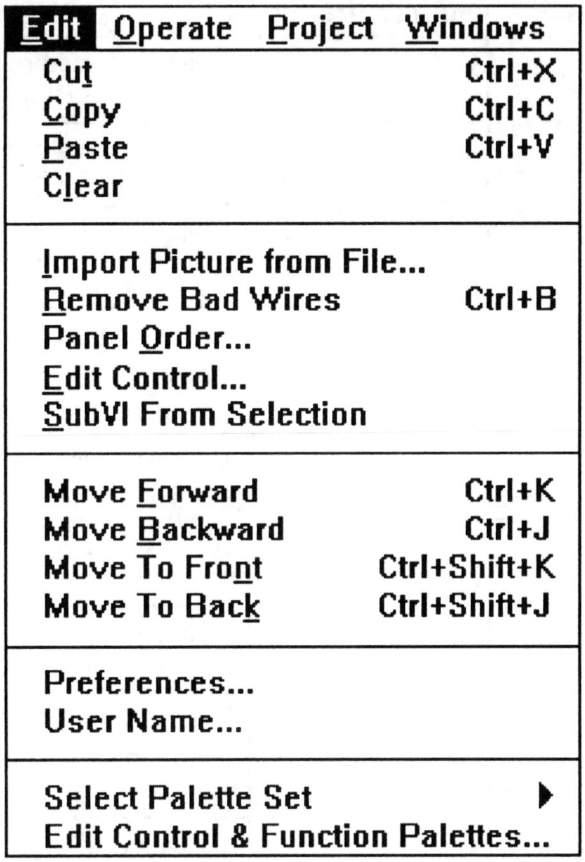

```
┌─────────────────────────────────────────────┐
│ │Edit│  Operate   Project   Windows          │
├─────────────────────────────────────────────┤
│    Cut                          Ctrl+X        │
│    Copy                         Ctrl+C        │
│    Paste                        Ctrl+V        │
│    Clear                                      │
├─────────────────────────────────────────────┤
│    Import Picture from File...                │
│    Remove Bad Wires             Ctrl+B        │
│    Panel Order...                             │
│    Edit Control...                            │
│    SubVI From Selection                       │
├─────────────────────────────────────────────┤
│    Move Forward                 Ctrl+K        │
│    Move Backward                Ctrl+J        │
│    Move To Front          Ctrl+Shift+K        │
│    Move To Back           Ctrl+Shift+J        │
├─────────────────────────────────────────────┤
│    Preferences...                             │
│    User Name...                               │
├─────────────────────────────────────────────┤
│    Select Palette Set                 ▶       │
│    Edit Control & Function Palettes...        │
└─────────────────────────────────────────────┘
```

Fig. 2-14 Edit Menu

Operate Menu

The Operate menu, shown in Fig. 2-16 provides tools for operating your VI. This includes running and stopping the VI, printing and logging the front panel, and logging data stored in front panel controls and indicators to a log file of your choice. As shown in Fig. 2-16, the data log option has a submenu that gives you a choice to log, retrieve, or purge data stored in the log file. Fig. 2-17 includes a description for each of the Operate menu options.

Edit Menu Options	Shortcut Key	Description
Cut	Ctrl+X	Delete selected region from window and move to the Clipboard.
Copy	Ctrl+C	Copy selected region to the Clipboard.
Paste	Ctrl+V	Copy contents of Clipboard to the active window.
Clear		Delete selected object or region.
Remove Bad Wires	Ctrl+B	Remove all improper wire connections that appear as dashed lines and those that are hidden behind objects.
Panel Order		Edit the order number assigned to objects in the front panel.
Import Picture from File...		Allows access to files for importing a picture.
Edit Control		Activates Control Editor. Advanced feature not covered in this workbook.
Move Forward	Ctrl+K	The selected object, one of several overlapping objects, is moved forward one position.
Move Backward	Ctrl+J	The selected object, one of several overlapping objects, is moved one position to the back.
Move To Front	Ctrl+shift+K	The selected object, one of several overlapping objects, is moved one position toward the front.
Move To Back	Ctrl+Shift+J	The selected object, one of several overlapping objects, is moved one position toward the back.
Preferences...		Offers the user to set his preference on front panel, block diagram, disk, debugging, fonts, printing, and others.
Edit Control & Functions Palettes		This option allows you to modify the Functions and Controls floating palettes. The VI, for example, that you created and are using frequently can be added for easy access.

Fig. 2-15 Edit Menu Options

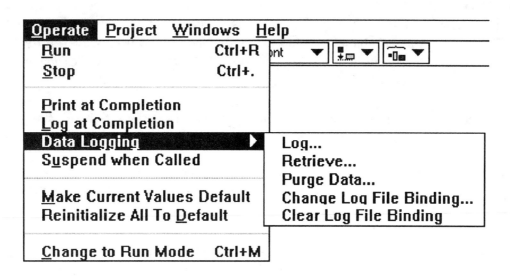

Fig. 2-16 Operate Menu

Operate Menu Option	Shortcut Key	Description
Run	Ctrl+R	Execute the active VI.
Stop	Ctrl+.	Terminate VI execution.
Print at Completion		Print front panel after VI completes execution.
Log at Completion		Log front panel after VI completes execution.
Data Logging		When VI executes, data in controls and indicators is logged to a log file of your choice.
Suspend when Called		Suspend VI execution when it is called. This option applies only to a VI that is used as a subVI.
Make Current Values Default		The values currently in controls and indicators on front panel are made default.
Reinitialize All To Default		Set controls and indicators to their normal default values.
Change to Run Mode	Ctrl+M	This option changes VI mode to Run. The default mode is edit.

Fig. 2-17 Operate Menu Options

29

Project Menu

The Project menu option, shown in Fig. 2-18, is included for the first time in version 4.0 of LabVIEW. This option is probably not very useful for one small VI. However, for a program that includes many VIs, the Project menu contains tools that simplify the task of navigating through those VIs, as shown in Fig. 2-19.

This menu includes the **Hierarchy** option with a graphical configuration of VIs and subVIs. It also includes a toolbar that can be used to perform a number of editing tasks on the configuration.

The Hierarchy provides information on VI's callers and subVIs and unopened subVIs. The **Find** option can be used to search for VIs as well as text; the report on matches found by LabVIEW is presented in the **Search Results** table.

Of particular importance is the **Show Profile Window** option. It helps you optimize the performance of your VI by timing its execution. A report including the number of runs for VI, time used to execute a subVI, time used to display information, and time used by you to interact with controls is presented by LabVIEW in the Profile Window shown in Fig. 2-20. As mentioned earlier, this option is very useful for optimizing the performance of a large VI file.

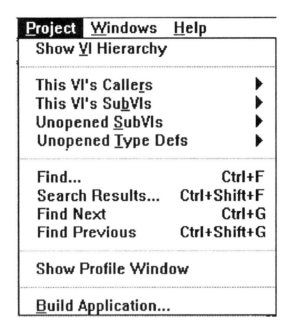

Fig. 2-18 Project Menu

Project Menu Option	Shortcut Key	Description
Show VI Hierarchy		The Hierarchy window shows all VIs and subVIs included in the active VI. This window has a toolbar that can be used to perform various editing and configuration tasks.
This VI's Callers		The submenu of other VIs that call the active or the currently running VI.
This VI's SubVIs		The submenu of all VIs that are the subVIs for the currently active or running VI.
Unopened SubVIs		The submenu of all subVIs in memory but unopened for the currently active or running VI.
Unopened Type Defs		A submenu of all unopened type definitions that belong to the currently active or running VI.
Find...	Ctrl+F	Popup menu that lets you find objects or text.
Search Results...	Ctrl+Shift+F	A listing of matches that LabVIEW found as a result of the Find inquiry.
Find Next	Ctrl+G	When you select (highlight) the match item in the Search Results listing of matches and invoke the Find Next option, LabVIEW opens the window and highlights the icon corresponding to the next match item on the list.
Find Previous	Ctrl+Shift+G	When you select (highlight) the match item in the Search Results listing of matches and invoke the Find Previous option, LabVIEW opens the window and highlights the icon corresponding to the previous match item in the list.
Show Profile Window		This option helps you optimize the performance of your VI by timing its execution. It calculates the number of runs for the VI, the time used to execute a subVI, the time used to display information, and the time used to interact with controls.
Build Application...		Create executable application file.

Fig. 2-19 Project Menu Options

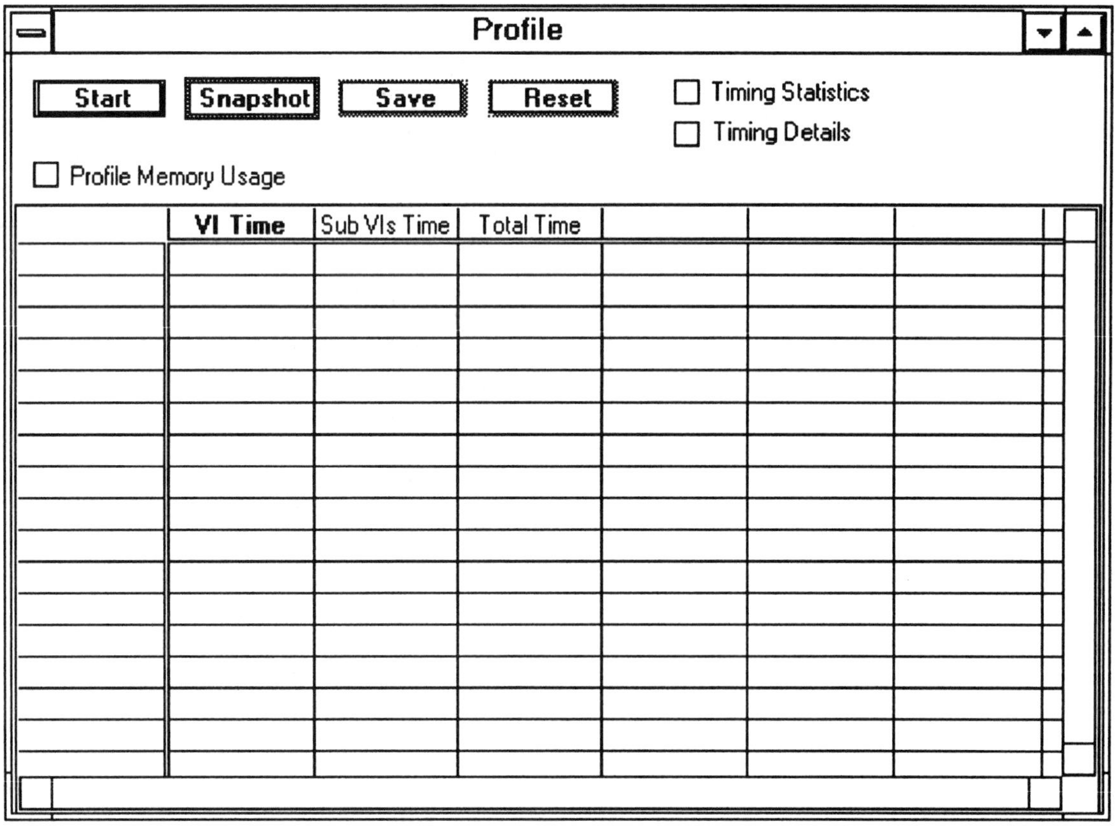

Fig. 2-20 Profile Window Shown Here Provides Performance Data on VI After Its Execution. This Information May Be Useful for Optimizing VI Performance.

Windows Menu

The Windows menu shown in Fig. 2-21 provides you with tools to operate and modify the LabVIEW window configuration and other special features. From this menu you can open floating palettes and view the clipboard or the error list. You can also type a VI description and special comments as well as the active VI history for future reference. Fig. 2-22 provides a brief description for each of the options in this menu.

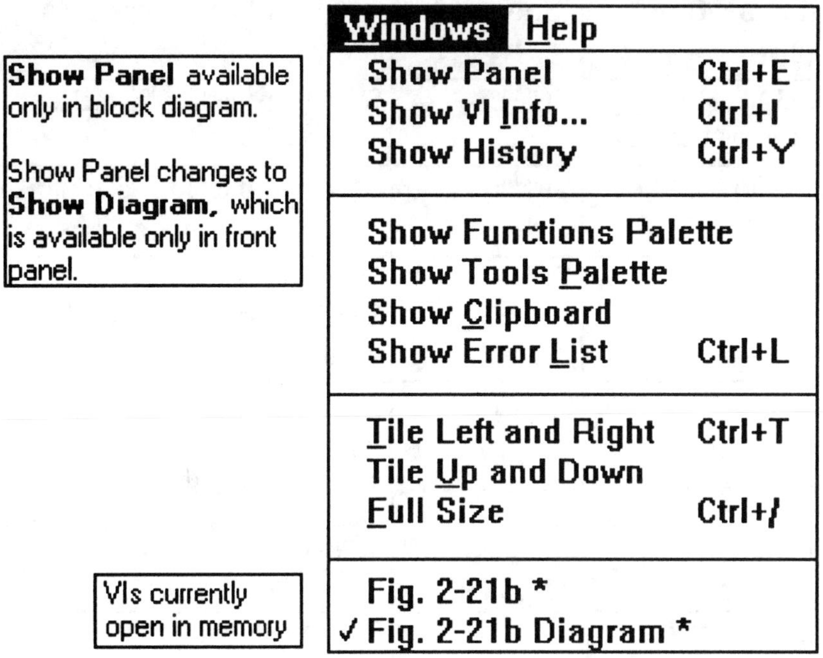

Show Panel available only in block diagram.

Show Panel changes to **Show Diagram**, which is available only in front panel.

Windows	Help	
Show Panel	Ctrl+E	
Show VI Info...	Ctrl+I	
Show History	Ctrl+Y	
Show Functions Palette		
Show Tools Palette		
Show Clipboard		
Show Error List	Ctrl+L	
Tile Left and Right	Ctrl+T	
Tile Up and Down		
Full Size	Ctrl+/	
Fig. 2-21b *		
✓ Fig. 2-21b Diagram *		

VIs currently open in memory

Fig. 2-21 Windows Menu

Windows Menu Option	Shortcut Key	Description
Show Panel (block diagram only)	Ctrl+E	Switch to the front panel.
Show Diagram (front panel only)	Ctrl+E	Switch to the block diagram.
Show VI Info...	Ctrl+I	Switch to VI popup menu. It shows the active VI path, memory usage, and the dialog box for the user to type the VI description.
Show History	Ctrl+Y	Open the History window pertaining to the active VI. This window includes a Comment dialog box and a History dialog box. The interactive dialog boxes allow you to type information that applies to the current VI for future reference.
Show Functions Palette (block diagram only)		Open the floating Functions Palette in the block diagram window.
Show Tools Palette		Open the floating Tools Palette. It can be used in the front panel and block diagram.
Show Controls Palette (front panel only)		Open the floating Controls palette in the front panel window.
Show Clipboard		Open and show the contents of the Clipboard window.
Show Error List	Ctrl+L	Open the list of errors incurred while wiring objects in the block diagram. When you select an error in the list and click on it, LabVIEW will open the appropriate window and highlight the object associated with that error.
Tile Left and Right		Arrange front panel and the block diagram windows horizontally and side by side.
Tile Up and Down	Ctrl+T	Arrange dront panel and the block diagram windows vertically.
Full Size	Ctrl+/	Switches the active window to full size so that it occupies the whole screen.

Fig. 2-22 Windows Menu Options

Help Menu

The Help menu, shown in Fig. 2-23, provides quick reference help for subVI nodes, functions, controls, and indicators. It is helpful not only in the course of VI development but also in obtaining information while browsing through a VI.

The **Help** window contains information about the object that you are interested in. To open the Help window, select **Show Help** from the Help menu or use the shortcut key **Ctrl+H** from the keyboard.

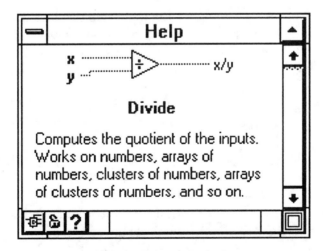

Help

Show Help	Ctrl+H
Lock Help	Ctrl+Shift +L
Simple Help	

| Online Reference... | Ctrl+? |
| Online Help for My Own VI | |

| About LabVIEW... | |

Fig. 2-23 Help Menu

When the Help window opens, it will look like Fig.2-24. It can be moved about as well as resized. In versions of LabVIEW earlier than 4.0, this window could not be resized. Note also the horizontal and vertical scroll bars allowing you to scroll through text in the window. In this simple illustration, the Help window includes help on the divide function. It shows the icon with inputs and outputs and a brief description of the function.

Help

x .... ÷ .... x/y
y ....

Divide

Computes the quotient of the inputs. Works on numbers, arrays of numbers, clusters of numbers, arrays of clusters of numbers, and so on.

Fig. 2-24 Help Window

Note the three buttons ⊞⊡⊡ in the lower left corner of the window in Fig. 2-24. The first button allows you to switch between simple and detailed or complex views of the Help window. The **Simple Diagram Help** ⊞ option described in Fig. 2-25 is particularly useful for a VI which is overwhelmingly complex; by excluding some of the less important connections, the diagram becomes easier to read and follow.

The **Lock/Unlock** ⊡ option serves to freeze the contents of the Help window. When locked, the Help window will not respond to any further requests. This is useful when you wish the window to remain unchanged for a while you work with a segment of a VI.

When you click on the last button, ⊡ described in Fig. 2-25, the Help window provides a link to a more detailed and indexed description for the selected object. This description is important when the information in the simple Help window is not sufficient for your needs. The Online Help window also has cross references to other related topics.

Help Window Button		Description
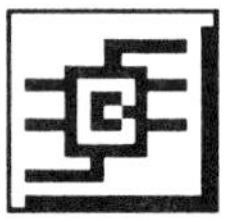 **Detailed Diagram Help** 	**Simple Diagram Help**	The Detailed and Simple Diagram Help toggle as you click on this button. **Detailed Diagram Help** provides a complex Help view showing all connections. **Simple Diagram Help** presents a simpler Help view where less important connections are excluded.
 **Unlocked Help** 	**Locked Help**	Unlocked and Locked Help toggle as you click on this button. **Unlocked Help** responds to new requests for help. **Locked Help** displays the last request before the Help window was locked. It does not respond to new requests. Shortcut key: **Ctrl+Shift+L**
 **Enabled**  **Disabled** **Online Help**		When this option is enabled, the Help window provides a link to the Online Help reference for the selected object. When you click on this button, a more detailed, indexed description of the selected object becomes available to you. This button assumes a disabled form when no objects are selected. Shortcut key: **Ctrl+?**

Fig. 2-25 Help Window Options

36

The *Simple Diagram Help* or *Detailed Diagram Help* can be selected from the Help window or from the Help menu. When the Simple Help option is enabled, a check mark will appear next to the Simple Help Option. If there is no check mark next to the Simple Help option, then the Help window will show the detailed diagram. In fact, the check mark will appear next to any option selected in the Help menu. You may note that the first four options in the Help menu may be enabled either through the use of the shortcut keys or option buttons on the Help window.

You can create *your own online help* document by using appropriate development tools. You must create a source file that links the help document to the VI for which it is intended. The source file for the help document must then be compiled to convert it to the object file or the executable help file. The help compiler may be obtained from a number of software manufacturers, including the Microsoft Corporation, who produce such compilers for Windows. All help compilers include tools to create help documents. The help document file will have the extension .hlp.

Once such a help document for a particular VI is available, you can then link it to the Help menu by first choosing the *VI Setup* from the front panel icon pane of the VI for which the help document is intended. Then select *Documentation* from the ring control of the VI Setup popup menu, click on the *Help Path* box, type the help file name, and click on the *Browse* button. *Select a Help file:* menu opens next, allowing you to choose the file that you presumably created before.

In Fig. 2-23 the help menu option *Online Help for My Own VI* would be gray if *My Own VI* didn't have the Online help file. Otherwise this option will be in solid letters, as shown in the illustration. If the option in the Help menu, or for that matter in any other menu, is gray, it is not available for selection.

Help Functions

For the first time, version 4.0 of LabVIEW includes Help functions located in the Advanced subpalette of the Functions palette. These Help functions, as all other functions, have icons and a connector. Therefore, they can be wired into the block diagram of your VI. These functions can be used to modify or check the status of the Help window as well as to control the online help.

Fig. 2-26 shows the three help functions with a brief explanation of their purpose.

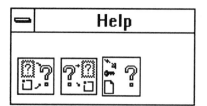

This floating Help palette includes three functions. It can be found in the Advanced subpalette of the Functions palette.

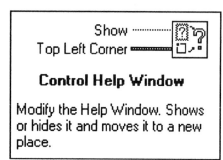

Control Help Window

Modify the Help Window. Shows or hides it and moves it to a new place.

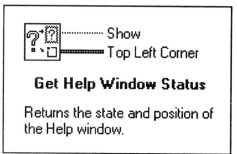

Get Help Window Status

Returns the state and position of the Help window.

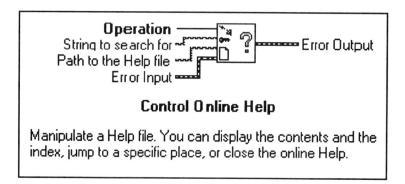

Control Online Help

Manipulate a Help file. You can display the contents and the index, jump to a specific place, or close the online Help.

Fig. 2-26 Help Functions

Editing Exercises

The task of editing arises in the process of building a VI or making changes to an existing VI. Such tasks as *selecting, moving, deleting, resizing, copying, labeling, arranging* objects inside either window, as well as several other tasks, are essential to a speedy and successful completion of a final product. The reader must therefore become familiar with these techniques. The editing exercises that follow offer the user an opportunity to practice some of the editing as well as other rules of the LabVIEW environment.

Throughout the exercises, the following terminology is often used and the user should be familiar with each:

Click on an object   Depress the left mouse button when the mouse cursor is over the object.

Pop up on an object   Depress the right mouse button when the mouse cursor is over an object. Popping up may also be done in an empty area of a window when you have to open the Controls or the Functions menu.

Dragging an object   Click on the object and, while holding down the left mouse button, move the mouse in any direction. The object will move on the screen as the mouse is moved.

Each exercise is started in an empty front panel and block diagram. Usually when LabVIEW is just launched, the empty front panel and block diagram become available immediately. But if other VI files have been opened before, then there may be no empty windows. In that case, choose *File>New*, and an empty panel window will appear.

Exercise 1:
Getting Objects from the Menu to the LabVIEW Window

In this exercise we will practice getting objects from the menu to the LabVIEW windows. You will begin by bringing a waveform chart into the front panel.

1.   Open a new front panel. Also open the Tools and Controls palettes if they are not open.

2.   Pop up on the *Graph* option in the Controls palette, and from the *Graph* subpalette

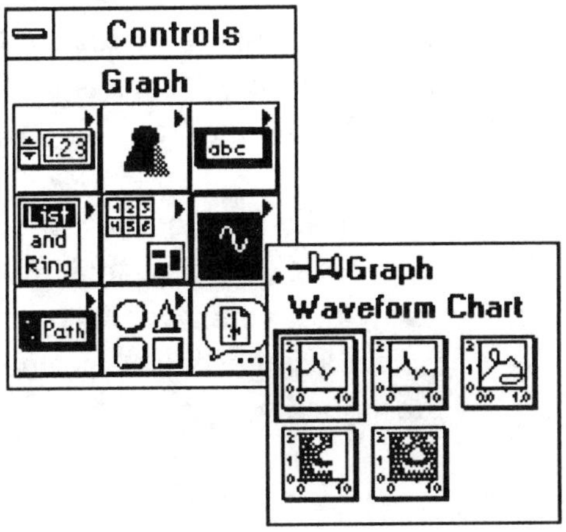

Fig. 2-27 Selecting the Waveform Chart from the Graph subpalette of the Controls Palette.

39

choose the *Waveform Chart* as shown in Fig. 2-27 and Fig. 2-28. Note that when you bring the mouse cursor over any object inside the subpalette, a frame forms around the object and the name of the object appears at the top of the subpalette.

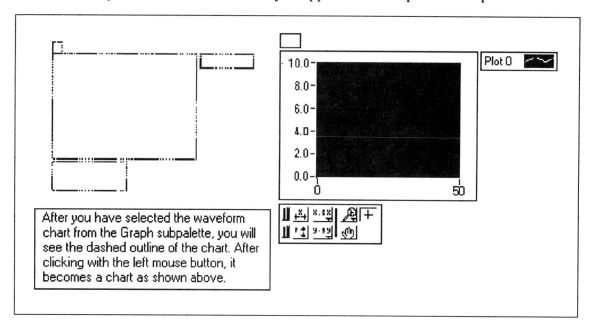

After you have selected the waveform chart from the Graph subpalette, you will see the dashed outline of the chart. After clicking with the left mouse button, it becomes a chart as shown above.

Fig. 2-28 Opening a Waveform Chart Inside the Front Panel

3. Practice by opening objects from other subpalettes of the Controls palette.
4. The procedure for opening objects inside the block diagram is same as that described above. For example, switch to the block diagram (recall the shortcut key Ctrl+E), open the Functions palette (click with the right right mouse button inside the block diagram), and select an object from one of the Functions subpalettes. Suppose you have to open the *Add function*. You can do that by going to the *Numeric* subpalette and then by selecting the *Add* function. You can see how simple this procedure is.

Exercise 2: Selecting and Deleting Objects

In order to perform an editing task on an object, you have to let the system know which object you want to work on. This is done by *selecting* the object. Let's try this on a square LED. First get the LED from the Controls palette:

1. Select the Positioning Tool from the Tools palette. It has the appearance of an arrow.
2. Choose **Controls>Boolean>Square LED**, as shown in Fig. 2-29.
3. Now that you have the square LED in the front panel window, it can be selected. You can select a single object or multiple objects by following one of the two procedures described below:

40

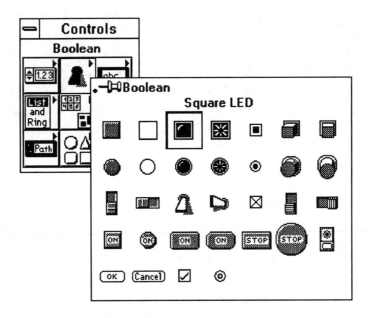

Fig. 2-29 Selecting a Square LED from the Boolean Subpalette

To Select a Single Object: Click on the object (left mouse button) and position the cursor close to the center of the object. If a *corner symbol* appears, reposition the cursor until the corner symbol disappears (it is used to resize the object only). Once the object is selected, a *dashed outline* appears around the object, indicating that the object has been selected.

To Select Multiple Objects: Position the cursor above and to the left of the objects to be selected. Press on the left mouse button (do not release it). The shape of the mouse cursor will change from an arrow to a cross. As you move the cursor, a dashed rectangle is formed and all objects inside the dashed rectangle will be selected. When you release the mouse button, all selected objects will have a dashed outline. Note that you can use this procedure also to select a single object.

To Deselect: Click outside the dashed outline. The dashed line will disappear and the object is thus deselected.

To Delete: First *select* the object to be deleted. Then press on the *Delete* key and the selected object will disappear.

4. Practice selecting, deselecting, and deleting objects in the front panel and in the block diagram. Do not save anything.

41

Note: *The rules for selecting and deselecting are the same for the front panel and the block diagram.*

In the block diagram some objects cannot be deleted. You can delete function and subVI icons as well as free labels. However, you **cannot** *delete* **control** *and* **indicator** *terminals nor are you allowed to delete* **owned labels** *associated with these terminals. The reason is that there must be a one-to-one relationship between the controls and indicators in the front panel and their associated terminals in the block diagram.*

If you wish to delete a control or an indicator, you must delete it in the front panel. If you simply want to remove the owned label from an object, pop up on the object and choose Show>Label. Repeat this procedure if you want the label back (Show>Label option toggles).

LabVIEW editor **does not** *have an* **Undo** *command; it takes too much memory. So anything that you delete from LabVIEW windows is gone. There is one exception to that. The graphics editor used for subVI icon design has an Undo option that will be covered later.*

Exercise 3: Moving, Duplicating, and Resizing Objects

When designing or modifying VIs, it is often necessary to change the size of objects or their position inside the window. Let's try this on a square LED. It was deleted last, so let's bring it back.

1.   Select the Positioning tool (the cursor has the shape of an arrow).
2.   Choose **Controls>Boolean>Square LED.** Once the LED appears in the front panel , it may be edited.

To Move an Object	*Select* the desired object, then *drag* the object. This means that as you click on the object, you must hold down the left mouse button. As you move the mouse, the object follows the motion of the cursor. Once again, when clicking, make sure that the corner symbol does not appear.
To Duplicate an Object	*Select* the desired object. While pressing the *Ctrl key* on the keyboard, *drag* or move the object in any direction, following the rules for moving. When you release the left mouse button, you will have a copy of the object.
To Resize an Object	Position the tip of the mouse *cursor over a corner* of the object. The cursor *arrow shape* changes to the *corner shape* (see Fig. 2-5 for a Positioning Tool cursor shapes description). While *holding down* the left mouse button,

move the cursor in an outward direction. You will notice the object increasing in size. When the left mouse button is released, the object will assume the enlarged size.

Note: *You can **move** objects in both the front panel as well as in the block diagram according to the rules described above.*

*In the block diagram, you are allowed to copy functions, labels, and subVIs; however, you are **not allowed** to **duplicate** any control or indicator terminal. The reason is that there must be a one-to-one relationship between the controls and indicators in both windows. If you want to copy a control or an indicator, you must do that in the front panel.*

You are not allowed to resize objects (with the exception of labels) in the block diagram.

3. Practice the moving, copying, and resizing rules on the square LED presently in the front panel or on other objects that you wish to bring into the front panel.

Exercise 4: Labeling

Labeling of objects is necessary for descriptive or identification purposes. For example, if there are two digital controls in the front panel, their counterparts, called **terminals** are in the block diagram. Unless they are labeled, one cannot tell them apart in the front panel or in the block diagram. This creates a problem because they probably have different functions. There are two types of labels: **owned labels** and **free labels**.

Creating an Owned Label
1. Click on the *Positioning Tool* in the Tools palette.
2. Pop up on the object such as the square LED and select **Show>Label** from the popup menu that opens.
3. As soon as you see a rectangle above the object, start typing the name of the object. The object's name that you type will appear inside the rectangle. This is illustrated in Fig. 2-30.

Note: *As soon as you bring an object to the front panel, the rectangle will be above the object. So if you start typing immediately, you may omit the above steps. Should you click anywhere in the window, the rectangle will disappear. To create the owned label, you will then have to follow the above steps.*

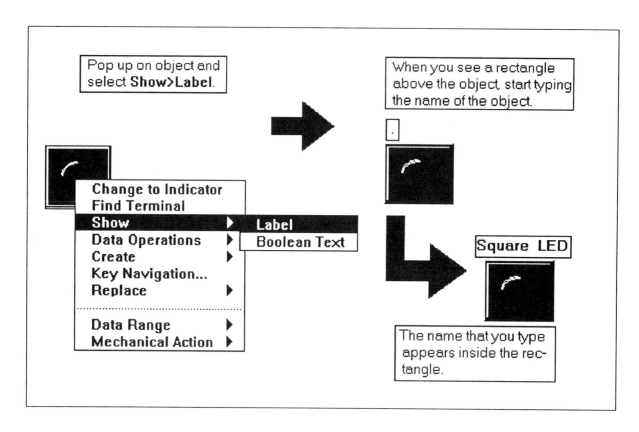

Fig. 2-30 Creating an Owned Label

Creating a Free Label

1. Click on the Labeling Tool in the Tools palette.
2. Click anywhere inside the window and begin typing. What you type will appear inside the rectangle. You can move this rectangle and place it anywhere inside the window.

> **Note:** *The **owned label** that you create for an object in the front panel will also appear in the block diagram over the corresponding terminal. Every object that you create in the front panel has a corresponding terminal that must be wired in the block diagram.*
>
> *This is not true for the **free label**. A free label that you create in the front panel will not appear in the block diagram. A free label is used for your convenience in providing additional information about the object. **The system does not associate the free label with the object.***

3. At this time, bring to the front panel the square LED or another object from the **Controls** palette.
4. Bring objects from another option in the Controls palette into the Panel Window. For example, open a Digital Control by choosing **Numeric>Digital Control** from the **Controls** palette.
5. Label the objects you selected with *owned label* and others with *free label*. Some objects

should have both labels.

6.   Select an object that has only an *owned* label. Move or reposition this object. Note that the owned label moves with the object.

7.   This time select only the label of the object in step 6. Try moving the label alone. Note that the label can be moved without the object. This means that the object's label may be moved to a more convenient position.

8.   Select an object that has both labels: *owned* and *free*. Try to move the object. Notice that the owned label moves with the object but the free label does not.

9.   Suppose that you would like to reposition or move

          (a) an object together with the free label **or**

          (b) several objects at the same time.

To accomplish this, follow the procedure outlined in Exercise 2 for selecting multiple objects. Select several objects or an object with a free label and try to move the selected group of objects to a different location in the window. After you select a group of objects, a dashed outline will appear around the selected group. Place the mouse cursor on any of the selected objects and drag that object (don't forget to hold down the left mouse button as you drag the object). Notice that as you drag one of the selected objects, the rest of the selected objects move with it.

Exercise 5: Coloring

The coloring option provides the user with the ability to color objects, giving them a distinctive appearance. This not necessarily done for cosmetic reasons, although if you have a color printer, coloring objects will add an attractive feature to the front panel and block diagram. But even if the printed copy was not of great concern, the appearance of the program on the screen, its readability, and the ability to follow data flow is enhanced when objects are colored. The diagram will not have that overall gray appearance where all objects seem to merge into the gray background. Also special emphasis may be given to some objects by coloring them.

You have to use the **Set Color** tool to color an object. The Set Color Tool is located at the bottom of the Tools palette. Notice the Foreground/Background rectangles in the Set Color tool icon. They store the colors for the foreground and the background of the object to be colored. You may set the Foreground/Background colors *directly* or by *copying* a color as described below.

Setting the Foreground/Background Colors Directly

These rectangles are in the Set Color Tool located at the bottom of the Tools palette. In order to color objects using the Foreground/Background colors, you must first set these colors.

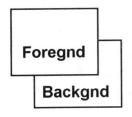

To Set the Background Color, click with the left mouse button on the Backgroundnd rectangle and the Colors palette appears as shown in Fig. 2-31. Move the mouse cursor (do not press any mouse buttons) over various colors of the palette. Note that as you pass over a particular color, that color appears in the *Color square* of the palette, giving you a preview of the color. When you click on the color of your choice, the Colors palette will disappear, and the Background rectangle of the Coloring Tool will assume the color that you picked. This is illustrated in Fig. 2-31.

To Set the Foreground Color, follow the procedure for setting the Background color, except, click first on the Foreground rectangle of the Coloring Tool.

You may also create **custom colors**. As shown in Fig. 2-31, when you click on the **More...** option in the Colors palette, a popup menu opens where you can specify percentages of red, green and blue in your custom color. The Foreground or Background rectangle will assume your special color mixture after you click on OK.

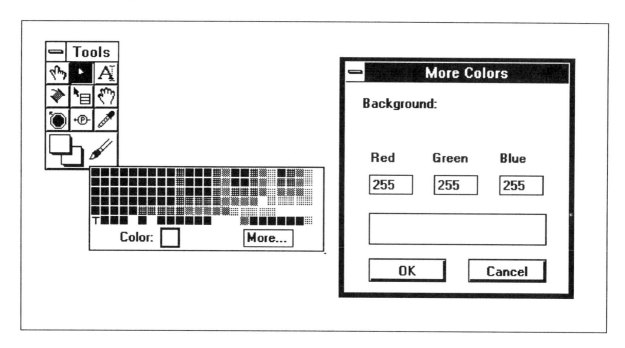

Fig. 2-31 Setting the Foreground/Background Colors Directly

Copying the Foreground/Background Colors

The *Get Color* tool of the *Tools Palette* is used to copy the color of any object in the window.

Get Color Tool

To Copy a Color, click on the **Get Color** tool in the Tools palette. With the pipette shaped cursor, click on an object whose color you wish to copy. The Foreground/Background rectangles of the *Set Color* Tool will assume the color of the object that you just clicked on.

Note: *If you click with the Get Color tool on an object such as a knob or a dial that has both foreground and background colors, both colors will be copied to the Foreground/Background rectangle of the Set Color tool. When you click with the Get Color tool on the object whose* *foreground and background are the same, the colors copied to the Set Color tool will also be the same.*

Set Color Tool

Coloring Objects

To Color an Object, click on the Set Color Tool in the Tools palette, then click on the object to be colored. The object will assume the color stored in the foreground rectangle or the background rectangle of the Set Color tool, as the case may be.

If you don't like the Foreground/Background colors of the Set Color tool, then enable the coloring tool by clicking on it and click using the right mouse button on the object that you wish to color. Choose the color from the Color palette that pops up. Notice that the Foreground/Background rectangle will assume the color that you just selected.

Note: *With the exception of some objects such as the dial or the knob, most objects have the same Foreground/Background colors.*

Making Objects Transparent

Note the letter **T** that appears on the left side of the Color palette. Choosing **T** instead of a color will make the object to be colored *Transparent*. This feature may be used to make the box around the label invisible.

We can now begin with the coloring exercise.
1.   If the Controls palette is not open, then open it from the Windows menu.
      Open in the front panel the square LED from **Controls>Boolean** subpalette, and the Dial from **Controls>Numeric** subpalette.
2.   Enlarge them so they appear more or less as shown in Fig. 2-32.
3.   Using the procedure described above, set the foreground color to black and the background color to red.
4.   If the Tools palette is not open, then open it from the Windows menu.
      Color the square LED by first clicking on the Set Color tool in the Tools palette and then on the square LED with the paintbrush cursor. Note that the LED assumed the Backgnd color.
5.   Click on the Set Color tool in the Tools palette. Let's try to color the square LED in a slightly different manner. Click with the right mouse button on the square LED and move the cursor over the various colors in the popup Colors palette. Note several things that are happening as you move over the colors:

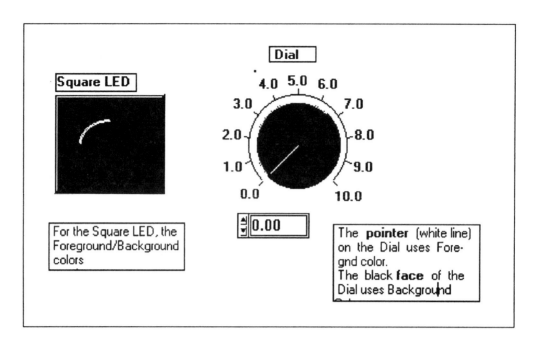

Fig. 2-32 Front Panel for Coloring Exercise

First, the square LED is changing colors and giving you a preview of the color that the mouse cursor is on at that instant.

Second, notice two squares labeled as Foreground and Background in the Colors palette. Both indicate the same colors as the object.

Decide on the color that you would like your object to be and click on it. The object as well as the Foreground/Background rectangles of the Set Color tool assume the color chosen by you.

6. Next, color the Dial. Note from the illustration in Fig. 2-32 that the Dial uses both the foreground and the background colors. Set the foreground color to *white* and the background color to *red* using the procedure described earlier.

    If you like using the shortcut keys, you may want to consider the following procedure. Enable the Set Color tool and click on the Dial with the right mouse button. Enter **f** from the keyboard. Note that as you move the cursor over various colors, only the color in the Foreground square of the Colors palette is changing. By clicking on a particular color, you are setting the foreground to that color.

    In a similar way you can use the **b** key to set the background color and **a** key to set both the foreground and the background to the same color.

7. Having set the foreground and the background colors white and red, respectively, enable the Set Color tool and paste the Foreground/Background colors on the dial by first clicking on the face of the dial and then on the indicator line. The indicator line is thin, so make sure that the tip of the paintbrush cursor is exactly on the line. The face of the Dial should be red and the pointer line white.

8. Set the Foreground/Background colors of the Set Color tool to *green.* Click on the Get Color tool and then click with the pipette cursor anywhere on the face of the Dial. Observe the change in the Foregnd/Backgnd colors of the Set Color tool. Notice that the Foreground/Background colors of the Dial have been copied to the Set Color tool.

9. Practice with other objects and other colors. Do not save anything.

Exercise 6: Editing Text

Editing text in LabVIEW is done frequently. Such operations as entering text into a label or identifying special features of your VI using free labels involve the use of text editor.

> **Note:** *In earlier versions of LabVIEW, there was an Edit/Run icon. In order to perform edit functions including editing text, you had to click on this icon. Version 4.0 of LabVIEW eliminates mode switching. When you first launch LabVIEW or open a VI, it opens in edit mode. When you run a VI, the Toolbar reflects that condition, and when execution is complete, it switches back to edit mode.*
>
> *Should you prefer that a VI opens in run mode, you must change the default setting to run mode from **Edit>Preferences>Miscellaneous** by selecting **Open VI in run mode** option.*

When editing text you will be using quite frequently the **Text Settings** pull-down menu in the Tool Bar (see Figs. 2-2 and 2-3). There you will find **Fonts, Size, Style and Color** options.

1. Let's begin this exercise by opening the **Waveform Chart** in the front panel. Make sure that the **Controls palette** as well as the **Tools palette** are open. You can get both palettes from the Windows menu. See Exercise 1 if you have forgotten how to open the Waveform Chart. The Path is **Controls>Graph>Waveform Chart**.

2. Now that you have the Waveform Chart opened, we can begin editing. First, enlarge the chart so that it is easier to work with. You resize the chart with the positioning tool. The chart should occupy more than half the screen.

3. Change the vertical (ordinate) and horizontal (abscissa) as follows:
    Ordinate: Max Value = **80**,   Min Value = **20**
    Abscissa: Max Value = **200**

Use *Edit Text Tool* from the Tools palette. Its cursor looks like this: 🛱
Before you can enter a new value, you must first delete the old one.
Place this cursor to the left of the maximum value on the vertical axis, click and hold down

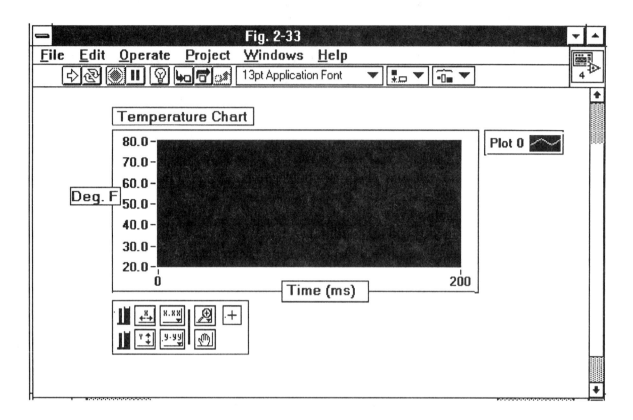

Fig. 2-33 Front Panel for the Editing Text Exercise

the left mouse button, and drag the cursor from left to right across the number to be deleted. You can also place the cursor on the right side of the number to be deleted and then drag the cursor from right to left. Observe that the background of the number became dark. Use the *Delete* key from the keyboard to erase the number. Now type **80** and either click on the *Enter* icon that shows up as the first icon on the left in the Toolbar, or use the *Enter* key from the keyboard. Notice that the rest of the scale has adjusted numerically.

An alternative way of deleting text is to click with the Edit Text cursor on the right side of the number to be deleted and then use the *Backspace* key on the keyboard to delete the number.

Repeat this procedure to enter **20** for the minimum value along the vertical scale and **200** for the maximum value along the horizontal scale.

4. Label the waveform chart with *owned label* as **Temperature Chart**. Refer to Exercise 4 for the labeling procedure.

5.   To give the chart a practical meaning, use *free* labels to label the vertical axis as **Deg. F** and the horizontal axis as **Time (ms)**. Refer to Exercise 4 for the labeling procedure.

6.   Using bold text enhances the appearance of the chart. ***Select*** the entire chart by clicking on it with the positioning tool ⬆, which you get from the Tools palette. Once selected, the chart will have a dashed outline around it. Enter from the keyboard ***Ctrl+3***, or ***Ctrl+2***, or select ***Bold*** from the ***Style*** submenu of the ***Text Settings*** pull-down menu. These options will change all the text in the Waveform Chart to bold. You have to select the free labels separately to change their text to bold.

7.   Suppose that you didn't want to convert all text in the Waveform Chart to bold but instead only some of it. You can make all the values along the vertical axis bold (you cannot make one value bold and the rest plain) by selecting any value with the operating tool ✋ or the edit text (labeling) tool ⬚ and then entering ***Ctrl+2*** or ***Ctrl+3*** from the keyboard or choosing ***Bold*** from the ***Style*** submenu of the ***Text Settings*** pull-down menu.

Try this on the Waveform Chart. If the text right now is bold, you can toggle it back to plain by first selecting the chart with the positioning tool and then choosing ***Plain*** from the ***Styles*** submenu of the ***Text Settings*** pull-down menu.

Notice that only the vertical scale changed the text style and the remaining text stayed the same. You can do the same thing to the horizontal axis, owned labels and free labels. *Using the positioning or the labeling tools, you first select the text that you wish to change and then apply the text changes from the Style submenu.*

8.   Suppose that you wish to change the size of the text. Let's make the owned label **Temperature Chart** larger. First, select it by clicking on it with the positioning tool. When you see a dashed outline around it, it has been selected. Next, depress the ***Ctrl*** key on the keyboard and press several times the (=) key until you see the text getting bigger. Conversely, if you select the label, depress the ***Ctrl*** key and depress several times the (-) key. You will see the text getting smaller. The alternative method of changing the text size is to choose the desired font size from ***Size*** submenu of the ***Text Settings*** menu. The final waveform chart configuration for this exercise is shown in Fig. 2-33.

9.   You can also change the ***text color***. Suppose that we would like to change the numbers along the vertical scale to **red**. First, select any number along the vertical scale by dragging the labeling tool cursor across it as described in step 3 of this exercise. Next, choose the ***Color*** option from the ***Text Settings*** menu. Incidentally if you double click on the Text Settings menu, a popup menu opens that, among other text options, also has a color option. From the ***Color palette*** choose red and OK. Notice that the vertical scale numerical values changed to red. You can change the horizontal scale values in exactly the same way.

To change the Temperature Chart label to green, select it in the usual way by clicking on it with the positioning tool until you see a dashed outline around the label. Then choose the green color from the color palette following the procedure of step 9. You can also change the color of the free labels by following the same procedure.

Note: *You must first select an object whose text is to be colored. For instance, if you click with the positioning tool on the chart, thus selecting the whole chart, and then choose a red color, you will color text along both axes and the text of the owned label (Temperature Chart) with red but not the free labels. They are separate objects. You have to select them and color their text separately with the same or a different color.*

However, if you wanted to color the text of several objects with the same color, select all objects following the procedure for multiple object selection as described in Exercise 2, and then choose the color from the color palette. The color that you choose will be applied to the text in all objects.

Remember also that we are coloring text and not the objects. Coloring of objects was done in a separate exercise.

10. Although this has nothing to do with coloring text, you may want to spend some time at this point coloring objects. Suppose it is required to color the screen of the waveform chart with the following custom color: **Red: 0; Green: 128; Blue: 128**. See if you can figure out how to do it! Clue: Use the More... option.

Exercise 7: Aligning and Distributing Objects

Alignment and Distribution options can be used to position objects inside the Panel or the Diagram windows. Objects can be arranged with a desired order or symmetry. These options are in the front panel and block diagram toolbars (see Figs. 2-2 and 2-4)

To see how these options work, let's try an experiment.

1. Open a **digital control** in the front panel. Choose the digital control from the *Numeric* subpalette of the *Controls* floating palette as shown in Fig. 2-34.

2. Once the Digital Control is in the front panel, make two copies of this control. Use the procedure in Exercise 3 for duplicating objects. You should now have three digital controls in the front panel. Move them around so that they are positioned vertically. Do not pay attention to the spacing between them. This is shown in Fig. 2-35 on the left side of the front panel. Also label them with *owned label*, so that the top digital control is **A**, the middle one is **B**, and the bottom digital control is **C**.

3. Next, select the three Digital Controls using the procedure described in Exercise 2 for selecting multiple objects. Each of the selected objects will be enclosed by a dashed border.

4. Click on the **Align Objects** tool in the Toolbar and choose **Left Edges** from the popup menu, as shown in Fig. 2-36. The selected objects will be aligned along the left edges.

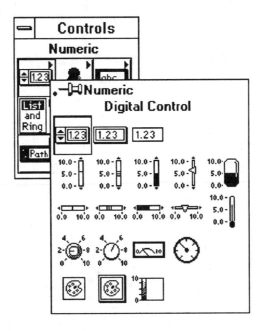

Fig. 2-34 Choosing the Digital Control from the Numeric Subpalette

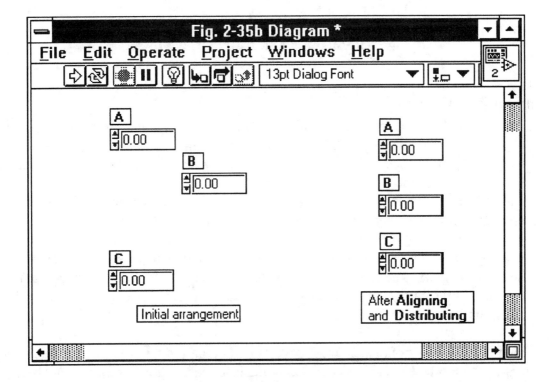

Fig. 2-35 Aligning and Distributing Objects Exercise

5. Select the three digital controls that are now aligned and click on **Distribute Objects** in the Toolbar, as shown in Fig. 2-36. Choose **Bottom Edges** from the popup menu, and three objects will be distributed with equal spacing between their bottom edges. The final arrangement of the three objects is shown in Fig. 2-35.

6. The Align and Distribute Objects menus in the Toolbar have options other than those used in this exercise. Practice using these other options on the three digital controls. After completing this exercise, do not save anything.

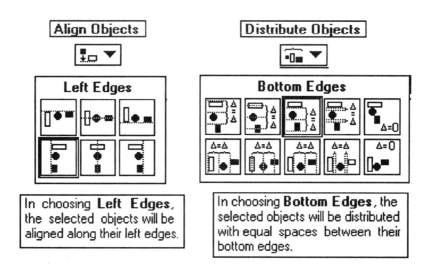

Fig. 2-36 Aligning and Distributing Objects

Exercise 8: Wiring

Thus far, we have focused on a variety of editing exercises that were done, as you might have noticed, in the front panel. But for every front panel there must also be a block diagram. As mentioned earlier, every VI must have a front panel and a block diagram. Although most of the editing techniques apply also to the block diagram, wiring of objects is done only in the block diagram. Objects such as functions, subVI nodes, and terminals must be connected or wired to allow the flow of data.

As we know, front panel objects consist of controls and indicators. Controls pass data to the block diagram. The block diagram, on the other hand, is a graphical program that manipulates the data it gets, and passes the results of program execution back to the indicators in the front panel.

Each object in the front panel must have its counterpart, a *terminal,* in the block diagram. It is very important to label each object in the front panel with an *owned label* because several objects of the same type, such as digital controls or digital indicators in the front panel, will have exactly the same symbolic representation in the block diagram.

54

Unless they are labeled with owned labels (not free labels) in the front panel, they cannot be distinguished in the block diagram. When an object is labeled with an owned label in the front panel, the same label will appear in the block diagram.

Wiring of objects in the Diagram Window is associated with *Data Flow* in the program. A wire connected from the output of one object to the input of another graphically represents the path that the data takes. More will be said later about the data flow and other functional aspects of a VI, but now our major concern here is to wire objects inside the block diagram.

Let's begin the wiring exercise.

1.　Open one **digital control** and one **digital indicator** in the front panel. Both the digital control and indicator are in the *Numeric* subpalette of the *Controls* palette. Copy each object so that you have two digital controls and two digital indicators.

2.　Label the digital controls with owned labels, one as **A** and the other as **B.**
Label the digital indicators with owned labels, one as **AB** and the other as **A+B.**

3.　Switch to the block diagram by using the shortcut keys **Ctrl+E.**
Open the **Add** and **Multiply** functions from the Arithmetic menu. The Add and Multiply functions are in the **Numeric** subpalette of the **Functions** palette (see Fig. 2-9).

4.　Arrange the objects as shown in Fig. 2-37. In Fig. 2-37 we now have two functions: the **Add** with (+) inside the icon will accept two inputs and produce a sum at the output. The **Multiply** with (x) inside the icon will accept two inputs and produce the product at its output. The *Digital Control* terminals **A** and **B** provide the numerical inputs from the front panel. The outputs from the **Add** and the **Multiply** functions are applied to the *digital indicator* terminals labeled **A+B** and **AB**. The *digital indicators* on the front panel will display the **Sum** and the **Product.**

As mentioned earlier, the wiring represents the data flow symbolically. In this case the digital control terminals A and B must be wired to the inputs of the Add and the Multiply functions, and the outputs from the Add and the Multiply functions must be wired to their respective *digital indicator* terminals.

To simplify the wiring process, any function icon can be changed to another form that shows the inputs be wired. To accomplish this, click (with the right mouse button) on the function icon and choose **Show>Terminals** from the popup menu, as shown in Fig. 2-38. When you release the mouse button, the icon changes to the terminal representation. Notice the two inputs and the output are indicated clearly. This option toggles, so if you click on the terminal and choose **Show>Terminals** again, the terminal representation will switch to icon form.

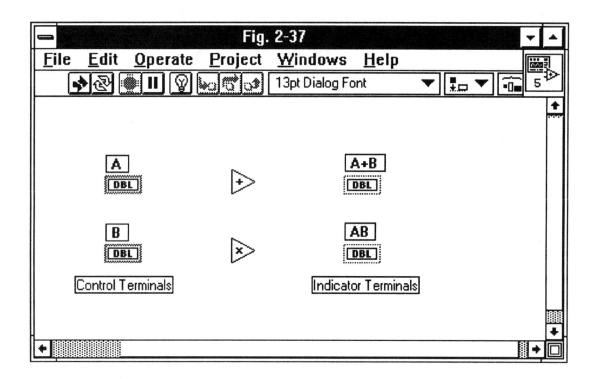

Fig. 2-37 Block Diagram for the Wiring Exercise

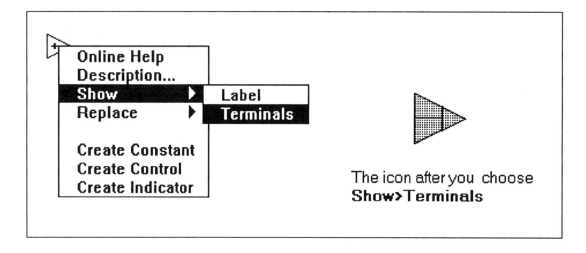

**Fig. 2-38 Choosing Show>Terminals Changes the Icon
Input/Output Terminal Representation**

5.	We are now ready to begin wiring. Click on the ***wiring tool*** 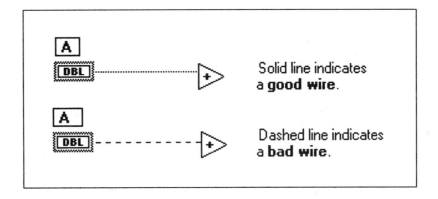 in the ***Tools palette***. Position the cursor (the tip of the wire) over digital indicator A and observe that it begins to blink. Click and hold down the right mouse button. Then drag the mouse to one of the inputs on the Add function terminal, making sure that the extended wire of the cursor is over the input. Notice again that once you are over the input, it begins to blink. Click the right mouse button only once and observe the orange wire in place between digital control A and one input of the Add function.

	If the wiring was successful, a solid wire will be in place. However, if you got a ***bad*** wire, it will appear as a *dashed line,* as shown in Fig. 2-39. Delete the bad wire by entering ***CTRL+B*** shortcut key from the keyboard or choose ***Remove Bad Wires*** from the ***Edit*** Menu and repeat the wiring process in step 5.

Fig. 2-39 A Dashed Line Indicates a Bad Wire

6.	Repeat the wiring process described in step 5 and wire the Digital Control B to one of the inputs of the Multiply function.

7.	A ***Wire Junction*** may be created as shown in the illustration below. It is useful when the data source such as the digital control A or B has to be wired to more than one terminal input.

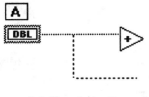

A Wire Junction

	To create a wire junction, click with the tip of the wiring tool on the wire where the junction is to be created and drag the cursor to the input of the terminal. As the input area of the terminal begins to blink, click with the left mouse button. Observe a solid wire that extends from the junction to the input of the terminal.

	Use this procedure to wire digital control A to the other input of the Multiply function.

8.	Repeat the procedure described in step 7 by creating a wire junction and wiring ***digital control B*** to the remaining input of the Add function.

9. Complete the wiring by connecting the output of the Add function to the **A+B** digital indicator and the output of the Multiply function to the **AB** digital indicator. Your completed wiring diagram should look like that shown in Fig. 2-40.

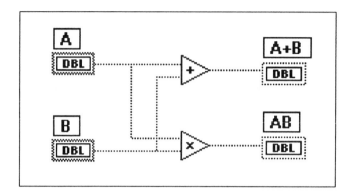

Fig. 2-40 Completed Diagram for the Wiring Exercise

More Wiring Tips

10. You can *Delete* one or more wire segments by first selecting them. To select a wire segment, click with the *Positioning Tool* ⬈ on the wire to be deleted. The selected wire becomes enclosed by dashed lines. You can select more than one wire segment, depending on how many times you click, as shown in Fig. 2-41. If you hold down the *Shift* key, all segments that you click on will be selected. A shortcut to selecting all segments connected by one or more nodes is to *click three times* on one of the segments.

> **One Click** – Select one segment
> **Three Clicks** – Select all segments joined by one or more junctions

By entering *Delete* from the keyboard, all selected wire segments will be deleted.

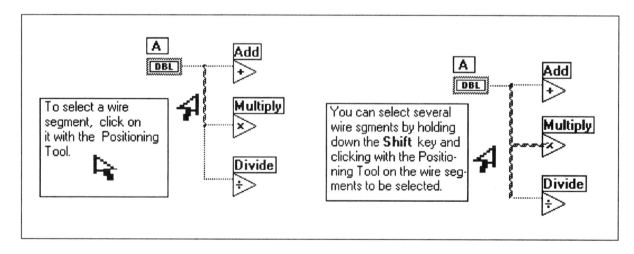

Fig. 2-41 Selecting Wire Segments

11. Sometimes the configuration that you are wiring forces you to change **wiring direction**. Wiring direction can be changed in one of two ways:

     A. Use the *Space Bar* on the keyboard during wiring.
         When not wiring, the Space Bar causes toggling between the *Operating Tool* and the *Wiring Tool*.

     B. After you started the wiring path and before you get to the end (terminal), *click and hold down* the left mouse button. This will freeze the wiring segment that you have made thus far. Change the direction at this point and continue with the wiring.

12. Check the wiring. If there are no broken wires, then you have completed your first VI. You can actually run it. Switch to front panel (*Ctrl+E*) and activate the *Operating Tool* 🖑 by clicking on the Operating Tool in the Tools palette. Use the Operating Tool to enter values into Digital Controls A and B. To increment or decrement values, click on the ⬍ *up/down* arrows of the digital control with the Operating tool. Another way to enter values into the digital control is to click with the Operating Tool cursor inside the Digital Control's window, erase with the *Backspace* key the current value, and type the new value. The *Labeling tool* A may also be used here in place of the Operating tool.

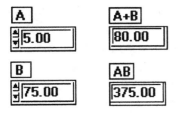

For example, enter **5** into Digital Control A and **75** into Digital Control B and run the VI by clicking on the **Run** ⇨ button in the Control Bar. The VI will execute once and display the **sum A+B** and the **product AB** as shown. Note the difference between the digital controls and the digital indicators.

Exercise 9: Saving VI to the Library File

All VIs that you build and would like to keep can be saved in some directory, as is common practice. In LabVIEW, however, you have another option. Your VI can be saved in a VI Library. The Library is not a directory, but rather it is a file that can contain many VI files. There are several advantages associated with a VI Library. Any VI stored in a Library can have a name that is up to 31 characters long instead of the usual 8 characters. To save disk space, all VIs are compressed when you save them and decompressed when you load them. Portability becomes simpler too because all the VIs are in the same file.

The VI Library must have a name 8 characters long or less and a **.LLB** extension. A VI file may have a name 31 characters long or less, as mentioned earlier, with a **.vi** extension.

Let's experiment with saving the VI that you just finished wiring.

1. Choose **Save As** from the **File** menu.
2. From the popup menu that opens, choose **New**.
3. **New Directory** or **VI Library** opens next. Type the VI Library name of your choice in the

dialog box. For example, if you typed **My_VIs**, it would appear as shown in Fig. 2-42. The VI Library will be created by LabVIEW after you click on the **VI Library** button.

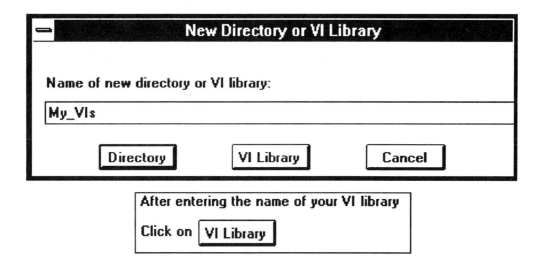

Fig. 2-42 Creating VI Library called My_VIs.LLB

4. As soon as you click on VI Library, the *File Dialog* menu opens. Notice that the VI Library that you just created appears in the directory box. Type the name of the VI that you wish to save in the newly created VI Library. Suppose that you want to save the VI that you just finished wiring and call it Add_Multiply. Type in the dialog box **Add_Multiply.vi** and choose OK. The path for your file is *LabVIEW>MyVIs.LLB>Add_Multiply.vi.*

> **Note:** *If you are saving a VI, you must type the* **.vi** *extension after the VI name. The system will not do it for you.*

5. To view the file that was just saved, choose *Open* from the *File* menu, choose **My_VIs.LLB**, and click on the **Add_Multiply.vi**.

Exercise 10: VI Documentation

Any VI that you create can be documented. Although this is not essential, it is often helpful, especially if the VI was constructed quite some time ago and you may have forgotten its objectives. Obviously if the VI is simple, documentation is not necessary. Let's go through the procedure on how to document a VI. You are documenting a currently open VI.

1. Open the VI that will be documented. Take, for instance, the VI that you just finished wiring, the Add_Multiply.vi. If it is already open, then proceed to the next step.
2. Choose *Show VI Info...* from the *Windows* menu.

3.   The popup menu that opens is called *VI Information*. Notice the VI name, at the top of the menu, followed by the VI path. The Current Revision box indicates the latest revision for this VI. If you click on *Explain*, the next popup menu will offer an explanation for the change, assuming that the VI documentation has been kept up.

In the *Description* box, type the most appropriate description for your VI. A sample description is offered in Fig. 2-43.

Memory Usage is also included here. Note that this tiny VI consumes about 10.7 Kbytes of RAM.

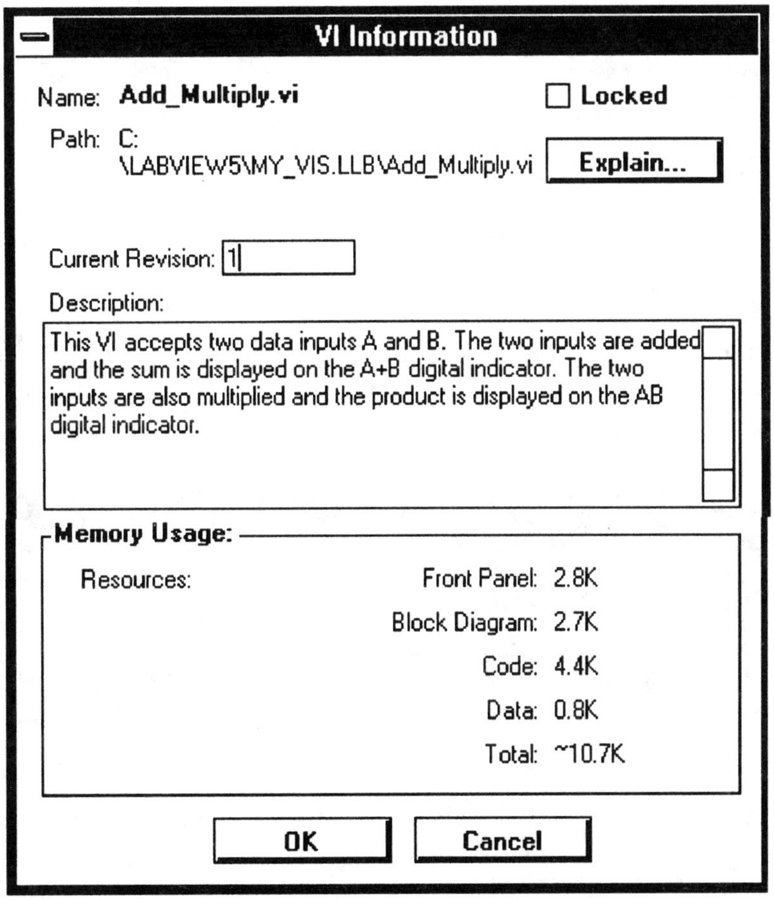

Fig. 2-43 VI Documentation

Object Documentation

Any object in the window of a VI that is presently open may also be documented for future reference. Suppose that a **Sum 3** subVI is in the block diagram and you wish to document it.

To document it, pop up on it (with the right mouse button) and choose *Description* as shown in Fig. 2.44.

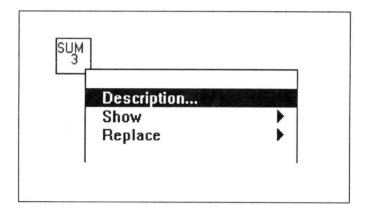

Fig. 2-44 Choosing the Description Option for Object Documentation

The *Description* menu pops up, allowing you to document the object in the dialog box, as shown in Fig. 2-45.

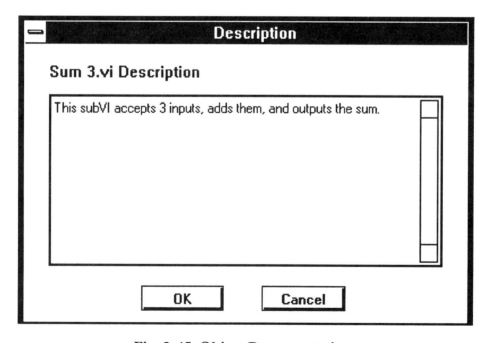

Fig. 2-45 Object Documentation

Summary

1. LabVIEW is a graphical programming environment. A program written in LabVIEW is called a virtual instrument (VI). Each VI must have a front panel and a block diagram. The front panel includes various controls and indicators, while the block diagram typically includes functions, terminals, and subVIs.

2. An object in the front panel has its counterpart, called a terminal, in the block diagram. All controls and indicators have their corresponding terminals in the block diagram. Because any two controls have exactly the same appearance in the block diagram, it is important to label them in the front panel, thus identifying them not only to the system but also to yourself, so that you can tell them apart in the block diagram.

3. There are two types of labels: *owned* and *free* labels. When you type an owned label over an object in the front panel, the same label will be attached to the corresponding terminal in the block diagram and the system is aware of that label. The free label is used for additional descriptive information. When you type the free label in the Front Panel, it will not appear in the block diagram.

4. The Toolbar serves as the user interface, providing tools for editing and running your VI. It includes the Text Settings pull-down text menu, as well as options for aligning and distributing objects and tools for debugging.

5. LabVIEW version 4.0 introduces graphical floating palettes. Controls, functions, and other tools that were previously in the pull-down text menus are now moved to the floating palettes. Floating palettes have graphical subpalettes that can be converted to floating palettes. Controls, Functions, and Tools floating palettes contain valuable resources for building a VI.

6. The Menu Bar includes options for file control, editing, operating a VI, window control, and many other options. Project and Options are of particular importance and usefulness. The Project option includes tools for optimizing the performance of your VI, while the Help option provides object description as well as in-depth on-line help.

7. A VI Library is a special feature of LabVIEW. A VI Library is not a directory but rather a file where you can store many VIs. It helps to save disk space because all VIs are compressed when saved and decompressed when loaded. It allows 31 characters for VI names, instead of the usual 8. Portability is simpler too because all VIs are in the same folder. All you need to do is to copy a VI Library and you have copied all VIs inside the library.

Chapter 3

Creating
and
Troubleshooting a VI

In this chapter you will learn:
How to create a VI
How to create a subVI
How to use a subVI
Data types and data representation
Format and precision
How to troubleshoot a VI

Introduction

The previous chapter was almost entirely devoted to the description of the LabVIEW environment. You have learned about the valuable resources in the floating palettes and the toolbar. Because wiring is an essential task in building any VI, it was discussed at great length. Wiring is a skill that you gain with practice. You also learned that a VI Library is a file that contains many other VI files.

As you progress through this workbook, you may need to refer back to Chapter 2. In time you will agree that Chapter 2 is a valuable resource on information about the LabVIEW environment. There are some aspects of LabVIEW that still need to be covered and that will be done in a more appropriate setting in future chapters.

In this chapter, however, you will embark on the task of creating a VI, using it, and interpreting the results. Probably one of the most frustrating experiences is to find that your VI is not working after you put in considerable effort building it. Fortunately LabVIEW has an impressive array of debugging tools, which will be covered in considerable detail in this chapter.

Exercise 1: Viewing a VI

Before building your own VI, you will open, run, and inspect a demonstration VI. You will find out the power and versatility of LabVIEW. Simulation is one of many things that can be done in LabVIEW, and this is exactly what our demonstration VI will do. Its name is ProjMotn.vi, and as you might have guessed from its name, it simulates projectile flight.

We know from physics that when a projectile is aimed at a given angle and given an initial velocity, its path through space will follow a parabolic path before descending back to earth. This is a simplistic model where drag forces due to friction are neglected. The **Range** is the distance along the ground between the starting point and the point where the projectile returns to ground, and the **Altitude** is the maximum vertical distance of the parabolic path.

The path for this VI is A:\Workbook.LLB\ProjMotn.vi. Actually Workbook.LLB is the suggested VI Library for saving all VIs that you will build.

You are not expected to understand at this time the design of this VI, although you can peek at the block diagram by entering Ctrl+E from the keyboard. The purpose of this exercise is to operate a typical VI, observe its response, and observe the various objects in the front panel.

So go to WorkBook.LLB and open the ProjMotn.vi. The front panel, as shown in Fig. 3-1, opens as soon as you open the ProjMotn.vi.

Note that the front panel contains controls and indicators. There are digital controls for inputting the angle and the initial velocity, and there are digital indicators for displaying the altitude, range, and the time of flight. There is also the X-Y graph for displaying the parabolic projectile path.

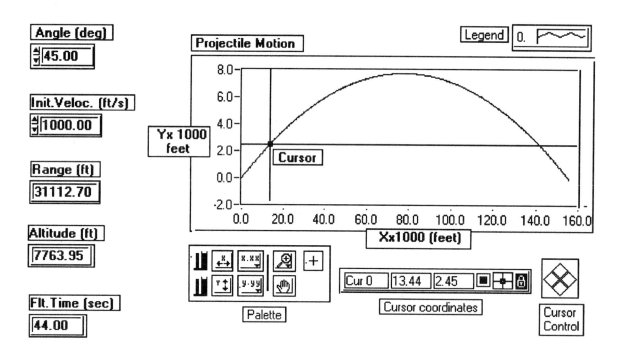

Fig. 3-1   Front Panel of the ProjMotn.vi

Run the VI by clicking on the **Run** button. As soon as you click on the Run button, a popup graph opens. This is an example of what can be done when you run out of space in the original front panel. Notice that in the front panel the X-Y graph displays a plot of the projectile's vertical position (along the Y-axis) versus its position along ground (along the X-axis). But suppose we also wanted to see how the projectile's vertical distance and its position along ground vary with time. Well, the popup graph does just that. When you are finished observing the popup graph, click on the **Done** button. The popup graph will disappear, and you are back to the front panel of the ProjMotn.vi.

Enter different values for the angle and the initial velocity, and run the VI again. Note different results for range, altitude, and time of flight.

Note the **Cursor Display** shown in Fig. 3-2. The cursor, which also rides the curve as shown in Fig. 3-1, can be controlled from the cursor bar and the cursor control located below the graph. You can move the cursor along the curve by clicking on the diamond shaped cursor control, and the x-y coordinate values are displayed in the cursor bar below. The cursor can also be locked and unlocked. Don't forget to use the Operating tool to operate the various cursor controls.

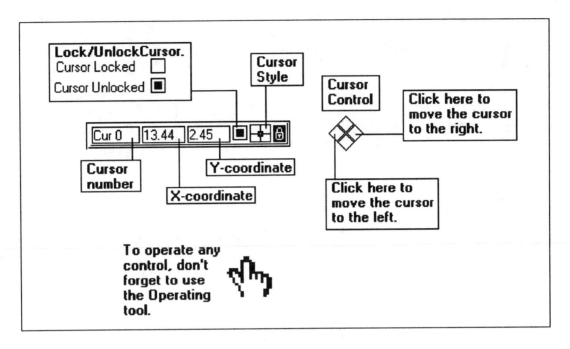

Fig. 3-2   The Cursor Display

Once you are finished with this VI, close it by choosing *Close* from the File menu or use the shortcut keys *Ctrl+W*. *Do not save* any changes that you might have made.

Exercise 2:   Creating a VI

Although you have already built a VI in the wiring exercise of the last chapter, the situation is slightly different here. The VI that you have to build has been configured. You are given its completed front panel and block diagram and now it is your job to build it.

The VI that you have to build, Sum4.vi, is shown in Fig. 3-3. This VI can add four numbers and output the sum. We will later create an icon and a connector for this VI. Since the conventional Add function can add only two numbers, this VI will be a handy icon for future applications.

The front panel includes 4 digital controls and one digital indicator, and the block diagram uses the 3 Add functions. You will find:

Digital Control and Indicator in *Controls>Numeric* floating palette.
Add function in *Functions>Numeric* floating palette.

Build the front panel and the block diagram as shown in Fig. 3-3.

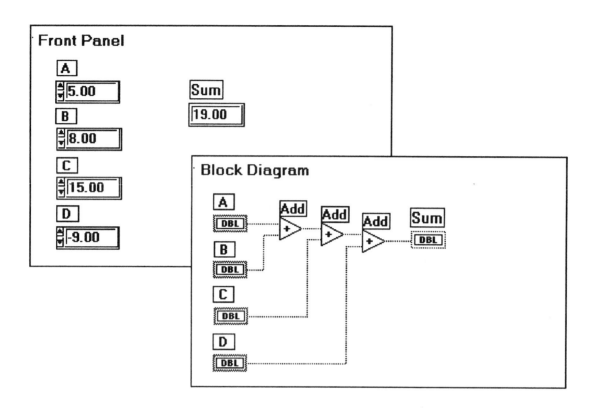

Fig. 3-3　Front Panel and Block Diagram for Sum4.vi

Run the Sum4.vi by clicking on the Run button. If the Run button is broken, your VI cannot be executed because it has errors. This is similar to syntax errors in a high-level language (such as C language) program. The errors must be corrected before your VI can be executed. Consult the troubleshooting section later in this chapter and correct all errors.

Provide a VI description. See Exercise 10 of Chapter 2.

Save Sum4.vi in WorkBook.LLB. If this VI Library does not exist, create it following the procedure of Exercise 9 in Chapter 2.

Exercise 3: Creating an Icon and a Connector for a VI

All VIs that you build are hierarchical in character. This means that any VI, regardless of how large it is, may be used as a *subVI* in another VI. This capability of LabVIEW permits a modular construction of a complex VI. A complex VI may include one or more subVIs, each with an icon and a connector, and each subVI is designed to perform a specific function. The modularization of a large VI makes it is easier to troubleshoot. If changes need to be made in a subVI, they can be handled without affecting the rest of the VI.

Any VI can be converted into a subVI. All it needs is an *Icon and a Connector*. This exercise will show you how to create an Icon and a Connector for a VI, and we will use the Sum4.vi that you just finished building as an example.

1. First open the Sum4.vi. Remember, it is in the Workbook.LLB VI Library.

2. Switch to the block diagram and **select** the three Add functions shown in Fig. 3-4. Consult Exercise 2 in Chapter 2 on how to select multiple objects.

3. Choose **subVI From Selection** from the Edit menu. The selected portion of the Sum4.vi has been converted to a subVI. This is shown in Fig. 3-4.

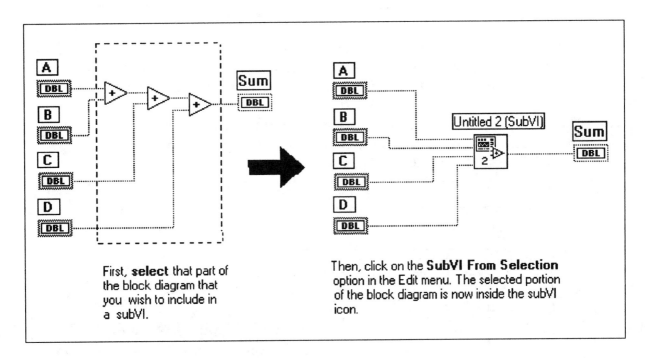

Fig. 3-4 Creating a subVI

69

4. *Pop up* (right mouse button) on the subVI icon and choose *Show>Terminals* from the popup menu. As illustrated in Fig. 3-5, the icon switches to a terminal configuration. This is a connector that has four input terminals (for A, B, C, D inputs) and one output terminal (for the sum output). If you wish to see the icon again, pop up on the connector and choose *Show>Terminals*; this option toggles, as you can see.

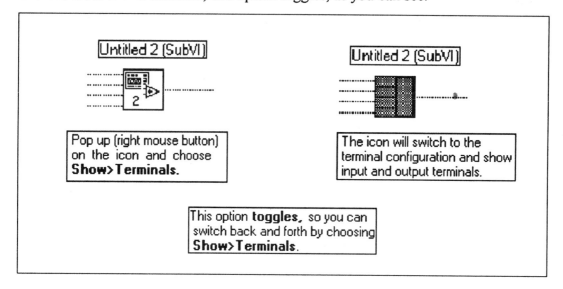

Fig. 3-5 Switching from Icon to Connector

5. When you created a subVI in step 3, the system created for you not only the connector but also a default icon. Generally the icon picture should reflect more or less the function of the VI. Since the default icon doesn't really do that, we should design our own.

Double click on the subVI icon to open its front panel. When the front panel of the subVI opens, click with right mouse button on *Icon Pane* and choose from the popup menu *Edit Icon*, as illustrated in Fig. 3-6.

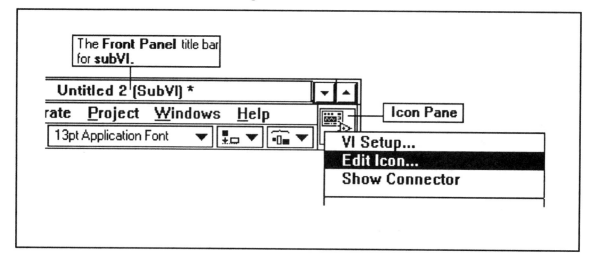

Fig. 3-6 Choosing Edit Icon from Icon Pane

70

6. The **Icon Editor** window shown in Fig. 3-7 opens as soon as you release the Edit Icon button. It has the working area where you can draw the symbol for your icon. The black and white and color options allow you to draw in black and white or in color.

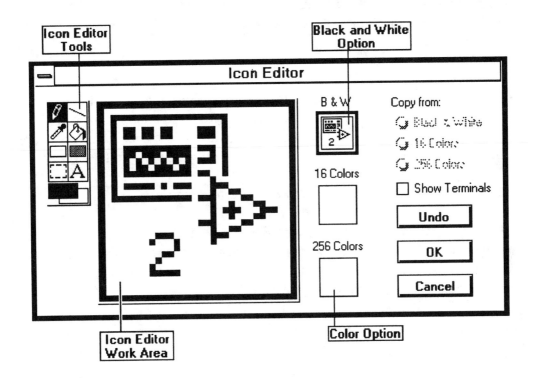

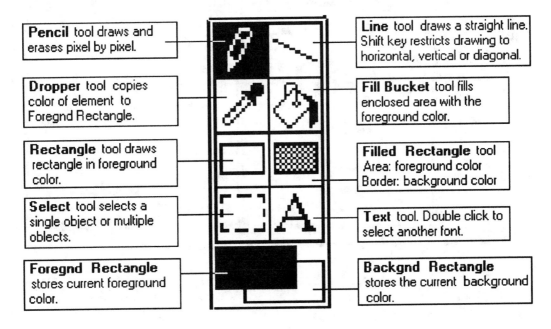

Fig. 3-7 The Icon Editor

71

You should become familiar with the tools the used to draw the icon symbol. A brief description of each tool is given in Fig. 3-7.

One tool used often is the *Select* tool. Select one or more objects by first clicking on this tool and then forming a dashed outline around the area to be selected. Once selected, the objects can be copied, moved, or deleted.

The *Text* tool allows you to add lettering to your symbol.

The *Foregnd/Backgnd* rectangles display the currently active colors. By clicking on one of the rectangles, you can change the active color from the popup color palette. You can also use the *Dropper* to change the foreground color by first clicking on the dropper icon and then on any area in the icon editor window to copy its color to the Foregnd Rectangle.

To draw a rectangle or a square, you use the *Rectangle* tool.

Most of your drawing is done either with the *Pencil* tool or *Line* tool. The Pencil tool draws pixel by pixel. If you create a pixel and then click on it again, you will erase it. The Line tool, on the other hand, draws linear shapes. To draw perfect vertical or horizontal lines, hold down the *Shift* key on the keyboard.

7. *Design* an icon symbol for Sum4.vi. A suggested design for the icon is shown in Fig. 3-8, but you can create your own.

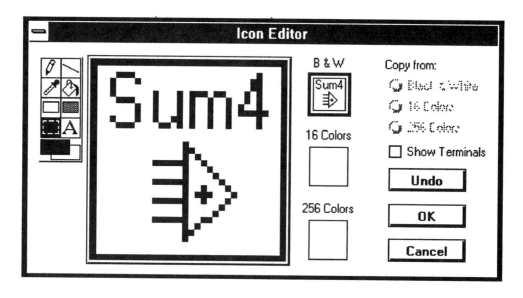

Fig. 3-8 Sum4.vi Icon Symbol

8. At this point, the Sum4.vi has been assigned a *connector* and you drew the symbol for the *icon*.

> **Note:** *In order for a VI to be used later as a subVI, it must have an icon and a connector.*

Suppose that the connector assigned by the system is not acceptable to you. Can it be changed? The answer is yes.

9. You may omit this step if you are not interested in changing the connector configuration. To change the connector configuration, first open the VI that already has a connector that you wish to change, or a VI that doesn't have a connector, and switch to front panel.

Next, click (the right mouse button) on the *Icon Pane* and choose *Show Connector* from the popup menu (see Fig. 3-6). The icon changes to the connector configuration.

Click (the left mouse button) on the *Icon Pane* and choose *Patterns* from the popup menu, as shown in Fig. 3-9. Choose the desired connector pattern and click on it. The pattern that you selected will appear in the Icon Pane.

The connector pattern that you selected may be rotated, flipped horizontally, or flipped vertically by choosing the appropriate options that appear below the Patterns option.

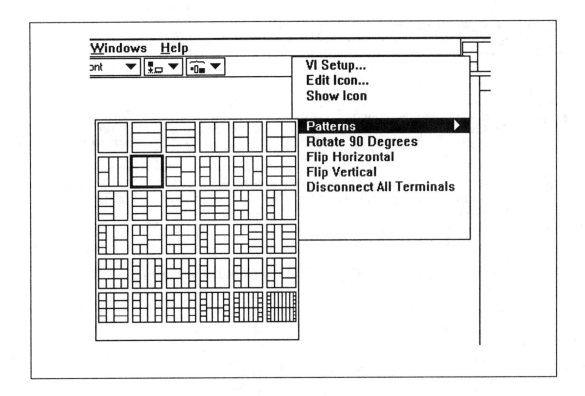

Fig. 3-9 Choosing a Connector Pattern

73

10.   Next, you must assign every control and indicator appearing in the front panel to the terminals on the connector. Follow the procedure as shown in Fig. 3-10.

The assigned terminals will appear as gray on the connector. You may have more terminals than there are objects. The unassigned terminals will not be used.

You may wish delete the terminal assignment. To do so, choose **Disconnect All Terminals** from the Icon Pane popup menu (see Fig. 3-9).

After completing the terminal assignment and icon symbol design, **save** the VI as, for example, Sum4icon.vi in *Workbook.LLB*. Note that Sum4.vi cannot be used as a subVI because it does not have an icon and a connector. Sum4icon.vi, on the other hand, can be used as a subVI.

We will next use Sum4icon.vi as a subVI.

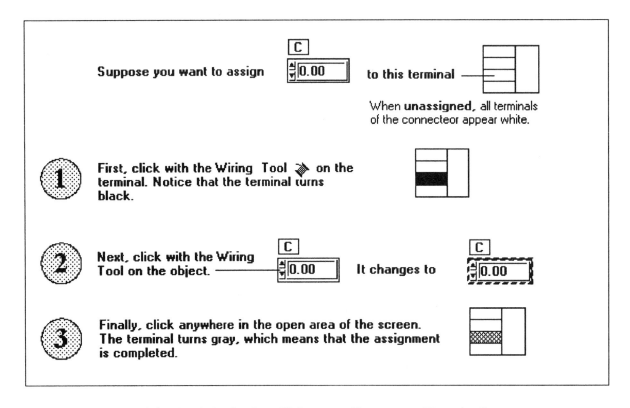

Fig. 3-10 Assigning Objects to Connector Terminals

74

Exercise 4: Using a VI as a SubVI

The purpose of this exercise is to demonstrate how a VI can be used as a subVI in another VI. As mentioned earlier, *a subVI must have an icon and a connector* if it is to be used in another VI. In Exercise 3, we created an icon and a connector for Sum4icon.vi. In this exercise we will use Sum4icon.vi as a subVI.

1. ***Open new VI*** by choosing *New* from the File menu.

2. Switch to the front panel, open four ***digital controls (Controls>Numeric palette)***, and label them with owned labels as **N1, N2, N3, N4**. Also open a digital indicator (from the same palette) and label it with an owned label as **Result**.

3. 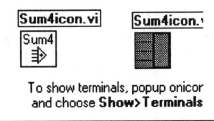 Switch to the block diagram (Ctrl+E) and click on the ***Select a VI...*** button in the Functions palette. The *Select a VI* window opens, giving you access to directories and files. Navigate to the place where you saved the Sum4icon.vi. If it was in the Workbook.LLB, then open the Workbook.LLB and double click on the Sum4icon.vi.

4. After clicking anywhere in the block diagram, you should see the familiar icon for the Sum4icon.vi. If its owned label is not shown, then you can open it by popping up on the icon and choosing ***Show>Label*** from the popup menu.

   You may also switch to the terminal representation, as shown in the illustration, by popping up on the icon and choosing the ***Show>Terminals*** option from the popup menu.

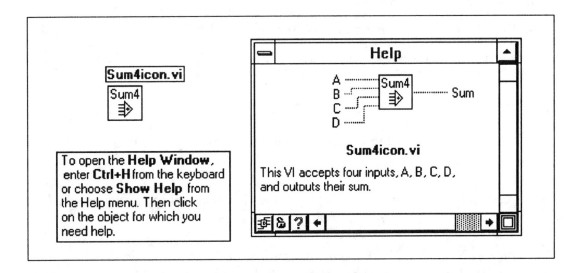

Fig. 3-11 The Help Window

75

5. The *Help Window* shown in Fig. 3-11 is one of the most useful features of LabVIEW. It provides object description as well as the connector configuration with inputs and outputs.

    To Open Help Window enter **Ctrl+H** from the keyboard, or choose **Show Help** from the Help menu. Once the Help window is open and you need help on a particular object, just click on that object. The description of the object will appear in the window. This is illustrated for Sum4icon.vi in Fig. 3-11.

    The Help window also assists you *in quickly identifying the terminal* being wired on a connector. For example, suppose you wire an object to terminal C on the Sum4icon subVI. As illustrated in Fig. 3-12, when the wiring tool is over the terminal, three things happen:

    The terminal on Sum4icon begins to blink.
    The corresponding terminal in the Help window begins to blink.
    The name of the terminal (C in the illustration) appears
    below Sum4icon.

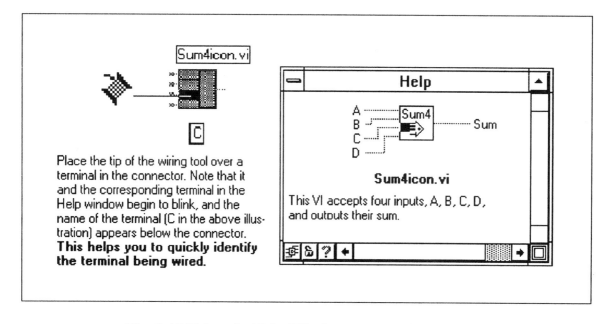

Fig. 3-12 Using the Help Window to Identify Terminals

    As discussed under Help menu in Chapter 2, the Help window can provide *Detailed Help*, *Simple Help*, or *On-line Help*, depending on the object.

6. *Wire* controls N1, N2, N3, N4 and the indicator Result to the Sum4icon.vi. Try to use the features of the Help window as described in step 5. The completed front panel and block diagram are shown in Fig. 3-13.

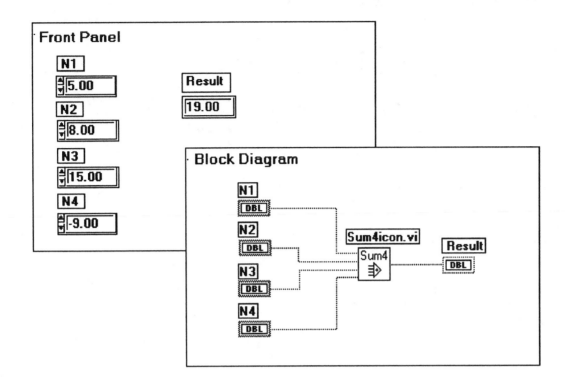

Fig. 3-13 Front the Panel and Block Diagram of Exercise 4

7. Once again, note the advantage of the subVI icon. Although this particular subVI doesn't contain a great deal of graphical code, in general a subVI can include a large and complex configuration. This helps to keep the block diagram neat and uncluttered. Also, it is easier to troubleshoot the configuration and make changes in individual subVIs without affecting too much of the rest of the diagram.

Broken buttoɪ

If the Run icon in the Control bar is broken, the VI cannot be executed. Consult the troubleshooting section later in this chapter.

Otherwise, *Run* this VI using different values in digital controls.
Save this VI as *Using Sum4icon.vi as a subVI.vi* in the Workbook.LLB.

Data Types

Objects in the block diagram are interconnected by wires, and wires carry data. Because there are several data types, a specific thickness and color are assigned to each data type. Fig. 3-14 includes a summary of wire shapes and colors for different data types. As shown in the table, blue is used for integers, orange for floating point numbers, green represents Boolean types, and purple is reserved for strings. The wires become thicker as you progress from scalars to two-dimensional arrays.

	Scalar	Array(1D)	Array(2D)	Color
Number	 ···· ············ ·	 ᵕᵕᵕᵕᵕᵕᵕᵕᵕᵕ	 :::::::::::::::::::	Integer: **Blue** Float: **Orange**
Boolean	 ···· ···········	 ᵕᵕᵕᵕᵕᵕᵕᵕᵕᵕᵕ	 ✕✕✕✕✕✕✕✕✕✕✕✕	Green
String	 ⌐⌐⌐⌐⌐⌐⌐⌐⌐⌐	 ⌷⌷⌷⌷⌷⌷⌷⌷⌷	 ▓▓▓▓▓▓▓▓▓	Purple

Fig. 3-14 Data Types Represented by Color and Thickness of Wires

Data Representation

Data Representation characterizes numerical data as

Floating Point Number
Integer
Unsigned Integer
Complex

A floating point number has as many decimal places as dictated by the *precision* that was assigned to that number, and the integer has no decimal places but can assume a positive or a negative sign. The unsigned integer must be positive only, and the complex number has the real and the imaginary components.

The amount of memory consumed by the data in a particular VI depends on the data type that you have chosen.

In the block diagram, wires that interconnect various objects carry data. The shape and color of the wire makes it easier for the user to identify the type of data that the wire carries. For example, when we see a thin orange wire, we know that it must be carrying floating point numerical data.

Wires don't produce data; they only transport data, and that data must originate at the source, to which one end of the wire is connected. If the source of data is a digital control, as was the case in the Sum4.vi that you built, then that digital control can be configured in several ways.

To configure a digital control, pop up on the digital control, choose ***Representation***, and then choose data representation from the submenu. If you choose a **DBL,** as shown in Fig. 3-15, the numerical value placed into the digital control will consume 8 bytes of memory. Other controls or indicators in the front panel can be configured in exactly the same way.

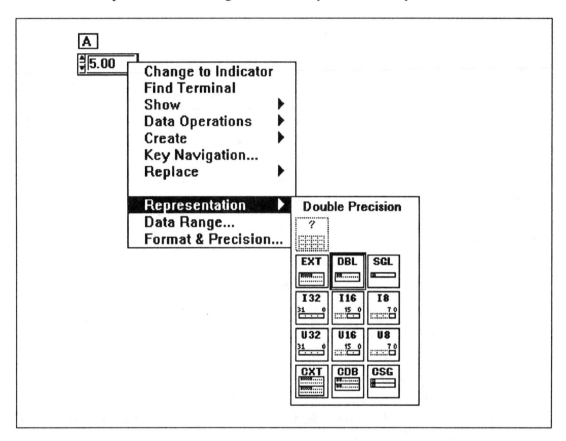

Fig. 3-15 Choosing Data Representation for a Digital Control

Note that the floating point numbers can be **SGL, DBL,** or **EXT.** Double is a default assignment to all floating numbers used in LabVIEW. So if you choose not to change that default assignment, a digital control that you bring to the Panel Window will have the DBL representation. This means that each number that you enter into that digital control will occupy 8 bytes (one byte is 8 bits) of memory space. It also means that you can use any number between 10^{-308} and 10^{308} with 7 digits of precision (up to 7 decimal places).

Numeric Data	Data Types		
Floating Point Numbers	**SGL** **4 bytes** 3.4 exp(−38) to 3.4 exp(+38)	**DBL** **8 bytes** 1.7 exp(−308) to 1.7 exp(+308)	**EXT** **10 bytes** 3.4 exp(−4932) to 3.4 exp(+4932)
Signed Integers	**I8** **Byte** **(1 byte)** −128 to +127	**I16** **Word** **(2 bytes)** −32,768 to +32,767	**I32** **Long** **(4 bytes)** −2 exp(9) to +2 exp(9)
Unsigned Integers	**U8** **Byte** **(1 byte)** 0 to +127	**U16** **Word** **(2 bytes)** 0 to +65,536	**U32** **Long** **(4 bytes)** 0 to +4 exp(9)
Complex Numbers	**CSG** **Single** 8 bytes	**CDB** **Double** 16 bytes	**CXT** **Extended** 20 bytes

Fig. 3-16 Data Representation Options

On the other hand, an **SGL** representation uses only 4 bytes in memory, allowing you to use numbers between 10^{-38} and 10^{38} also with 7 digits of precision.

Similarly **I8** occupies only 1 byte in memory, allowing you to use integer values between −128 and +127. **U8** (unsigned), on the other hand, also occupies 1 byte in memory and allows you to use values from 0 to 255. Note that between −128 and +127, there are the same number of integer values as between 0 and 255. That's why both I8 and U8 occupy 1 byte of memory. **I16**, on the other hand, needs 2 bytes of memory, allowing you to use integer values between −32, 768, and 32,767. **U16** also uses 2 bytes of memory, offering a range of 0 to 65, 535.

The complex form of data uses twice as much memory as does the corresponding floating point number. Thus a double precision complex data point requires 16 bytes of memory, while the double precision floating point number need 8 bytes.

Thus, the data representation that one chooses can have a great effect on memory consumption. This may not be a consideration if the VI does not process a great deal of data. However, if the VI application is data intensive with large files, choosing the appropriate data representation can be an important consideration.

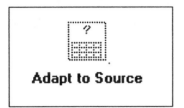

The *Adapt to Source* option at the top of the Representation submenu, if selected for a control object, will automatically adapt to the data source during program execution.

Format and Precision

Precision indicates the number of decimal places in a floating point number. Up to 7 decimal places are possible with *DBL* or *SGL* representation, while the *EXT* representation allows up to 15 decimal places. Format options include:

> **Floating Point Notation**
> **Scientific Notation**
> **Engineering Notation**
> **Relative Time (sec)**

To set Format and Precision for an object in the front panel, pop up on the object (with the right mouse button) and click on the *Format* and *Precision* option in the popup menu The window that opens is shown in Fig. 3-17, and it allows you to select the format and the precision for the object. The illustration shows 2 digits of precision and the floating point notation. However, if you want to change the precision, just type another number in the *Digits of Precision* box. You can also change the *Format* by clicking on another option.

Fig. 3-18 shows the effect of precision choice on the digital indicator display. In all illustrations the input to be displayed is 123.4567. In the case of the floating point display, the entire value is displayed when 4 digits of precision are used, and when 2 digits of precision are used, the second decimal place is rounded off to 6. The scientific notation places the decimal point after the first digit, and the precision you select determines the number of decimal places; a precision of 4 displays 123.46, rounding off the second decimal place to 6, and the precision of 2 displays 123, truncating completely all decimal places.

When engineering notation is used with a precision of 4, the display is 123.4567. When the precision is changed to 2, 123.46 is displayed, rounding off once again the second decimal place to 6.

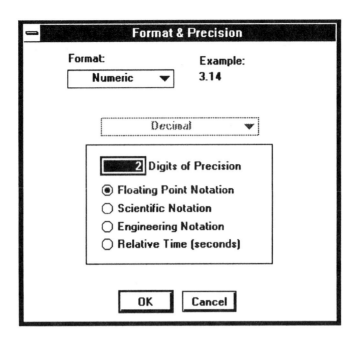

Fig. 3-17 Format and Precision Menu

The relative time option treats the number as seconds and converts it to a hr:min:sec format. The precision of 2 rounds off the second decimal place to 6, and the precision of 4 displays the entire number.

Format	Precision	Digital Display
Floating Point	4	123.4567
Floating Point	2	123.46
Scientific	4	1.2346E+2
Scientific	2	1.23E+2
Engineering	4	123.4567E+0
Engineering	2	123.46E+0
Relative Time (seconds)	4	2:03.4567
Relative Time (seconds)	2	2:03.46

Fig. 3-18 Format and Precision Example
(The number to be displayed in each case is 123.4567.)

Exercise 5: Troubleshooting a VI: Single Stepping a VI

In LabVIEW execution of a VI is driven by the flow of data. A typical block diagram includes control terminals, indicator terminals, function nodes, subVI nodes, and others. All objects are interconnected by wires, which provide the path for data. *Any node will execute if data is present at all its input terminals.* After the node executes, it provides data at its output terminal, which becomes the source of data for the next node.

Consider the Sum4.vi block diagram shown in Fig. 3-19. Digital control terminals A, B, C, and D are the sources of data. When execution begins, A and B apply data to the Add function S1, C applies data to S2, and D applies data to S3 at the same time. Nodes S2 and S3 cannot execute because they don't have all the data at their input terminals. However, S1 can execute because both of its input terminals have data. As soon as S1 executes, the data at its output terminal is passed to the input of S2. Now S2 executes because it has data at both of its input terminals. After S2 executes, it passes

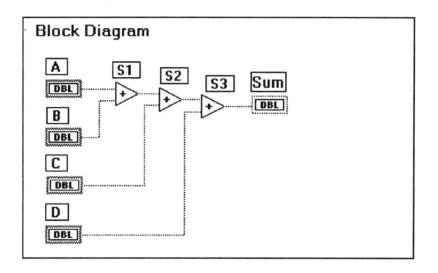

Fig. 3-19 Data Flow Example

its data to S3, which executes last. This process continues until all nodes have executed.

In high-level programming there are generally two types of errors: syntax errors and run-time errors. Syntax errors occur because some programming rules have been broken. Syntax errors must be corrected before a program can be executed. Run-time errors, however, can be very frustrating. For example, if you wrote in your program $z = x/y$ and it should have been $z = x*y$, the computer will execute the division anyway because there are no syntax errors, and you will have incorrect results after the execution. It is up to you at that point to find the errors, and there is always the chance that you will overlook them no matter how many times you review the code.

Single stepping through the program is one troubleshooting technique that is extremely effective. LabVIEW offers this technique, which involves executing one node at a time. After each execution, numerical values will be shown at input and output terminals. This technique allows you to see VI execution in slow motion. After each node executes, a value produced by that node will be shown. You have to decide at this time whether that value is correct. As the execution proceeds from node to node, an inspection of node output values will allow you to catch any run-time errors in the VI.

We shall next try the *single stepping* technique on the Sum4.vi.

1. Open the Sum4.vi, enter the values of your choice into digital controls A, B, C, and D, and then switch to the block diagram. The following values were used in the illustrations below: A = 10, B = 6, C =1 2, D = -9.

2. Click on the **Highlight Execution** button in the Toolbar: 💡 It changes to 💡 .

3. To begin **single stepping**, click on either of these stepping buttons ⬇️➡️ in the Toolbar. Notice that as single stepping begins, **bubbles** representing data start to flow along the wires, and the **Run** button ➡️ indicates that VI is being executed.

4. As single stepping begins, the values that you entered into digital controls A, B, C, and D will appear at their corresponding terminal outputs in the block diagram. As shown in the

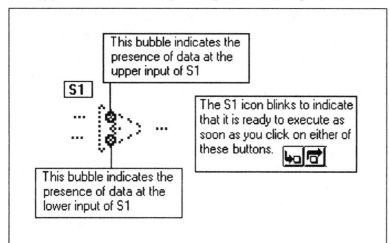

illustration, bubbles arrive at the two inputs of the S1 Add function, and the S1 icon begins to blink, indicating that it is ready to execute.

S1 will execute when you click on one of the stepping buttons, as you did in step 3, and the value of the addition will appear at the output of S1.

As shown in the illustration below, upon completing its execution, S1 outputs a value of 16, which is available at the input to S2. S2 now has the data at both of its inputs, one

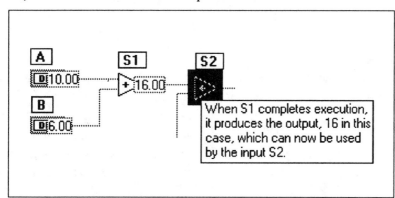

value from S1 and the other value from terminal C. S2 now begins to blink, thus indicating that it is ready to execute. S2 will execute when you click on one of the stepping buttons as you did in step 3 above.

5. Continue to single step through the VI until all nodes have been executed.

6. This is the *Pause/Continue* button ▐▐, located in the Toolbar. When you click on it during the single stepping of the VI, the execution will continue to the end without stopping instead of pausing at each node. Try it. Single step through the VI again, but this time click on this control after the first pause.

7. The *Abort Execution* button, when VI is not running, looks like this ▧ , and when VI is running, it changes to this ◉ . Use this control by single stepping the VI again. While single stepping, click on this button and observe what happens.

8. The *Step Out* button in the Toolbar that looks grayed out ▣ when VI is not running, changes to ▣ when VI is being executed. When you click on this button, the VI finishes execution without pausing. Single step through the Sum4.vi and use this control. Do not close Sum4.vi; we will use it in the next exercise.

Exercise 6:   Troubleshooting: Using Breakpoints and Probes

When you set a breakpoint in the VI, the execution will proceed up to the breakpoint, allowing you to inspect data. When you click on the Continue button, the execution resumes until the next breakpoint is reached, pausing once again. You can either terminate execution at some breakpoint or continue until all nodes have executed.

To Set a Breakpoint, follow the procedure illustrated in Fig. 3-20. When the breakpoint is set on a:

Block Diagram	Execution pauses when all nodes inside the block diagram have been executed once.
Node	Execution pauses just before executing the node with the breakpoint.
Wire	Execution pauses immediately after data passes on the wire with the breakpoint.

To Delete the Breakpoint, click with the breakpoint tool on the wire, node, or block diagram as the case may be, and the red outline or the red dot will disappear.

To begin the breakpoint/probe exercise:

1. Switch to the block diagram of Sum4.vi and set the breakpoint on the wire connected   to the output of S2. To do this, click on the Set/Clear Breakpoint tool ◉ in the Tools

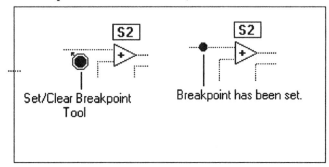

palette. As illustrated here, click with the arrow part of the tool on the wire where you want to set the breakpoint. After clicking, a red dot will appear to indicate that the breakpoint has been set. If you wish to clear the breakpoint, click with the same tool on the red dot and it will vanish.

86

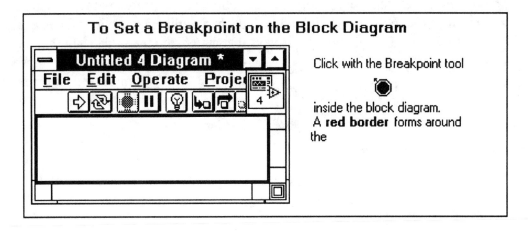

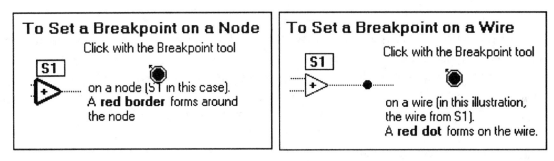

Fig. 3-20 Setting Breakpoints

2. *Probe is used to monitor data on wires.*

   Set the probe on the wire connected to S2 in Sum4.vi. To accomplish this, click on the Probe Data tool ➔Ⓕ in the Tools palette and then click with the probe tool on the wire

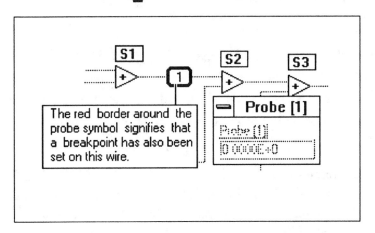

connected to S1. As shown in the illustration, the probe symbol is enclosed by a red border ⎯ ⟦1⟧ ⎯ . The red border is there because of the breakpoint that has been set there earlier in step 1. Otherwise the probe symbol would appear as ⎯ 1 ⎯ . You may delete the probe by clicking on the ⊟ button in the probe window.

3. *Run* the VI by clicking on the Run button ⇦ in the Toolbar. The Run button changes to ⇨ , thus indicating that the VI is being executed.

87

Upon reaching the breakpoint, the VI execution pauses, as shown in the illustration. The wire with the breakpoint is highlighted by a dashed outline, the node to be executed next (S2) begins to blink, and the probe displays the value from the node (S1) that executed last. Note by observing the Run button that the VI is still running.

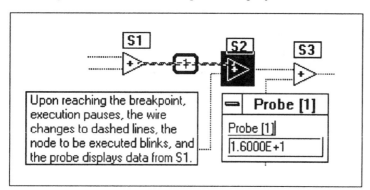

Remember that the use of a probe, the breakpoint, or both is a troubleshooting technique that helps you to find run-time errors in a faulty VI.

When the VI pauses execution because of the breakpoint, as is the case in this example, you may inspect the probe display; more than one breakpoint and certainly more than one probe may be used in complex VIs. You may choose to use probes only, without breakpoints, run the VI, and inspect the probe values upon completion of execution. You may also choose to set the breakpoint on the entire block diagram by clicking with the breakpoint tool anywhere in the open area of the block diagram. The actual troubleshooting approach depends on the particular situation.

Having inspected the probe value, click on the Continue button ▐▐ , thus allowing the VI to go on to the next breakpoint or, as is the case in this exercise, complete the execution.

Close the probe, delete the breakpoint, and close the Sum4.vi. Do not save any changes. We will consider next how to single step a subVI icon. For the most part, the procedure is similar to what has been covered in this exercise.

Exercise 7: Troubleshooting: Single Stepping a SubVI

1. **Build** the front panel and the block biagram as shown in Fig. 3-21. In the front panel, there are two digital indicators with owned labels *Total* and *Root* and one digital control with owned label *N*. Digital controls and indicators are in the *Numeric* subpalette of the *Controls* floating palette.

In the block diagram you must open the *icon* of the *Sum4icon.vi*. To accomplish this, click on the *Select a VI...* button in the *Functions* floating palette. This gives you access to drives, directories, and files. Navigate to the directory where you saved the Sum4icon.vi and open it. The *icon* of Sum4icon.vi will appear in the block diagram.

Notice that if you opened the Sum4icon.vi from the File menu using the Open option, you would open the front panel of the Sum4icon.vi and *not its icon*.

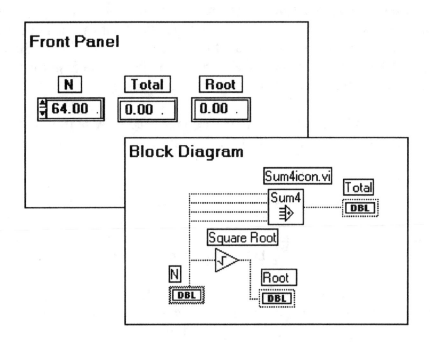

Fig. 3-21   Front Panel and Block Diagram of Math.vi of Exercise 7

Next, open the *Square Root* function ⊳ from the *Numeric* subpalette of the *Functions* floating palette. Complete the wiring as shown in Fig. 3-21. Enter the value into digital control *N*. In this illustration, N was set to 64.

Save this VI as **Math.vi** in Workbook.LLB. Do not close this VI because we will use it in the next step. Next, we will explore *stepping into* and *single stepping* a subVI.

2.   Switch to the block diagram (Ctrl+E). If you are already in the block diagram, then click on either of these buttons in the Toolbar. Notice that when you have the cursor over either of these buttons, a yellow banner that reads *Start Single Stepping* appears below the button. Also click on the *Highlight Execution* button .

As soon as you click on one of the buttons, they *assume a different role*. As shown in this illustration, the *Step Into* button allows you to step inside the subVI (it will not allow you to step inside a function). The *Step Over* button lets you go over the subVI. The *Step Out* button is used to complete execution of the block diagram.

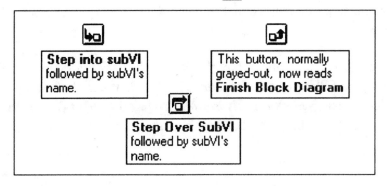

Upon clicking on the **Single Stepping** button, one of the nodes in the block will begin to blink. Because VI execution is driven by the availability of data at the node input, it is not possible to predict which node will execute first (Square root function or Sum4icon subVI). If it is absolutely necessary that a particular node execute first, then the sequence structure (one of the topics in the next chapter) must be used.

If the Square Root node begins to blink, click on the *Step Over* button. In this case the *Step Into* button also acts as a *Step Over* because the system won't let you step into a function.

Once the Sum4icon subVI begins to blink, click on the *Step Into* button. Notice that the yellow banner below the button reads *Step Into subVI Sum4icon.vi.* As shown in Fig.3-22, the block diagram of the subVI Sum4icon opens and you can begin single stepping by clicking on the stepping button in the Sum4icon block diagram.

Continue to click on the Step Into button in the Sum4icon.vi block diagram until the last node executes. Notice the execution image that overlays the subVI Sum4icon.vi icon in the calling VI, Math.vi. As as shown in the illustration, it indicates that the subVI is presently running.

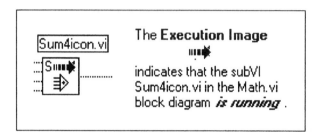

The **Execution Image**

indicates that the subVI Sum4icon.vi in the Math.vi block diagram *is running* .

After the last node in the Sum4icon subVI has executed, the value (in this example, 256) is returned to the calling

Math.vi and appears at the output of the icon. Also the Square Root icon begins to blink.

Click on this button in the Math.vi block diagram. Notice that the yellow banner below this icon reads *Step Over the Square Root* when the mouse cursor is over this icon, indicating once again, that the system does not allow stepping into a function. This causes the Square Root function to execute and output a value of 8. The entire block diagram begins to blink. Place the mouse cursor over this icon and observe the yellow banner that read *Finish VI "Math.vi"*. Clicking on it completes the single stepping of Math.vi. The button that is generally called *Step Into*, as you can see, has played different roles.

3. You should be familiar with other features associated with single stepping a subVI. In this step we shall explore a single stepping feature that lets you decide how far you want the single stepping to progress.

Return to the Math.vi block diagram, and turn ON the *Highlight Execution* button (if it is not ON). Begin single stepping following the procedure in step 2. When the block diagram of subVI Sum4icon opens, *click on this button* and hold it down. Make sure that you click on this button in the Sum4icon block diagram.

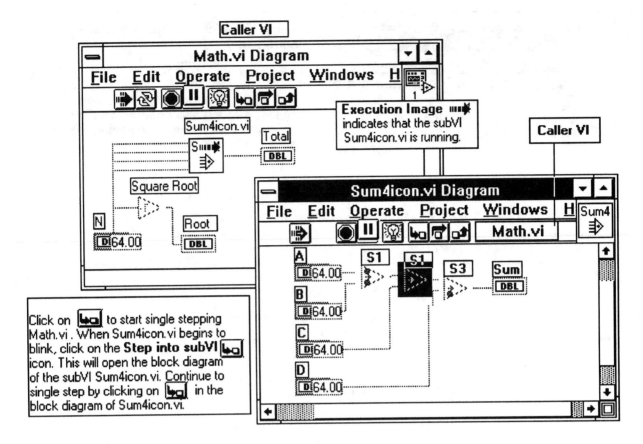

Fig. 3-22 Single Stepping SubVI Sum4icon.vi

As illustrated in Fig. 3-23, a popup menu with several options opens:

Current Block Diagram   Execution pauses in Sum4icon (this is the current block diagram) after all nodes in this block diagram have been executed.

VI "Sum4icon.vi"   Execution pauses in the caller block diagram (Math.vi) after Sum4icon.vi has been executed.

VI "Math.vi"...   Execution stops after all nodes in Math.vi have been executed.

Select first the *Current Block Diagram* and single step to the end. Observe the effects of this selection. Repeat single stepping two more times, once for *VI "Sum4icon.vi"* and once for *VI "Math.vi"*. Observe in each case the effect of your selection of single stepping.

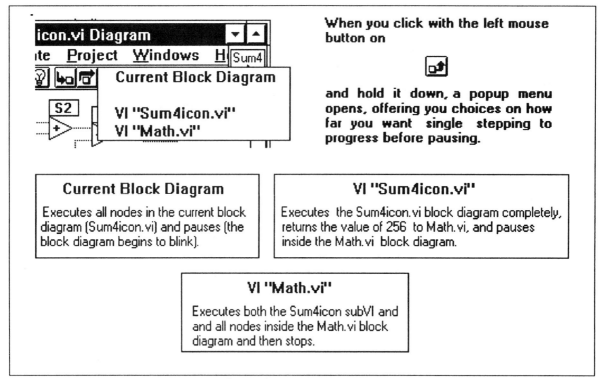

When you click with the left mouse button on

and hold it down, a popup menu opens, offering you choices on how far you want single stepping to progress before pausing.

Current Block Diagram

Executes all nodes in the current block diagram (Sum4icon.vi) and pauses (the block diagram begins to blink).

VI "Sum4icon.vi"

Executes the Sum4icon.vi block diagram completely, returns the value of 256 to Math.vi, and pauses inside the Math.vi block diagram.

VI "Math.vi"

Executes both the Sum4icon subVI and and all nodes inside the Math.vi block diagram and then stops.

Fig. 3-23   Choosing How Far to Single Step

4.   In this step we will explore the *Hierarchy Window* and the information that it provides on Math.vi. Return to the block diagram of Math.vi and single step it. When you get inside the Sum4icon.vi, open the Hierarchy Window by choosing ***Show VI Hierarchy***

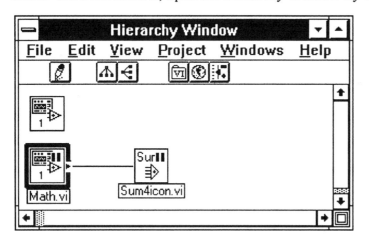

from the Project menu. As shown in the illustration, Sum4icon is the subVI of the Math.vi. Notice that Math.vi has a ***red arrow button*** on its right side. This is an indication that it has a subVI. To open or close the Sum4icon subVI, just click on the *red arrow button*.

When you move the mouse cursor over the icon, its name appears below the icon. The default form is the way it's shown in the Hierarchy Window illustration. However, if you want to see the VI path instead of its name, choose *Full VI Path in Label* from the *View* menu of the Hierarchy Window, as shown in this illustration.

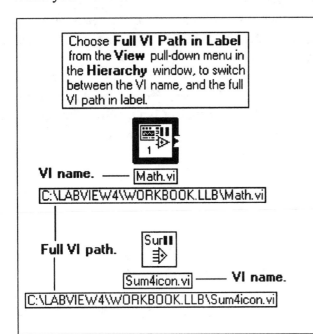

Choose **Full VI Path in Label** from the **View** pull-down menu in the **Hierarchy** window, to switch between the VI name, and the full VI path in label.

VI name. —— Math.vi
C:\LABVIEW4\WORKBOOK.LLB\Math.vi

Full VI path.

Sum4icon.vi —— VI name.
C:\LABVIEW4\WORKBOOK.LLB\Sum4icon.vi

The *paused glyph* symbol **II** appears in the upper righthand corner of the VI icon, as shown in the illustration here.

The *red* glyph indicates that VI is currently paused.

The *green* glyph indicates that VI is not currently paused.

The Hierarchy window has other tools, as shown in this illustration. *Horizontal/Verical Layout* allows you to place VI icons horizontally or vertically. If you moved icons inside the window, the *Redo Layout* button places them in the original order.

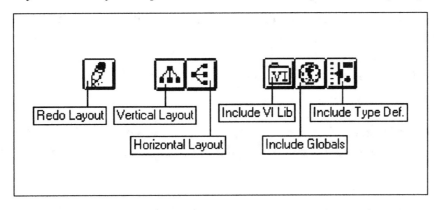

Redo Layout   Vertical Layout   Include VI Lib   Include Type Def.

Horizontal Layout   Include Globals

The three *Include* tools, *VI Lib*, *Type Def.*, and *Global variables*, are more appropriate for larger and more complex VIs.

Redraw   Ctrl+D
Show All VIs   Ctrl+A

Vertical Hierarchy
√ Horizontal Hierarchy

Include VIs in vi.lib
Include Globals
Include Type Defs

Full VI Path in Label

When you click anywhere in the open area of the Hierarchy window, a popup menu like the one shown here opens, giving you additional options.

Most of these are in the Hierarchy Window toolbar. The *Show All VIs* option will open other VIs or subVIs not shown in the current window.

The *Full VI Path in the Label* option will display the path for the VI when you place the mouse cursor over its icon. This option was illustrated earlier.

Summary

1. Any VI must have a front panel and a block diagram. All controls and indicators are in the front panel. The block diagram contains terminals from the front panel, functions, and subVI nodes that are interconnected by wires.

2. Any VI that you create can also be used as a subVI. A subVI must have an icon and a connector. A subVI is a space saver in the block diagram. Also it offers the ability for the user to modularize various components of a large VI. It easier to troubleshoot and modify individual modules without affecting others.

3. Use the Select a VI... button in the Functions palette to open the subVI icon. Opening the same VI using the File>Open option will open that VI's front panel.

4. To edit the VI icon, click on the Edit Icon in the Icon Pane of the front panel. The Icon Editor has tools for drawing and entering text in color or black and white.

5. The Help Window provides a simple or an in-depth object description and can be used effectively when wiring objects inside the block diagram.

6. Objects in the block diagram are linked by wires and wires carry data. The thickness and color of the wires represent different data types.

7. Numerical data in LabVIEW is represented as floating point numbers, signed or unsigned integers, or complex numbers. The amount of memory that will be consumed depends on your choice of data representation. For instance, using EXT to represent a numerical value will require 10 bytes in memory, while using SGL to represent the same value will consume only 4 bytes of memory.

8. Format allows you express numbers using floating point notation, scientific notation, or engineering notation. The relative time format option converts a numeric value in seconds to a format of hrs:min:sec.

    Precision, on the other hand, specifies the number of decimal places in the number. Precision depends on representation; a DBL or SGL representation offers up to 7 decimal places, while EXT offers up to 15 decimals places.

9. Troubleshooting a VI is necessary when the VI does not run because it has either syntax errors or run-time errors. Single stepping, breakpoints, and probes help the troubleshooting task.

10. Single stepping is a very effective troubleshooting tool that can be used in single stepping a block diagram or a subVI. The use of a probe lets you monitor data on wires. Breakpoints force the execution to pause and inspect the results. You can set a breakpoint on a block diagram, a node, or a wire.

Chapter 4

Structures

In this chapter you will learn about the:
>   While Loop
>   For Loop
>   Shift Register
>   Case Structure
>   Sequence Structure
>   Formula Node

Introduction

It has been said that the entire C programming language can be broken down into three *Control Structures* and that any C program can be written in terms of these structures (except Formula Node which is not in C). These structures are:

> Repetition Structure
> Selection Structure
> Sequence Structure
> Formula Node

LabVIEW also has these structures. It has two repetition structures: the ***While Loop,*** which is equivalent to Do/While in C language, and the ***For Loop.*** The *Case* structure in LabVIEW, which can do single or multiple selections, is an example of a Selection Structure. The Sequence Structure, which occurs naturally in C language because all instructions are executed in sequential order, is given special attention in LabVIEW. As you may remember from the last chapter, the execution order in LabVIEW is based on data flow; a node can execute only if data is available at all input terminals. Therefore, LabVIEW has a special node called the ***Sequence*** structure that is intended for special sequence operations. LabVIEW also includes the ***Formula Node*** for mathematical and logical operations.

Repetition Structures

The While Loop

Consider the concept of the repetition structure shown in Fig. 4-1. The program instructions are executed once before the condition is tested. If the result of the test is *true*, the program instructions

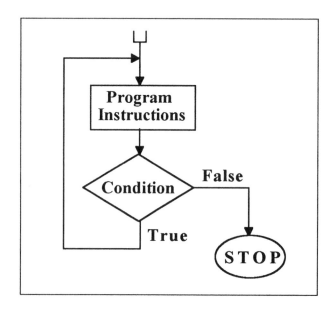

Fig. 4-1 The Do/While Repetition Structure

will be executed again. If it is *false,* the next statement following the loop will be executed in C language and in LabVIEW the loop terminates. This type of repetitive execution of a group of program instructions is called the ***Do/While*** structure in C language, and in LabVIEW it is known as the ***While Loop.***

To Open the While Loop, click on the While Loop option with the *positioning tool* in the *Structures* subpalette of the *Functions* menu, as illustrated in Fig. 4-2.

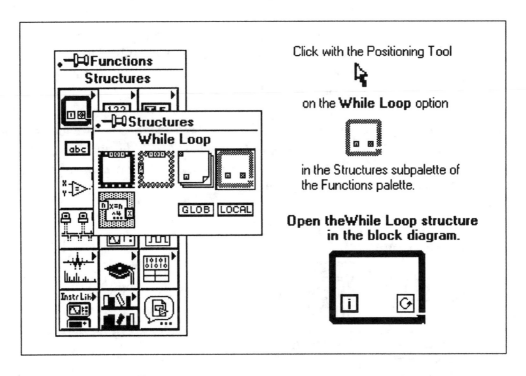

Fig. 4-2 Opening the While Loop in LabVIEW

As shown in the illustration, the While Loop has an iteration terminal **i** that counts the number of times the loop has executed. The ***Condition*** terminal ⌖ expects a *true* or *false* input. A *true* input forces the While Loop to run indefinitely, and a *false* input terminates execution.

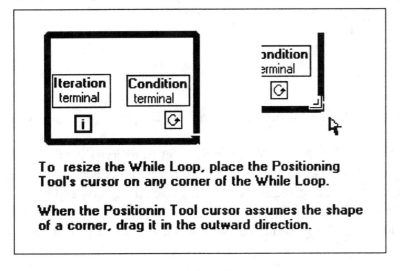

As shown in the illustration, the While Loop may be resized by placing the Positioning Tool's cursor over any corner of the loop. When the cursor assumes the shape of the corner, drag it in the outward direction.

To move the loop, catch the border of the loop with the positioning tool's cursor and drag it to a new position.

97

Exercise 1: Using the While Loop (Lottery Game)

In this example we will consider an application of the While Loop. You will create a lottery game. The VI, which we will call Guess_3, will guess the three numbers that you pick and will indicate to you how many tries it took to guess the numbers.

But first, you will build a VI, including wiring, with an icon and a connector that will be used as a subVI in our game.

1.   Construct the front panel and the block diagram shown in Fig. 4-3.

        Front panel objects: *Digital control* is in the *Numeric* subpalette of the *Controls* palette, and the **Square LED** is in the *Boolean* subpalette of the Controls palette.

        Block diagram objects: *Numeric* subpalette of the *Functions* palette includes the following objects: **Random Number, Multiply**, and **Round To Nearest**. The **Equal?** function is in the *Comparison* subpalette of the Functions palette.

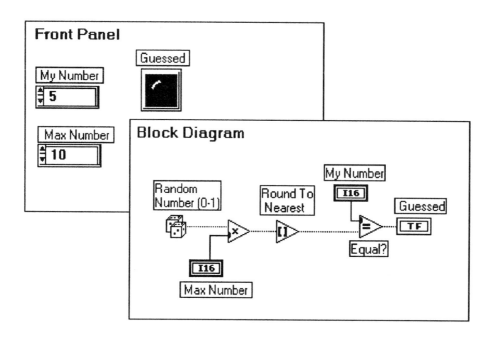

Fig. 4-3 Front Panel and Block Diagram of Guess_Number.vi

2.   Next create the connector and the icon for this VI. You should refer to exercise 3 of Chapter 3 on how to create an icon and a connector for a VI. To create a connector, select the entire block diagram of this VI (the dotted rectangle must include all objects) and choose **subVI From Selection** from the *Edit* menu.

    Create the icon for this VI by double clicking on the icon that was just created and choosing

Edit Icon from the *icon pane* in the front panel. The *Icon Editor* that opens allows you to edit the icon. Edit the icon by entering text as shown in the illustration. Choose OK and close the Icon Editor.

Save this VI as **Guess_Number.vi** in the Workbook.LLB library. Close this VI.

3.   Construct the VI whose front panel and block diagram are shown in Fig. 4-4.

The front panel includes three *digital controls* and one *digital indicator*. Label with owned labels the digital controls and the indicator, as shown in Fig. 4-3. Choose *I-16* from the popup palette for each of these by clicking with the right mouse button on the digital control and indicator object.

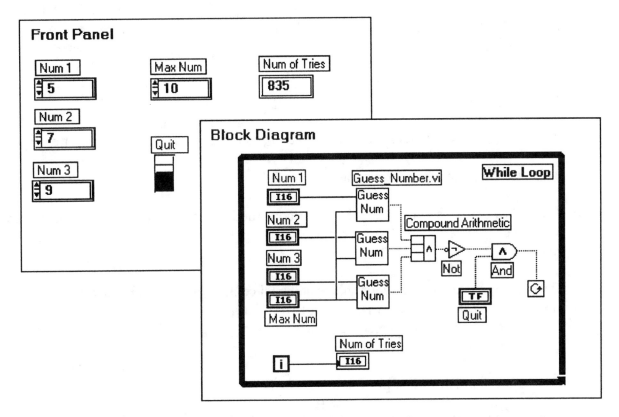

Fig. 4-4 Front Panel and Block Diagram of Guess_3.vi

The switch shown in the front panel is the *Vertical Switch,* which is in the *Boolean* subpalette of the Controls palette. Click on the switch with the *Positioning* tool found in the Tools palette to move it to the upper position, as shown in Fig. 4-3. Click on the switch (the right mouse button) and choose *Latch When Pressed* from the *Mechanical Action* popup menu.

Also choose *Make Current Value Default* from the **Data** *Operations* option in the popup menu for this switch. Label the switch, with an owned label, as *Quit*.

4.   Turning now to the **block diagram**, open the icon of the Guess_Number.vi. As indicated before, you open the icon of a VI by clicking on the *Select A VI...* button in the Functions palette. This gives you access to directories and files. Choose *Guess_Number.vi* from the Workbook.LLB (assuming that you saved it there). The icon appears in the Block Diagram. Duplicate this icon so that you have a total of three.

The *Compound Arithmetic* function is in the *Numeric* subpalette of the Functions palette.

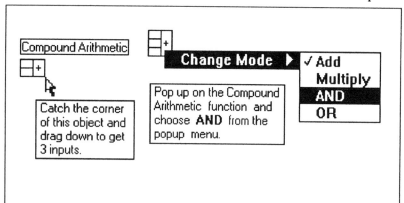

Configure the Compound Arithmetic function as a three input *And* gate. As shown in the illustration, resize the Compound Arithmetic icon for three inputs, pop up on the icon, and choose *AND* from the popup menu.

The *Not* and *And* functions are in the *Boolean* subpalette of the Functions palette.

Wire all objects in the block diagram of Fig. 4-4.

5.   If the *Run* button is not broken, then your construction is successful. If it is broken, then you have syntax errors. Correct them following the procedure of the Troubleshooting section in Chapter 3.

Enter the three numbers of your choice in digital controls Num1, Num2 and Num3. Also enter the value for Max Num. Try Max Num of 10 . A larger value for Max Num means that the VI will take a longer time to guess your numbers. Don't forget that the three numbers you pick cannot be larger than Max Num. Run the VI.

Play the game also with larger values of Max Num.

Save this VI as **Guess_3.vi** in Workbook.LLB and close it.

The For Loop

Another instance of the repetition control structure is the For Loop. As in the case of the While Loop, the For Loop can execute a group of instructions repetitively. The While Loop checks the state of the condition with each iteration and as long as the condition is true, it continues the repetitive execution of the instructions. It stops execution as soon as the condition becomes false.

The For Loop, on the other hand, executes a group of instructions a *fixed number* of times. It initializes a counter to N=0, as shown in Fig. 4-5, checks the counter against a user supplied value C, and then executes a group of instructions that are inside the For Loop. The counter is then incremented and the procedure repeats. As soon as the value of the counter is equal to C, the loop stops.

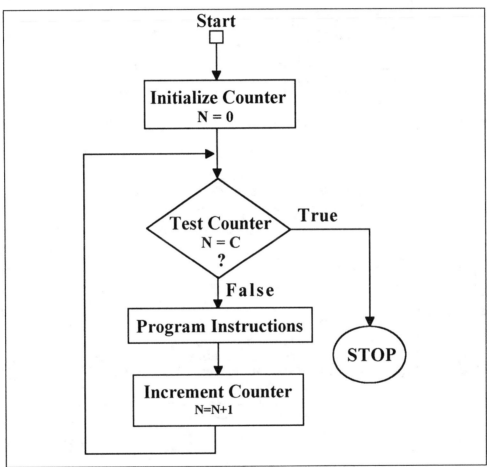

Fig. 4-5 The For Loop Repetition Structure

Note: *The For Loop outputs values only after it completes executing N times the program that is inside the boundary of the loop. The loop stops execution when the loop counter N reaches the value supplied by the user. Thus, if you wired a value of 50 to the loop counter, the loop will begin with N=0 and continue through N=49. On the count of N=50, the loop stops execution and only now will be able to pass values to objects outside the loop.*

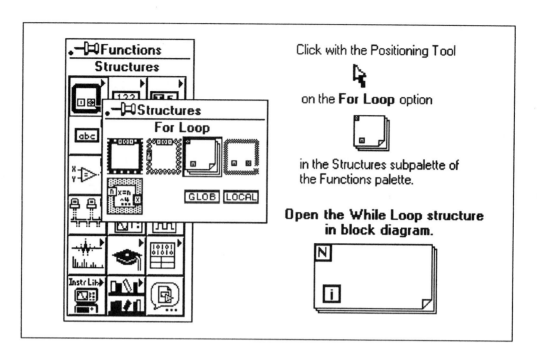

Fig. 4-6 Opening the For Loop in LabVIEW

To Open the For Loop, click with the *positioning tool* in the *Structures* sub-palette of the *Functions* menu on the For Loop option, as illustrated in Fig. 4-6.

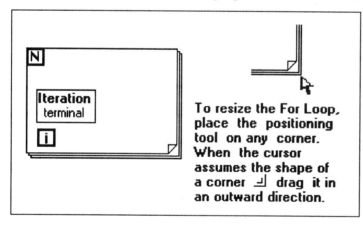

As shown in the illustration, the For Loop has the iteration terminal **i**, which counts the number of times that the loop has executed; **i** can be used as an output to a digital indicator.

It also has the Loop Counter **N**. This is an input that the user must provide to specify the number of times that the loop must execute. N must be an integer number.

To move the For Loop to a new location in the window, place the cursor of the positioning tool on the border of the loop and drag the loop to the new location.

To copy the For Loop select the loop, hold down the ***Ctrl*** key, and drag the loop.

The Replace Option. If you completed all the code inside the For Loop and then realized that a While Loop might do better, you can make the switch easily using the *Replace* option. Pop up with the positioning tool cursor on the border of the loop and choose Replace from the popup menu. While still holding down the right mouse button, navigate to the Functions palette and make another choice from the Structures subpalette. If you choose **Remove the For Loop** from the popup menu, you will delete the For Loop in your Block Diagram.

Incidentally, the *Replace* option can be applied to any object in the Front Panel or in the Block Diagram.

Exercise 2: Using the For Loop (Motor Control Simulation)

In this exercise you will build a VI that simulates the control of a DC motor. The staircase

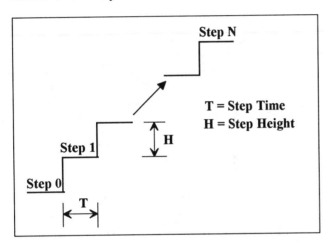

waveform shown in this illustration is used as a voltage input to the motor and also as a motor speed response.

If you had a data acquisition (DAQ) board installed, then one of the D/A ports could be used to output this waveform and drive a DC motor.

You will also learn in this exercise how to use *Local Variables*.

1. **Build** the VI whose Front Panel and Block Diagram are shown in Fig. 4-7. The following information will help you in finding objects:

Front Panel

Digital Control and **Digital Indicator** are in the Numeric subpalette of the Controls palette. *Step Time* and *Iteration Number* are **owned** labels and *msec* is the *free* label.

> **Change the Representation** for the digital control and indicator to **I16** by popping up on the control and indicator, choosing **Representation**, and then clicking on **I16** in the Representation palette.

The Meter, as shown here in the illustration, is in the Numeric subpalette of the Controls palette. You will need two such meters, one to indicate motor speed and the other to indicate

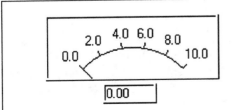

the motor input voltage.

Using **owned** labels, label one meter as *Motor Speed* and the other as *Motor Input Voltage*. The *RPM* and *Volt* are *free* labels, as shown in Fig. 4-7.

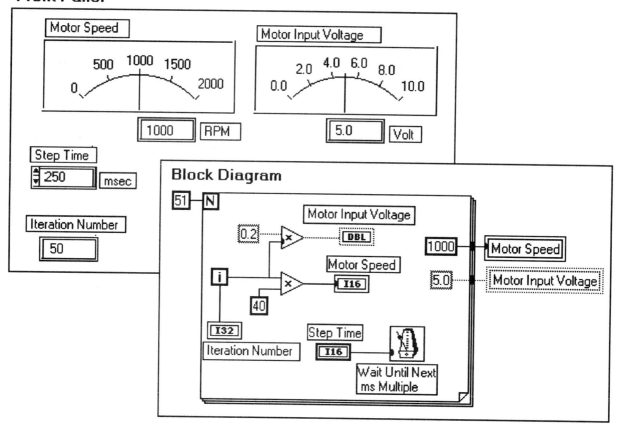

Fig. 4-7 Motor Operation Simulation VI

You must also change the scale of the Motor Speed meter. One way to accomplish this is to use the Labeling tool ⌨ . Click on the labeling tool in the Tools palette, then click with this tool (hold down the mouse button) immediately to the left of **10** on the Motor Speed scale, and drag the cursor across 10. Note that 10 will appear as white on a black background. Now type **2000** and click on the *Enter* button in the Toolbar immediately to the left of the Run button.

Change *Precision* on the Motor Input Voltage meter. Pop up inside the meter (right mouse button), choose the *Format and Precision...* option from the popup menu, and *type* in the *Digits of Precision* box **1**. Repeat this procedure for the digital indicator to the left of the Volt free label and also type **1**.

Choose Representation for the Motor Speed meter. Pop up on the meter, choose the *Representation* option from the popup menu, and click on **I16** from the Representation palette.

Block Diagram

Numeric Constant is in the Numeric subpalette of the Functions palette. You need five such numeric constants: **.2**, **5.0**, **40**, **51** and **1000**, as shown in the Block Diagram of Fig. 4-7. When you fetch the numeric constant object from the Numeric subpalette and it appears in the Block Diagram, immediately type the desired value. If you click somewhere else in the Block Diagram, you will have to use the labeling tool to type the value in the numeric constant box.

The Multiply function is in the Numeric subpalette of the Functions palette. You will need two multiply functions.

Wait Until Next ms Multiple function is in the *Time & Dialog* subpalette of the Functions palette.

Local Variable. There are situations when you need more than one instance or a copy of a control object. In our exercise, when the loop completes execution, we have to output 1000 to the Motor Speed digital indicator, and 5.0 to the Motor Input Voltage digital indicator. Since you cannot duplicate digital control or indicator terminals in the block diagram, the use of a *local variable* is the only way that we can solve this problem.

To Create a Local Variable for the Motor Speed digital indicator, click on the Motor Speed

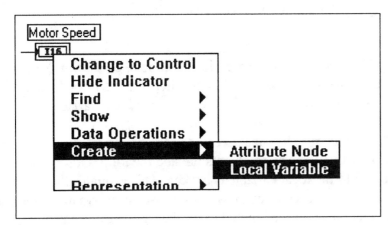

terminal, as shown in this illustration, and choose **Local Variable** from the **Create** option of the popup menu. The local variable symbol that has the following appearance

pops up in the Block Diagram. Move this local variable outside the For Loop in preparation for wiring.

Repeat the above procedure and create the local variable for the *Motor Input Voltage* digital indicator.

The *local variable* can be either a *Write to* or *Read from* type. By default it is a *Write Local*, which is exactly what we need in this exercise because 1000 must be passed to the Motor Speed local variable when the For Loop completes execution. If in another situation you have to change it to a *Read from* local variable, simply pop up on the local variable and choose *Change To Read Local* from the popup menu.

Wire all objects in the block diagram, as shown in Fig. 4-7. Insofar as the wiring of the two local variables to their respective constants is concerned, you must be aware of certain properties of the For Loop (that also apply to the While Loop).

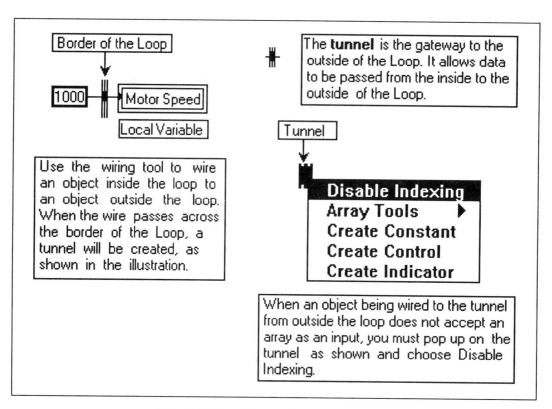

Fig. 4-8 The Tunnel in the Loop

For example, when wiring 1000 to the Motor Speed local variable, click with the wiring tool on the 1000 constant and drag the wire across the loop border to the Motor Speed local variable. When the tip of the wiring tool is over the Motor Speed local variable, click again.

Notice that the *tunnel* (black rectangle) has been created in the border of the For Loop. As shown in Fig. 4-8, the tunnel is the gateway to objects outside the loop. Observe also that the wire connecting the tunnel to the local variable is broken. This is due to the mismatch in data types. This will be explained in greater detail when we discuss arrays in a later chapter. But for now, to fix this problem, click on the tunnel (with the right mouse button) and choose *Disable Indexing*. This will change the broken wire to a solid wire.

Complete wiring the Block Diagram. A broken Run button means that you have syntax errors. Refer to the Troubleshooting section of Chapter 3 and fix all errors.

2.　　Switch to the Front Panel and enter 250 in the *Step Time* digital control.

This VI makes use of the *Iteration Terminal* **i** to create the staircase waveform. Each time the loop executes all nodes inside its border, i increments. When we multiply the value of i by a constant, the result is a step whose height is equal to that constant. The duration of the step is accomplished by the *Wait Until Next ms Multiple* function. It forces the loop to halt execution for the time specified by the *Step Time* digital control. This occurs for each value of i.

On the first iteration, the loop reads the input 51 and stores it in the N loop counter. This will be the only time that the loop will read this value because once the loop starts execution, it will not read any inputs external to the loop nor will it output any values to objects outside the loop.

Each time the loop executes all nodes inside its border, the value of **i** increments. Thus, the value of the iteration terminal i advances from 0 to 50, forcing the loop to execute 51 times. The loop stops when i takes on a value of 51 and in the process 50 steps would have been created.

3. **Run** the VI, and experiment with different values of constants as well as with different values of the step time.
Save this **VI as Motor_Control.vi** in Workbook.LLB and close it.

Exercise 3: Using the For Loop (Tank Control Simulation)

In this exercise we will simulate the draining of a tank. In some respects this exercise resembles the previous exercise, where the positive slope staircase was the basis of control. The staircase waveform is used once again, except this time we will use a staircase with a declining, or negative slope to drain the tank.

1. **Build** the VI whose Front Panel and Block Diagram are shown in Fig. 4-9. The following information will help you in finding objects:

Front Panel
Tank indicator is in the *Numeric* subpalette of the Controls palette. When you open the tank indicator in the front panel, do the following:
Change its *Representation* to I16 by following the procedure of the previous exercise.
Change the default maximum value of 10 to **1000** using the labeling tool and the procedure of the previous exercise.
Tank is the owned label and **gal** is a free label.

The two remaining digital controls are in the *Numeric* subpalette of the Controls palette. **Drain Interval** and **Drain Level** are owned labels and the **gal, sec** and **scaled time: 1 sec=1 msec** are free labels.

Block Diagram
Subtract and **Multiply** are in the *Numeric* subpalette of the Functions palette.
Greater? is in the *Comparison* subpalette of the Functions palette.
The two constants **20** and **50** are in the *Numeric* subpalette of the Functions palette.
Select function is in the *Comparison* subpalette of the Functions palette.
Wait Until Next ms Multiple is in the *Time & Dialog* subpalette of the Functions palette.

Complete wiring the block diagram. A broken Run button means that you have syntax errors. Refer to the Troubleshooting section of Chapter 3 and fix all errors.

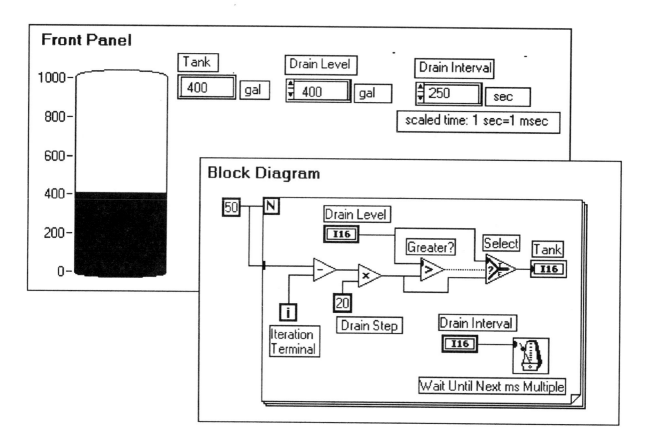

Fig. 4-9 Tank Control VI

2.   Switch to the front panel and enter 250 in the *Drain Interval* digital control and 400 in
the *Drain Level* digital control. ***Run*** this VI.

As in the previous exercise, the iteration terminal is used to create a staircase waveform. This
time the staircase waveform has a negative slope because it is declining with each iteration of
the loop. On the first iteration the loop reads the value of 50 and sets the loop counter N to
this value. This value is also applied to the subtract function with the iteration terminal as the
other input.

On the first iteration of the For Loop, the value of i = 0; hence, the output of the subtract
function is 50 – 0, or 50. The value of 50 is then multiplied by 20, the size of the drain step in
gallons, resulting in the product of 1000 at the output of the multiply function. The *Greater?*
comparison function compares 1000 with the *Drain Level* value, which is set to 400 and
outputs a *false*.

As shown in this illustration, The *Select* function has three inputs. The Boolean input **?**

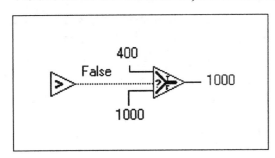

determines which of the two input values is passed to the output. In this case a False causes the 1000 to be passed to the output and displayed on the tank indicator.

When the output of the *Greater?* comparison function is *True,* then 400 will be passed to the output and displayed on the tank indicator.

On the next iteration the value of **i** is incremented to a 1 and 49·20, or 980 will be displayed on the tank indicator. With each successive iteration the tank level will drop by 20 gal., giving the appearance of the tank being drained. The *Drain Interval* setting determines the time delay between iterations and hence the rate at which the tank is being drained.

When **i = 31**, the multiply function will output (50−31)·20 = 380, the comparator will output a *true,* and the *Select* function will pass 400 (the drain level setting) to the Tank indicator. For all remaining values of **i**, the *true* from the comparator will force the *Select* function to output 400 to the Tank indicator. The Tank liquid level will appear to have stabilized at the Drain Level (front panel control) setting of 400.

3. *Experiment* with different values of the *Drain Level* and *Drain Interval. Save* this VI as **Tank_Control.vi** in Workbook.LLB and close the VI.

The Shift Register

A shift register is a device that can store data that has occurred in the past. This concept is similar to a shift register moving or shifting binary data from one stage to the next in a digital circuit. But in a digital circuit the shifted data is restricted to the binary type only. In the LabVIEW shift register, however, the data may be of any type including strings, floating point, and so on. The shift register in LabVIEW may be implemented in a For Loop or a While Loop.

To Create a Shift Register, open the ***For Loop*** or the ***While Loop***; the shift register can be created in either the For Loop or the While Loop. To open the For Loop in the block diagram, choose *For Loop* from the *Structures* subpalette of the Functions palette.

As shown in Fig. 4-10, click on the border of the For Loop (either the right side or the left side but not the top or the bottom) and choose ***Add Shift Register*** from the popup menu. As soon as you release the mouse button, two shift register terminals appear, one on the right side and the other on the left side.

Data is applied to the left terminal. At the end of the iteration (in one iteration all nodes inside the loop border are executed), this data is stored in the left terminal and is available at the left terminal at the beginning of the next iteration.

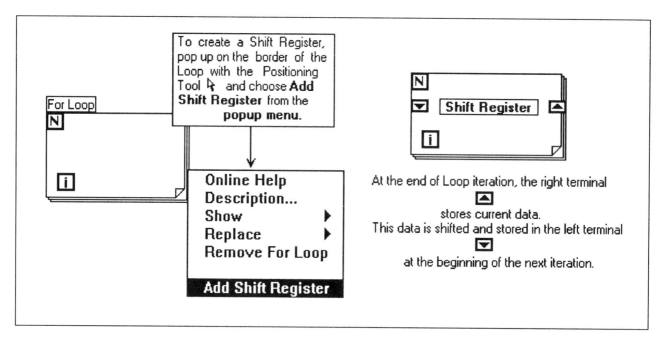

Fig. 4-10   Creating a Shift Register

A single terminal on the left side of the loop is capable of storing only one value from the previous iteration. If you want to store values from two iterations ago, you need two terminals on the left side of the loop and three terminals to accommodate values from the three previous iterations. You can have as many terminals as the room on the left side of the loop allows. The more past history that you want to store, the more terminals you will need.

110

To Add a Shift Register Terminal, pop up on the terminal, as shown in this illustration, and choose *Add Element* from the popup menu. The second terminal will appear on the left side of the For Loop. Repeat this process if you want to add more elements to the Loop.

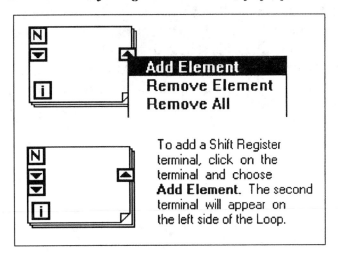

To add a Shift Register terminal, click on the terminal and choose **Add Element**. The second terminal will appear on the left side of the Loop.

To Delete Terminals, pop up on the terminal and choose from the popup menu *Remove Element* to delete the last element that was added or *Remove All* to delete all terminals.

An example of a Shift Register operation is shown in Fig. 4-11. Notice that this shift register is initialized.

To Initialize a Shift Register, wire a value from outside the Loop to all terminals on the left side of the Loop. In this example the shift register has been initialized to 10.

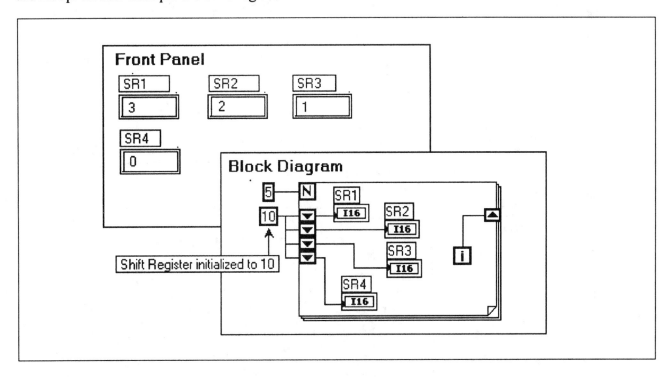

Fig. 4-11   Shift Register Example

Note: *Uninitialized shift registers can lead to ambiguous results because the values from a previous operation of the loop are stored in the shift register terminals on the left side of the Loop. These values will be used for the next operation. To avoid this problem, wire a constant from outside the Loop to all terminals on the left side of the Loop.*

In this example the iteration terminal **i** is wired to the right terminal of the For Loop and the digital indicators SR1, SR2, SR3 and SR4 are wired to the four shift register terminals on the left side of the loop. At the beginning of loop operation, **i=0**, 10 is moved in the four left terminals, and a 0 is stored in the right shift register terminal. When i is incremented to 1, 0 is shifted to the SR1 terminal, and 1 is shifted to the right terminal. This process continues until i=4, and by that time SR1=3, SR2=2, SR3=1 and SR4=0. As i is incremented to 5, the value of 4 is not stored in the shift register because the loop counter N=5 and therefore the loop must terminate execution. Fig. 4-11 shows the values stored at the end of loop operation.

Exercise 4: Using the Shift Register

In this exercise the For Loop is used as a shift register. This VI will generate four random numbers between 0 and 101 (floating point), and find and display their sum and their average value.

1. ***Build*** the Front Panel and the Block Diagram of the VI shown in Fig. 4-12.
    The **front panel** has two digital indicators, which are found in the *Numeric* subpalette of the Controls palette. Label these with owned labels as ***Sum*** and ***Average***.

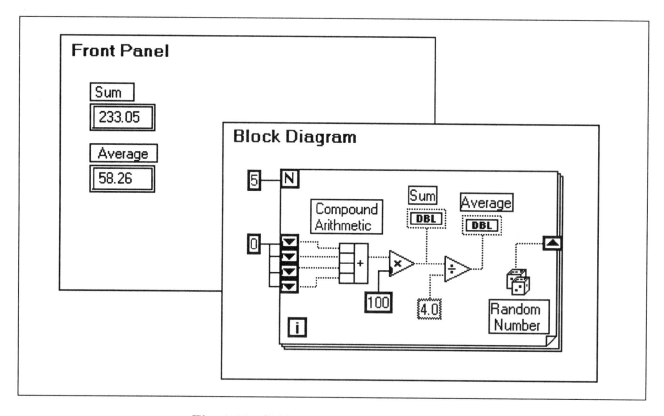

Fig. 4-12   Shift Register for Exercise 4

112

Block Diagram

For Loop is in the *Structures* subpalette of the Functions palette. Open the For Loop in the Block Diagram and configure it as a *Shift Register* with four terminals on the left side of the Loop. Follow the procedure described in the Shift Register section preceding this exercise.

Initialize the shift register to **0** by wiring a **0** *numeric constant* to each shift register terminal on the left side of the loop. Also wire a constant value of **5** to the loop counter **N**. The *Numeric Constant* can be found in the *Numeric* subpalette of the Functions palette.

Compound Arithmetic Function is in the *Numeric* subpalette of the Functions palette. Resize this icon to accommodate four inputs. To resize the Compound Arithmetic function, catch the lower corner with its icon and drag in the downward direction until you get four inputs.

Multiply , **Divide** , **and the Random Number Generator** are all found in the *Numeric* subpalette of the Functions palette.

2. **Run this VI.** You may want to practice your VI single stepping skills and single step this VI. Single stepping will reveal in slow motion how the values are shifting through the terminals on the left side of the For Loop.

Save this VI as **Shift Register.vi** in Workbook.LLB. Close the VI.

Selection Structures

The If/Else Selection Structure

The double selection structure in a high-level programming language such as C has the configuration shown in Fig. 4-13. This is the If/Else selection structure. The condition is first tested and if the result is *true*, all program statements that are included in task 1 are executed. If the result of the test is *false*, all program statements that are included in task 2 are executed.

The If/Else selection structure offers the programmer a branching option. The outcome of the condition test determines which of the two program segments is to be done next.

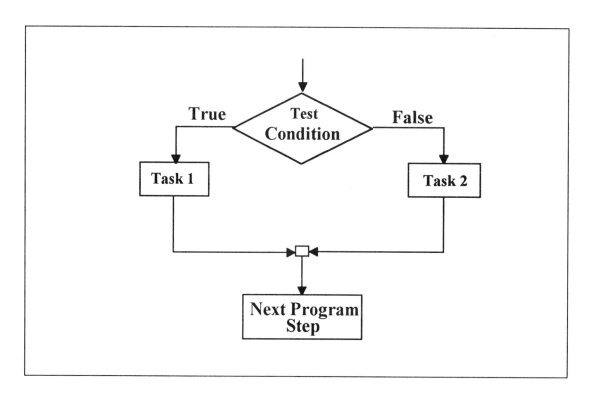

Fig. 4-13 The If/Else Selection Structure

The Nested If/Else Selection Structure

The If/Else structures may also be *nested*. This means that one If/Else structure is inside the other. The flowchart shown in Fig. 4-14 illustrates the nested If/Else structure, and the table lists the tasks to be selected on the basis of the condition tests.

As you can see either from the table or from the flowchart, task 1 will be executed if both conditions 1 and 2 test as true. If, on the other hand, both conditions 1 and 3 test as false, then task 3 will be executed.

A single If/Else statement shown in Fig. 4-13 offers a choice of two tasks to be executed. Notice that by nesting If/Else statements, a greater range of tasks is possible. By nesting two If/Else statements, shown in Fig. 4-14, we made four tasks available. Eight tasks are possible by nesting three If/Else structures, and so on.

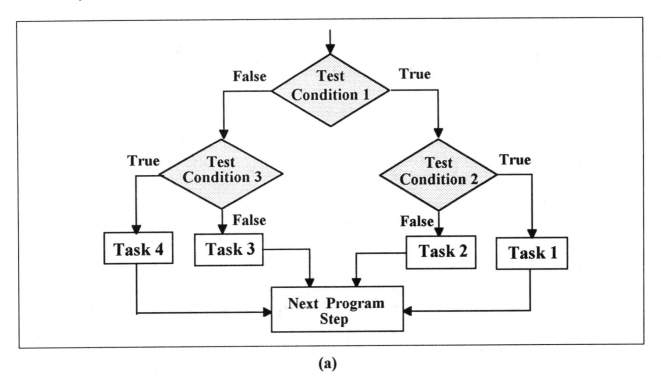

(a)

Task	Condition 1	Condition 2	Condition 3
Task 1	True	True	
Task 2	True	False	
Task 3	False		False
Task 4	False		True

(b)

Fig. 4-14 (a) If/Else Nested Selection Structures (b) Condition/Task Table

The Boolean Case Structure in LabVIEW

In the previous section we considered If/Else as well as the nested If/Else selection structures through the perspective of a high-level programming language such as the C language. LabVIEW also has this structure and it is called the *Case Structure.* Case structure can be of the Boolean type or the Numeric type. Let's consider first the Boolean type.

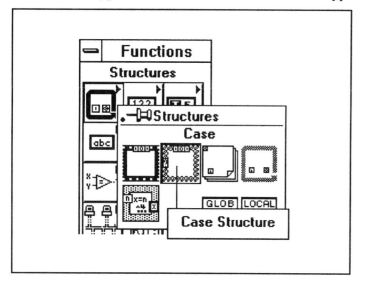

To Open the Boolean Case Structure, choose *Case* from the *Structures* subpalette of the Functions palette, as shown in this illustration.

When you open the *Case* structure in the Block Diagram, it has the appearance shown in this illustration.

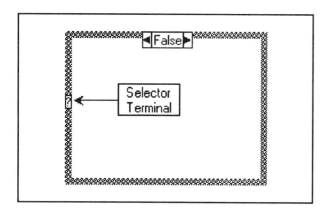

Actually, there are two overlapping frames: the ***true*** frame and the ***false*** frame.

To switch between them, click on the button to the left ◀ or on the button to the right ▶ of the False/True window at the top of the frame.

The Boolean input to the ***Selector Terminal*** determines which of the two frames will be executed. A *true* input will cause the *true* frame to be executed and a *false* input will force execution of the *false* frame.

Fig. 4-15 compares the IF/Else structure that can be implemented in a high-level language such as the C language with the Case structure in LabVIEW. A closer inspection of the two shows that both accomplish the same objective. In LabVIEW the test condition is implemented in a Boolean control such as a switch tested by the Case structure for a *true* or a *false*. The result of the test determines which of the two Case frames will be executed.

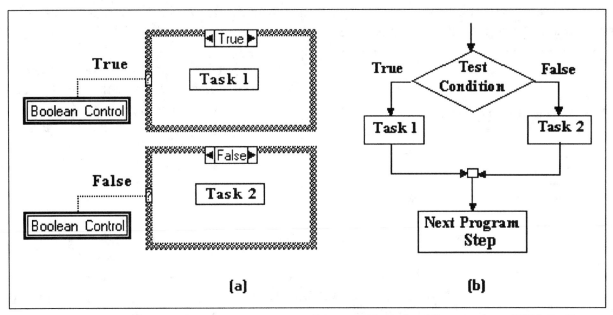

Fig. 4-15 (a) A True or False Input to the Selector Terminal Determines Which Case Window Will Be Executed (b) If/Else Selection Structure from Fig. 4-13

The Numeric Case Structure in LabVIEW

Conditional branching need not be limited to a choice of two tasks. When a Boolean control is wired to the selector terminal, you are led to only two Case structure frames. But suppose that you needed more than two Case frames because you have more than two tasks to be done. The solution is a *Numeric Case Structure*.

To Open a Numeric Case Structure, follow the procedure for opening a Boolean Case structure.
As shown in this illustration, the Boolean format is the default for the Case structure. But as soon as you wire a digital control to the *Selector (?)* Terminal, the Case structure becomes Numeric.

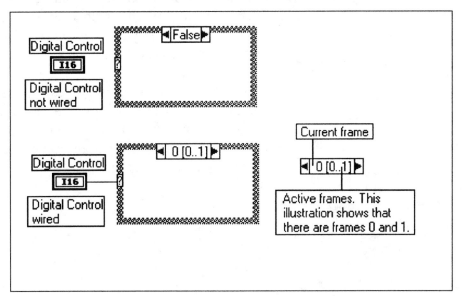

Note the window at the top of the frame. It indicates the current frame and the range of active frames that are below the current frame.

To Advance to the next or to the preceding frame, click in the frame window either on the right arrow button ▶ or the left arrow button ◀ .

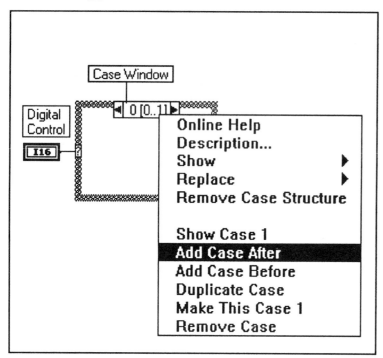

To Add a Case Frame, click anywhere inside the Case window and choose *Add Case After* from the popup menu. This will add a Case frame after the current frame. Choosing *Add Case Before* will add a Case frame before the current frame.

Note the other options in the popup menu. *Make This Case 1* will change the current frame to frame number 1. *Remove Case* will delete the current frame. *Duplicate Case* will copy the current Case frame.

Note: *All Case structure frames are stacked one on top of the other. They cannot be separated and placed next to each other. To access a particular frame for the purpose of viewing it or for building a VI, you must use the arrow buttons inside the Case window.*

Suppose that there are a large number of active frames. In this illustration the Case structure has 10 active frames, with number 1 as the current frame, and you wish to open and view frame number 9.

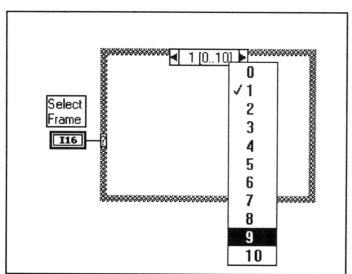

Instead of clicking many times on the arrow button, click (with the left mouse button) inside the Case window and choose 9 from the popup menu, as shown in this illustration.

Exercise 5: Using Boolean Case Structure

This exercise illustrates the use of the Boolean Case structure. The front panel and the block diagram of the VI that you will build is shown in Fig. 4-16. This VI will make use of the For Loop shift register from Exercise 4.

1. Copy the block diagram of the Shift Register.vi of Exercise 4. Open the block diagram of the *Shift Register* that you built in Exercise 4. Copy the VI in the block diagram. To copy the Shift Register block diagram, *select* the entire For Loop, including the constants **0** and **5**. When selected, the objects will have dotted lines around them. Enter *Ctrl+C* from the keyboard and close the Shift Register.vi.

2. Open a new VI and switch to the block diagram. Click anywhere in the center of the block diagram and then enter from the keyboard *Ctrl+V*. The Shift Register block diagram should now appear in the block diagram. Switch to the front panel and observe that the *Sum* and the *Average* digital indicators have also been copied.

3. Add to the front panel two **Vertical Switches**. Vertical switches can be found in the *Boolean* subpalette of the Controls palette. With *owned* labels, label one switch as the **Function** and the other as *QUIT*. As shown in Fig. 4-16, add free labels **Sum** and *Average* to the Function switch. Also configure *both* switches as follows:
    Pop up on the switch and choose **Mechanical Action>Latch When Pressed** from the popup menu.
    Use the Operating Tool and move the switch to the upper position so that it

    appears like this ▐ , then pop up on the switch and choose **Data Operations>Make Current Value Default**.

4. *Switch to the block diagram*. The Shift Register that you just copied should be inside the block diagram at this time. Open next the *Case* structure. The Case structure is in the *Structures* subpalette of the Controls palette. As soon as you click on the Case structure in the Structures subpalette, the cursor changes to

    > |?|

    Place this dashed rectangle cursor above and to the left of the For Loop shift register (slightly above and to the left of constant 5). Click and *hold down* the left mouse button. Drag the cursor down and to the right so that the dashed outline completely encloses the entire shift register. When you release the mouse button, the shift register will be inside the *False* frame of the Case structure.

    Remove the *Sum* terminal and place it outside the Case structure. Delete any bad wires (Ctrl+B).

5. Switch to the *true* frame of the Case structure by clicking on the arrow button in the Case window.

119

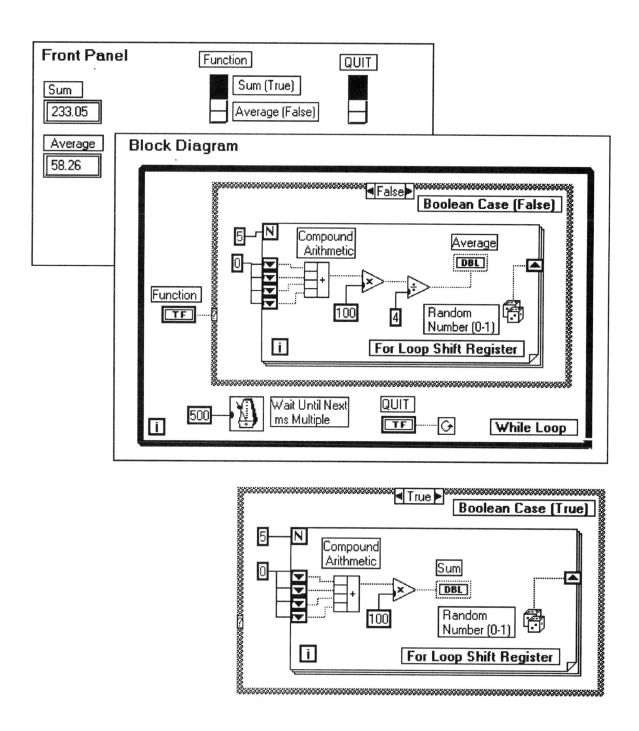

Fig. 4-16   The Front Panel and Block Diagram for Exercise 5

Copy the For Loop shift register to the *True* frame of the Case structure. At this point, the best way to accomplish this is to pop up in the *False Case* window and choose **Duplicate Case**. Notice that the *True Case frame* now contains the same thing as the *False* frame minus the digital indicator *Average* terminal.

Delete the *Divide* function and the **4** numeric constant, and wire the *Sum* digital indicator terminal to the output of the *Multiply* function, as shown in Fig. 4-16 for the True frame.

6.   Wire the **Function** Boolean terminal to the *Selector Terminal* of the Case structure.

7.   Open the **While Loop**. You will find the While loop in the *Structures* subpalette of the Functions palette. As described in step 4 of this exercise, place the rectangular dashed line cursor outline above and to the left of the Case structure, then drag it (continue to hold down the mouse button) downward and to the right until the entire Case structure is enclosed. Leave some room inside the While loop for other objects. When you release the mouse button, the While loop will be in place.

8.   Open the **Wait Until the Next ms Multiple** function from the *Time & Dialog* subpalette of the Functions palette and wire to it a numeric constant of 500. You can either copy the numeric constant from the current block diagram or get it from the *Numeric* subpalette of the Functions palette.

9.   Wire the **QUIT** Boolean terminal to the *Condition* terminal of the While Loop.

10.   Switch to the front fanel and **Run** the VI. Make sure that the *Quit* vertical switch in the front panel is in the *up* or *True* position. Switch the *Function* to *Sum* and *Average* positions and observe the indicator displays.

The Function switch decides which of the two Boolean Case frames will be executed. The While loop provides a continuous operation, allowing you to change the function switch setting while the VI is running.

The *Wait Until the Next ms Multiple* provides a 500 ms time delay between iterations, giving you an opportunity to view the display. Increasing the 500 value will make the delay longer, and vice versa.

Save this VI as **Boolean_Case.vi** in Workbook.LLB and close it.

Exercise 6: Using the Numeric Case Structure

This VI illustrates the use of the Numeric Case Structure. In the previous exercise we used the Boolean Case structure, which has only two frames, *True* and *False*. When there are more than two tasks that must be done, the Boolean Case structure cannot be used. The Numeric Case structure has as many case frames as you need. In this exercise we have three tasks to be executed.

Two random integer numbers are generated inside the While loop and applied to the Case structure. The setting of the Function switch (menu ring) determines which frame will be executed.

1.   The **front panel** includes five digital indicators. Digital Indicators are in the *Numeric* subpalette of the Controls palette. Label them with owned labels, as shown in Fig. 4-17.

The **Vertical Switch** is in the *Boolean* subpalette of the Controls palette. Configure the switch according to the procedure described in step 3 of Exercise 4 and label it *QUIT* using an owned label.

The **Menu Ring** that we are using in the front panel under the owned label of ***Function*** is a

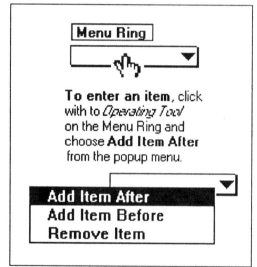

To enter an item, click with to *Operating Tool* on the Menu Ring and choose **Add Item After** from the popup menu.

new control that you haven't used before. It is located in the *List & Ring* subpalette of the Controls palette.

To Enter an Item into the Menu Ring, click with the Operating Tool, as shown in this illustration, on the Menu Ring button and choose ***Add Item After*** from the popup menu. The face of the button becomes white. Type the item name.

Type ***Sum*** as the first item. Repeat the above process, and type ***Math Average*** as the second item. Repeat this process once more and type ***Geom Average***.

Note other options in the popup menu that allow you to ***Add Item Before*** and to ***Remove Item.***

To Operate the Menu Ring, click with the Operating Tool on the Menu Ring button and choose from the menu one of the items that you typed.

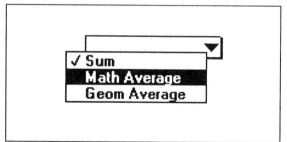

When you select *Sum,* the first item, the Menu Ring (being a control object) outputs a **0**. It outputs a **1** when you select *Math Average* and a **2** when you select the *Geom Average*.

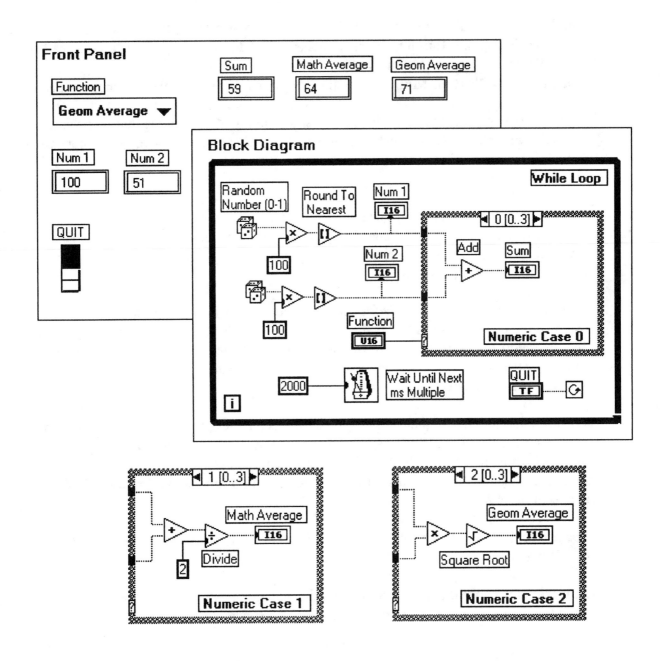

Fig. 4-17   Using the Numeric Case Structure of Example 6

2.   In the **block diagram:**

Case Structure is in the *Structures* subpalette of the Controls palette. When you wire the *Function* terminal to the *Selector* terminal, the Boolean Case structure will change to the Numeric Case structure. Notice that Fig. 4-17 shows all three Case frames. To access frames 1 and 2, use the arrow button in the Case window.

123

The *Numeric* subpalette of the Functions palette contains most of the remaining items in the block diagram: **Random Number** generator, **Add, Multiply, Divide, Square Root, Round to Nearest, Numeric Constant**.

Wait Until the Next ms Multiple is in the *Time & Dialog* subpalette of Functions palette.

3.   *Wire* all objects inside the block diagram as shown in Fig. 4-17. Notice that when you extend a wire into the Case structure, a **tunnel** in the shape of a black rectangle appears. The tunnel is the means of passing data to and from a structure. This was true also for the While and the For loops.

4.   This VI begins its operation by generating two random integer inside the While Loop. Actually the *Random Number* generator outputs random values between 0 and 1. But after being multiplied by 100 and after passing through the *Round To Nearest* function, they fall into the range of 0 to 100.

The *Wait Until Next ms Multiple* function provides a delay between iterations. In this example the delay is set to 2000 milliseconds, or 2 seconds. The delay pauses the execution and gives you an opportunity to view the data. You can change the delay to another value. In fact, instead of using the numeric constant, you can create a digital control and thus change the delay time from the front panel.

The *Function* terminal in the block diagram outputs an integer value corresponding to your choice in the Menu Ring. If you select the *Sum*, the Menu Ring outputs a **0** and applies it to the Case structure, causing the execution of frame **0**. Similarly when you choose *Math Average,* the menu Ring outputs a **1** and Numeric frame **1** and Geom Average will result in in execution of frame 2.

The use of the While Loop will execute all code repeatedly until you stop execution with the QUIT switch.

Run the VI. Choose different options from the Function menu and note the results.
Save this VI as **Numeric_Case.vi** in Workbook.LLB and close it.

Sequence Structure

Thus far we spoke of programming tools that provide branching and a repetitive execution of a group of instructions. The Sequence structure is different. In most high-level languages the sequence or the order in which instructions are executed is simply the order in which the instructions are written. Therefore in the high-level language there is no concern about sequence.

In LabVIEW the order in which nodes in the Block Diagram are executed depends on the availability

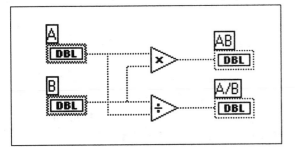

of data at the input terminals of that node. A particular node will execute only if data is available at each terminal of that node. In this respect LabVIEW differs from the traditional high-level language.

In this illustration, for example, it would be difficult to predict which operation, multiplication or division, will be done first.

The Sequence Structure can easily resolve this problem.

To Open the Sequence Structure, click with the *Positioning Tool* on the *Sequence* option in the *Structures* subpalette of the Functions palette, as shown in Fig. 4-18.

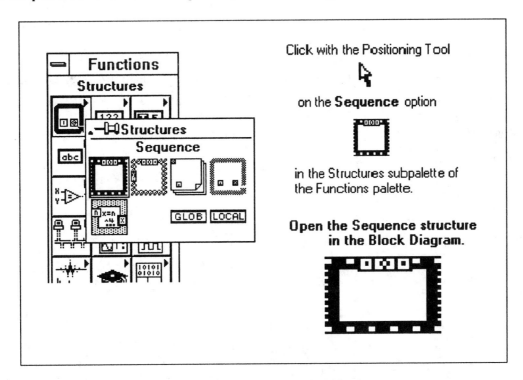

Fig. 4-18   Opening the Sequence Structure

Once opened in the block diagram, the Sequence structure can be ***moved*** or ***resized*** in the usual way.

125

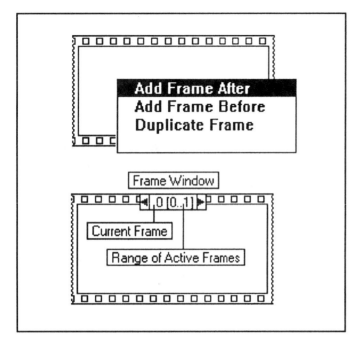

To Add a Frame, click (with the right mouse button) on the Sequence structure border and choose **Add Frame After** from the popup menu. This popup menu also allows you to **Add Frame Before** the current frame as well as to copy a frame.

This creates the **Frame Window,** as shown in the illustration. Notice that the Frame window is similar to that of the Numeric Case structure. As shown in this illustration, it indicates the current frame and, in the brackets [0..1], it shows the range of all active frames. The 0..1 indication means that there are frames 0 and 1.

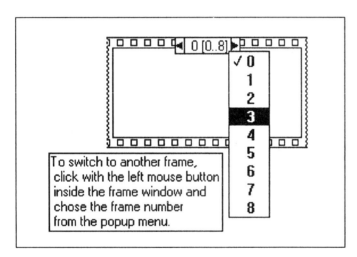

To switch to another frame, click with the left mouse button inside the frame window and choose the frame number that you wish to open from the popup menu.

Note once again that the frames of the Sequence structure are stacked one on top of the other. In this illustration there 9 active frames (0 to 8) and there could be more if you need them.

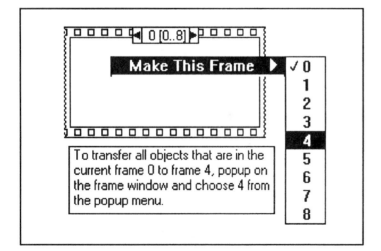

If for some reason you wish to **transfer** all objects in the current frame to another frame, there is an easy way of doing so.

Pop up on the window and choose **Make This Frame** from the pop up menu. Then choose the frame number from the submenu. In this illustration all code will be transferred from frame 0 to frame 4. All other frames will adjust accordingly.

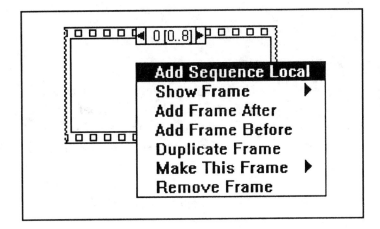

To Add a Sequence Local, pop up on the frame window and choose *Add Sequence Local* from the popup menu.

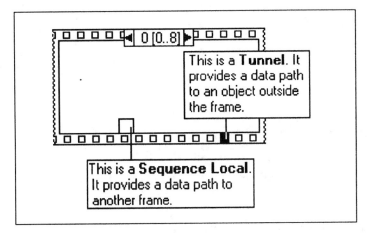

The *Sequence Local* provides a data path to any other active frame. In contrast, a *Tunnel* provides a data path to another object outside the frame. Note the difference in appearance between the tunnel and the Sequence Local, as shown in this illustration.

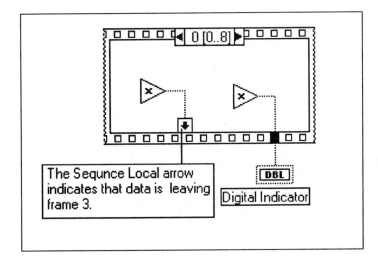

When an object is wired to the Sequence Local, an arrow inside the Sequence Local points to the outside the frame, thus indicating that the data is leaving frame 3, as shown in this illustration. This data will be available in all frames higher than frame 3 and will not be available in any of the preceding frames.

This illustration also shows the tunnel that provides a data path to an object outside the frame.

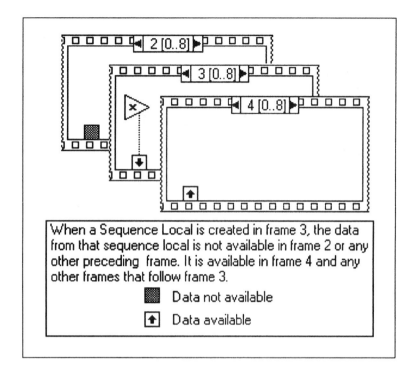

When you create a Sequence Local in a frame, the data from that Sequence Local is not available in any of the preceding frames. It is available, however, in all other frames that follow the frame where you created the Sequence Local, as shown in this illustration.

Exercise 7: Using the Sequence Structure (Motor Speed Profile)

In this exercise we will use the Sequence Structure as well as the For and the While loops to simulate the motor speed profile. As you will see shortly, the Sequence structure makes possible the execution of a specific sequence of different tasks.

The motor speed profile shown graphically in Fig. 4-19 includes the following tasks:

1. Ramp at fast rate the motor speed to 2000 rpm
2. Remain at 2000 rpm for 5 seconds
3. Ramp down at slow rate to 1000 rpm
4. Remain at 1000 rpm for 4 seconds
5. Ramp down at medium rate to 0 rpm
6. Calculate the operation time

1. The **front panel** includes the **Meter** and a **Digital Indicator**. Both are in the *Numeric* subpalette of the Controls palette. Label the *Meter* with an owned label as **Motor Speed** and add the **RPM** free label as shown in Fig. 4-20. Change the scale maximum point to 2000 and choose the *Representation* as **I16.** See Exercise 2, step 1.

    Label the digital indicator with an owned label as **Operation Time** and use **sec** as the free label.

2. The **block diagram** includes a **Sequence** structure that has 7 frames.
    Open the *Sequence* structure, which you will find in the *Structures* subpalette of the Functions palette. Following the procedure described earlier, open **Frame 0.**

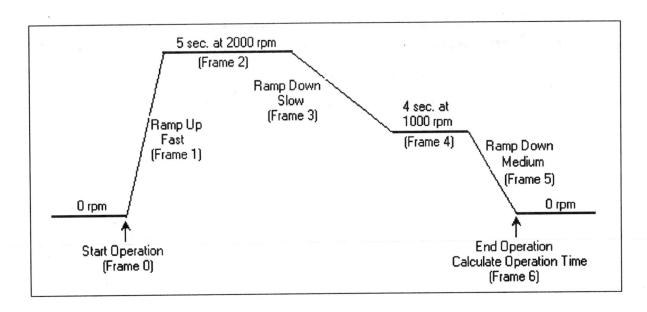

Fig. 4-19 Motor Speed Profile

The **Tick Count** ⏱ timer is in the *Time & Dialog* subpalette of the Functions palette.
Open it inside *Frame 0*. Add *Sequence Local* and wire the *Tick Count* timer to the
Sequence Local. Your frame 0 should look like that shown in Fig. 4-20. Note that the *Start
Time* is a free label and it is not essential to the operation.

As shown in Fig. 4-19, when frame 0 executes the relative time marking the start of the
operation is recorded.

3. Click on the *arrow button* at the top of the frame window and open **Frame 1**.
    Inside this frame are the following objects:
    > **For Loop** that is in the *Structures* subpalette of the Functions palette.
    > Three **Numeric Constants** (40, 51 and 100), which can be found in the *Numeric*
    > subpalette of the Functions palette.
    > **Multiply** function, which is in the *Numeric* subpalette of the Functions palette.
    > **Wait Until Next ms Multiple** timer, which is in the *Time & Dialog* subpalette
    > of the Functions palette.

    Wire these objects as shown in *Frame 1* of Fig. 4-20.
    When frame 1 is executed, the fast ramping task will be accomplished as shown in Fig. 4-17.
    Notice that the Iteration terminal is used as a counter to generate a ramping waveform.

4. Click on the *arrow button* at the top of the frame window and open **Frame 2**.

    This frame includes the **Wait** ⌚ timer found in the *Time & Dialog* subpalette of the
    Functions palette and the **Numeric Constant** (5000) from the *Numeric* subpalette
    of the Functions Palette.
    Wire the constant as shown in Frame 2 of Fig. 4-20. This frame, when executed, provides a
    5 second (5000 msec.) time delay. See Fig. 4-19.

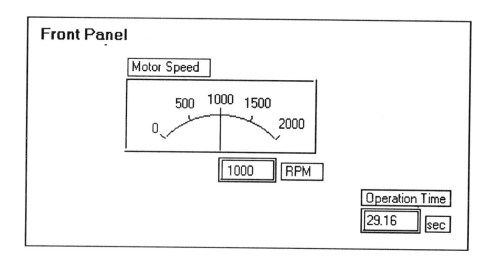

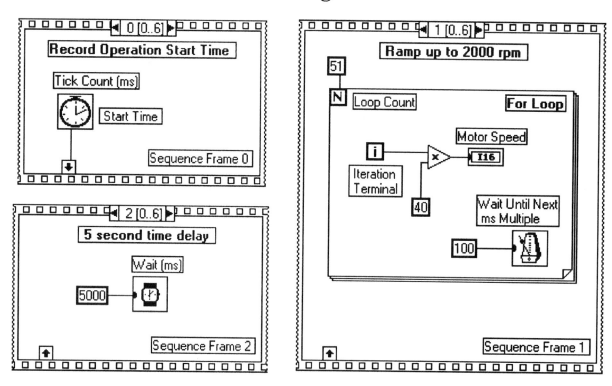

Fig. 4-20 The Front Panel and Block Diagram of Exercise 7

130

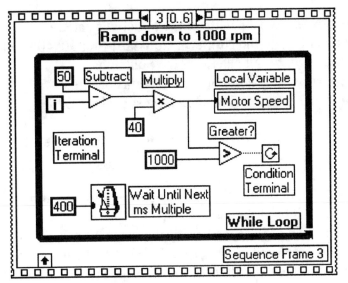

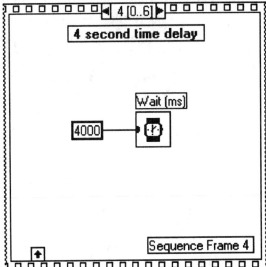

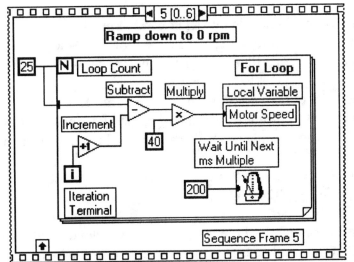

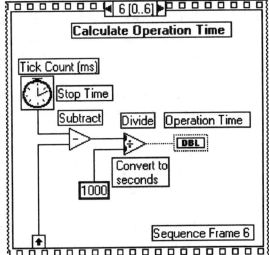

Fig. 4-20 The Front Panel and Block Diagram of Exercise 7 (continued)

5. Click on the *arrow button* at the top of the frame window and open **Frame 3**.
The following objects are in *Frame 3*:

> The **While Loop** found in the *Structures* subpalette of the Functions palette.
> **Subtract** function, **Multiply** function and the **Numeric Constant** (40, 50, 400 and 1000) can be found in the *Numeric* subpalette of the Functions.
> **Greater?** is found in the *Comparison* subpalette of the Functions palette.
> **Wait Until Next ms Multiple** timer is in the *Time & Dialog* subpalette of the Functions palette.
> **Motor Speed** local variable. See Exercise 2 on how to create a local variable.

Wire all objects as shown in Frame 3 of Fig. 4-20.

The 400 numeric constant provides a 400 millisecond time delay between loop iterations. The 40 numeric constant determines the height of the ramping step.
This frame creates the ramping down portion of the speed profile between 2000 rpm and 1000 rpm. As long as the motor speed is greater than 1000 rpm, the Greater? comparison function outputs a *true*, which is applied to the *Condition Terminal*. When the speed reaches 1000, the comparator outputs a *False* to the *Condition Terminal* and that stops the loop. By adjusting the value of the 400 constant, you will control the ramping slope or the rate of ramping down.

6. Click on the *arrow button* at the top of the frame window and open **Frame 4**.
Duplicate frame 2 and set the numeric constant to 4000. See Frame 4 of Fig. 4-20.
This frame, when executed, provides a 4 second time delay, as shown in Fig. 4-19.

7. Click on the *arrow button* at the top of the frame window and open **Frame 5**.
This frame includes the **For Loop** from the *Structures* subpalette of the Functions palette. Most of the objects inside the For Loop are exactly the same as those of Frame 3 (refer to step 5).
The **Increment** function is found in the *Numeric* subpalette of the Functions palette.
Wire all objects as shown in Frame 5 of Fig. 4-20.

When executed, this frame accomplishes the task of ramping down as was done in Frame 3, except here the ramping starts at 1000 rpm and ends at 0 rpm. Frame 3 uses the While Loop to accomplish the ramping down task. Do you think that a For Loop could have been used there?

8. Click on the *arrow button* at the top of the frame window and open **Frame 6**.
There are no new objects in this frame. Build this frame as shown in Frame 6 of Fig. 4-20.

This is the last frame. The only thing that is done in this frame is the computation of the Operation Time. Recall that in Frame 1 the Start time was recorded and applied to the sequence local. Notice that this sequence local also appears in Frame 6 but with the arrow pointing inside the frame ⬆, indicating that data from Frame 0 is available here.

The *Tick Count* timer in frame 6 records the *Stop Time* (Stop Time in frame 6 is a free label). The difference between the two times is the Operation Time. It is divided by 1000 to convert it to seconds and displayed on the **Operation Time** digital indicator.

Note that the *Tick Count* timer does not output real time. Its output is relative time. If you converted its output from frame 0, the result would be meaningless. The time reference is lost, of course, when you subtract the two time readings. The time difference is real, however, and you can check that on your watch.

9.   **Run** the VI. Experiment with different values of iteration delays and the 4 and 5 second time delays.
    Save this VI as **Motor Speed Profile.vi** and close it.

Exercise 8:   Using the Sequence Structure (Liquid Level Control)

In this exercise the Sequence structure is used once again in the liquid level control of a chemical processing tank simulation. Imagine a large 2000 gallon chemical mixing tank where chemicals are added. In the process the tank volume has to be adjusted to a desired level and a specific rate.

The VI that simulates this operation can be exactly the same as the VI of the previous exercise with only a slight modification in the front panel and the block diagram, shown in Fig. 4-21. As you can see, the only change that you have to do is to replace the *Meter* indicator with the *Tank* indicator.

1.   The best way to accomplish this with a minimum of work is, first, to open the *Speed_Profile.vi* and then choose *Save As...* from the File menu.
    Save this VI as **Tank_Processing.vi** in Workbook.LLB.

2.   Next, in the front panel replace the *Meter* indicator with the *Tank* indicator. As shown in Fig. 4-21, change the scale, replacing the 10 with 2000, and change the labels as shown. You will have to rewire the tank terminal (Liquid Level) that will appear in frame 1. Create Liquid Level local variables and wire them in frames 3 and 5.

3.   *Run* the VI, experimenting with different values for rates and delays. Close it.

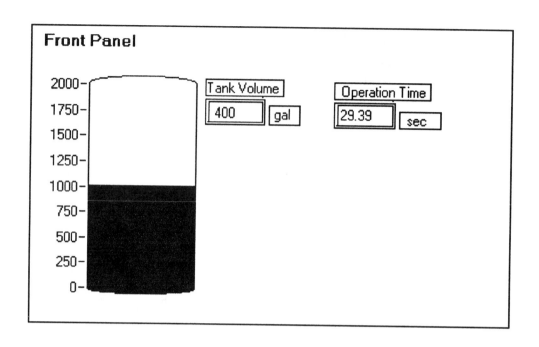

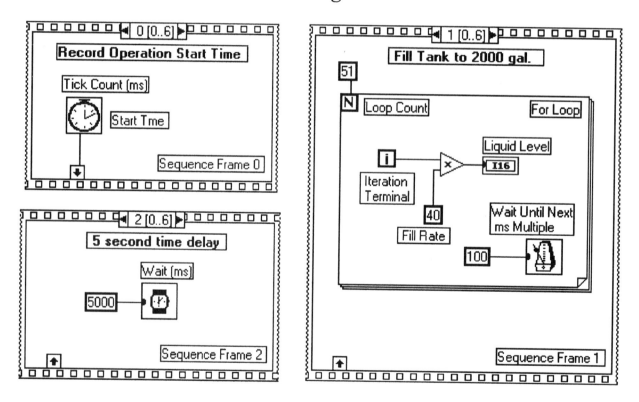

Fig. 4-21 Liquid Level Control of Exercise 8

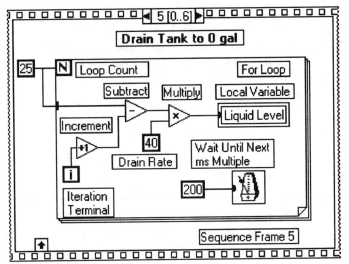

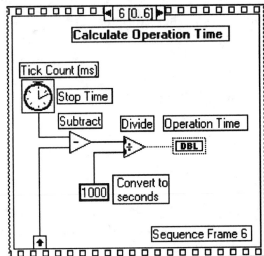

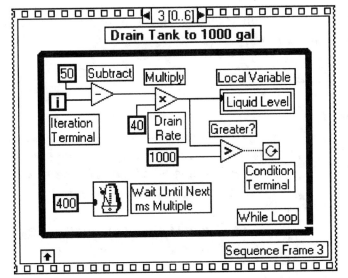

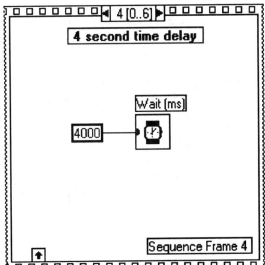

Fig. 4-21   Liquid Level Control of Exercise 8 (continued)

Formula Node

A Formula Node is a rectangular structure into which you enter formulas following the specific syntax rules. These formulas are done at execution time. It's true that an equation such as $y = 2 + x^3$ can be synthesized using add and multiply function blocks, as shown in this illustration.

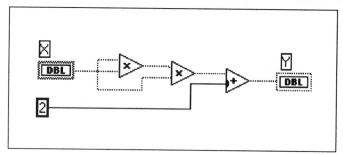

However, there is another option: type the formula inside the Formula node rectangular box and the Formula node will execute it for you. It is an option for the user and very often a convenient one.

To Open the Formula Node, choose ***Formula Node*** from the *Structures* subpalette of the Functions palette. When you open the Formula Node inside the block diagram, it looks like simple rectangular box, as shown below.

But you also need input and output terminals to pass parameter values into the *Formula Node* and to pass calculated values to objects outside the *Formula Node*.

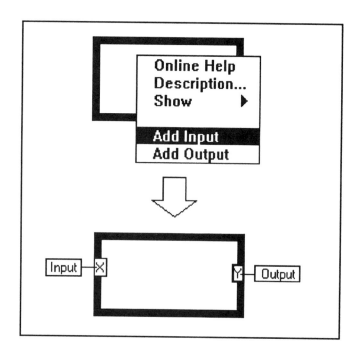

To Create Input Terminal, pop up (with the right mouse button) on the *border* of the Formula Node and choose ***Add Input*** option from the popup menu.

To Create Output Terminal, repeat the above procedure and choose ***Add Output.***

To Enter Equation into the Formula Node, click on the Labeling Tool ⒶⅠ in the Tools palette, then click inside the Formula Node with the labeling tool's cursor and start typing.

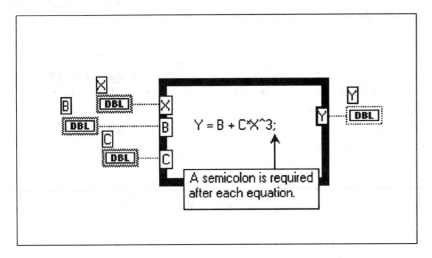

Don't forget about the semicolon, because one is required at the end of each equation.

As shown in this illustration, the Formula node will output the value of the Y variable when you supply the X variable value.

In this illustration, the front panel digital control X supplies the X value and the digital controls B and C provide the parameter values B and C. The front panel indicator Y displays the values that the Formula Node outputs.

The syntax or the rules that you must follow are shown in Fig. 4-22. As you can see, the set includes

```
Formula Node operators, lowest precedence first:
assignment   =
conditional   ? :
logical OR    ||   logical AND    &&
relational    == != > < >= <=
arithmetic    + - * / ^
unary         + - !

Formula Node functions:
abs acos acosh asin asinh atan atanh ceil
cos cosh cot csc exp expm1 floor getexp getman
int intrz ln lnp1 log log2 max min mod rand
rem sec sign sin sinc sinh sqrt tan tanh
```

Fig. 4-22 Formula Node Syntax Table

the hierarchy of the operators, from the assignment with the lowest precedence to the unary operator having the highest precedence. The set also includes an array of functions that you can use.

To Open Formula Node Syntax Table, enter *Ctrl+H* from the keyboard and then click with the positioning tool on the Formula Node.

Exercise 9:   Using the Formula Node

This exercise illustrates the use of the Formula Node. You will build a VI that solves the quadratic equation when the roots are real. When the roots are imaginary, it will display a message to that effect.

1.   The **front panel** includes three digital controls, two digital indicators and a vertical switch. You will find the digital controls and indicators in the *Numeric* subpalette of the Functions palette and the vertical switch in the *Boolean* subpalette of the Functions palette.
    Set the vertical switch to the *up* or *true* position, then pop up on the switch and choose *Mechanical Action>Latch When Pressed*, as you have done in step 3 of Exercise 1.

2.   Switch to **block diagram** and open the **While Loop**. The While Loop is in the *Structures* subpalette of Functions palette. Enlarge it so it takes up most of the window.

3.   Inside the While Loop open the first **Formula Node**. As shown in Fig. 4-23, add three *Input* terminals along the left edge and label them A, B and C. Add also the *Output* terminal and label it X. Wire the digital control terminals A, B, C to their corresponding inputs on the Formula Node.

    Using the Labeling tool, enter the equation X = B^2 - 4*A*C; inside the Formula Node.

4.   Open the **Case structure** inside the While Loop. The Case structure is in the *Structures* subpalette of the Functions palette. Enlarge the Case structure so that you can fit another Formula Node inside it. Make sure that the *false* frame is open and if not, click on the arrow button in the case window.

5.   Open a **Formula Node** inside the Case structure. Create three inputs along the left edge of the Formula Node, as shown in Fig. 4-23, and label them as **A, B** and **X**. Also create two outputs and label them as **RT1** and **RT2**.

    Enter into the Formula Node the following equations:
        RT1 = (−B + sqrt(X))/(2*A);
        RT2 = (−B − sqrt(X))/(2*A);

6.   *Wire* the digital control terminal A to the A input of the Formula Node inside the Case structure. As you pass the wire across the border of the Case structure, a tunnel (black rectangle) will be formed in the wall of the Case structure.

    In a similar fashion wire the digital control terminal B to the B input of the Formula Node inside the Case structure. Also wire the X output of the first Formula Node to the X input of the Formula Node inside the Case structure.

    Wire the RT1 and RT2 digital control terminals to the outputs RT1 and RT2.

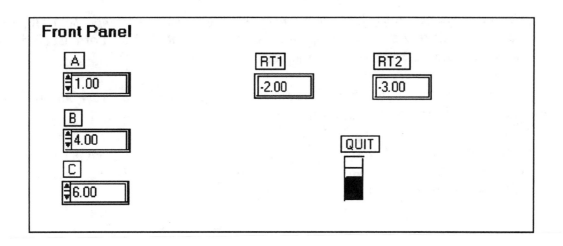

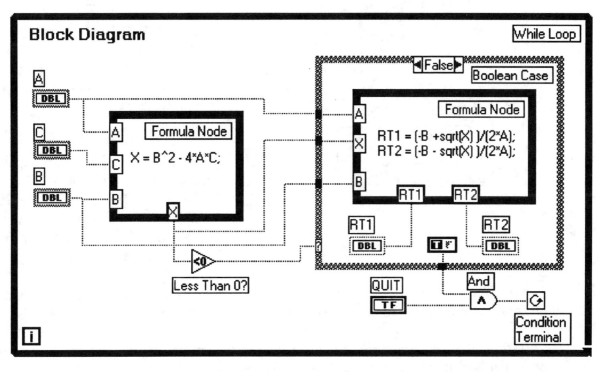

Fig. 4-23 The Front Panel and Block Diagram of the Root.vi in Exercise 9

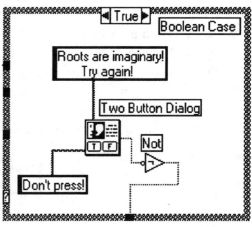

7. Open the **Less than 0?** <img_1 comparison function. It is in the *Comparison* subpalette of the Functions palette. As shown in Fig. 4-23, wire the output X of the Formula Node to the Selector Terminal **?** of the Case structure.

8. Switch to the *true* frame of the Case structure by clicking on the arrow button in the Case window at the top of the Case structure.

Open the **Two Button Dialog** . It is in the *Time & Dialog* subpalette of the Functions palette. As shown in this illustration, the *Two Button Dialog icon* has two buttons. One button is labeled as *T* and the other as *F.*

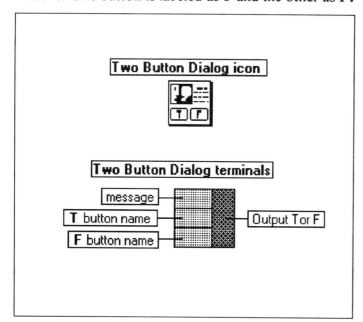

The terminal version of the Two Button Dialog (which you get by popping up on the icon and choosing *Show Terminals* from the popup menu) has three inputs and one output.

The *message* input is a required input and must be provided by the user.

Both the *T* and *F* button inputs are optional. The default name for the former is *OK* and for the latter, *Cancel*. You can, however, provide your own T and F button names if you don't like the default ones.

When the *Two Button Dialog* function executes, it outputs to the screen a dialog box with your message and two buttons whose names are either default or the ones you specified.

To create a message you must first open the **String Constant** ☐ , which looks like a purple rectangular box. It is located in the *Strings* subpalette of the Functions palette.

Open the **String Constant** from the *Strings* subpalette of the Functions palette in the block diagram. Immediately start typing (do not click with the mouse button anywhere).
Type the following: **Roots Are Imaginary!**
                             Try again!

It will look like this when you are done:

> **Roots Are Imaginary!**
> **Try again!**

140

Next wire this string constant to the *message input* of the Two Button Dialog function. Notice the color of the wire; it's purple, which is appropriate for strings.
Get another string constant, type **Don't Press** and wire it to the *F* input of the Two Button Dialog. Leave the T input unwired unless you don't like the *OK* name.

Select the two strings and the Two Button Dialog objects using multiple object selection rules. When selected, each object will be surrounded by dashed lines. Move the strings and the objects in the **True** frame of the Case structure.

9.   *Open* the **Not** inverter inside the True frame of the Case structure and an **AND** gate inside the While Loop.

Wire the output of the Two Button Dialog to the input of the Not and the output of the Not to the one input of the AND gate. Notice the tunnel that was formed when you moved the wire across the boundary of the Case structure to make the connection to the AND gate.

Wire the **QUIT** Boolean terminal to the other input of the AND gate.
Wire the output of the AND gate to the *Condition Terminal.*

10.   Assuming that you have followed the above directions and wired everything correctly, you should have at this time a broken Run button [⇥] , indicating that you have syntax errors. You can click on the Run button and find out where the errors are. The system will tell you that you are "missing assignment to tunnel" in the Case structure.

After a closer look, you will observe that the other three tunnels in the Case structure appear as **black rectangles**, but the tunnel wired to the output of the **Not** inverter appears as a **white rectangle**. The white rectangle is an indication that one input is missing. Certainly the True Case frame provides an input but the False frame doesn't.

The best way to handle this problem without affecting anything else is to use a **Boolean Constant**. It can be found in the *Boolean* subpalette of the Functions palette. Its default form will appear as [?F] . Click with the operating tool ⌐ᵐ on the Boolean Constant and it will change to [T?] .

Place [T?] in the *false* frame of the Case structure and wire it to the white tunnel of the Case structure. Notice that the tunnel changed to black and the broken Run arrow became solid. You are now ready to run the VI

11.   The first Formula Node calculates the value of $B^2 - 4*A*C$ and equates it to X. The sign of X is tested by the *Less Than 0?* comparator. If X is positive, the *False* frame of the Case structure will be executed, and the roots RT1 and RT2 will be calculated and displayed on their respective front panel digital indicators.

But if X is negative, the *True* Case frame will be executed, and the Two Button Dialog function will be executed, displaying a dialog box as shown in this illustration.

When you click on OK button, the Two Button Dialog function will output a *true*, which is inverted, and the *false* from the inverter is applied to the AND gate. The AND gate in turn will apply a *false* to the Condition Terminal. This will force the While Loop to stop execution.

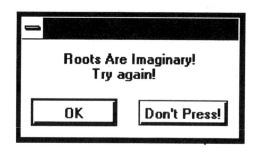

Should you click on the *Don't Press*, nothing will happen because the Two Button Dialog will output a *false*, which is inverted, resulting in a *true* input to the AND gate.

You can also stop the execution by clicking on the QUIT vertical switch in the front panel with the operating tool.

Run the VI. Try different values of A, B, C.
Save this VI as **Root.vi** in Workbook.LLB. Close it.

142

Exercise 10:   Craps Game

This exercise combines the use of the While Loop, For Loop, shift register and a Sequence structure in a game of chance, a simulation of a craps game. In this exercise you will explore on a larger scale the interactive aspects of structures and functions.

1.   Before building the craps game VI, you must first build another VI that will be used later as a subVI. The front panel and the block diagram for this VI are shown in Fig. 4-24.

Build the front panel and the block diagram shown in Fig. 4-24. You will find the *Random Number* generator in the *Numeric* subpalette of the Functions palette and the *To Unsigned Word Integer* in the *Conversion* subpalette of the Numeric subpalette of the Functions palette.

The front panel includes three digital indicators, as shown in Fig. 4-24.

Refer to Chapter 3 on how to create an icon and a connector for this VI. A suggested icon may look like this Roll 2 Dice .

Save this VI as **Roll 2 Dice.vi** in Workbook.LLB and close it.

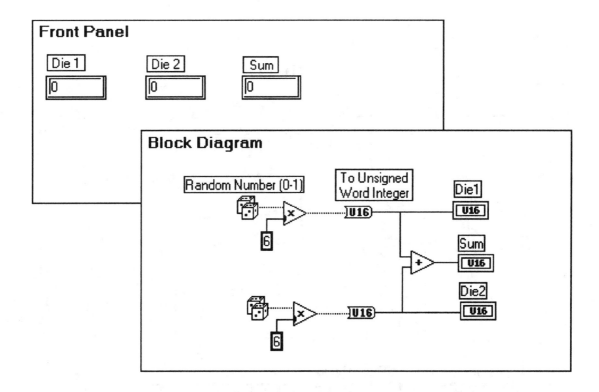

Fig. 4-24   Roll 2 Dice.vi to Be Used Later As a subVI

2.   *Build* the Front Panel of the Craps game VI as shown in Fig. 4-25. As you can see, it
      includes five digital indicators and a Boolean vertical switch.

3.   *Build* the Block Diagram as shown in Fig. 4-25. The block diagram consists of Sequence
      Frames 0, 1 and 2. Notice that the subVI Roll 2 Dice is used in frames 0 and 2. All
      objects in the block diagram have been covered before, so this is your challenge:
      build this VI all by yourself.

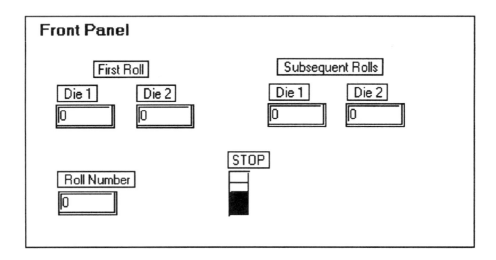

Block Diagram

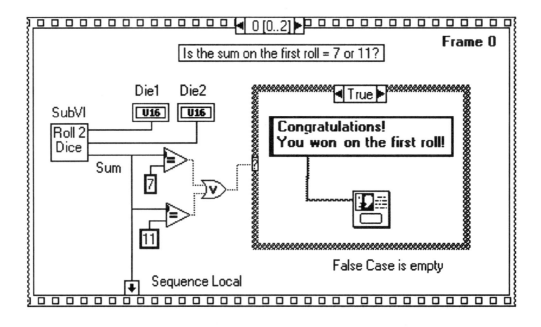

Fig. 4-25 Front Panel and Block Diagram of Exercise 10

144

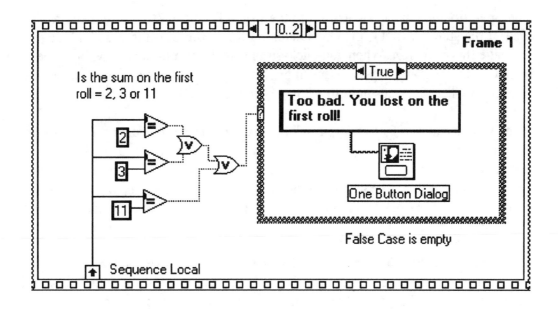

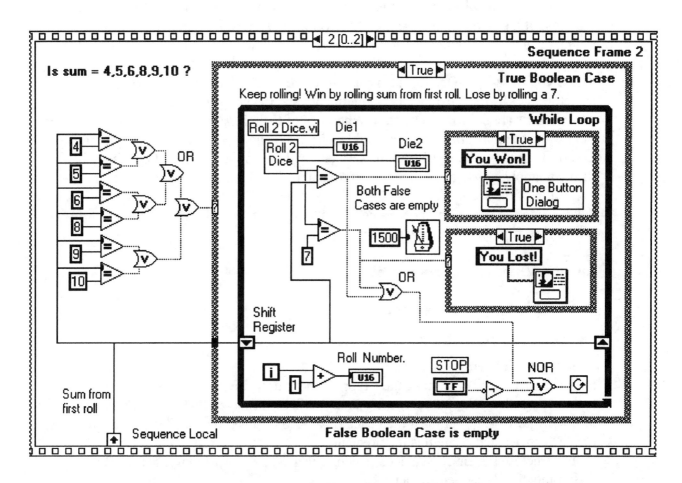

Fig. 4-25 Front Panel and Block Diagram of Exercise 10 (continued)

145

4.   The operation begins in Frame 0 when the Roll 2 Dice subVI simulates the rolling of two dice. If the sum is 7 or 11, the One Dialog button in the Boolean case will display the message that you won. When you click on the OK button in the dialog box, the sum will be tested in frames 1 and 2, where the empty *False* case will be executed. The VI terminates its execution when all nodes in Frame 2 have been executed.

If the sum is equal to 2, 3 or 12, it will be tested in Frame 0 forcing the execution of the empty *False* case, but in the sequence of Frame 1, the *True* case will be executed, displaying the message that you lost. After you click on the OK button in the dialog box, sequence Frame 3 will be tested, forcing the execution of the empty *False* case. At this point the VI will terminate its execution because all frames of the Sequence structure have been executed.

On the other hand, if the sum of the two dice on the first throw is 4, 5, 6, 8, 9, or 10, the empty *False* case will be executed in Frame 0 and nothing will happen. This sum will also be tested in Frame 1, forcing the execution of the empty *False* case and again nothing will happen. The sum will next be tested in Frame 2, forcing the execution of the *True* case. Notice that inside the *True* case the While Loop shift register recirculates the sum and compares it on each iteration with the new sum from the subVI Roll 2 Dice. The object of the game at this point is to match the old sum on a subsequent throw of the dice. You lose if you throw a 7. One Boolean case structure checks for a 7 and the other Case structure checks for the match between the old and the new sums. Both of these comparisons are fed to the OR gate. When one of them is *true* (you roll a 7 or match the old sum), the appropriate message will be displayed and the While Loop will terminate execution because the *true* from the OR gate will be applied to the NOR gate, which in turn will apply a *false* to the condition terminal of the While Loop. This will complete execution of the sequence Frame 2 and thus terminate VI execution. Notice the 1.5 second delay inside the While Loop of Frame 2. It allows you to watch the subsequent throw of the dice on the front panel in slow motion.

Run this VI and after you are done.

Save it as **Craps.vi** in Workbook.LLB.

Additional Challenge Exercise
Suppose that we wish to make the Craps VI more user friendly so that after the game is finished, whether you win or lose, a message will be displayed that reads: *Would You Like to Play Again?* The user must then click on a YES or a NO button. Make changes in the Craps.vi to accommodate this requirement.
[Hint: Enclose the entire sequence structure in a While Loop and use a Two Button dialog function in sequence Frame 2.]

Summary

1. The *While Loop* is a repetition structure. The loop executes all nodes inside the loop repeatedly as long as the Boolean input to the Condition terminal is *true*. When it becomes *false*, the loop terminates execution. Usually a Boolean control such as a switch in the front panel is used to provide the input to the Condition terminal in the block diagram.

2. The *For Loop* is also a repetition structure. It executes all code inside the loop border a fixed number of times, as dictated by the user supplied value to the loop counter N.

3   One property that applies to the While Loop as well as to the For Loop is that the loop does not accept inputs or output data during execution time. At the beginning of its execution, the loop reads values external to the loop and then begins execution. It is only when the loop completes its execution that data can be passed from inside the loop to objects outside the loop.

4. The iteration counter *i* can serve as a counter in practical applications. We have used it to generate a staircase waveform in several simulation exercises.

5. A *Shift Register* can be implemented in the While Loop as well as in the For Loop. It can store data that has occurred one iteration ago, two iterations ago, etc. It can be used to find the average of several values.

6. The *Case structure* is a selection structure that corresponds to the If/Else structure in a high-level language. When a Boolean value is applied to the *Selector terminal (?)* in the border of the Case structure, the Case structure becomes a Boolean type with two Case frames, one *True* and the other *False*. The Boolean input determines which frame will be executed.

    When the input to the Selector terminal is numeric, the Case structure changes to the Numeric type. The case window at the top of the frame indicates the current frame as well as the range of active frames. The numeric input to the selector terminal dictates which frame will be executed.

7. The *Sequence structure* consists of frames beginning with frame 0. When executed it will execute all code in frame 0 and will continue to execute all remaining frames in sequence. Because the order of node execution in LabVIEW depends on the availability of date at the input to the node, there are situations when it is not possible to predict which node in the block diagram will execute first. Most of the time the order in which nodes execute is not important. However, as was illustrated in exercise 6, where the order of execution of specific tasks is essential, the sequence structure was used to solve that problem.

8. The *Formula Node* is a structure used to execute mathematical equations and logical operations. Although many times the same code can be synthesized using the function blocks, the Formula Node is a convenient alternative option for the user.

9. A terminal in the block diagram that corresponds to the front panel object cannot be duplicated. But there are situations when you need a copy of a terminal. As was demonstrated in the exercises, the *Local Variable* is the answer.

10. The *Select* function has three inputs, one input being Boolean. The Boolean input (?) determines which of the remaining two inputs will be passed to the output. This function was used effectively in the Tank Control simulation of exercise 3 to maintain the liquid level at a desired level as the loop completes its execution.

11. The timers are useful in providing a time delay or marking time. The *Tick Count* timer may be used to time the operation, the *Wait* timer is useful in generating accurate time delays, and the *Wait Until Next ms Multiple* timer can also be used to provide time delays or time between loop iteration delays.

12. The *Two Button Dialog* function is useful in displaying messages. It has two buttons, *T* and *F*. The default names for the T and F buttons are OK and Cancel, respectively but the user can change the default names by providing appropriate string inputs. When the Two Button Dialog function is executed, the message that the user created is displayed on the screen. It outputs a *true* when you click on the T button, and *false* when you click on the F button. In the last exercise this function was used to alert the user to the fact that the roots are imaginary.

Chapter 5

Arrays

In this chapter you will learn how to:
  Create an array control or indicator
  Create a one-dimensional array
  Create a two-dimensional array
  Use array functions

Introduction

One-Dimensional Arrays

An array is a collection or an orderly arrangement of objects. The objects may be numbers, square LEDs, switches and many others. In LabVIEW the members of an array may not be arrays, charts or graphs. A one-dimensional array of integers may look like this:

4 3 1 0 12 15 9 6

There are eight integer values in this array. Each member is identified by its value and by its numerical position within the array. Let's give this array a name, ***Bunch***. Now each member of this array can be uniquely identified. For example:

Bunch[0] = 4
Bunch[3] = 0
Bunch[5] = 15

and so on. Notice that all members of the array have the name Bunch. What sets them apart is the ***index*** value. The index is the number inside the brackets. Arrays are zero based, which means that the maximum index value is one less than the size of the array. For an eight member array such as the array Bunch above, the index range is from 0 to 7.

> **Note:** *Members of an array must be a homogeneous collection of objects. This means that if an array is composed of integer values, as is array Bunch, every member must be an integer. For example, an array made up of integer numbers, floating point numbers and square LEDs would be illegal.*

Two-Dimensional Array

A two-dimensional array has rows and columns, thus resembling a rectangular structure. For example, a 4 x 6 array of integers may look like this:

7	3	12	0	10	9
0	7	20	6	4	1
3	6	4	2	19	0
6	9	5	12	16	7

Suppose that the name of this array is ***Box***. Therefore all members of this array must have the name Box. Two indexes, one for the row and one for the column, must be attached to Box in order to identify uniquely each member of the array. Hence, Box[i,j] can uniquely identify any member of the array Box; the **i** index is used for the row and the **j** index is used to represent the column.

150

Here are some members of the array Box:

$$Box[0,3] = 0$$
$$Box[1,4] = 4$$
$$Box[2,5] = 0$$
$$Box[3,2] = 5$$

and so on. Notice, once again, that both indexes are zero based; the first row is row 0 and the first column is column 0, so Box[0,0] = 7. That means that the first index i can take on values from 0 to 5 in the above example, and the second index j can take on values from 0 to 3.

The preceding discussion singled out the integer value arrays. However, exactly the same can be said for an array made up of floating point numbers, or for an array consisting of square LEDs. A 3 x 5 array of square LEDs is shown below:

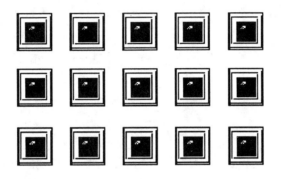

Arrays in LabVIEW

Array Controls and Indicators

To Open an Array Shell in the Front Panel, click on the *Array and Cluster* subpalette in the Controls palette and choose ***Array***,

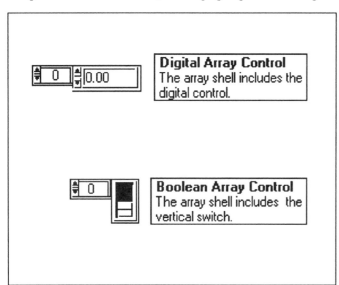

as shown in this illustration.

When you open the array shell in the front panel, it will look like this:

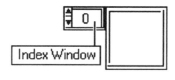

To Create Array Control/Indicator, open an empty array shell in the front panel as was shown in the previous illustration, then pop up with the positioning tool ⊹ inside the array shell and choose the desired object from a subpalette of the Controls palette. This illustration shows two Array Controls, one Boolean and the other digital.

The *digital array control* was created by popping up inside the empty array shell and then by choosing *digital control* from the *Numeric* subpalette of the Controls palette.

The *Boolean array control* was created in a similar fashion, except the vertical switch was chosen from the *Boolean* subpalette of the Controls palette.

This illustration shows two *array indicators*, one *Digital* and the other *Boolean*. To create the

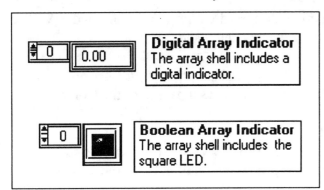

Digital Array Indicator
The array shell includes a digital indicator.

Boolean Array Indicator
The array shell includes the square LED.

digital array indicator, pop up inside the empty array shell and choose the *digital indicator* from the *Numeric* subpalette of the Controls palette

In the case of the *Boolean array indicator*, choose *LED* from the *Boolean* subpalette of the Controls palette.

Objects other than those shown in the above illustrations could also be used inside the empty array shall to create array control or array indicator. An array, chart or graph are the only objects that cannot be used inside an empty array shell.

The examples above show *one-dimensional array* controls and indicators. *To create a two-dimensional array control or indicator*, you must add a dimension to the one-dimensional array shell.

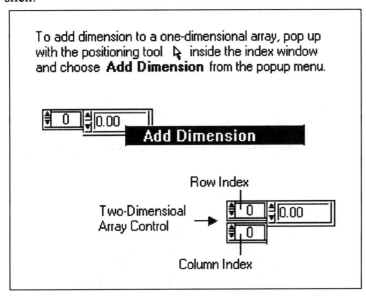

To add dimension to a one-dimensional array, pop up with the positioning tool inside the index window and choose **Add Dimension** from the popup menu.

Add Dimension

Row Index

Two-Dimensioal Array Control →

Column Index

To Add Dimension to the one-dimensional array, pop up with the positioning tool inside the index window and choose ***Add Dimension*** from the popup menu.

As shown in this illustration, another index window will be added. The top window indicates the row and the lower window indicates the column. The two indexes uniquely identify the position of an element within a two-dimensional array.

Exercise 1: One-Dimensional Array

This exercise illustrates some of the array properties discussed earlier. You will build a VI that creates a one-dimensional array of five random integers between 0 and 20.

1.   The **front panel** shown in Fig. 5-1 includes only one object, the *Digital Array Indicator*. You will find the *array* in the *Array & Cluster* subpalette of the Controls palette. Open it in the front panel.

    Pop up inside the array shell and choose **Digital Indicator** from the *Numeric* subpalette of the Controls palette. Move the digital indicator (dotted outline) into the array shell and click.

    Pop up inside the array window on the digital indicator and choose *Representation>I16*. This will change the representation of the digital indicator to a two byte integer.

    Label the array as **Bunch** with an owned label.

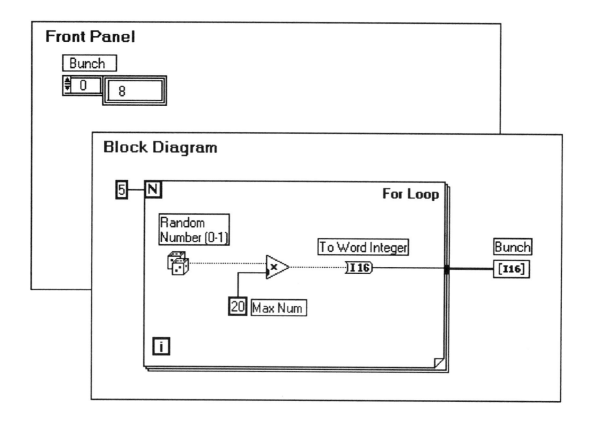

Fig. 5-1 One-Dimensional Array VI for Exercise 1

Block Diagram

2. You will find all objects shown in the block diagram in the *Numeric* subpalette of the Functions palette. This includes the *Random Number, Numeric Constant and Multiply*.

The **To Word Integer** ⸱⸱⸱**I16** conversion function is in the *Conversion* subpalette of the Numeric subpalette. It converts a floating point input to a two byte integer.

3. *Wire* the block diagram as shown in Fig. 5-1.

4. The numeric constant 20 multiplies the output from the random number generator, thus ensuring that the output from the Multiply function will be in the range of 0 to 20 and will not exceed 20. The *To Word Integer* converts this floating point value to an integer.

As the For Loop executes, it accumulates array data **at the boundary** of the loop. Only after the loop completes execution is the array applied to the *Bunch*, the digital array indicator.

The ability of the For Loop to index and acquire array data at its boundary is called **auto-indexing**. Auto-indexing is enabled by default in the For Loop; in a While Loop you must enable it.

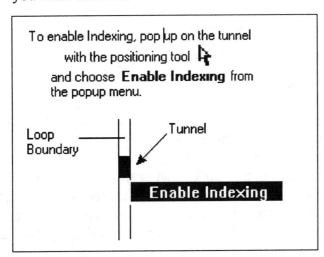

To Enable Indexing, pop up on the tunnel in the border of the loop with the positioning tool, as shown in this illustration, and choose *Enable Indexing* from the popup menu.

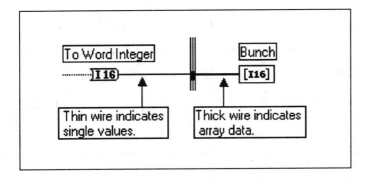

When you wire the digital array indicator Bunch to the tunnel, the wire becomes thick, indicating that the data on that wire is an array data, as shown in this illustration.

Should you wire an object from inside the For Loop to an object such as the simple digital indicator where the data passed *is not an array*, you will have a bad wire. To correct this, pop up with the positioning tool on the tunnel and choose ***Disable Indexing***.

> **Note:** *Auto-indexing is enabled in the For Loop by default, but in the While Loop it is disabled by default. When enabled, auto-indexing allows the loop to accumulate and index array data at its boundary.*

Run the VI.

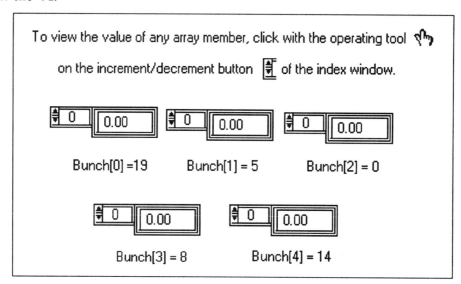

To view the array values, click with the operating tool on the increment/decrement button of the index window, as shown in this illustration,

or

you can resize the digital array indicator in the front panel as shown in the illustration below to view the entire array. When you catch the corner of the array to resize it, this cursor will appear for resizing the array shell instead of the usual corner cursor for resizing objects. Note the gray elements Bunch[5] and Bunch[6], indicating that there are no values there because the array Bunch has only 5 values. Resizing the array for the purpose of viewing element values will obviously not work for large arrays.

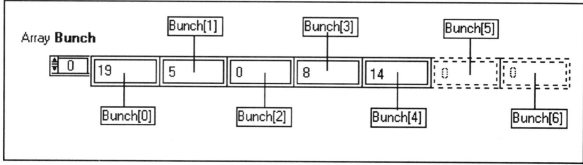

Save the VI as **1-D Array Example.vi** in Workbook.LLB and close it.

Exercise 2: Two-Dimensional Array

In Exercise 1 we considered a one-dimensional array. You constructed a one-dimensional array of random numbers. By its very nature, a one-dimensional array is limited to accumulating data in only one dimension. A group of numbers or objects laid out along a straight line represents one dimension.

In practice, however, we will find applications more often for a two-dimensional array. A table of values, for example, is a two-dimensional array.

In this exercise you will build a two-dimensional array that accumulates the values of a sinewave. We will discuss later some of the array properties as well as its objects. In this exercise you will learn how to use a sinewave function.

1.   The front panel contains only one object and that is the two-dimensional **digital array indicator**. The *digital array indicator* has been discussed and illustrated earlier. Open the digital array indicator *shell* in the front panel. You will find it in the *Array & Cluster* subpalette of the Controls palette.

Click inside the shell with the positioning tool and choose *digital indicator* from the *Numeric* subpalette of the Controls palette. Leave the representation as is, because the default is *DBL,* which is fine for this application.

Click inside the *index window* with the positioning tool and choose **Add Dimension** from the popup menu. Notice that another index window is added to represent the columns.

Block Diagram

2.   Switch to the block diagram (Ctrl+E) if you are not there already. The block diagram includes the following objects:

For Loop	*Structures* subpalette of the Controls palette.
Numeric Constant	*Numeric* subpalette of the Functions palette. There are four numeric constants in this Block Diagram (3, 6, 6, 18).
Pi Constant ⊓	Choose **PI** constant from the [π] *Additional Numeric Constants* subpalette of the *Numeric* sub-palette of the Functions palette.
	Note that The Additional Numeric Constants is a *subpalette* of the Numeric *subpalette.* It contains many universal constants such as π, the speed of light, the Planck constant, and others.

157

Add, **Multiply**, **Divide**	These functions are in the *Numeric* subpalette of the Functions palette.
Sine function	This function is in the *Trigonometric* subpalette of the *Numeric* subpalette of the Functions palette.

x (radians) ......SIN...... sin(x)   As shown in this illustration the input to the sine function is in radians.

3.   *Wire* the block diagram objects as shown in Fig. 5-2.

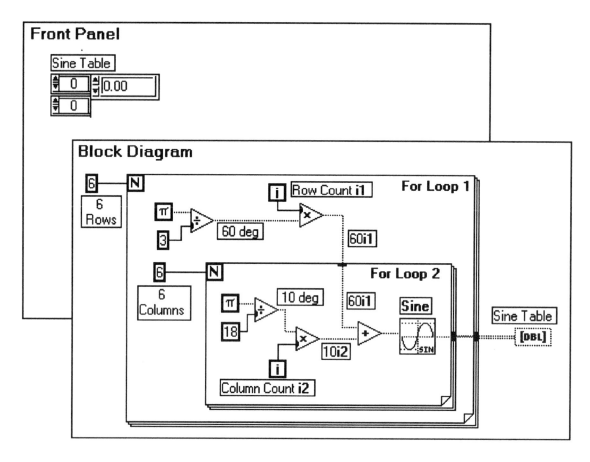

Fig. 5-2 Two-Dimensional Array VI of Exercise 2

4. Let's look at the basic approach to generating a two-dimensional array. Fig. 5-3 shows an abbreviated version of Fig. 5-2 for the purposes of explanation.

To Create a Two-Dimensional Array, you need two loops, which can be For Loops or While Loops, one inside the other. As shown in Fig. 5-3, each loop goes through 6 iterations; in other words, each loop executes 6 times (0 through 5).

For each iteration of Loop 1, Loop 2 executes 6 times. Notice the thickness of the wires from the sine function, from Loop 1, and from Loop 2. The sine function outputs 6 values that are accumulated at the boundary of Loop 2 as a one-dimensional array. Loop 2 accumulates 6 one-dimensional arrays at its boundary as a two-dimensional array. Notice that there are a total of 36 iterations because for each value of i in Loop 1, Loop 2 must execute 6 times. And when both loops finish execution, the two-dimensional array of sine values is passed as a table to the digital array indicator *Sine Table.*

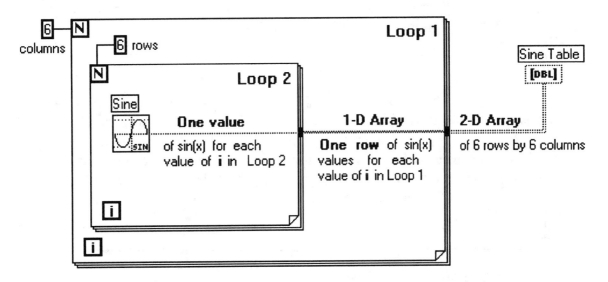

**Fig. 5-3   Creating a Two-Dimensional Array, Abbreviated Block Diagram
(See Fig. 5-2 for details)**

As shown in Fig. 5-2, Loop 1 generates the value **60i_1** and passes this value to Loop 2, where it is added to **10i_2** . The sum ($10i_2 + 60i_1$) is applied to the sine function.

The operation begins with $i_1 = 0$ in Loop 1 and i_2 stepping through six values from 0 to 5 and generating 6 angle values: 0°, 10°, 20°, 30°, 40°, and 50° (in radians) that are applied to the sine function. The sine function, in turn, calculates 6 values, one for each angle, and applies them to the border of Loop 2, where they become a one-dimensional array which is then passed to the border of Loop 1, where the two-dimensional array is being formed.

Next $i_1 = 1$ and the above process repeats, except this time the 10° steps are added to 60° (the value in radians passed from Loop 1). As i_1 steps once again from 0 to 5, the 10° increments are added to 60° and then applied to the sine function. Thus, the second row of the table is generated and accumulated at the boundary of Loop 1. Notice that one-dimensional arrays (rows) are accumulated at the boundary of Loop 1.

The above process continues as each row of the table is accumulated at the boundary of Loop 1, with the last row generated when $i_1 = 5$. When both loops complete their execution, the two-dimensional array of sin(x) values is passed to the digital array indicator *Sine Table*.

5. ***Run*** this VI. You may view the individual elements of the Sine Table array by clicking with the operating tool on the increment/decrement arrows of the index windows.

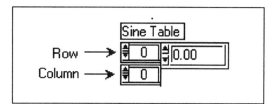

Remember that the upper index is Row and the lower index is Column, as shown in this illustration.

You may also view all values of the *Sine Table* array by resizing the digital array indicator in the front panel. In step 4 of the preceding exercise, you resized a one-dimensional array by dragging the array corner in the horizontal direction. You may also resize a two-dimensional array by catching the lower right corner and then by dragging it downward and to the right until you see all elements of the array. Fig. 5-4 shows the result of a run. The array shows values of sin(x) in 10° increments from 0° to 350°.

Sine Table						
0.00	0.17	0.34	0.50	0.64	0.77	0.00
0.87	0.94	0.98	1.00	0.98	0.94	0.00
0.87	0.77	0.64	0.50	0.34	0.17	0.00
0.00	-0.17	-0.34	-0.50	-0.64	-0.77	0.00
-0.87	-0.94	-0.98	-1.00	-0.98	-0.94	0.00
-0.87	-0.77	-0.64	-0.50	-0.34	-0.17	0.00
0.00	0.00	0.00	0.00	0.00	0.00	0.00

Fig. 5-4   Sine Table of the Two-Dimensional Array.vi

160

Exercise 3: Viewing the Creation of the Two-Dimensional Array

If you would like to see the elements of the last exercise created one by one in slow motion, then you can modify the VI of Exercise 2 by adding three digital indicators to the front panel and the time delay to the block diagram as shown in Fig. 5-5.

When you run this VI, you will be able to observe the creation of an element value in the Sine Table array once every second. The row and column of the element being created will also be displayed.

This exercise is optional, and when you are done with it, do not save any changes.

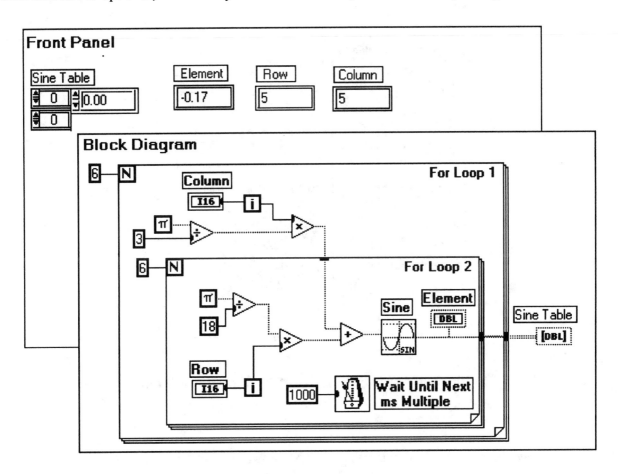

Fig. 5-5 The Front Panel and Block Diagram of Exercise 3

161

Exercise 4: Using Array Functions 1

The *Array* subpalette of the Functions palette includes many array functions that are useful in performing various operations on arrays. There are functions that find maximum and minimum values in an array, slice away and return a row or a column from a two-dimensional array, find the size of an array, or build array. In this exercise and in the exercise that follows, we will sample some of these functions to show you how they work. Fig. 5-6 shows the Array subpalette where these functions are to be found.

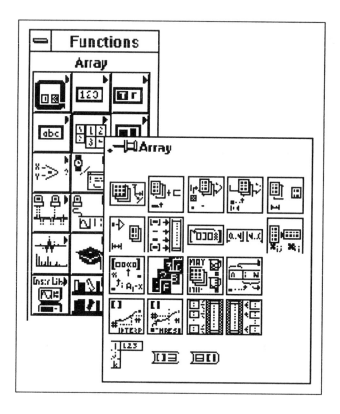

Fig. 5-6 Array Subpalette of the Functions Palette

In this VI we will use two array functions: **Array Max & Min** and **Array Size**.

Front Panel

1.   In the front panel you have three *digital indicators* and two *digital array indicators*. The **digital indicators** are in the *Numeric* subpalette of the Controls palette and the **array** is in the *Array & Cluster* subpalette of the Controls palette.

Open the following objects in the front panel and label them with owned labels as shown in Fig. 5-7:

The **Random Number Array** is a two-dimensional array. Pop up (with the right mouse button) inside the index window with the positioning tool and choose *Add Dimension* from the popup menu. To convert this array to *digital array indicator*, pop up inside the array shell with the positioning tool and choose *digital indicator* from the *Numeric* subpalette of the Controls palette, then drag and drop the digital indicator inside the array shell. Pop up on the digital indicator inside the array shell and choose *Representation>I8* from the popup palette. Finally, resize this array so that you can view a 5 x 3 (5 rows, 3 columns) array of elements.

The **Size 2** array is a one-dimensional array. For the most part, repeat the above procedure and resize the array so that you can see two elements.

The **Max Value**, **Min Value**, and **Size 1** digital indicators have *Representation* set to I8.

Block Diagram

2. Open the **For Loop** (you may want to label it with a free label as For Loop 1, as shown in Fig. 5-7). For Loop 1 includes the following objects:

> **Random Number (0-1)** generator is in the *Numeric* subpalette of the Functions palette.
>
> **Multiply** function is in the *Numeric* subpalette of the Functions palette.
>
> **Numeric Constant** is in the *Numeric* subpalette of the Functions palette. Use labeling tool to enter 40 into one constant and 3 into another.
>
> **To Byte Integer** conversion function is in the *Conversion* subpalette of the *Numeric* subpalette of the Functions palette. This function converts the floating point input from the multiply function to a one byte integer.

> *Wire* all objects inside For Loop 1 as shown in Fig. 5-7. Wire the output of the *To Byte Integer* to the tunnel at the boundary of For Loop 1 (the tunnel will be created automatically when you wire to the For Loop boundary). Don't forget to wire the *Columns* numeric constant to the loop counter terminal *N*.

3. Open another **For Loop** and label it with a free label as *For Loop 2*. This loop must be positioned so that it includes Loop 1 inside its boundary.

> **The Array Size** function is in the *Array* subpalette of the Functions palette. The Array Size function returns the number of elements in each dimension of input.

Complete the wiring as shown in Fig. 5-7. Wire also the *Rows* numeric constant set to 5 to the loop count terminal of For Loop 2. Notice that the wire from the tunnel of the For Loop 1 to the tunnel of the For Loop 2 is thicker. That is because the data on that wire is a one-dimensional array.

4.   There are four objects outside the For Loop 2.

     Array Size is the same object as in step 3 above except this time it is wired to the *Size 2* digital indicator terminal (counterpart of the front panel object).

The **Array Max & Min** function is in the *Array* subpalette of the Functions palette. The *Array Max & Min* function searches the input array for the maximum and the minimum values and outputs these values at their respective terminals.

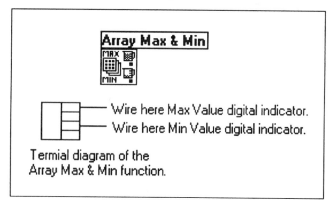

Termial diagram of the
Array Max & Min function.

Wire the *Max Value and Min Value* terminals as shown in this illustration.

Complete wiring the block diagram as shown in Fig. 5-7. Notice the *thick wires* from the For Loop 2 that appear as double lines. These carry the two-dimensional array data. **Run** the VI.

The operation begins as both loops read their respective N (loop count) values. The value of N is set to 3 in the For Loop 1 and to 5 in the For Loop 2. Initially **i=0** in the For Loop 2, while For Loop 1 executes 3 times generating an array of three numbers. This array is accumulated at the boundary of the For Loop 1. When For Loop 1 completes execution, it is passed to the boundary of the For Loop 2.

Next **i** is set to **1** in For Loop 2 and For Loop 1 generates three more numbers (second row). This process continues until the array of five rows is completed. You can view the entire array in the front panel as well as the display of the maximum and minimum values of the array. Notice that *Size 1* indicator displays 3 because the input to the *Array Size function* in loop 2 is a one-dimensional array of 3 values. On the other hand, *Size 2* array indicator displays 5, 3 because the input to the *Array Size* function is a two-dimensional array with 5 values in each column and 3 values in each row.

Save this VI as **Array Functions 1.vi** in Workbook..LLB and close it.

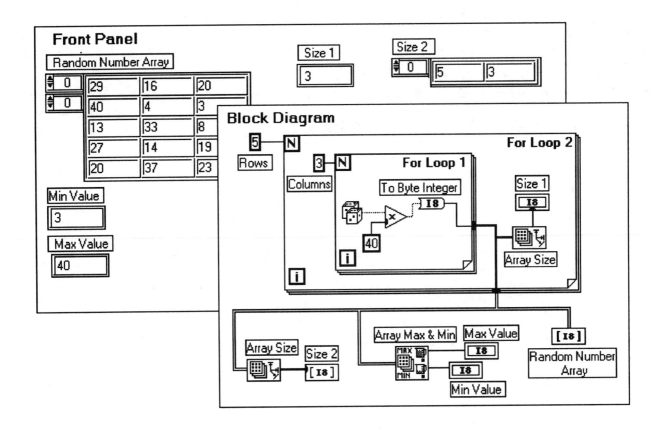

Fig. 5-7 The Front Panel and Block Diagram of Exercise 4

Exercise 5:   Using Array Functions 2

In this exercise you will build a VI that illustrates the use of the **Build Array** function.

Front Panel

1.   **Array** is in the *Array & Cluster* subpalette of the Controls palette. As shown in Fig. 5-8, you will need three arrays. The arrays A and B are *digital array controls*. You create a digital array control by popping up inside the array with the positioning tool shell and choosing *digital control* from the *Numeric* subpalette of the Controls palette.

Similarly you create the *digital array indictor* by popping up inside the array shell with the positioning tool and then choosing *digital indicator* from the *Numeric* subpalette of the Controls palette.

2.   **Digital Control** C is found in the *Numeric* subpalette of the Controls palette.

165

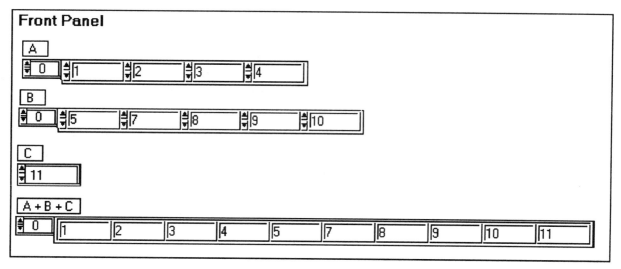

Fig. 5-8   The Front Panel and Block Diagram of Exercise 5

Set the Representation on all objects inside the front panel. Resize the arrays as shown in Fig. 5-8.

Block Diagram

3.   The **Build Array** function can be found in the *Array* subpalette of the Functions palette. As shown in this illustration, the Build Array function must be resized to include three

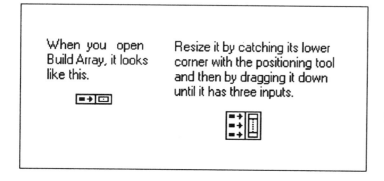

When you open Build Array, it looks like this.

Resize it by catching its lower corner with the positioning tool and then by dragging it down until it has three inputs.

inputs. The inputs to the Build Array function must be configured to accommodate the input data. If the data input is an array, then the input on the Build Array function must be changed accordingly.

166

In this exercise two of the inputs are arrays. Changing of the inputs to accommodate arrays is shown in this illustration. Simply pop up with the positioning tool (right mouse button) on the input and choose *Change to Array* from the popup menu.

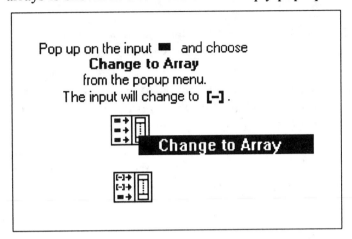

Pop up on the input ■ and choose
Change to Array
from the popup menu.
The input will change to **[-]** .

Change to Array

The third input on the Build Array function gets its data from the digital control C, therefore it doesn't have to be changed.

4.　*Complete the wiring* of the block diagram as shown in Fig. 5-8.

5.　*Enter* the numerical values into the two digital array controls A and B and the digital indicator C, as shown in the front panel of Fig. 5-8. To enter values click with the positioning tool on the increment/decrement arrows on the left side of the digital control window. You can also use the Labeling tool to type in the values.

　　Run the VI. Notice that the two arrays and the digital control's C value have been combined into a single one-dimensional array, as displayed by the digital array indicator A + B + C.

　　Save this VI as **Array Functions 2.vi** in Workbook.LLB and close it.

Exercise 6:　Using Array Functions 3

In this exercise you will build a VI that will use and illustrate the properties of two array functions: **Index Array** and **Transpose 2D Array**.

Front Panel

1.　The front panel includes four arrays and one digital indicator.
　　Array is in the *Array & Cluster* subpalette of the Controls palette. Open the array shell in the Front Panel. Pop up inside the shell and choose *digital indicator* from the *Numeric* subpalette of the Controls palette. Drag and drop the digital indicator into the array shell.

　　Choose Representation>I8 for the digital indicator inside the shell. Click inside the index window and choose *Add Dimension* to make this array two-dimensional.

Label the array with an owned label *as Random Number Array.*
Resize the array to 5 rows by 3 columns as shown in Fig. 5-9.

2. Follow the procedure in step 1 and create a two-dimensional array *Transposed Random Number Array.* Resize this array to show 3 rows and 5 columns.

3. Follow the procedure in step 1 and create two one-dimensional arrays. As shown in Fig. 5-9, resize one to show 5 elements and label it with an owned label as *Column 2*, and resize the other to show 3 elements and label it as *Row 3.*

4. Open a **digital indicator** (*Controls>Numeric*) and label it with an owned label as *Element 4,1.* Also choose *Representation>I8* for this indicator.

Block Diagram

5. As shown in Fig. 5-9, build For Loop 1 inside For Loop 2. Note that For Loop 1 is exactly the same as that shown in Fig. 5-7.

6. Open **Index Array** function. You will find it in the *Array* subpalette of the Functions palette. When you first open the Index Array, it will have only one index terminal, the black rectangle in the lower lefthand corner of the icon. Resize the icon to include two index terminals, as shown in this illustration.

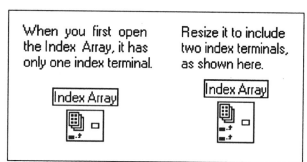

    To increase the number of index terminals, catch the lower corner of the icon with the positioning tool and drag in the downward direction.

You can also accomplish the same thing by popping up on the index terminal (right mouse button) and choosing *Add Dimension* from the popup menu.

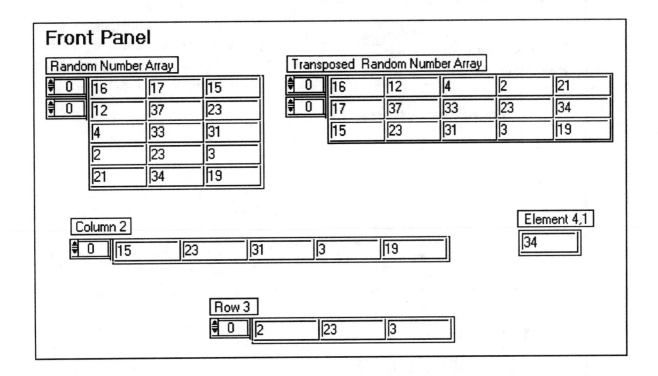

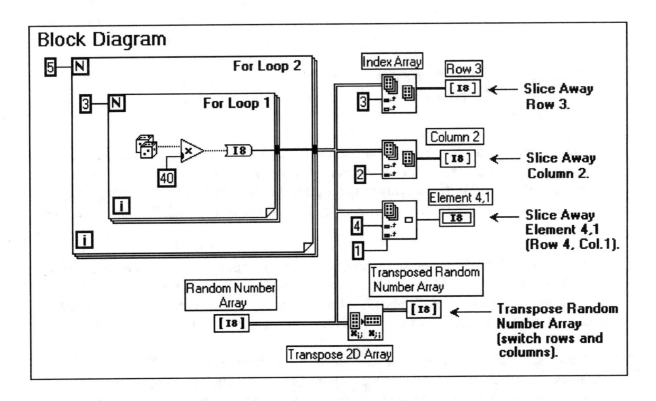

Fig. 5-9 The Front Panel and Block Diagram of Exercise 6

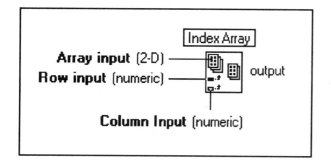

As shown in this illustration, you must wire a two-dimensional array to the input terminal of Index Array and a numeric integer value to either one or both index inputs.

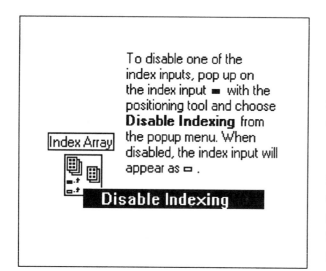

When you have to slice away a row or a column from a two-dimensional array, one of the index inputs must be disabled. In this illustration the column index input is disabled, but you can disable the row index input instead.

To Slice Away a Column from a two-dimensional array, you must disable the row index input and apply the numeric value (of the column that you wish to slice away) to the column index input.

To Slice Away a Row from a two-dimensional array, you must disable the column index input, and apply a numeric value (of the row that you wish to slice away) to the row index input.

7. Following the guidelines for configuring the Index Array function in step 6, disable the column input and wire a *Numeric constant* whose value is **3** to the row index input, as shown in Fig. 5-9. Wire the array output of For Loop 2 (at the tunnel of For Loop 2) to the array input of the Index Array function, and its output to the *digital array indicator* terminal *Row 3*.

8. Repeat step 7 above, except this time disable the row index input and wire the numeric constant **2** to the column index input. The output of this Index Array function is wired to the digital array indicator *Column 2*. As shown in Fig. 5-9, wire the two-dimensional array from the tunnel of For Loop 2 to the array input of this Index Array function.

9. You need one more Index Array function with both indexes enabled. Wire **4** to the row index input and **1** to the column index input. As was done before, wire the array from the tunnel of For Loop 2 to the array input of this Array Index function. Also wire the output to the *Element 4,1* digital indicator terminal.

10. Open the **Transpose 2D Array** function, which is in the *Array* subpalette of the Functions palette. This function transposes a two-dimensional array by switching rows and columns. Wire the array from the tunnel of Loop 2 to the input of the Transpose 2D Array function and its output to the *Transposed Random Number Array* indicator terminal, as shown in Fig. 5-9.

11. *Wire* the array from the tunnel of Loop 2 to the *Random Number Array* digital array indicator terminal, as shown in Fig. 5-9.

12. **Run** this VI.

As the VI begins execution, For Loops 1 and 2 form a 5 x 3 array, which is accumulated at the boundary of the For Loop 2. The top Index Array function in Fig. 5-9 slices away row 3 of the array. Next Index Array function slices away column 2, and the last function slices away a single element located in row 4, column 1. Element values of row 3 and column 2 are displayed on the front panel digital array indicators, and the value of the element 4,1 is displayed on the digital indicator.

Note the element values of the transposed array indicator. It now has 3 rows and 5 columns.

Save this VI as **Array Functions 3.vi** in Workbook.LLB and close it.

Exercise 7: Using Array Functions 4

In this exercise you will build a VI that explores the properties of the *Array Subset* function. In Exercise 5 we used the *Build Array* function to combine arrays A and B plus a digital constant into one array called A + B + C. We can now use the *Array Subset* function to extract the arrays A and B and the constant C from the one-dimensional array A + B + C.

Front Panel

1. As shown in Fig. 5-10, the front panel contains arrays A + B + C, A, and B, as well as the digital indicator C.

    Array A + B + C is a one-dimensional *digital array control*.
    Arrays A and B are one-dimensional *digital array indicators*.
    C is a *digital indicator*.

    Build the front panel as shown in Fig. 5-10. Refer to Exercise 5 for creating array objects in the front panel.

Block Diagram

2. The **Array Subset** function is in the *Arrays* subpalette of the Functions palette. As shown

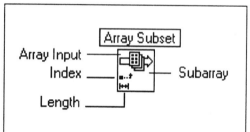

    in this illustration, it requires an *array input* as well as the **Index** and the **Length** inputs. Its output is the extracted subarray.

    The *Index* specifies the point at which to begin subarray extraction, and the *Length* specifies the number of elements (beginning at the index value) to be extracted.

    Open three Array Subset functions. *Complete wiring* the block diagram as shown in Fig. 5-10.

3. As shown in the block diagram of Fig. 5-10, the top Array Subset function extracts array A from array A+B+C because its index is set to **0** and its length to **4**; that means elements 0, 1, 2 and 3 will be extracted. In a similar fashion the middle Array Subset function begins with element **4** and extracts the **5** elements beginning with element 4. Finally the bottom Array Subset function extracts the last element of array A+B+C.

    Run this VI after entering the values into the array A+B+C, as shown in the front panel.

    Save this VI as **Using Array Functions 4.vi** in Workbook.LLB and close it.

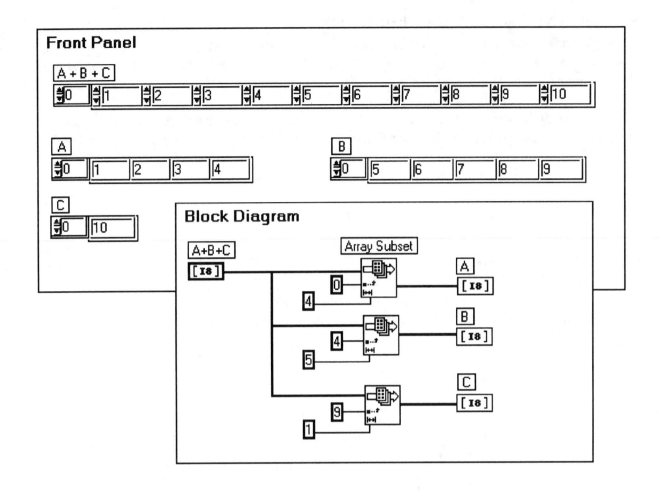

Fig. 5-10　The Front Panel and Block Diagram of Exercise 7

Exercise 8: Using Array Functions 5

In this exercise we will create a VI that illustrates the **Array Subset** function. In some respects this function bears resemblance to the *Index Array* function, except that the Index Array function slices away or extracts one row, one column, or one element from an array.

While the Array Subset function can do all that, its more important use is to extract a subset that is a two-dimensional, from another two-dimensional array. In the preceding exercise we used the Array Subset function on a one-dimensional array, and in this exercise we will use it on a two-dimensional array. Incidentally, it can be used on arrays of any dimension.

Front Panel

1.　As shown in Fig. 5-11, the front panel contains arrays *Input Array* and *Subarray*, and four digital controls.
　　Input Array　is a two-dimensional *digital array control*.
　　Subarray is a two-dimensional *digital array indicator*.
　　Row, Column, Num. Rows, Num. Columns are digital controls.

　　Build the front panel as shown in Fig. 5-11. Refer to Exercise 5 for creating array objects in the front panel.

Block Diagram

2.　*Build* the block diagram as shown in Fig. 5-11. Note that the Array Subset function must be resized to include the second dimension.

　　To resize the Array Subset function, catch the lower corner of the icon with the positioning tool cursor. When the cursor changes its shape to a corner, drag it down until you see two dimensions. Remember that each dimension must include the *Index* and *Length* input terminals.

3.　Before you run this VI, you should be aware of several things. First of all, the Array Subset function extracts a portion (called a subset) of a two-dimensional array. This subset is also a two-dimensional array.

　　In order to slice away this smaller array from a larger array, you must tell the VI where to begin and how far to go. For example, suppose you enter

$$Row = 1 \qquad Column = 0$$
$$Num. Rows = 3 \qquad Num. Columns = 2$$

into the digital controls on the front panel as shown in Fig. 5-11. You are telling the VI to begin with row 1, column 0, and to include 3 rows (that means rows 1, 2 and 3) and two columns (that means columns 0 and 1). The VI as shown in Fig. 5-11 was executed

174

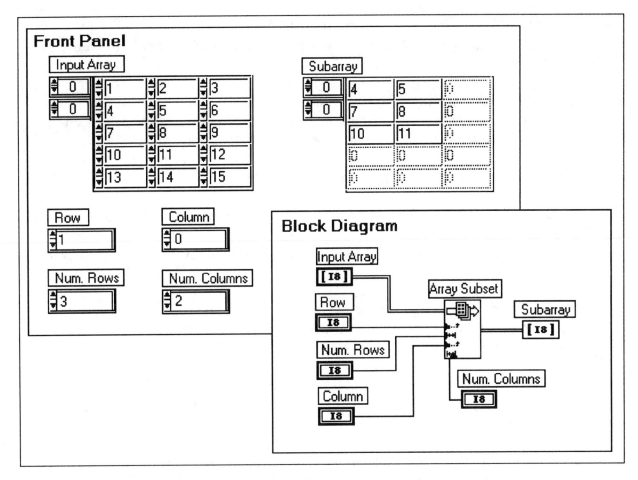

Fig. 5-11   The Front Panel and Block Diagram of Exercise 8

using these values, and the resulting subset that was extracted from the *Input Array* is displayed inside the *Subarray* digital indicator. Notice that the values displayed by the Subarray digital indicator is the intersection of rows 1, 2, 3 and columns 0, 1 of *Input Array*.

Enter values into Input Array as shown in the Front Panel of Fig. 5-11 or use values of your own choice.

Run the VI. Experiment with different values in the Front Panel digital controls.

Save this VI as **Using Array Functions 5.vi** in Workbook.LLB and close it.

Summary

1. An array is a collection of objects such as numbers, square LEDs, Boolean switches, or other objects.

2. In a one-dimensional array objects are placed along a straight line. A two-dimensional array is made up of rows and columns. A three-dimensional array may be likened to a book, where a two-dimensional array is included on a given page and the page number represents the third dimension. Arrays of dimension higher than 3 are difficult to visualize, although they can still be treated mathematically.

3. In LabVIEW you open an array shell in the front panel. It can be made an array control or an array indicator depending on the type of object that you drop into the shell. By adding a dimension to the array shell, it becomes a two-dimensional array control or array indicator.

4. The For Loop or While Loop is used to create an array. You use one loop to create a one-dimensional array and a nested arrangement of two loops to create a two-dimensional array.

5. Auto-indexing is a feature of the loop that allows accumulation of an array at its boundary. In the For Loop auto-indexing is enabled by default, but in the While Loop it must be enabled.

    When auto-indexing is enabled, an array will be accumulated at the loop's boundary. By disabling the auto-indexing, you can pass single data points to an object outside the loop.

6. LabVIEW has a wide variety of array functions that you can use in your VI to manipulate arrays. The Index Array function, for example, can be used to slice away a row, a column, or a single element. The operation of many of these functions has been explored in several exercises.

Chapter 6

Charts and Graphs

In this chapter you will learn about:
Waveform chart
Waveform graph
X-Y graph

177

Waveform Chart

A Waveform is an indicator for displaying one or more waveforms. It has three update modes. The strip chart mode resembles the old paper strip chart with the scrolling display.

To Open, a waveform chart, choose ***Waveform Chart*** from the *Graph* subpalette of the Controls palette as shown in this illustration.

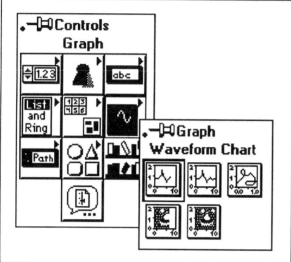

When you open the waveform chart in the front panel, it will appear as shown in Fig. 6-1. It has several features that you should be familiar with. Let's first consider the **Palette** shown in the illustration.

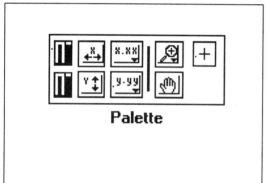

Palette

To enable AutoScale Y, click with the positioning tool 🖑 on the ⬛ button next to the ⬛ button. The scale along the vertical scale will adjust automatically to fit the data being displayed.

In the same manner you can also enable the ***AutoScale X*** by clicking on the ⬛ button next to the ⬛ button.

Another way to set the *AutoScale is* by popping up inside the waveform screen and then by choosing *Y Scale>AutoScale Y* or *X Scale>AutoScale X.*

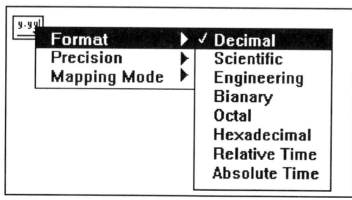

When you click with the positioning tool on the ⬛ button or the ⬛ button in the *Palette* window, a popup menu opens. By clicking on the ***Format*** option, as shown in this illustration, the second menu opens, allowing you to choose the desired format. The default is the *Decimal* format.

178

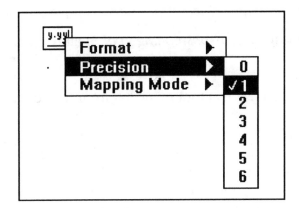

When you click on the *Precision* option, the second menu allows you to choose the precision, number of decimal places, as shown in this illustration.

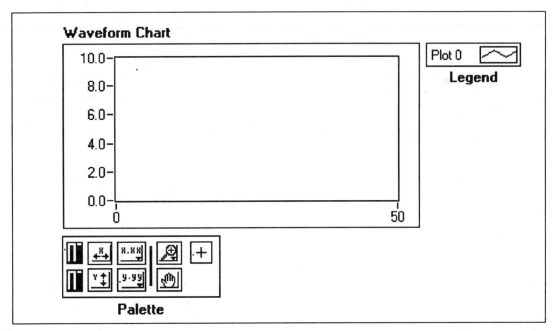

Fig. 6-1   The Waveform Chart

The magnifying glass 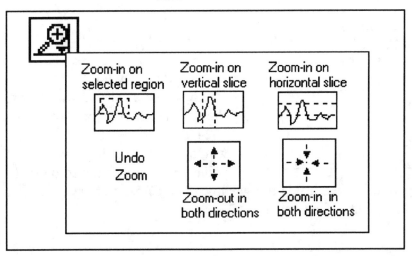 button inside the palette is the *zooming tool*. As shown in this illustration, by clicking on the zoom button, you open a palette from which you can choose a variety of zooming options.

179

The extended hand ⌷ button inside the palette is the *waveform positioning tool*. It allows you to move the display horizontally as well as vertically.

The cross hair +⌷ button is the *graph cursor*. You can use this tool to switch from the zoom mode ⌷ or the waveform positioning mode ⌷.

The *Legend* ⌷Plot 0 ⌷ that opens by default on the upper righthand side of the waveform chart shows the characteristics of the waveform that the chart displays. The default name of the waveform is Plot 0; however, you can delete Plot 0 and, using the labeling tool, type the name for the displayed waveform. This legend window can be resized (by catching the lower corner with the positioning tool and dragging it down) to accommodate additional waveforms.

This window ⌷ inside the legend window indicates the *point style* and the *color* of the plot.

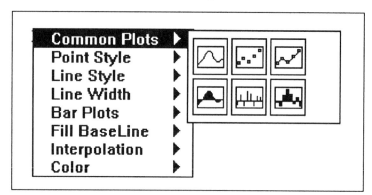

Additional Plot Options, including those of point style and color, are accessed by clicking inside the legend window with the operation tool and choosing the desired option from the popup menu. This illustration shows the *Common Plots* palette.

To access various plot setting accessories, pop up inside the waveform chart window and choose *Show* from the popup menu. A submenu with additional options opens, as shown in this illustration.

For example, when you click on the *Scrollbar* option, the scrollbar shown below will appear below the waveform chart.

Scrollbar

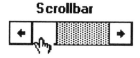

Use the operating tool 🖑 to scroll through the displayed waveform. Waveform chart stores the last 1024 data points. Since the chart window may not display all 1024 points, you can use the scrollbar to show that part of the plot that is not displayed inside the window. The *Chart History Length...* option allows you to change the 1024 point default value.

The **Digital Display** option, when activated, opens the digital indicator next to the legend. It indicates the value of the current point being plotted.

To Format the Y scale, pop up inside the waveform chart and choose **Y Scale>Formatting ...** from the popup menu. The *Y Scale Formatting window* opens, giving you various formatting options as shown in this illustration.

As you can see from this window, you can choose *scale style, linear or logarithmic mapping*, the desired *format* and *precision*. The *Grid Options* give you several choices of grid type and color that you can select individually for the X axis and the Y axis.

Click on this icon to display the grid options, and on this icon to display the color palette for choosing the grid color. After making all desired selections, click on OK.

You will get almost the same formatting window when you choose **X Axis>Formatting...** from the pop up menu.

Update Mode

Waveform Chart has three update modes:

Strip Chart
Scope Chart
Sweep Chart

To Access the Update Mode Palette, pop up inside the Waveform Chart and choose *Update Mode* from the *Data Operations* popup menu. The Update Mode palette opens, allowing you to access one of three charts as shown in this illustration. The default is the *Strip Chart.*

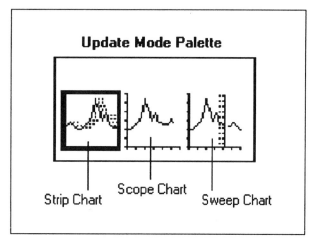

To access the Update Mode palette during VI execution, pop up on the chart and choose Update Mode from the popup menu.

Strip Chart resembles the old paper strip chart that has a scrolling display. As the display reaches the right edge of the display window, it scrolls off and continues to display new data.

Scope Chart has a retracing display that is similar to an oscilloscope. When the display reaches the right edge of the screen, the screen is cleared and the display begins to scroll from the left side of the screen. The screen is cleared every time the display reaches the right edge.

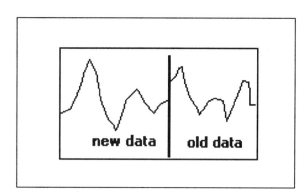

Sweep Chart has a retracing display also, except that the screen is not cleared when the display reaches the right edge. Instead, the vertical line, as shown in this illustration, moves along with the display, adding new data. The plot to the right of the display represents the old data.

Because the strip chart has more software overhead, its display is significantly slower than that of the scope or the sweep charts.

Exercise 1:   Using the Waveform Chart

In this exercise you will build a VI that illustrates the use of the waveform chart. In this VI the chart will be used to display several cycles of sine and cosine waveforms.

Build this VI. The front panel and the block diagram are shown in Fig 6-2. The following guidelines will help you in the VI construction.

Front Panel

1. **Digital Indicators** are in the *Numeric* subpalette of the Controls palette. Label these with owned labels as shown in Fig. 6-2.

    Vertical Switch is in the *Boolean* subpalette of the Controls palette. Label the switch as *Quit* using an owned label.

    Waveform Chart is in the *Graph* subpalette of the Controls palette. Label the chart with an owned label as *Sine/Cosine Chart*. Resize the *Legend* (that currently shows Plot 0) to include two plots. To resize the legend, catch its lower corner with the *Positioning Tool* and drag it down until you see Plot 0 and Plot 1 inside the legend window. Use the *Labeling Tool* to delete and type *Sine* in place of Plot 0 and *Cosine* in place of Plot 1. Pop up inside the legend window of the Sine waveform and click on the *Color* option from the popup menu. Choose the desired color for the Sine waveform. Repeat this for the Cosine and choose its color. The Default color is white.

    Pop up on the chart, and choose *Show>Digital Display*. Pop up on the chart once more and choose *Show>Scrollbar*.

    When you are done, your waveform chart will resemble that of Fig. 6-2. You may want to resize the waveform chart to make the display larger.

Block Diagram

2. **Multiply, Divide** functions are in the Numeric subpalette of the Functions palette.

    2   constant is in the *Additional Numeric Constants* subpalette of the *Numeric* subpalette of the Functions palette.

    Sine and **Cosine** functions are in the *Trigonometric* subpalette of the *Numeric* subpalette of the Functions palette.

    Bundle structure is in the *Cluster* subpalette of the Functions palette. The bundle structure is used to combine two or more plots to be displayed. It can be resized by dragging down its lower corner with the *Positioning Tool* to accommodate more than two inputs.

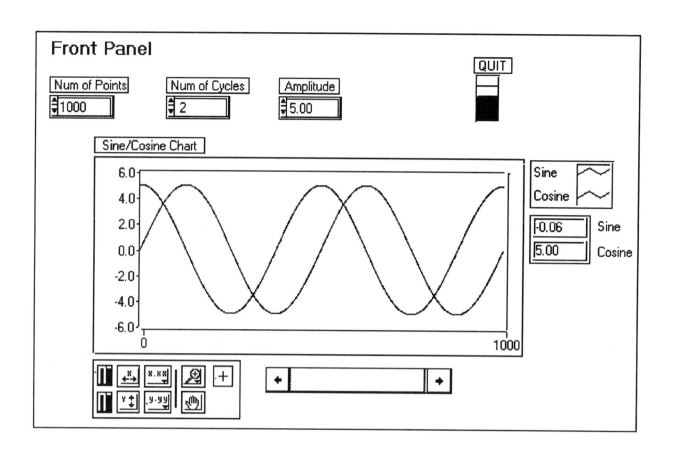

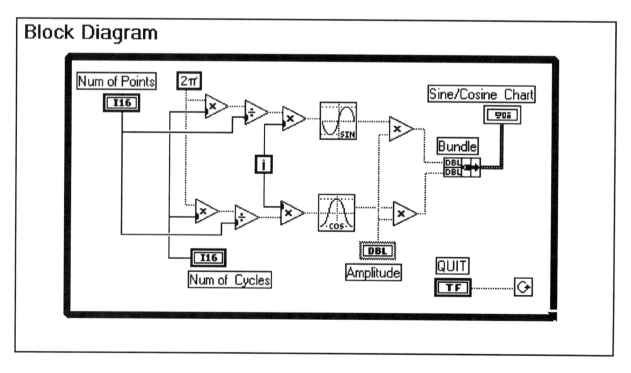

Fig. 6-2　The Front Panel and Block Diagram of Exercise 1

3. **Wire** all objects inside the Block Diagram as shown in Fig 6-2.

4. The input to the sine and cosine functions, which is also their argument, must be in radians. In this VI, the argument is $2\pi(N_{cycle} \cdot i/N_{points})$. As the iteration variable i counts from 0 to N_{points}, the value of the argument varies from 0 to $2\pi N_{cycle}$. Since 2π is the period of one cycle of the sine or the cosine wave, it is clear that N_{cycle} is the multiplier (front panel digital control) that determines the number of cycles of the waveform to be displayed.

Set the front panel digital controls to the values shown in Fig. 6-2.

Configure the Vertical Switch as follows:
    Move the switch to the *up* or *true* position with the *Operating Tool*.
    Pop up on the switch and choose *Mechanical Action>Latch When Pressed*
        Latch When Pressed mechanical action of the switch which is often used
        to stop the While Loop, works as follows: when you click with the *Operating Tool* on the switch as the While Loop is running, the switch will move
        down to its *false* position and stay there until VI reads it once. As soon
        as VI takes the *false* value reading, the switch will return to its *true*
        position. It doesn't matter how many times you click on the switch; the
        VI will take the reading only once.

    Pop up on the switch again and choose *Data Operations>Make Current Value Default* from the pop up menu.

Set the maximum value to 6 and the minimum value to −6 on the Y-axis of the
    waveform chart.
Set the maximum value to 1000 on the X-axis of the waveform chart.

Disable the AutoScale for the X and Y axes.

You may want to change the waveform chart window color from the default black.
To change the screen color, use the *Set Color Tool* in the Tools palette. If the Tools palette is not open, you can access it by choosing *Windows>Show Tools Palette*.

5. *Run* the VI. Experiment with different settings of the front panel digital controls.
    While the VI is running, pop up on the waveform chart and choose the *Update Mode* option. Select the *Scope Chart* or *Sweep Chart* from the palette that opens. Observe the difference in execution speeds as compared to the *Strip Chart*. As was mentioned earlier, the strip chart is slower because of its software overhead.

Save this VI as **Sine/Cosine Chart.vi** in the Workbook.LLB and close it.

Waveform Graph

The Waveform Graph's appearance in the Front Panel is similar to that of the Waveform Chart. However, there are significant differences between the two.

To Open Waveform Graph, choose *Waveform Graph* from the *Graph* subpalette of the Controls palette. As shown in Fig. 6-3, the waveform graph is very similar in appearance to the waveform chart shown in Fig. 6-1.

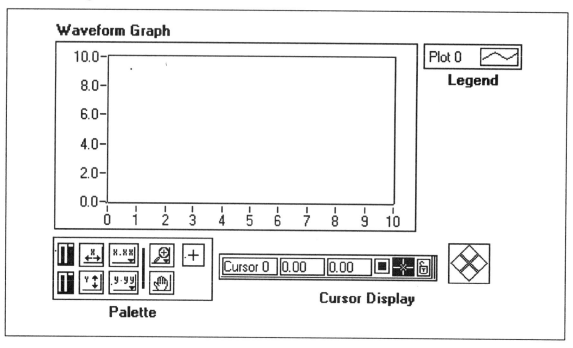

Fig. 6-3 Waveform Graph

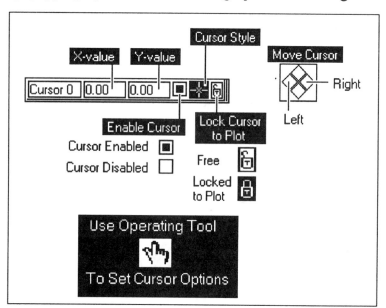

By popping up on the waveform graph and choosing ***Show***, you will observe that most of the options are the same as that of the waveform chart. Notice that the ***Cursor Display*** is an option for the waveform graph and not for the waveform chart.

As shown in this illustration, the X-value, Y-value digital indicators provide precise values of the cursor coordinates.

The ***Enable/Disable*** button allows you to enable or disable the cursor. This control toggles.

When you click on the **Lock Cursor to Plot** button, a menu opens with several options. The *Lock to Plot* option forces the cursor movement along the waveform. The *Free* option restricts the cursor movement along the X-axis and not along the waveform.

The **Cursor Style** menu allows you to choose, among other things, cursor shape, its point style, and its color.

To **Move** the cursor, click with the positioning tool inside *the Move Cursor* diamond.

To **Remove the Cursor** from the display, click on the Cursor Style button and choose **none** from the *Cursor Style* palette and **none** from the *Cursor Point* palette.

> *The most important difference between the Waveform Chart and the Waveform Graph is in the type of applied data. The Waveform Chart accepts data on a point by point basis. The Waveform Graph, however, accepts data only in an **array** form.*

The waveform graph can display a single plot or multiple plots. The single plot and multiple plot graphs require special consideration, as discussed below.

Single Plot Waveform Graph

Probably the simplest way of applying the array data to the Waveform Graph terminal inside the

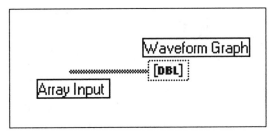

block diagram, as shown in this illustration, is to wire the array data directly to the terminal. In this case the default scaling of the X-axis will set Xo = 0, and ΔX=1. This means that the plot will begin at the origin with unity spacing between the X values. Notice that the Waveform Graph terminal assumes the one-dimensional array symbol [DBL].

You can, however, specify the initial value of X as well as the ΔX value, as shown in this

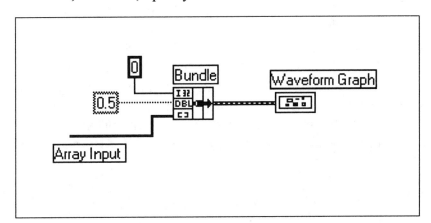

illustration. To combine this information you need a bundle structure. In this illustration the initial value of 0 for X is wired to the upper terminal of the Bundle structure, the delta X of 0.5 is wired to the middle terminal, and the array (Y-values) is wired to the bottom terminal. Because the Bundle combines the different data types, it creates a *Cluster*

(a cluster of values) and the Waveform Graph icon assumes the cluster symbol [≡] (the wire between the bundle and waveform graph will be purple).

187

Multiple Plot Waveform Graph

When two or more waveforms are to be displayed, you need a **Build Array** structure that combines the input arrays into a multidimensinal array. In this illustration each of the

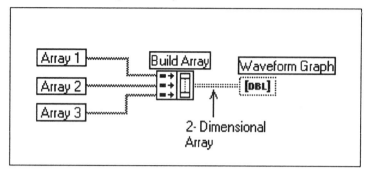

one-dimensional input arrays (Arrays 1, 2 and 3) represents a plot or a waveform to be displayed on the Waveform Graph. As shown, they are applied to the *Build Array* structure, which combines them into a two-dimensional array that is applied to the Waveform Graph terminal.

Notice the difference in the wire thickness of the one-dimensional and two-dimensional arrays. Also note the difference in the icons representing the one-dimensional and two-dimensional array terminals. The one-dimensional array terminal was shown in the preceding illustration as [DBL], and the two-dimensional array terminal [DBL], is shown in the above illustration. This may be a subtle point, but what makes them different is the thickness of the brackets ([ ] versus [ ]). If you wire the arrays as shown in the above illustration, the initial value of X will be taken as 0 and the spacing (ΔX) will be taken as 1.

If you want to use custom settings for the initial X value and the spacing, you have to use the

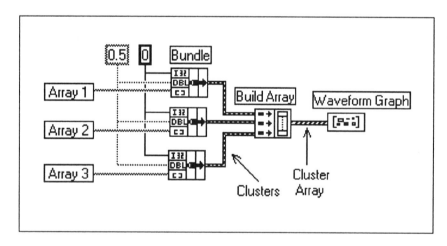

Bundle structure again. As shown in this illustration, each input array has its own Bundle structure. The same value of $X_o = 0$ and $\Delta X = 0.5$ is applied to the three Bundle structures, and the respective arrays are applied to the bottom terminal of each Bundle structure.

The output from each Bundle is a *cluster* of 0, 0.5

and the array data. The three clusters are applied to the *Build Array* structure, which creates a *Cluster Array*. The Cluster Array that includes the X-axis settings and data for three individual plots is finally applied to the Waveform Graph terminal. Note once again the wire thickness of the data lines as well as the color, which you will be able to see once you build a VI. Also notice the cluster representation of the Waveform Graph icon.

Instead of using *Build Array* after the *Bundle* structure, as was done in the preceding illustration, just the opposite may be done, which eliminates two *Bundle* structures and renders a less cluttered configuration. As shown in this illustration, the three input arrays are converted to a two-dimensional array by the *Build Array* structure.

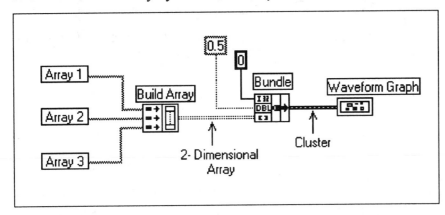

Then the *Bundle* structure combines the two-dimensional array with the X-axis settings into a cluster, which is applied to the Waveform Graph terminal.

Exercise 2: Using the Waveform Graph (Motor Control Simulation)

In this exercise we will revisit Exercise 2, the Motor Control simulation exercise that you built in Chapter 4. In Chapter 4 the *meter* was used as the indicator. Here we will use the waveform graph to display the motor speed response curve.

Most of the front panel and the block diagram remains unchanged, with only a few minor alterations.

Open the Motor Control.vi, which is in the Workbook.LLB. Using the following guidelines make the modification as shown in Fig. 6-4.

Front Panel

The fastest way to replace the Motor Speed Meter indicator is to pop up on the meter indicator and choose **Replace** from the popup menu. When the Controls palette opens, choose *Waveform Graph* from the *Graph* subpalette.

Modify the maximum values for the Y and X scales to **2000** and **100,** respectively.

Using free labels, label the Y-axis with *RPM* and the X-axis with *Time* **x 0.1 sec.**
Disable the *AutoScale* for the X and Y axes.

Block Diagram

Move the Motor Speed waveform graph terminal outside the For Loop.

Open the **Build Array** structure outside the For Loop. The *Build Array* structure, which was discussed in Exercise 5 of Chapter 5, can be found in the *Arrays* subpalette of the Functions palette. Resize the Build Array by dragging down its lower corner with the positioning tool so that it includes two inputs.

Complete the *wiring* as shown in Fig. 6-4.

The *Build Array* structure combines the 50 point array generated by the multiply function and the 50 point array of the numeric constant 1000 into a two-dimensional array. The top input to the Build Array will be displayed first, followed by the bottom input. In this exercise the ramp waveform must be displayed first, followed by the constant 1000 line.

Run this VI. Experiment with different values of the front panel Controls. You may want to place all objects in the block diagram into a While Loop to create an interactive configuration.

Save this VI as **Motor Control 2.vi** in Workbook.LLB and close the VI.

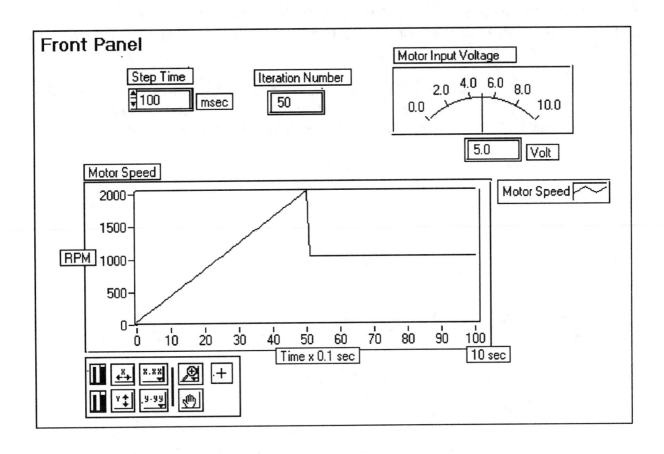

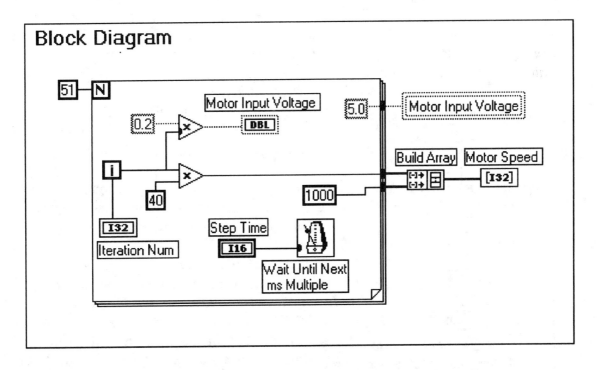

Fig. 6-4   The Front Panel and Block Diagram of Exercise 2

191

Exercise 3: Using the Waveform Graph (Amplitude Modulation)

In this exercise we will build an amplitude modulation VI that uses the waveform graph. Included in this VI are three AM options:

DSBFC   Double sideband full carrier. It includes the carrier, one upper sideband (USB), and one lower sideband (LSB) frequency components.

DSBFC2   Double sideband full carrier. It includes two sideband frequency components on each side of the carrier.

DSBSC   Double sideband suppressed carrier.

The Menu Ring used in this VI provides the means of choosing one of the above options to be executed.

Two waveform graphs are used, one to display the time domain waveform and the other to display the amplitude spectrum.

Build the VI as shown in Fig. 6-5, using the following guide.

Front Panel

1.   **Waveform Graph** is located in the *Graph* subpalette of the Controls palette.
   Open two waveform graphs and resize them. See Fig. 6-5.
   Rescale both graphs as shown in Fig. 6-5.
   Disable AutoScale for the X and Y axes in both graphs.
   Label both graphs as shown in Fig. 6-5. Use owned labels for *Time Domain Wave* and *Amplitude Spectrum*. Use free labels for *Time (msec.)* and *Frequency (Hz)*.

   Digital Control is found in the *Numeric* subpalette of the Controls palette
   Open five digital controls.
   Label them with owned labels as shown in Fig. 6-5.
   Representation is **I16** for f_c, f_s and f_{s2}. Representation for the remaining two digital controls is *DBL* by default. To change the Representation, pop up on the digital indicator and choose *Representation>I16* from the popup palette.

   Vertical Switch is located in the *Boolean* subpalette of the Controls palette.

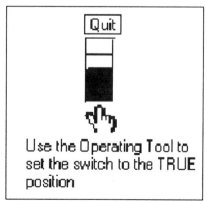

Set switch to the *true* position using the *Operating Tool,* as shown in this illustration.

Mechanical Action: Latch When Pressed.
Pop up on the switch and choose *Mechanical Action> Latch When Pressed* from the popup palette.

Set Default: Pop up on the switch and choose *Data Operations>Make Current Value Default* from the popup menu.

192

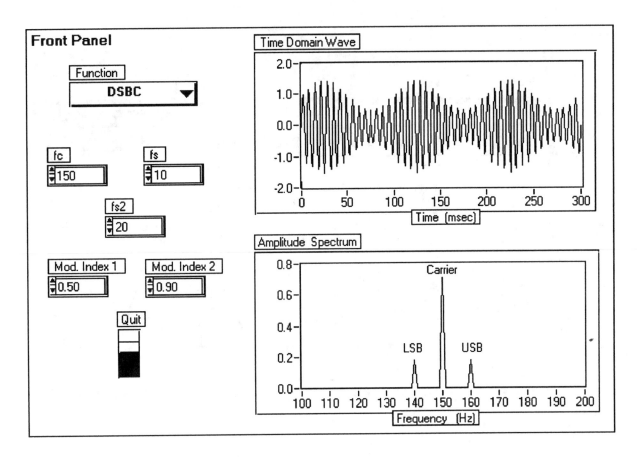

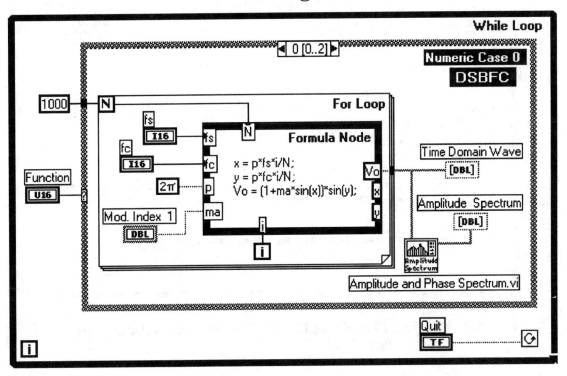

Fig. 6-5 The Front Panel and Block Diagram of Exercise 3.

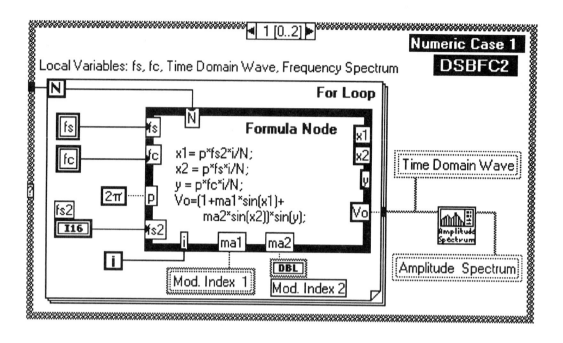

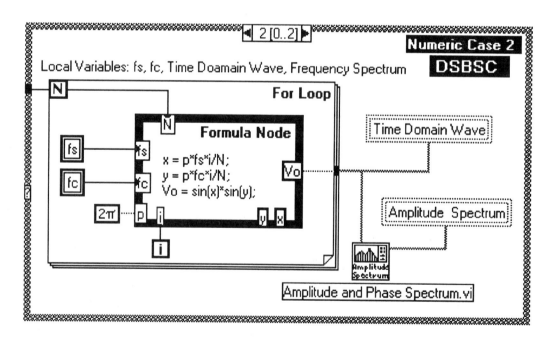

Fig. 6-5 The Front Panel and Block Diagram of Exercise 3 (continued)

Although the switch setting procedure is not absolutely necessary to operate this VI, it makes the *true* position of the switch the default position. Next time you open this VI, the switch will be in the correct position to run the VI. The *Latch When Pressed* mechanical action of the switch as described in Exercise 1 of this chapter works well with While Loops.

Menu Ring is in the *List & Ring* subpalette of the Controls palette.
Label the Menu Ring as **Function** using an owned label.

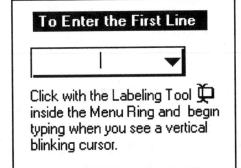

Enter Menu Options into the menu ring as follows: **DSBFC, DSBFC2** and **SSBSC**.

To enter the first option, click with the *Labeling Tool* inside the Menu Ring. The face of the Menu Ring changes from gray to white. Begin typing the first entry (which is DSBFC in this exercise) as soon as you see the blinking vertical line cursor.

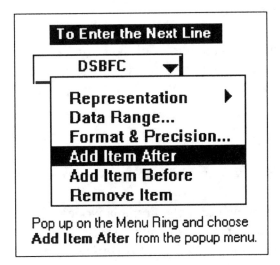

To enter the second option, pop up on the Menu Ring and choose *Add Item After* from the pop up menu. Begin typing as soon as you see the vertical blinking cursor. Use this procedure to enter all subsequent menu ring options

To Delete an entry, pop up on the menu ring and choose *Remove Item*. The entry presently in the menu ring window will be deleted.

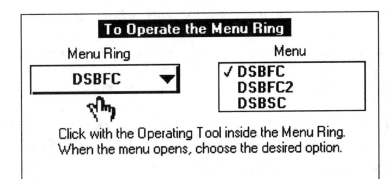

To Choose Menu Ring Option, click with the *Operating Tool* on the Menu Ring. Choose the desired option from the menu that opens.

195

Block Diagram

2. **While Loop** and **Case Structure** are in the *Structures* subpalette of the Functions palette.

  Open the While Loop and the Case structure inside the While Loop.

  Resize the Case structure and the While Loop to fill the screen.

  Wire the *Function* terminal to the Selector terminal of the Case structure. The Case structure, Boolean by default, now becomes Numeric Case Structure.

  Wire the *Quit* Boolean terminal to the Condition terminal of the While Loop.

  Next, three frames of the Case structure must be constructed.

3. ## <u>Numeric Case 0</u> (DSBFC)

  For Loop is located in the *Structures* subpalette of the Functions palette.

  Open the For Loop inside Numeric Case 0.

  Numeric Constant is in the *Numeric* subpalette of the Functions palette.

  Open the numeric constant, set its value to 1000 (with the Labeling Tool) and wire it to the loop counting terminal N of the For Loop, as shown in Fig. 6-5.

  Formula Node is in the *Structures* subpalette of the Functions palette.

  Open Formula Node inside the For Loop.

  Add Inputs/Outputs to the Formula Node as shown in Fig. 6-5.

  To add an input/output, pop up on the border of the Formula Node and choose ***Add Input*** or ***Add Output*** from the popup menu.

  Inputs: f_c , f_s , p, ma, i and N

  Outputs: V_o , x and y

  Wire various terminals to the Formula Node inputs and the V_o output to the border of the For Loop, as shown in Fig. 6-5. The 2π constant is found in the *Additional Numeric Constants* subpalette of the *Numeric* subpalette of the Functions palette.

  Type with the Labeling Tool the formulae inside the Formula Node as shown in Fig. 6-5. *Don't forget the semicolon at the end of each formula.*

  Wire V_o from the border of the For Loop to the *Time Domain Wave* terminal.

Amplitude and Phase Spectrum.vi is in the *Measurements* subpalette of the *Analysis*

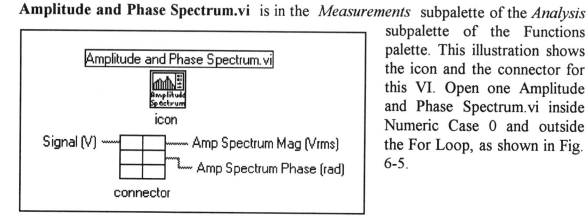

subpalette of the Functions palette. This illustration shows the icon and the connector for this VI. Open one Amplitude and Phase Spectrum.vi inside Numeric Case 0 and outside the For Loop, as shown in Fig. 6-5.

Signal (V) is an input array that includes the time domain signal. In this VI the time domain signal is the **Vo** array created at the border of the For Loop.

Amp Spectrum Mag (Vrms) is the Fast Fourier Transform of the input signal. It is the single-sided amplitude spectrum magnitude in volts rms if the input signal is in volts.

Amp Spectrum Phase (radians) is the single-sided amplitude spectrum phase in radians.

Wire V_o from the border of the For Loop to the *Signal (V)* input terminal of the *Amplitude and Phase Spectrum.vi*.

Wire the *Amp Spectrum Mag (V_{rms})* output from the *Amplitude and Phase Spectrum.vi* to the *Amplitude Spectrum* terminal, as shown in Fig. 6-5.

4. ## Numeric Case 1 (DSBFC2)
Open **Numeric Case 1** frame by clicking on the arrow button in the case window.
Open **For Loop** inside Numeric Case 1 frame.
   Wire the 1000 numeric constant from the *tunnel,* which is in the left border of the Case structure, to the loop counter N terminal of the For Loop.
Open **Formula Node** inside the For Loop.
   Add all inputs and outputs to the Formula Node as shown in Fig. 6-5.
   Type all formulae inside the Formula Node as shown in Fig. 6-5.

Creating a Local Variable
Terminals such as f_s, f_c, Time Domain Wave and others are front panel controls that can be used only once in the block diagram. Most of these terminals we have already used in Numeric Case 0 and we need them again in Case 1. Local variable provides the means of creating another instance of a terminal.

To Create a Local Variable, choose *Local Variable* **LOCAL** from the *Structures* subpalette of the Functions palette. When you bring it to the block diagram, it will have this appearance ⟦?⟧ .

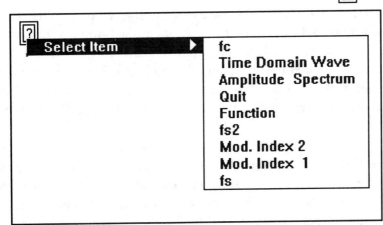

Pop up on the *Local Variable* icon and click on *Select Item*. A menu opens, isting all front panel controls and indicators, as shown in this illustration.

Choose the name for your local variable.

197

Local variables are classified as *Read Local* or *Write Local*.
The Read Local means "read from a front panel control."
The Write Local means "write to a front panel indicator."
Hence, the local variable representing a front panel control must be a
Read Local and the local variable representing a front panel
indicator must be a Write Local.

Note: *When you first open a local variable, it is by default*
a Write Local (to be used for an indicator). To change
it to a Read Local, pop up on the local variable icon
and choose Change to Read Local from the popup menu.

Create f_s, f_c, and **Mod Index 1** as read local variables and
Time Domain Wave, **Amplitude Spectrum** as write local variables.

Complete Wiring all objects inside Numeric Case 2, as shown in Fig. 6-5.

5. **<u>Numeric Case 2</u> (DSBSC)**
    Open **Numeric Case 2** frame by popping up inside the Case window (at the top of the
        structure) and choosing *Add Case After* from the popup menu.
    Complete the wiring of all objects in Numeric Case 2 as shown in Fig. 6-5. There is
        nothing new in this case frame. Refer to the preceding cases for help.
    This completes the VI construction.

6. *Enter* values into the front panel digital controls, as shown in Fig. 6-5.

    By choosing an item from the Function (Menu Ring) you indirectly specify the Numeric
    Case frame to be executed. For example, the Function terminal in the block diagram will
    assume a value of 1 when you select DSBFC2 from the Function menu in the front panel.
    This means that Numeric Case 1 will be executed only if push the Run button. Similarly
    the DSBSC selection in the front panel will cause Numeric Case 2 to be executed.

    The three numeric cases (Case 0, Case 1 and Case 2) are configured in a similar way.
    The For Loop is used to acquire a 1000 point array of data at the border of the For Loop.
    The array data is then applied directly to the Time Domain Wave waveform graph for
    time domain display. It is also applied to the Amplitude and Phase Spectrum.vi, whose
    output is applied to the Amplitude Spectrum waveform graph for the frequency domain
    display. You can change the 1000 numeric constant if you want the size of the array
    to be larger or smaller.

    The Formula Node in each of the case frames dictates the type of data. In Numeric Case 0
    we have the classical expression of the AM wave that yields the carrier and one sideband
    on each side of the carrier. Numeric Case 1 is an extension of Case 0 in because it
    produces two sidebands on each side of the carrier. In Numeric Case 2 the product of two

sinewaves produces the sum and the difference frequencies without the carrier, hence DSBSC (double sideband suppressed carrier).

You may have noticed that in each Formula Node there are two or more outputs that are not wired to anything. The reason for this has to do with Formula Node syntax rules; creating an output such as x or y in Case 0 and not creating the corresponding output terminal at the border of the Formula Node leads to syntax errors. The reason for creating the intermediate expressions such as x or y is to minimize the clutter in the main expression for V_o.

Once again we place the Numeric Case structure inside the While Loop. This provides an interactive environment, allowing you to change parameter values while the VI is running and to see the immediate results.

The use of Menu Ring has helped us use the front panel space in the most economical way. We would otherwise need six waveform graphs, two for each AM option.

Run this VI. Experiment with Function menu options and different parameter values. For example, by clicking with the Operating Tool on the increment arrow button on the side of the f_s digital control, you will observe the two sidebands shifting away from the carrier.

Similarly by clicking with the Operating Tool on the increment/decrement arrow buttons on the side of the Mod. Index 1 digital control, you will observe the change in shape of the time domain display. If the increments in Mod. Index 1 value are too large, pop up on the digital control and choose *Data Range*. Data Range window opens. Type in the Increment box the desired value, such as 0.01, 0.05, or 0.1, and then choose OK. This will adjust the increment jumps to your satisfaction.

Save this VI as **Amplitude Modulation.vi** in Workbook.LLB and close it.

Exercise 4: Using the Waveform Graph (AM Demodulation)

In this exercise we will build a VI that simulates the process of AM demodulation. Only the DSBFC and DSBSC cases will be considered. The VI that we built in the preceding exercise will also be used here to save us some time.

We will first build a VI that will be used as a source of amplitude modulated signal. Actually we already built a VI that does exactly that in Exercise 3. So let's rename it, modify it, and create an icon and a connector for it so that later we can use it as a subVI. Modularization, as mentioned earlier, is a good way of writing software. Not only is it easier to modify and troubleshoot but it also makes the overall VI look simpler. In this particular exercise, if it weren't for the subVI, the total code would be overwhelming.

AM.vi

1.   *Open* the *Amplitude Modulation.vi* from Workbook.LLB. This is the VI that you built in Exercise 3.

   Save As AM.vi in Workbook.LLB. Now you can close Amplitude Modulation.vi.

   Delete **the While Loop** in the block diagram.

      To delete the While Loop, click on the border of the While Loop and choose *Remove While Loop* from the popup menu.

   Delete **the Quit** vertical switch from the front panel.

      To remove bad wires, enter *Ctrl>B* from the keyboard.

   Delete **Case 1** from the Numeric Case structure.

      To delete the Case 1 frame, pop up on the border of the Case structure and choose *Remove Case* from the popup menu. Be careful: there is an option Remove Case Structure in the same menu - *that's not the one you want* because that one will delete the entire case structure instead of one frame.

   Delete f_{s2} **digital control** from the front panel. It was used in Numeric Case 1, which is why we don't need it anymore.

   Delete **Mod. Index 2** from the front panel. This digital control was also used in Case 1.

   Add **Carrier Out** indicator to the front panel as follows:

      Choose **Array** from the *Array & Cluster* subpalette of the Controls Palette.

      Pop up (with the right mouse button) inside the empty array shell and choose **Digital Indicator** from the *Numeric* subpalette of the Controls palette.

      Drop the Digital Indicator inside the empty array shell. You now have the digital array indicator.

      Label the array digital indicator as *Carrier Out* using an owned label.

   Do the following for the Formula Nodes in Numeric Case 0 and Case 1:

      Add c = sin(y); inside the Formula Node.

      Pop up on the border of the Formula Node and choose *Add Output*.

      Label the output as **c**.

   Wire the **c** output of the Formula Node to the *Carrier Out* terminal in both Case 0 and Case 1. In Case 1 you have to create a local variable called *Carrier Out*. Make sure that the Carrier Out terminal is inside the Case structure and outside the For Loop.

You are now finished with the modifications of the front panel and the block diagram. Save the changes (Ctrl>S is the quickest way).

The front panel and the block diagram of the AM.vi is shown in Fig. 6-6.

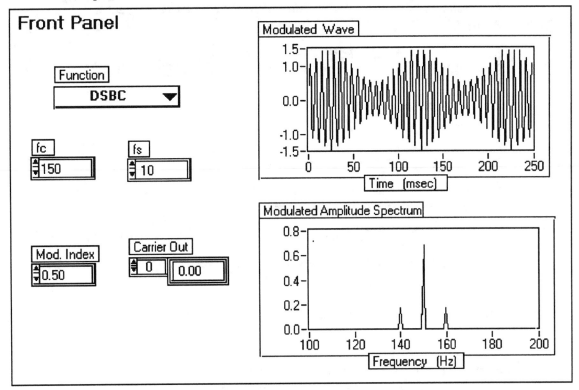

Block Diagram

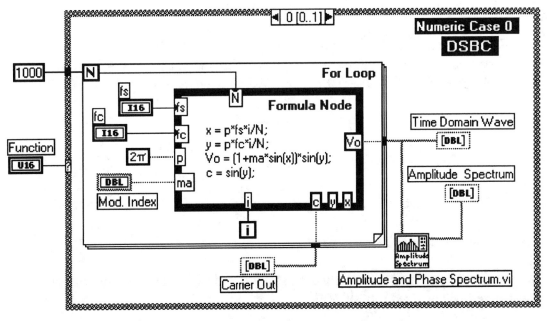

Fig. 6-6 AM.vi Used As a SubVI in the AM Demodulation of Exercise 4

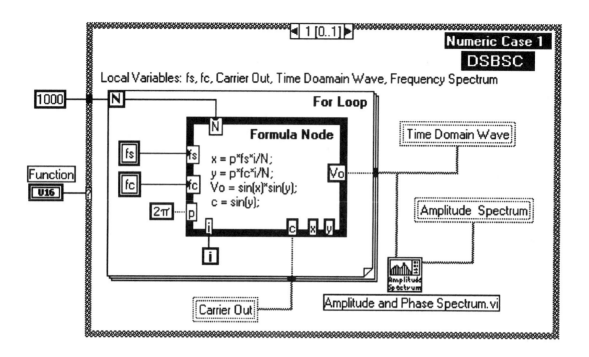

Fig. 6-6 AM.vi Used As a SubVI in the AM Demodulation of Exercise 4 (continued)

2.   You are now ready to create an *icon* and a *connector* for this VI.
   Select the entire block diagram of the AM.vi using the *Positioning Tool* and choose
      SubVI From Selection from the Edit menu. You will get several warnings as soon
      as you click on *SubVI From Selection*. In all cases click on OK.
      You have just created the *connector* for AM.vi.
   Now you can design the Icon.
   Double click on the default icon now in the block diagram. When the
      opens, click on Icon Pane in the upper righthand corner of the front panel and
      choose ***Edit Icon***. Design the icon. A suggested icon design is shown below.

   Refer to Exercise 3 of Chapter 3 for additional information on Icon Editor.

Save changes and close this VI.

Next, we will build the main VI, the AM Demodulation VI. The AM.vi that was just
constructed will be used as a subVI later.

Front Panel

1. *Open and Configure* the following objects as required in the front panel (see Fig. 6-7):

   Waveform Graph   is located in the *Graph* subpalette of the Controls palette.
   Open four waveform graphs.
   Label the graphs as follows:
      Owned Labels: Modulated Wave, Demodulated Wave, Modulated
                      Frequency Spectrum, Demodulated Frequency
                      Spectrum.
      Free Labels: Time (msec.), Frequency (Hz).
   Disable AutoScale X and *AutoScale Y* in all graphs.
   Digital Control is located in the *Numeric* subpalette of the Controls palette.
   Open five digital controls.
   Label the digital controls with an owned label as shown in Fig. 6-7.
   Representation:
      I16 for: f_s, f_c, Filter Order digital controls.
      DBL for: Mod. Index, Sample Freq. digital controls.
         To set representation, pop up on the digital control, click on
         Representation in the popup menu, and choose the desired
         representation from the palette.
   Data Range:
      Increment: 0.05 for Mod. Index digital control
                   0.5   for Sample Freq. digital control
                   To set increment, pop up on the digital indicator, click
                   on *Data Range,* and type the desired value in the Increment
                   box of the palette that opens.
   Menu Ring is found in the *List & Ring* subpalette of the Controls palette.
   Open one Menu Ring.
   Label the Menu Ring as **Wave to Demodulate** using an owned label.
      Enter into the Menu Ring the following:
         First Item: **DSBFC**
         Second Item: **DSBSC**
   Vertical Switch is in the *Boolean* subpalette of the Controls palette.
   Label the switch as **Stop** using an owned label.
   Mechanical Action: **Latch When Pressed**
      To set mechanical action, pop up on the switch, click on *Mechanical*
      Action and choose *Latch When Pressed* from the palette.
      Also choose *Data Operations>Make Current Value Default*.

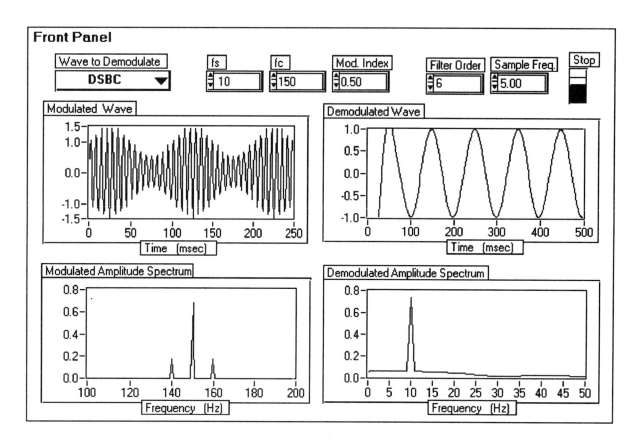

Block Diagram

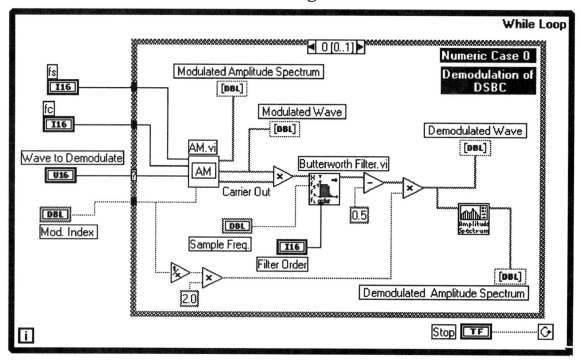

Fig. 6-7 The Front Panel and Block Diagram of Exercise 4

204

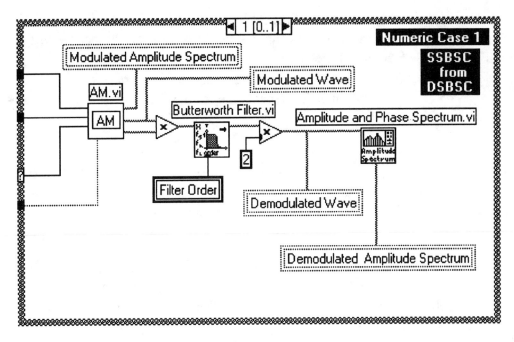

Fig. 6-7 The Front Panel and Block Diagram of Exercise 4 (continued)

Block Diagram

2. *Open* the **While Loop** and the **Case structure** inside the While Loop, as shown in Fig. 6-7. Resize both loops as necessary.

    Wire the *Wave to Demodulate* terminal to the *Selector* terminal [?] of the Case structure.

3. ### Numeric Case 0

    Open **Case 0** (if it is not open) by clicking on the arrow button in the case window.

    Open and wire the following objects inside Numeric Case 0:

    #### AM.vi

    To open the AM.vi icon, click on the *Select a VI...* button in the Functions palette. This will give you access to directories and files. Navigate to the Workbook.LLB and double click on AM.vi.

    Wire all objects to the AM.vi connector as follows:

    f_s, f_c terminals (through the border of the Case structure) to their terminals on the AM.vi connector.

    Wave to Demodulate terminal to the selector terminal [?] of the Case and then to the *Function* terminal of the AM.vi.

    Mod Index terminal to the corresponding terminal on AM.vi.

    Amplitude Spectrum output terminal of AM.vi to the *Modulated Amplitude Spectrum* terminal.

    Carrier Out and the *Time Domain Wave* outputs of the AM.vi to the multiply function (open multiply function).

205

Time Domain Wave output of the AM.vi to the *Modulated Wave* terminal.
Butterworth Filter.vi is in the *Filters* subpalette of the *Analysis* subpalette of the Functions palette. Open one Butterworth.vi .

> *Wire Sample Freq.* and *Filter Order* terminals to the *Sampling freq.:f$_s$* and *Order* input terminals, respectively, of the Butterworth Filter.vi, as shown in Fig. 6-7.

> *Filtered X* output terminal of the Butterworth Filter to the *Subtract* function. The bottom input to the Subtract function is 0.5 numeric constant.

Amplitude and Phase Spectrum.vi is in the *Measurements* subpalette of the *Analysis* subpalette of the Functions palette. Open one Amplitude and Phase Spectrum.vi.

Wire the *Mod Index* to the **1/x** function (this function is in the Numeric subpalette of the Functions palette) and the output of the 1/x function to the input of the Multiply function. The bottom input to the Multiply function is the numeric constant 2.0.

Wire the remaining objects inside the Numeric Case 0 as shown in Fig. 6-7.

4. ## Numeric Case 1

> *Open* **Numeric Case 1** by clicking on the arrow button in the Case window at the top of the structure.
> *Wire* all objects inside Numeric Case 1. The objects inside Case 1 are similar to those of Case 0. Refer to Case 0 above if necessary.
> The Modulated Amplitude Spectrum, Modulated Wave, Demodulated Wave, and the Demodulated Amplitude Spectrum are all *local variables*.

Wire the Stop terminal to the Condition terminal of the While Loop.

5. As in Exercise 3, the Wave to Demodulate (Menu Ring) decides which case will be executed. Case 0 demodulates the DSBFC AM wave by beating (multiplication) of the AM wave with the carrier and then applying to a low pass filter. The output of the filter is the demodulated signal. The demodulated signal is then scaled by first subtracting from it the DC value (0.5) and then by multiplying it by 2/(Mod. Index) (because modulation produces amplitudes of (Mod. Index)/2 for the sideband frequency components). The scaled demodulated wave is finally applied to the Demodulated Wave waveform graph for the time domain display and to the Amplitude and Phase Spectrum.vi, whose output is displayed on the Demodulated Amplitude Spectrum waveform graph in the frequency domain.

The process of demodulating DSBSC is similar to that described above. The DSBSC wave is multiplied by the carrier, filtered, scaled and displayed on the Demodulated Wave waveform graph in the time domain. The output of the Amplitude and Phase Spectrum.vi is displayed on the Demodulated Wave waveform graph in the frequency domain.

In this VI we use four waveform graphs. Two graphs are used to display the modulated and the demodulated waves in the time domain. The other two waveform graphs are used to display the amplitude spectrum of the modulated and demodulated waves.

Enter the values into the digital controls as shown in Fig. 6-7.

Run this VI. Experiment with different parameter values as the VI is running and observe the results. You may have to fine-tune the value of the Sample Freq. digital control to optimize the shape of the demodulated wave.

Save this VI as **AM Demodulation.vi** in Workbook.LLB and close it.

Exercise 5:   Using the Waveform Graph (Frequency Modulation)

In this exercise we will illustrate the use of the waveform graph in simulating frequency modulation. Two waveform graphs are used, one to display the time domain wave and the other to display the amplitude spectrum in the frequency domain. The VI that you are to build is shown in Fig. 6-8. The following guide will help you construct this VI.

Front Panel

1. **Waveform Graph** is in the *Graphs* subpalette of the Controls palette.

Open two waveform graphs and resize them as necessary.

Disable AutoScle for the X and Y axes in both graphs.

Change scale on both graphs to that shown in Fig. 6-8.

Label the graphs as follows:

Owned Labels: Modulated Wave, Amplitude Spectrum

Free labels: Time (msec.), Frequency (Hz).

Digital Control is located in the *Numeric* subpalette of the Controls palette.

Open three digital controls.

Label the digital controls with owned labels, as shown in Fig. 6-8.

Representation: **I16** for all digital controls.

Vertical Switch is in the *Boolean* subpalette of the Controls palette.

*Mechanical Action: **Latch When Pressed.***

Block Diagram

2. **While Loop** and **For Loop** are in the *Structures* subpalette of the Functions palette.

Open the For Loop inside the While Loop and resize as necessary.

Multiple, Divide and **Add** functions are in the *Numeric* subpalette of the Functions palette. The **2π** constant is in the *Additional Numeric Constants* subpalette of the *Numeric* subpalette of the Functions palette.

Open these functions as required in the block diagram of Fig. 6-8.

Sine and **Cosine** functions are in the *Trigonometric* subpalette of the *Numeric* subpalette of the Functions palette.

Open these two functions.

Amplitude and Phase Spectrum.vi is in the *Measurements* subpalette of the *Analysis* subpalette of the Functions palette.

Open this VI.

Wire all objects inside the block diagram as shown in Fig. 6-8.

3. The For Loop acquires 1000 data points for $V_o = \cos[2\ if_c/N + m_f\sin(2\ if_s/N)]$ where $m_f = $ (Max. Deviation)/f_s is the modulation index. The array of 1000 data points of V_o, acquired at the border of the For Loop, is then applied to the Modulated Wave waveform graph to be displayed in the time domain, and to the Amplitude and Phase Spectrum.vi, whose output is displayed by the Amplitude Spectrum waveform graph in the frequency domain.

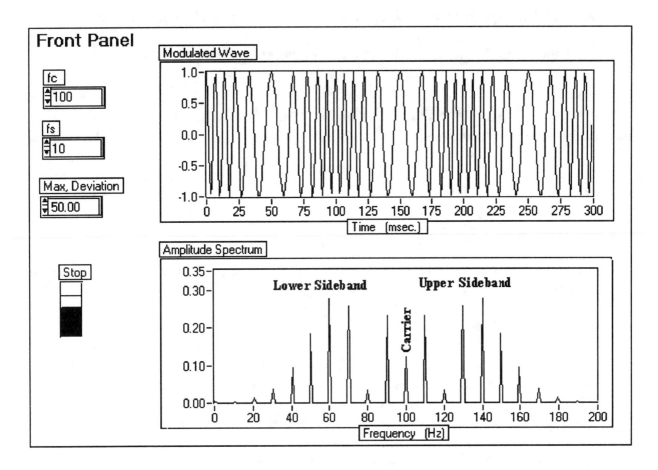

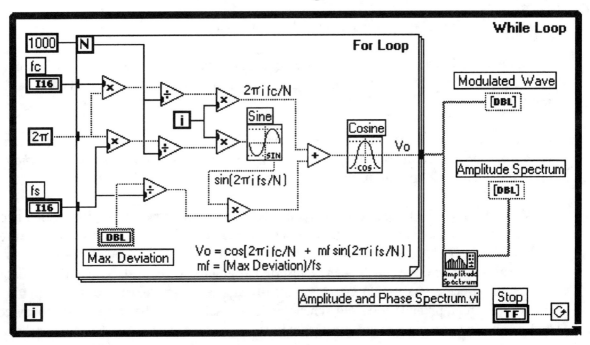

Fig. 6-8 Frequency Modulation.vi of Exercise 5

Run the VI. Experiment with different values of the Front Panel digital controls.

Save this VI as **Frequency Modulation.vi** in Workbook.LLB and close it.

Exercise 6:   Using the Waveform Graph: A Control?

One expects that a waveform graph will be used for display purposes only. However, the plot that is displayed is also stored by the waveform graph. If that is the case, then it should be possible to output the plot from the waveform graph, using it as a control object rather an indicator object. You may wonder, why do it in the first place? What's the point of that? A possible use of this technique will be discussed at the end of this exercise.

Build this VI as shown in Fig. 6-9.

1.   Inside the *front panel* open two **Waveform graphs**, a **Digital Indicator** and the **Vertical switch**, and configure them as shown in Fig. 6-9.

2.   *Switch* **to the** *block diagram*.
        Open the **While Loop** and inside it, open the **Sequence structure**. Pop up on the border of the Sequence structure and choose *Add Frame After* from the popup menu. Click on the left arrow button inside the sequence frame window that just appeared to select frame 0.
        Open the **For Loop** inside frame 0 and wire all objects inside frame 0 as shown in Fig. 6-9.
        Open frame 1 and inside it open and wire all objects as shown in Fig. 6-9.
        In frame 2 create a local variable for the *Waveform Graph Indicator* and make it a *Read Local.*
         Complete wiring all objects inside the Block Diagram.

3.   In frame 0 the For Loop acquires a 1000 point sinewave array at the border of the For Loop. It is displayed, when the loop completes execution, on the Waveform Graph Indicator.

        Frame 1 produces a 2 second delay and in frame 3 the waveform graph indicator, which is now a control, outputs the array generated in frame 0 to the *Waveform Graph Indicator Output* waveform graph for display.

        This VI appears to be useless from a practical standpoint; however, it has interesting and important use in data acquisition applications. In data acquisition applications where the software is unable to keep up with the rate at which data is being acquired due to its overhead, the concept of this VI can be inserted as an intermediate step, making the data acquisition process quasi-real time. A sample of data, for example, can be stored first in the waveform graph and processed. Then the second sample can be stored and processed, and so on. This is a topic of an advanced nature.

        Run this VI, and **save it** as **Waveform Graph Control.vi** in Workbook.LLB and close it.

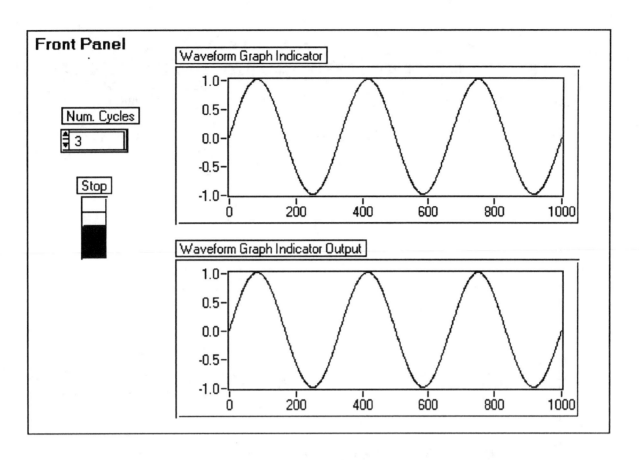

Block Diagram

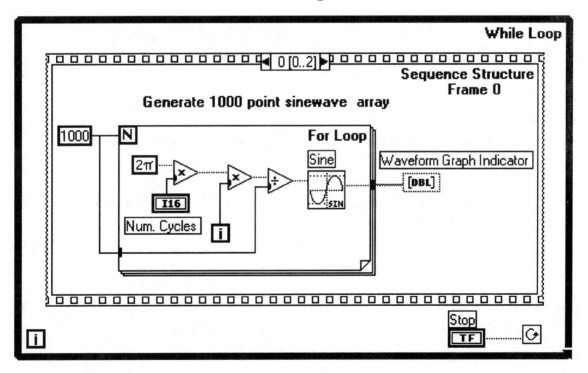

Fig. 6-9 Waveform Graph Control of Exercise 6

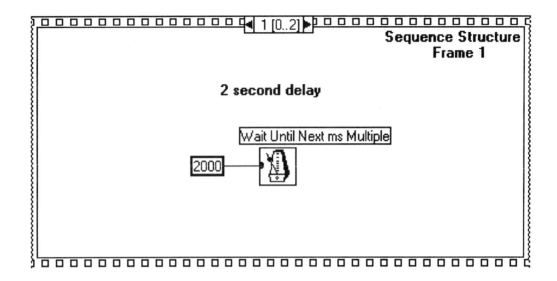

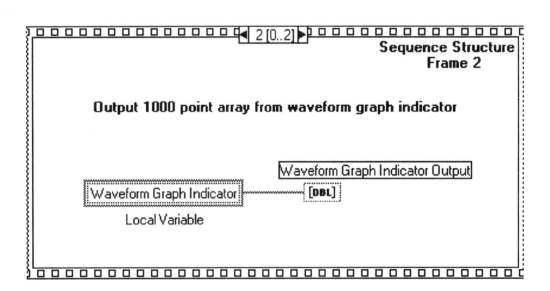

Fig. 6-9 Waveform Graph Control of Exercise 6 (continued)

Exercise 7:   Using the Waveform Graph (Fourier Spectrum)

In this exercise we will illustrate the use of the waveform graph in yet another practical VI. Any periodic waveform can be expressed, according to Fourier, as an infinite sum of sines and cosines. The closeness of the Fourier approximation to the actual waveform depends on the number of terms being added. The more terms you add, the better is the approximation. In this VI you will be able to add as many terms as you like and see the resulting Fourier approximation.

Our main VI, called Fourier.vi, has two subVIs: the *Amplitude.vi* and the *cos(x).vi*. As you know, any VI can be used as a subVI as long as it has the *connector* and the icon, although the icon has a more cosmetic rather than functional value.

The first item on the agenda is to build two VIs with an icon and a connector so that later they can be used as subVIs. The first of these subVIs to be built next is the Amplitude.vi.

Amplitude.vi

The front panel and the block diagram for the Amplitude.vi is shown in Fig. 6-10. Build this VI, then create the connector and design the icon. The suggested icon is shown below.

Refer to Exercise 4 of this chapter or to Exercise 3 in Chapter 3 for information on creating an icon and a connector.

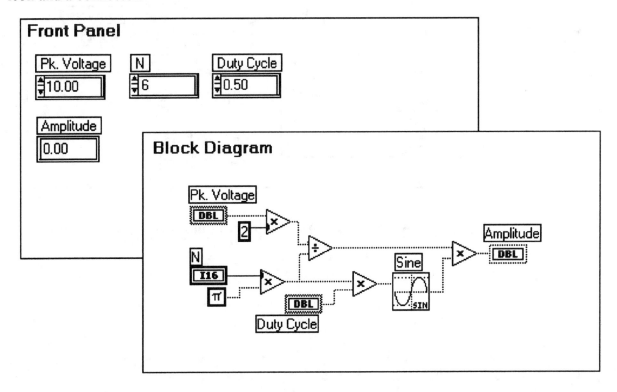

Fig. 6-10 Amplitude.vi to Be Used As a SubVI in Fourier.vi

213

Cos(x).vi

This the second VI that will be used later as a subVI. The front panel and the block diagram for this VI is shown in Fig. 6-11. Build this VI, create the connector, and design an icon. A suggested icon for this VI is shown below.

Refer to Exercise 4 of this chapter or to Exercise 3 in Chapter 3 for information on creating an icon and a connector.

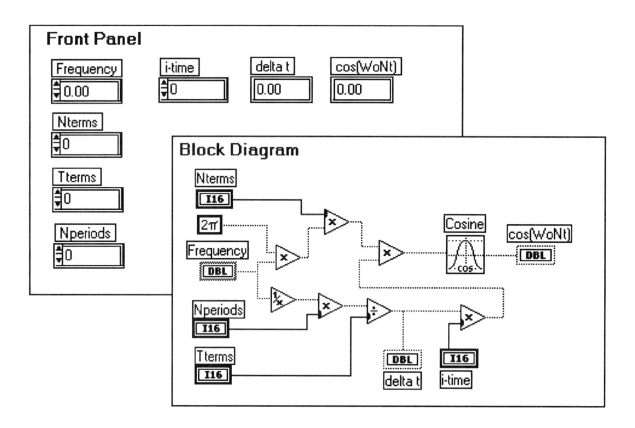

Fig. 6-11 Cos(x).vi Used As a SubVI in Fourier.vi

Now let's return to the main VI of this exercise, the Fourier.vi. The front panel and the block diagram are shown in Fig. 6-12. Consider the front panel first.

Front Panel

1.   The following objects are required in the front panel:

Waveform Graph is in the *Graphs* subpalette of the Controls palette. Configure the waveform graph as follows:

Scale: Enter the X and Y min/max values as shown in Fig. 6-12.

AutoScale: Disable for the X and Y axes.

Remove from the screen the waveform graph's Palette and Legend.

Label: Fourier Wave using owned and Time (seconds) using free labels as shown in Fig. 6-12.

Color: Use *Set Color* Tool from the Tools palette to change the plot background color and the Color palette from the Legend to change plot color.

Six **Digital Controls**. They are found in the *Numeric* subpalette of the Controls palette. The *Representation* for 5 controls is *I16* and *DBL* for the Duty Cycle digital control.

Block Diagram

2.   *The following objects are required in the block diagram*:

One **Sequence structure** and four **For Loops**. They are found in the *Structures* subpalette of the Functions palette. Two *For Loops* are required in Frame 0 and two *For Loops* in Frame 1.

Multiply, Add and Increment ▷ functions are found in the *Numeric* subpalette of the Functions palette.

SubVIs: Amplitude.vi and Cos(x).vi . Click the *Select a VI...* button in the Function palette and navigate to the Workbook.LLB where these VIs are stored.

Index Aray, Array Subset, Transpose 2-D Array and **Array Constant** are found in the *Array* subpalette of the Functions palette.

When you open the *Array Constant*, drop the Numeric Constant 0 inside the empty array shell to set its constant value to 0.

When you open the *Index Array*, resize it to include two index inputs, disable the row (upper) index, and wire **i** to the column index (lower), as shown in Fig. 6-12. For more information, see Exercise 6 in Chapter 5.

Build Array is in the *Cluster* subpalette of the Functions subpalette. Resize it to include three inputs. You will need it in Frame 2 of the Sequence structure.

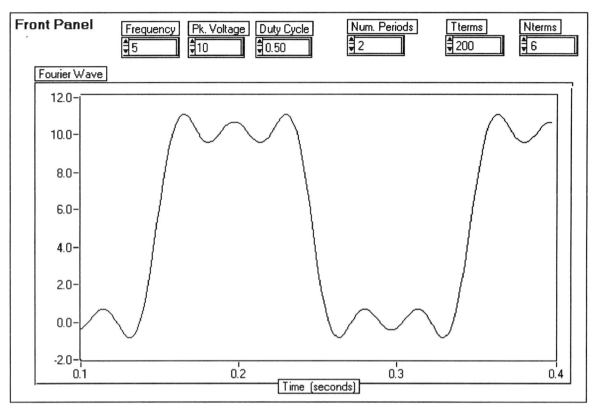

Block Diagram

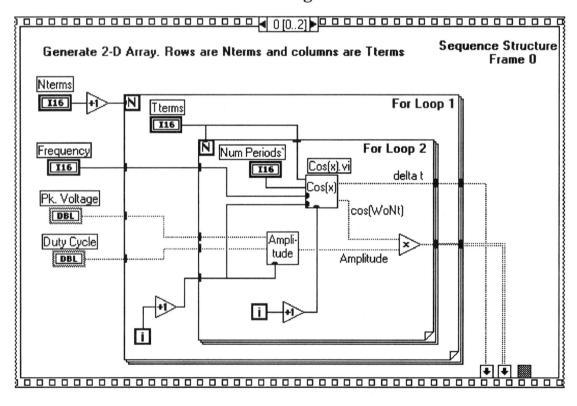

Fig. 6-12   Fourier.vi of Exercise 7

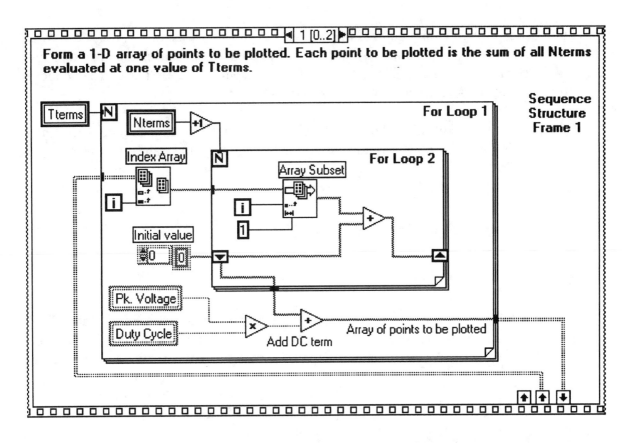

Form a 1-D array of points to be plotted. Each point to be plotted is the sum of all Nterms evaluated at one value of Tterms.

Sequence Structure Frame 1

Tterms

Nterms

Index Array

For Loop 1

For Loop 2

Array Subset

Initial value

Pk. Voltage

Duty Cycle

Add DC term

Array of points to be plotted

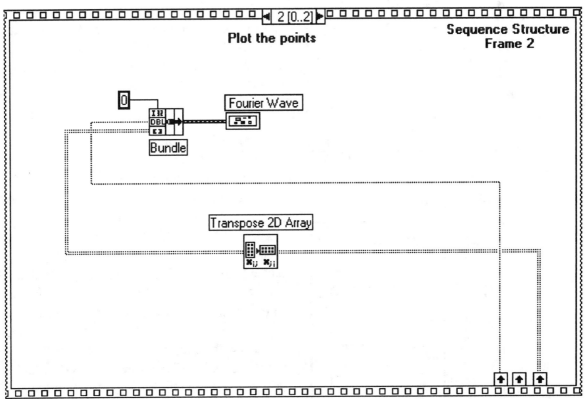

Plot the points

Sequence Structure Frame 2

Fourier Wave

Bundle

Transpose 2D Array

Fig. 6-12 Fourier.vi of Exercise 7 (continued)

Four **Local Variables** are required in Frame 1. Local Variable is found in the *Structures* subpalette of the Functions palette. As was mentioned before, you have to pop up on the local variable and choose *Select Item* from the popup menu. Then choose the local variable name from the menu that opens.

Sequence Local, as mentioned before, provides a means of passing data between frames. This sequence local ⊞ indicates that data is entering the frame and this one ⊞ indicates that data is leaving the frame. The direction arrow as well as its color representing the data type will appear as soon as you wire something to it.

To create a sequence local pop up on the border of the sequence structure and choose *Add Sequence Local*.

3. *Wire* all objects as shown in Fig. 6-12.

4. The objective of Frame 0 is to generate the two-dimensional array of Fourier data. For each value of Nterms (front panel control) in For Loop 1, Loop 2 executes Tterm (front panel control) number of times, thus generating a row of values, as shown by the darkened row in this illustration. When Loop 2 completes execution, all rows in this two-dimensional array will be filled.

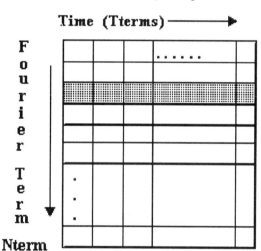

The two-dimensional array is acquired at the boundary of For Loop 2. When the loop completes execution, the two-dimensional array is passed over the sequence local to frame 1 to be processed.

The size of this array is (Nterms)(Tterms).

The objective of Frame 1 is to create an array of points to be plotted in the time domain.

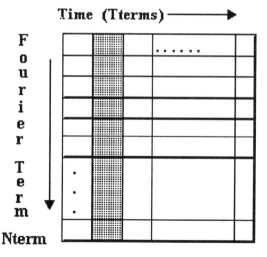

The way to do this is to slice away a column (such as the darkened column in this illustration) and add all the terms in that column. The sum represents one point to be plotted. The Index Array accomplishes the slicing away task in For Loop 1 of Frame 1. The one-dimensional array is then passed to For Loop 2, where all elements in that array are added with the help of the Array Subset structure and the shift register. As the point to be plotted exits, the DC value is added in For Loop 2. This point and all remaining points generated as For Loop 2 executes Tterm

218

number of times are acquired at the boundary of For loop 2. This one-dimensional array is then passed to Frame 2. The Transpose two-dimensional Array structure switches the rows and columns of the array, a formatting step necessary for displaying the array on the waveform graph. The Bundle structure combines the array of points to be plotted, the initial value of X, and the time values generated in Cos(x).vi at which the Y points to be plotted are evaluated.

Enter parameter values as shown in the front panel of Fig. 6-12.

Run the VI. Experiment with different parameter values in the Front Panel.

Shown below is the Fourier Wave plots with different settings of Nterms. Notice how the Fourier approximation approaches the squarewave as the sum of the Fourier terms is increased.

Save this VI as **Fourier.vi** in Workbook.LLB and close it.

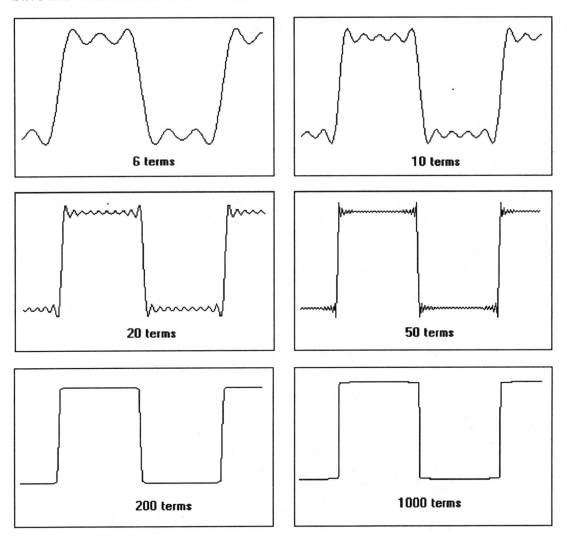

Exercise 8: Using the Waveform Graph (Waves)

In this exercise we will build a VI that uses the waveform graph to plot some of the popular waveforms in electronics. These waveforms include the square wave, the triangle wave and the sawtooth wave. This will be a relatively simple VI to build because you will use some VIs from the Analysis library that generates these waveforms.

The front panel and the block diagram of the VI that you are to build next is shown in Fig. 6-13.

Front Panel

1. **Waveform Graph** is in the *Graphs* subpalette of the Controls palette. Open one Waveform Graph and configure it as follows:
   Scale: Enter the Y min and max values as shown in Fig. 6-13.
   AutoScale: Disable the Y-axis only. The X-axis autoscale will be enabled by default.
   Label the graph as shown in Fig. 6-13:
       Owned Label: Waveform Graph
       Free Label: Samples

   Menu Ring is in the *List & Ring* subpalette of the Controls palette. Open one Menu Ring and *label it using an owned label* as ***Wave Menu***. Using the labeling tool, type into the Menu Ring the following items in the following order:
       Square Wave
       Triangle Wave
       Sawtooth Wave
   Remember that you have to enter these items one at a time. After adding an item, pop up on the Menu Ring and choose ***Add Item After*** from the popup menu.

   Digital Control is in the *Numeric* subpalette of the Controls palette. Open three digital controls and label them with owned labels, as shown in Fig. 6-13.
   Representation: **I16** for *Num Samples* digital control.
   Increment:
       5 for *Amplitude* digital control.
       50 for *Num Samples* digital control.
       To set the increment, pop up on the digital control, choose ***Data Range...*** from the popup menu and type the desired value in the Increment box.

   Vertical Switch is in the *Boolean* subpalette of the Controls palette. Open one Vertical Switch and label it using an owned label as **STOP**.
   Mechanical Action: **Latch When pressed**.
   Choose ***Data Operations>Make Current Value Default*** from the popup menu.

Block Diagram

2.　Open the **While Loop** and the **Case structure** inside the While Loop as shown in Fig. 6-13. Resize both structures as necessary.
Wire the *STOP* terminal to the condition terminal of the While Loop.

Wire the *Wave Menu* terminal to the *Selector* [?] terminal of the Case structure.

Numeric Case 0

Open **Square Wave.vi**. It is in the *Signal Generation* subpalette of the *Analysis* subpalette of the Functions palette (Functions>Analysis>Signal Generation).
Wire all terminals to the Square Wave.vi as shown in Fig. 6-13. To identify the terminal to be wired on the connector, place the tip of the wiring tool over the terminal, which will begin to blink, and the banner with the terminal name will appear below the icon.

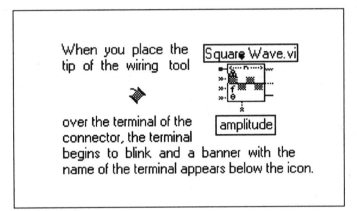

In this illustration the tip of the wiring tool was placed on the terminal labeled as A, and the banner with the name Amplitude appeared below the icon.

Wire the Samples, Amplitude and Duty Cycle (%) terminals to the corresponding terminals on the Square Wave.vi connector and the *Square Wave* output terminal to the *Waveform Graph* terminal, as shown in Fig. 6-13.

Numeric Case 1

Open the *Numeric Case 1* frame by clicking inside the numeric case window at the top of the structure.
Open the **Triangle Wave.vi**, which is found in the *Signal Generation* subpalette of the *Analysis* subpalette of the Functions palette.
Wire all terminals inside the *Numeric Case 1*, as shown in Fig. 6-13. Note that *Samples, Amplitude and Waveform Graph* terminals are all local variables.

Numeric Case 2

Open Numeric Case 2 by popping up inside the case window at the top of the structure and then by choosing ***Add Case After*** from the popup menu.
Open the **Sawtooth Wave.vi**, which is found in the *Signal Generation* subpalette of the *Analysis* subpalette of the Functions palette.
Wire all terminals inside the *Numeric Case 2*, as shown in Fig. 6-13. Note that *Samples, Amplitude and Waveform Graph* terminals are all local variables.

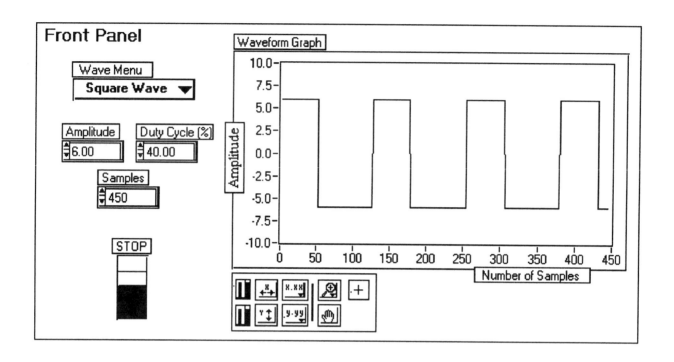

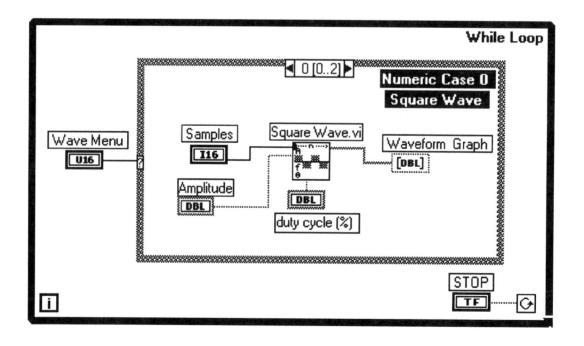

Fig. 6-13 Waves.vi of Exercise 8

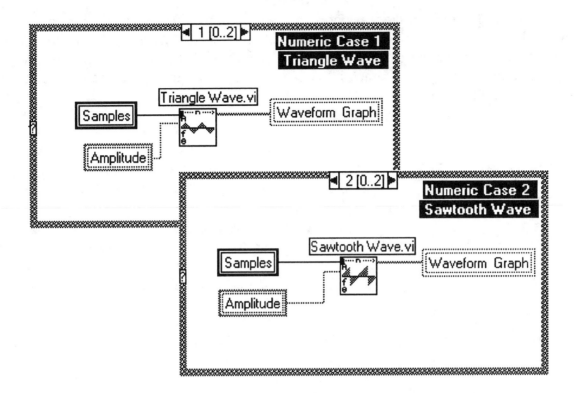

Fig. 6-13 Waves.vi of Exercise 8 (continued)

3.   *Enter* the values of the front panel digital controls as shown in Fig. 6-13.

4.   To select a wave to be displayed on the waveform graph, click with the *Operating Tool* on the Wave Menu (menu ring) and choose an item. Once again, the While Loop is used to create a user interactive environment where you can enter new parameter values, as the VI is running, and immediately see the results.

Each of the subVIs, the Square Wave, Triangle Wave, or the Sawtooth Wave, requires 128 samples to make up one cycle of a waveform. The square wave display shown in Fig. 6-13 shows slightly more than three cycles over 450 samples. The number of samples is the front panel digital control, which you can adjust to display a fewer or greater number of cycles. The Amplitude is a front panel digital control as well, and the duty cycle digital control works only for the square wave.

Run the VI.

Save this VI as **Waves.vi** in Workbook.LLB and close it.

X-Y Graph

The X-Y graph differs from the waveform chart or the waveform graph that was just covered because it is used for plotting curves on the Cartesian coordinates. When you open the X-Y graph in the front panel it will have the appearance of the waveform graph shown in Fig. 6-3. The associated terminal for the X-Y graph in the block diagram has the appearance of the following cluster-like symbol [⚏] .

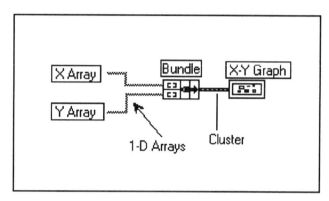

The type of inputs required by the X-Y graph makes it very different compared to the Waveform Graph and the Waveform Chart. As shown in this illustration, both inputs to the X-Y graph must be arrays, one array for the X-axis and the other for the Y-axis. The arrays must be combined in the Bundle structure before being applied to the X-Y graph. This configuration is used for one plot.

When two or more plots are to be displayed on the X-Y graph, then you need three pairs of

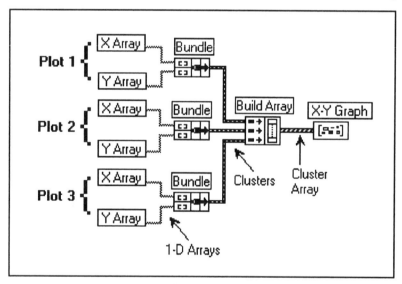

arrays, as shown in this illustration. Each pair is first combined in the Bundle structure and then applied to the Build Array structure. The output from the Build Array structure, as shown in the illustration, is a cluster array.

Exercise 9:   Using the X-Y Graph (Polynomial Plot)

This VI provides another illustration in the use of the X-Y graph. As mentioned, the X-Y graph uses the Cartesian coordinates to create the plot. In order for the X-Y graph to work properly, you must generate the X-array of points and Y-array of points and apply them to the X-Y graph terminal as inputs. The two arrays are combined by the Bundle structure whose output, a cluster, is applied to the X-Y terminal. As you build this VI, note the color and the thickness of the wires at various points. They represent the type of data that these wires carry.

Build the VI whose front panel and block diagram are shown in Fig. 6-14.

Front Panel

1.   The **X-Y Graph** is in the *Graph* subpalette of the Controls palette. Open one X-Y graph
            and configure it as follows:
            Scale: Enter the minimum and maximum X-axis values (-5 and 5). Don't worry
                    about the Y-axis.
            AutoScale: Disable for the X-axis and enable for the Y-axis (enabled by default).
            Label: Polynomial Plot with owned label; X, Y with free labels.

        Digital Control is in the *Numeric* subpalette of the Controls palette. Open ten digital
            controls and configure them as follows:
            Representation: **DBL** for all digital controls (DBL is the default setting).
            Increment: **0.5** for the X-Range digital indicator and 1 for all remaining digital
                    indicators (1 is the default setting). For information on increment setting,
                    refer to Exercise 8.
            Label: Label all digital controls with owned labels, as shown in Fig. 6-14.

        Vertical Switch is in the *Boolean* subpalette of the Controls palette. Open one vertical
            switch and configure it as follows:
            Label: **STOP** using owned label.
            Mechanical Action: **Latch When Pressed**.
            Data Operations (from popup menu): Choose *Make Current Value Default*.
            All other labels inside the front panel are free labels and are optional.

Block Diagram

2.   **While Loop, For Loop and Formula Node** are all in the *Structures* subpalette of the
        Functions palette. Open the While Loop, the For Loop inside the While Loop,
        and the Formula Node inside the For Loop. Resize all structures as necessary.

        Wire the numeric constant whose value is **1000** to the loop counter *N*. You will find
            the numeric constant in the *Numeric* subpalette of the Functions palette.

        Wire the **STOP** terminal to the condition terminal of the While Loop.

225

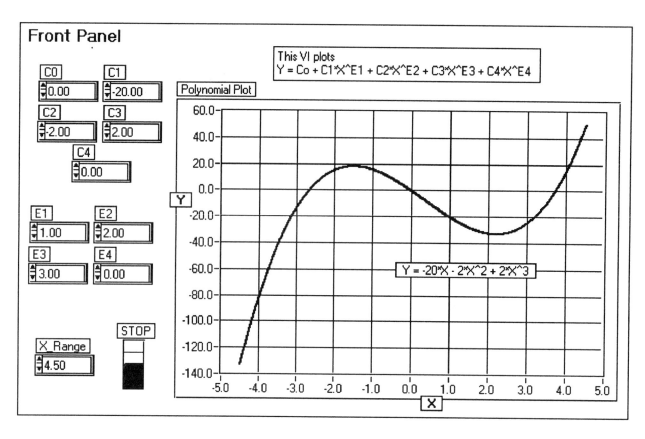

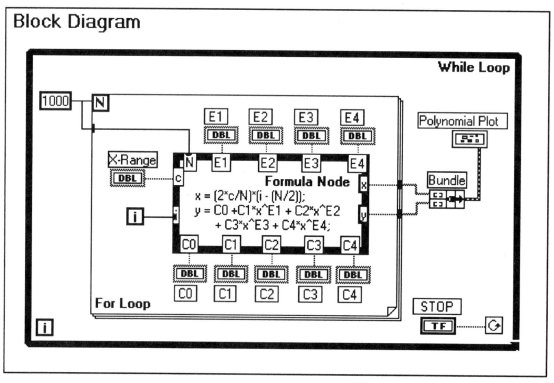

Fig. 6-14   Polynomial Plot.vi of Exercise 9

Add the following to the Formula Node border:

> *Inputs:* i, c, N, C0, C1, C2, C3, C4, E1, E2, E3, E4.
> *Outputs:* x, y.
>> To add input or output to the formula node, pop up on the border of the Formula Node and choose *Add Input* or *Add Output* as the case may be.

Type the x and y expressions, as shown in Fig. 6-14, inside the Formula Node using the Labeling Tool.

Wire all terminals to the Formula Node inputs as shown in Fig. 6-14. Also wire the x, y outputs to the border of the For Loop.

Bundle structure is in the *Cluster* subpalette of the Functions palette. Open one Bundle structure and wire to its inputs the x and y arrays from the tunnels of the For Loop. Wire the output of the Bundle structure to the *Polynomial Plot* terminal.

3.   *Enter* all values into the front panel digital controls as shown in Fig. 6-14.

Note how the X-array is generated. We use the expression $X = (2 c/N)[i - N/2]$ that we have used before to generate an array of points ranging from $-c$ to $+c$, where the value of c is the setting of the X-range front panel digital control. Notice that this range is independent of the value of N, the number of samples or data points. For example the X-Range setting in Fig. 6-14 is 4.5, and the number of data points is 1000 (the numeric constant wired to the iteration counter N of the For Loop). This means that there will be an array of 1000 points between -4.5 and $+4.5$ (for each value of x, one value of y will be calculated inside the Formula Node, thus forming a 1000 point y array). Should you change the value of 1000 to, say, 5000 in the block diagram, the X range will remain unchanged, extending from -4.5 to $+4.5$, with more points that are closer together. The advantage of this approach is that we deal only with the values of x in decimal format, as we have always done, without worrying about the sampling rates and the arrays of samples that make up our plots.

Run this VI. Experiment with different parameter values.

Save this VI as **Polynomial Plot.vi** in Workbook.LLB and close it.

Exercise 10: Using the X-Y Graph (Conic Sections)

In this exercise we will once more illustrate the operation of the X-Y graph. You will build a VI that will plot a straight line and some conic sections. As mentioned earlier the X-Y graph differs considerably from other graphs because it requires array inputs for the X and the Y axes. The X-Y graph uses Cartesian coordinates to plot single-valued as well as multi-valued functions.

You are to build the VI whose front panel and block diagram are shown in Fig. 6-15.

Front Panel

1.   **X-Y Graph** is in the *Graph* subpalette of the Controls palette. Open the X-Y graph and configure it as follows:

Scale: Enter the minima and maxima (−10, +10) X-axis and Y-axis values as shown in Fig. 6-15.

Resize: Resize the X-Y graph to the shape of a *square*. It is important that the X-axis and the Y-axis are the same length; otherwise a circle will appear as an ellipse.

AutoScale: Disable auto-scale for both the X and Y axes.

Label: *X-Y Graph* is an owned label.

Palette: Disable (optional).

Plot Settings: Resize the Legend to accommodate two plots and label them using the labeling tool as **y1** and **y2**, as shown in Fig. 6-15.

Pop up on the *Legend* and choose one of the following settings from the popup menu options:

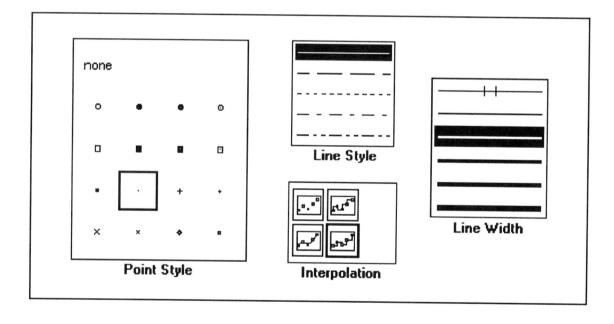

Point Style

Line Style

Interpolation

Line Width

Digital Control/Indicator is in the *Numeric* subpalette of the Controls palette. Open nine digital controls and three digital indicators, and configure them as follows:

Representation: **I16** for *Num Data Points* digital control and **DBL** for the remaining digital controls and the digital indicators.

Increment: Configure all digital controls as follows:

Increment = 1 for Xo, Yo, Cx, Cy.

Increment = 0.5 for m, b, X-Range and p.

Increment = 500 for Num Data Points.

*To set the increment, pop up on the digital control, choose **Data Range...** from the popup menu, and type the desired value in the **Increment box**.*

Menu Ring is in the *List & Ring* subpalette of the Controls palette.

Label the *Menu Ring* with an owned label as ***Plot Menu***. Using the labeling tool, type into the menu ring the following items in the given order:

> *Line*
> *Parabola (Y-axis)*
> *Parabola (X-axis)*
> *Ellipse/Circle*

Remember that you have to enter these items one at a time. After adding an item, pop up on the *Menu Ring* and choose ***Add Item After*** from the popup menu.

Vertical Switch is in the *Boolean* subpalette of the Controls palette.

Label the switch as **Stop** using an owned label.

Mechanical Action: **Latch When pressed**

Choose ***Data Operations>Make Current Value Default*** from the popup menu.

Block Diagram

2.   **While Loop** and the **Case structure** are in the *Structures* subpalette of the Functions palette. Open the *While Loop* and the *Case structure* inside the While Loop. Resize both as necessary.

Wire the **Plot Menu** terminal to the *Selector terminal* [?] of the Case structure.
Wire the **Stop** terminal to the *Condition* terminal of the While Loop.

Next, you are to build the four frames of the Numeric Case.

Numeric Case 0

For Loop is in the *Structures* subpalette of the Functions palette. Open the For Loop inside the Numeric Case 0 and resize it as necessary.

Wire the *Num Data Points* terminal to the loop iteration counter N through the border of the Numeric Case as shown in Fig. 6-15.

Build Array structure is in the *Array* subpalette of the Functions palette.

Bundle structure is in the *Cluster* subpalette of the Functions palette.

   Open one *Build Array* and one *Bundle* structure inside Numeric Case 0 and outside the For Loop, as shown in Fig. 6-15.

Formula Node is in the *Structures* subpalette of the Functions palette.

   Open Formula Node inside the For Loop and resize it as necessary.

   Add Inputs and Outputs to the Formula Node as shown in Fig. 6-15.

   *To add an input or an output, pop up on the border of the Formula Node and choose **Add Input** or **Add Output** from the popup menu.*

   Inputs: m, i, c, b, N, Xo, Yo

   Outputs: x , y

Wire all terminals to the Formula Node inputs, as shown in Fig. 6-15. As shown, the Xo and Yo terminals are wired from outside the For Loop.

Wire the x and y outputs to the border of the For Loop.

Type with the *Labeling Tool* the formulae inside the Formula Node as shown in Fig. 6-15. *Don't forget the semicolon at the end of each formula.*

Wire x and y outputs from the border (tunnels) of the For Loop to the *Bundle* structure.

Wire the output of the *Bundle* structure to the input of the *Build Array* structure and the output of Build Array to the *X-Y Graph* terminal, as shown in Fig. 6-15.

Numeric Case 1

Open Numeric Case 1 by clicking inside the case window at the top of the structure.

For Loop is in the *Structures* subpalette of the Functions palette. Open the For Loop inside Numeric Case 1 and resize it as necessary.

   Wire the *Num Data Points* terminal to the loop iteration counter *N* from the tunnel in the border of the Numeric Case, as shown in Fig. 6-15.

Build Array structure is in the *Array* subpalette of the Functions palette.

Bundle structure is in the *Cluster* subpalette of the Functions palette.

   Open one *Build Array* and one *Bundle* structure inside Numeric Case 1 and outside the For Loop, as shown in Fig. 6-15.

Formula Node is in the *Structures* subpalette of the Functions palette.

   Open Formula Node inside the For Loop and resize it as necessary.

   Add Inputs and Outputs to the Formula Node as shown in Fig. 6-15.

   *To add an input or an output, pop up on the border of the Formula Node and choose **Add Input** or **Add Output** from the popup menu.*

   Inputs: i, c, p, N, Xo, Yo

   Outputs: x, y, Xf, Yf

Wire all terminals to the Formula Node inputs, as shown in Fig. 6-15. As shown, the Xo and Yo terminals are *Local Variables* that are wired from outside the For Loop.

Before wiring Xo , popup on Xo and choose *Change to Read Local* otherwise you will get a bad wire. Recall that the local variables are *Write Locals* by default when you open them. Do the same for Yo. See Exercise 3, step 4 for information on local variables.

Wire the **x** and **y** outputs to the border of the For Loop.

Wire the Xf, Yf outputs of the Formula Node to the Xf, Yf terminals, which are *local variables* outside the For Loop. Pop up on the tunnel used by the Xf wire in the border of the For Loop and choose **Disable Indexing** from the popup menu. Do the same for the Yf wire tunnel.

Type with the *Labeling Tool* the formulae inside the Formula Node as shown in Fig. 6-15. *Don't forget the semicolon at the end of each formula.*

Wire **x** and **y** outputs from the border (tunnels) of the For Loop to the *Bundle* structure.

Wire the output of the *Bundle* structure to the input of the *Build Array* structure and the output of Build Array to the *X-Y Graph* terminal, as shown in Fig. 6-15. Note that the X-Y graph terminal is a local variable.

Numeric Case 2

Open **Numeric Case 2** by popping up inside the case window at the top of the structure and choosing **Add Case After.**

For Loop is in the *Structures* subpalette of the Functions palette. Open the For Loop inside Numeric Case 2 and resize it as necessary.

Wire the *Num Data Points* terminal to the loop iteration counter *N* from the tunnel in the border of Numeric Case, as shown in Fig. 6-15.

Build Array structure is in the *Array* subpalette of the Functions palette.

Bundle structure is in the *Cluster* subpalette of the Functions palette.

Open one *Build Array* and two *Bundle* structures inside Numeric Case 2 and outside the For Loop, as shown in Fig. 6-15.

Formula Node is in the *Structures* subpalette of the Functions palette.

Open Formula Node inside the For Loop and resize it as necessary.

Add Inputs and Outputs to the Formula Node as shown in Fig. 6-15.

*To add an input or an output, pop up on the border of the Formula Node and choose **Add Input** or **Add Output** from the popup menu.*

Inputs: i, c, p, N, Xo, Yo.

Outputs: x, y1, y2, Xf, Yf.

Wire all terminals to the Formula Node inputs, as shown in Fig. 6-15. As shown, the Xo,Yo, p and X-Range terminals are *Local Variables* that are wired from outside the For Loop.

Before wiring Xo, pop up on Xo and choose *Change to Read Local*; otherwise you will get a bad wire. Recall that the local variables are *Write Locals* by default when you open them. Do the same for Yo, p and X-Range. See Exercise 3 for information on local variables.

Wire the x, y1 and y2 outputs to the border of the For Loop.

Wire the Xf, Yf outputs of the Formula Node to the Xf, Yf terminals, which are *local variables* outside the For Loop. Pop up on the tunnel in the border popup menu. Also disable Indexing for the Yf wire tunnel.

Type with the *Labeling Tool* the formulae inside the Formula Node as shown in Fig. 6-15. *Don't forget the semicolon at the end of each formula.*

Wire x, y1, and y2 outputs from the border (tunnels) of the For Loop to the *Bundle*, as shown in Fig. 6-15.

Wire the two outputs of the *Bundle* structures to the input of the *Build Array* structure and the output of Build Array to the *X-Y Graph* terminal, as shown in Fig. 6-15. Note that the X-Y graph terminal is a local variable.

Numeric Case 3

Open **Numeric Case 3** by popping up inside the Case window at the top of the structure and choosing *Add Case After*.

For Loop is in the *Structures* subpalette of the Functions palette. Open the For Loop inside Numeric Case 2 and resize it as necessary.

Wire the *Num Data Points* terminal to the loop iteration counter N from the tunnel in the border of Numeric Case, as shown in Fig. 6-15.

Build Array structure is in the *Array* subpalette of the Functions palette.
Bundle structure is in the *Cluster* subpalette of the Functions palette.

Open one *Build Array* and two *Bundle* structures inside Numeric Case 2 and outside the For Loop as shown in Fig. 6-15.

Formula Node is in the *Structures* subpalette of the Functions palette.

Open Formula Node inside the For Loop and resize it as necessary.

Add Inputs and Outputs to the Formula Node as shown in Fig. 6-15.

*To add an input or an output, pop up on the border of the Formula Node and choose **Add Input** or **Add Output** from the popup menu.*

Inputs: i, c, Cx, Cy, N, Xo, Yo.

Outputs: x, y1, y2, f.

Wire all terminals to the Formula Node inputs, as shown in Fig. 6-15. As shown, the Xo, Yo, and X-Range terminals are *Local Variables* that are wired from outside the For Loop.

232

Before wiring Xo , pop up on Xo and choose **Change to Read Local**; otherwise you will get a bad wire. Recall that the local variables are *Write Locals* by default when you open them. Do the same for Yo, f and X-Range. See Exercise 3 for information on local variables.

Wire the x, y1 and y2 outputs to the border of the For Loop.

Wire the f output of the Formula Node to the *Distance between foci* terminal outside the For Loop. Pop up on the tunnel in the border of the For Loop used by the f output wire and choose **Disable Indexing** from the popup menu.

Type with the *Labeling Tool* the formulae inside the Formula Node as shown in Fig. 6-15. *Don't forget the semicolon at the end of each formula.*

Wire x, y1, and y2 outputs from the border (tunnels) of the For Loop to the *Bundle* structures, as shown in Fig. 6-15.

Wire the two outputs of the *Bundle* structures to the input of the *Build Array* structure and the output of Build Array to the *X-Y Graph* terminal, as shown in Fig. 6-15. Note that the X-Y graph terminal is a local variable.

3.   The combination of the *Menu Ring* and the *Numeric Case* are used once again in this exercise in order to use a single X-Y graph for displaying a variety of plots.

Each Numeric Case frame has a Formula Node inside a For Loop. You type inside the Formula Node the equations representing the curves or plots that are to be displayed on the X-Y graph.

The For Loop is used for the sole purpose of creating the X-array and Y-array associated with the plot to be displayed. Notice that the y-output and the x-output are wired from the Formula Node to the border of the For Loop, where the array is created. The number of points in the array is set by the user in the *Num Data Points,* a front panel digital control. For each plot, the X-Y graph requires an X-array and a Y-array as its inputs.

The X-array is created in a special way. The formula $x = (2 c/N)(i - N/2)$ produces an array of N points ranging from $-c$ to $+c$. Both N and c are front panel digital controls; *Num Data Points* is wired to N and *X-Range* is wired to c. In this arrangement the x-values will always fall between $-c$ and $+c$, and the end points $-c$ and $+c$ are independent of N. The value of N determines only the number of data points between $-c$ and $+c$.

Functions that we plot in this VI can be either single valued or double valued. As shown in this illustration, a *single valued* function such as a straight line or a parabola symmetric about the Y-axis has one value of y for each value of x.

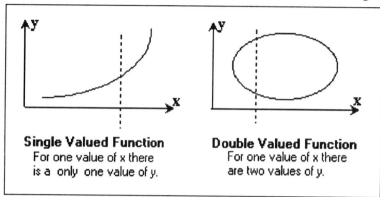

Single Valued Function
For one value of x there is a only one value of y.

Double Valued Function
For one value of x there are two values of y.

A *double valued* function, on the other hand, such as a circle or an ellipse, has two values of y for each value of x.

When we plot a double valued function such as an ellipse or a parabola symmetric about the x-axis, we generate the y1 segment to represent the upper part of the curve, the y2 segment to represent the lower part of the curve. When the two are plotted, they are joined to form the whole curve. See the illustration.

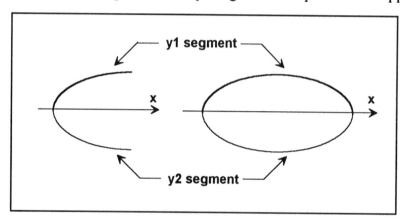

y1 segment

y2 segment

Both Numeric Cases 2 and 3 of Fig. 6-15 must plot double valued functions. This illustration shows a portion of Numeric Case 3, where the arrays y1 and y2 are combined

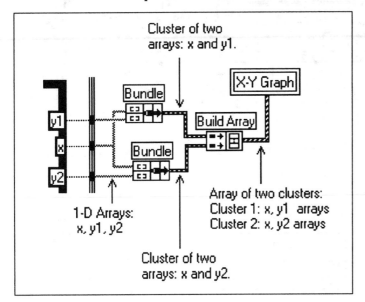

Cluster of two arrays: x and y1.

X-Y Graph

Bundle

Build Array

Bundle

1-D Arrays: x, y1, y2

Array of two clusters:
Cluster 1: x, y1 arrays
Cluster 2: x, y2 arrays

Cluster of two arrays: x and y2.

with the x-array in the *Bundle* structure. The *Cluster* outputs of the *Bundle* structures are then combined in the *Build Array* structure before being applied to the X-Y graph.

Note the *data types* at each point. Data from the tunnels of the For Loop are *one-dimensional arrays*. The Bundle structure outputs *clusters of arrays*. The upper Bundle outputs a cluster of y1 and x arrays, and the lower Bundle outputs a cluster of y2 and x arrays. The Build Array structure outputs an *array of two clusters*: the first cluster contains the x and y1 arrays, and the second cluster includes the x and y2 arrays.

It is possible to apply the output of the Bundle structure, whose **output data type is cluster of arrays**, directly to the X-Y graph. It is also possible to apply the output of the Build Array structure, whose **output data type is array of clusters**, to the X-Y graph. But it is not permissible to apply the two different data types to the same X-Y graph. Notice that Numeric Case 0 uses the X-Y graph terminal, but Numeric Cases 1, 2 and 3 use the local variables associated with that terminal.

This means that if you wired Bundle output in Numeric Cases 0 and 1 to the X-Y graph and the output of the Build Array structure to the X-Y graph in Numeric Cases 2 and 3, you will get a bad wire because two different data types are applied to the same X-Y graph. To remedy this problem, a single input Build Array structure is inserted between the X-Y graph and the Bundle structure in Numeric Cases 0 and 1 to adjust the data type so that the data type applied to the X-Y graph is an array of clusters in all Numeric Cases.

Enter the numeric values into digital controls in the front panel, as shown in Fig. 6-15.

Run the VI. Experiment with different values and different plots while VI is running.

Save this VI as **Conics.vi** in Workbook.LLB and close it.

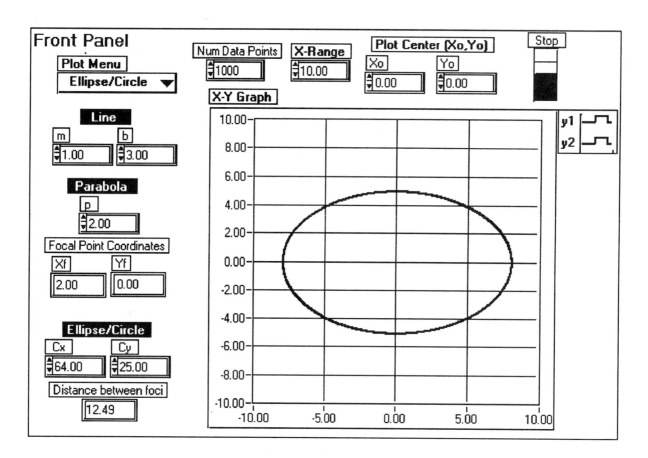

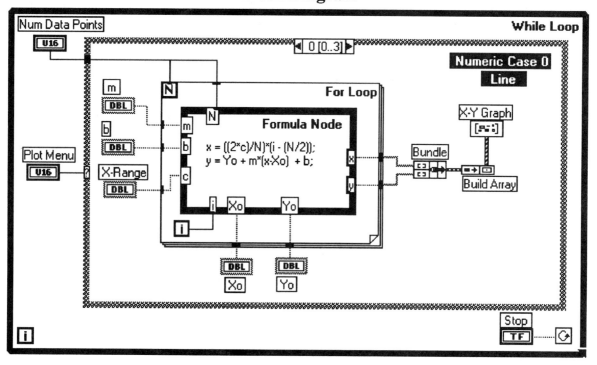

Fig. 6-15 Conics.vi of Exercise 10

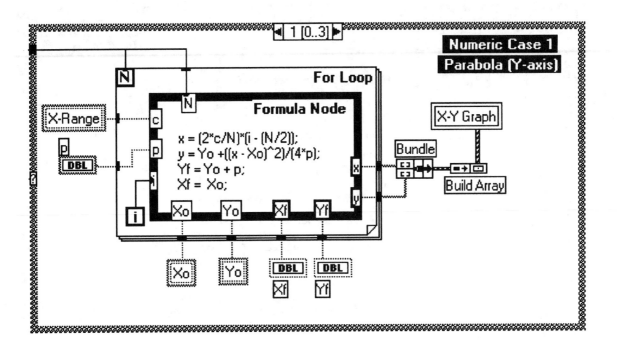

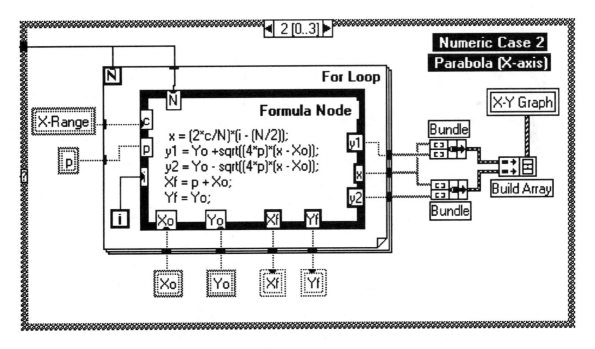

Fig. 6-15   Conics.vi of Exercise 10 (continued)

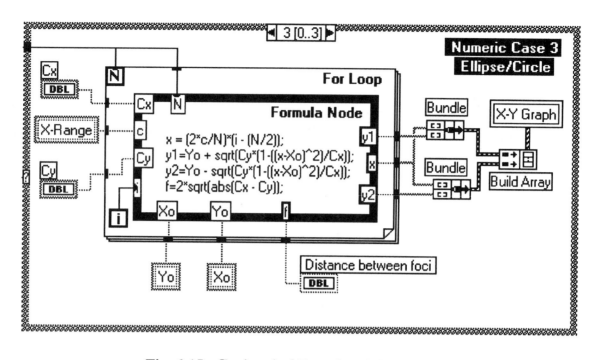

Fig. 6-15   Conics.vi of Exercise 10 (continued)

238

Summary

1. A Waveform Chart is used to display one or more waveforms. It has three update modes.

    The *Strip Chart* update mode resembles the old paper strip chart with the scrolling display. When the display reaches the right edge of the screen, it scrolls off the screen and continues to display new data.

    The *Scope Chart* update mode has a retracing display similar to that of an oscilloscope. When the display reaches the right edge of the screen, the screen is cleared and the display begins to scroll from the left side of the screen. The display is erased every time it reaches the right side of the screen.

    The *Sweep Chart* update is similar to the Scope Chart because it has a retracing display. However, it differs from the Scope Chart in the execution of the retracing display. When it reaches the right edge of the screen, the screen is not cleared. Instead, a vertical line moves along with the display, adding new data. The data on the left side of the line is new data and the data on the right side of the line is the old data. As the line moves, it erases some of the old data to make room for the new data.

2. Waveform Graph is also used to display waveforms. The data to be displayed on the waveform graph must be in the form of an array. The x-axis scale will be the default setting or it can be specified by the user. The default sets the initial value to 0 and the interval between points to 1. The user may change the default settings by using the Bundle structure. The Bundle icon is resized to accommodate three inputs, one for the initial value of x, one for delta x, and the bottom input is reserved for the wave array.

    When two or more waveforms are to be displayed on the same waveform graph, the arrays for each waveform are first combined in the Build Array structure, and the output of the Build Array, a two-dimensional array, is then applied to the waveform graph. The scale for the x-axis will assume the default setting as mentioned above. The user may change the default setting by using the Bundle structure. Each array will require one Bundle structure with three inputs, and the Bundle outputs are combined in the Build Array structure.

3. The X-Y graph differs considerably from the waveform chart or the waveform graph because it is used to plot mathematical functions or curves using the Cartesian coordinates. The X-Y graph requires two arrays as its inputs: one array for the Y-axis and the second array for the X-axis. Since a point in the Cartesian system is described by the (x,y) coordinate pair, it is assumed that for each value in the X-array there is a corresponding value in the Y-array.

    To display a single plot on the X-Y graph, the X-array and the Y-array are first combined in the Bundle structure, and then the output of the Bundle is wired to the X-Y graph terminal in the Block Diagram. The output of the Bundle structure in this case is a cluster of two arrays (x-array and y-array). To signify this, the X-Y graph icon assumes a cluster symbol.

To display two or more plots on the same X-Y graph, the x-array/y-array pair associated with a plot is combined in the Bundle structure. The next x-array/y-array pair is also combined in the Bundle, as are all remaining pairs. The outputs of the bundles are applied to the Build Array. Finally, the Build Array output is applied to the X-Y graph terminal.

At each level of this combining process the *data type* is different. The inputs to the Bundle structure are one-dimensional arrays, while the outputs from the Bundle structures are clusters of one-dimensional arrays. The output of the Build Array structure is an array of clusters.

4.   The Waveform chart, Waveform graph, as well as the X-Y graphs have a number of interesting accessories. These are special tools that help you to configure and operate the chart or the graph. Most of these are common to the chart and the graph.

The *Palette* is one such tool. The controls on the palette can be used to choose precision or format, to set the auto scale of the X and Y axes, or to enable zooming.

The *Legend* is another tool. It can be used to identify displayed plots as well as to choose plot characteristics such as point and line style, line width, type of interpolation between points, plot color, and so on.

The *Scrollbar* tool is used to scroll the display on the Waveform chart. Waveform Chart stores the last 1024 data points. Since the chart window may not display all 1024 points, you may use the scrollbar to show that part of the plot not shown inside the window. The *Chart History...* option in the popup menu allows you to change the 1024 point default value.

The *Cursor Display* tool is available only in the Waveform graph and the X-Y graph from the popup menu (*Show>Cursor Display*). You can place a cursor on the plot and move it along the plot. The coordinates of the cursor are displayed with any degree of precision on the X-value, Y-value digital indicators.

C h a p t e r   7

Strings

In this chapter you will learn about:

241

What Is a String?

A string is a sequence or a group of ASCII characters. When a character is encoded with the ASCII code, it is represented by a sequence of 0's and 1's (the eighth bit is usually the parity bit used for checking transmission errors). The upper case A, for instance, is represented by the ASCII code 1100001 in binary or 61 hex (usually written 61H). And so it is for most of the other characters on the keyboard: each character is assigned an ASCII code. The ASCII code is one of the most popular codes (another code that is also used quite frequently is the eight bit EBCDIC code) used in transporting information from one point to another. You will find other characters in the ASCII table such as SOH, STX, ETX, ACK that are used in network protocols.

In LabVIEW a string is a collection of ASCII characters. LabVIEW uses strings for:
    Text messages.
    Instrument control: data and control string messages are transported over the
        GPIB interface between the instrument and the computer.
    Storing numeric data to disk.

Storing information as strings of ASCII characters makes it easily accessible by other programs.

String Controls and Indicators

String controls and indicators are front panel objects. String controls are used to pass data to the block diagram, and string indicators display data generated by the block diagram.

To Open the String Control or Indicator, choose *String Control* or *String Indicator* from the *String & Table* subpalette of the Controls palette. This illustration shows the appearance of the String Control and the String Indicator as you open them in the Front Panel. Notice that the string indicator has a bar on the left side.

If the text inside the String Control takes too much space and is off the display area, you may resize it. This illustration also shows the String Control and the String Indicator after resizing.

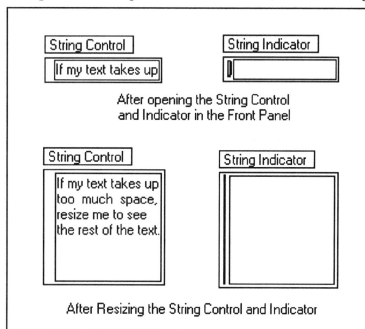

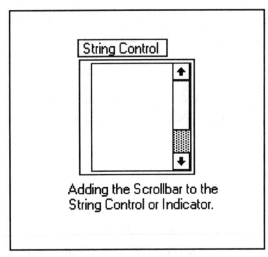

Adding the Scrollbar to the
String Control or Indicator.

To Activate Scrollbar, pop up on the String or a Control Indicator and choose **Show>Scrollbar**. You can type a lot of text into a small size display area and then use the Scrollbar to scroll through the text.

In the exercises that follow, you will build VIs that use various string functions.

Exercise 1: Using String Functions 1

In this exercise you will build a VI that illustrates the use of string functions **String Subset** and **String Length**, as well as the **String Control** and the **String Indicator**.

Build the VI whose front panel and block diagram are shown in Fig. 7-1.

Front Panel

1.   **String Control/Indicator** objects are in the *String & Table* subpalette of the Controls palette. Open one string control and two string indicators and configure them as follows:

    Label: string control as **Input text**, one string indicator as **Output Text**, and the other string indicator as **String Subset** using owned labels.

    Text: type the text as shown in Fig. 7-1 into the Input Text string control using the *Labeling Tool*. Resize the string control so that the text fits in two lines, as shown in Fig. 7-1.

    Resize the *Output Text* string indicator to be the same size as the *Input Text* string control.

    Digital Control/Indicator objects are in the *Numeric* subpalette of the Controls palette. Open two digital controls and one digital indicator and configure them as follows:

    Label: the two digital controls as **Length** and **Offset** and the digital indicator as **Num. ASCII Char.** using owned labels.

    Representation: **I16** for the two digital controls and the digital indicator.

    Vertical Switch is in the *Boolean* subpalette of the Controls palette. Configure the switch as follows:

    Label: **STOP** using an owned label.

    Mechanical Action: **Latch When Pressed**

    Setting: Using the *Operating Tool*, set the switch to *true* (up). Pop up on the switch and choose **Data Operations>Make Current Value Default**.

Block Diagram

2. **While Loop** is in the *Structures* subpalette of the Functions palette. Open one While Loop and resize it as necessary.

   String Length and **String Subset** functions are in the *String* subpalette of the Functions palette. Open String Length and the String Subset functions in the Block Diagram.

   String Length function has one input and one output. Its output is a count (integer) of the number of ASCII characters in the input string.

   String Subset is a function that slices away a portion of the input string. The integer applied to the *offset* input (shown in this illustration) determines where in

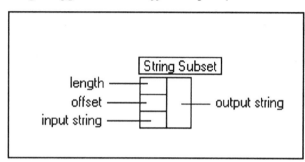

the input string slicing begins, and the **length** input, also an integer value, specifies the number of characters to slice away. The **output string** contains the portion of the input string that was extracted.

3. *Wire* all objects as shown in the block diagram of Fig. 7-1.

4. When executed, this VI displays in the Output Text string indicator the text that you type in the Input Text string control. It also counts and displays on the Num. ASCII Char. digital indicator the number of ASCII characters in the input string. The integer values that you enter in the Length and Offset digital controls specify the portion of the Input Text to be extracted. For example, when you set Length = 9 and Offset = 14, Chapter 7 will be extracted from the input string. The use of the While Loop provides an interactive environment where you make front panel adjustments and see the immediate results while the VI is running.

   Run this VI and experiment with different input texts and Offset and Length values.

   Save this VI as **Strings 1.vi** in Workbook.LLB and close it.
   When you close this VI and open it again later, the text that you entered into the Input Text string control and numeric setting in digital controls will be gone.
   If it is important for you that this information be retained next time you open this VI, pop up on the object and choose *Data Operations>Make Current Value Default* before closing the VI.

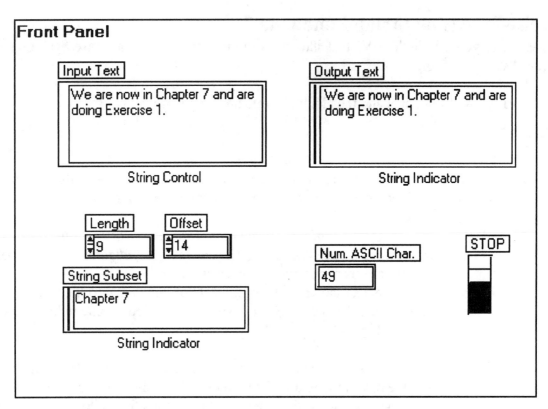

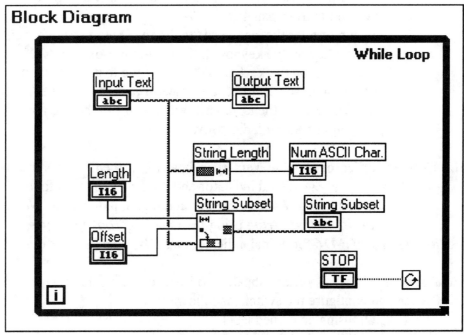

Fig. 7-1   Strings 1.vi of Exercise 1

Exercise 2:   Using String Functions 2

In this exercise you will build a VI that illustrates the use of the **Concatenate Strings** and **To Fractional** string functions.

Build the VI whose front panel and the block diagram are shown in Fig. 7-2.

Front Panel

1.   **String Control/Indicator** objects are in the *String & Table* subpalette of the Controls palette. Open one string control and one string indicator and configure them as follows:

   Label: String control as **Dialog** and label the string indicator as **Output String** using owned labels. The *String Control, String Indicator* are free labels intended as object descriptive information.

   Text: type the text as shown in the front panel of Fig. 7-2 into the Dialog string control using the *Labeling Tool*. Resize the Output String indicator as shown in Fig. 7-2.

   This part is optional but if you wish, you can separate the numerical value from the rest of the text in the Output String indicator. Notice that the 35.13 value is displayed in the middle of the line that follows the text, as shown in the front panel of Fig. 7-2. To accomplish this, place the *Labeling Tool* cursor after the last word "to" in the Dialog string control and press the *Enter* key on the keyboard, then enter approximately 28 spaces using the space bar on the keyboard. To make the text inside the Output String indicator bold, select the string indicator and choose the *Dialog Font* or enter *Ctrl+3* from the keyboard. When you run the VI, the text displayed by the Output String indicator will be bold.

   Digital Control/Indicator is in the *Numeric* subpalette of the Controls palette. Open one digital control and one digital indicator and configure them as follows:

   Label: digital control as **Pick a Number** and digital indicator as **Num. ASCII Char. in Output String** using the *Labeling Tool* and owned labels.

   Representation: **I16** for digital indicator and **DBL** (default) for digital control.

   Vertical Switch is in the *Boolean* subpalette of the Controls palette. Open one Vertical Switch and configure the switch as follows:

   Label: **STOP** using an owned label.

   Mechanical Action: **Latch When Pressed**

   Setting: Using the *Operating Tool,* set the switch to *true* (up). Pop up on the switch and ***choose Data Operations>Make Current Value Default.***

Block Diagram

2. **While Loop** is in the *Structures* subpalette of the Functions palette. Open one While Loop and resize it as necessary.

Concatenate Strings is in the *String* subpalette of the Functions palette. As shown in this illustration, the Concatenate Strings function concatenates input strings into a single output string.

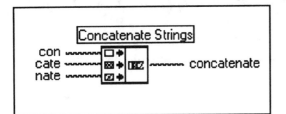

Open one Concatenate Strings function.

To Fractional is in the *Additional String to Number* subpalette of the *String* sub-palette of the Functions palette. Open one *To Fractional* string function. As shown in this illustration, the inputs to this string function are *number*, *width*, and *precision*.

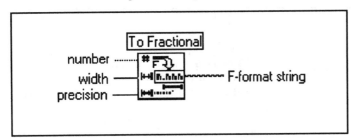

Number input is an integer or a floating point numeric value that is to be converted to a string.

Width is an integer representing the width of the output string. It defaults to **0** if you leave it unwired, which will make the output string as small as possible.

Precision is an integer that determines the number of decimal places allowed in the output string for the *number* input.

F-format string is the output that represents the input number converted to a fractional format floating point string.

String Length is in the *String* subpalette of the Functions palette. Open one *String Length* string function.

Square Root is in the *Numeric* subpalette of the Functions palette. Open one Square Root function.

3. *Wire* all objects as shown in the Block Diagram of Fig. 7-2. Notice that a numeric constant, whose value is **2**, is wired to the Precision input of the *To Fractional* function, thus allowing the number input two decimal places in the output string. The Numeric Constant can be found in the *Numeric* subpalette of the Functions palette.

4. As this VI begins execution, the Square Root function calculates the square root of the number that you enter into the *Pick a Number* digital control in the front panel. This number is converted to a string and is concatenated with the string from the *Dialog* string control. The resulting string is displayed by the *Output String* string indicator. The number of ASCII characters in the output string is determined by the *String Length* string function and displayed on the *Num. ASCII Char. in Output String* digital indicator.

The use of the While Loop provides for you once again an interactive environment that allows you to make front panel adjustments and see the immediate results.

Run this VI. Experiment with different values.

Save this VI as **Strings 2.vi** in Workbook.LLB and close it.

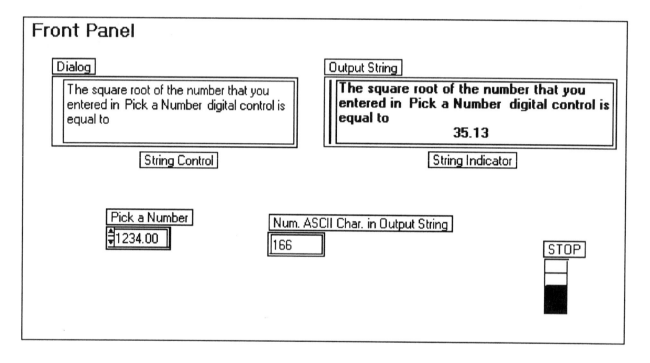

Fig. 7-2 Strings 2.vi of Exercise 2

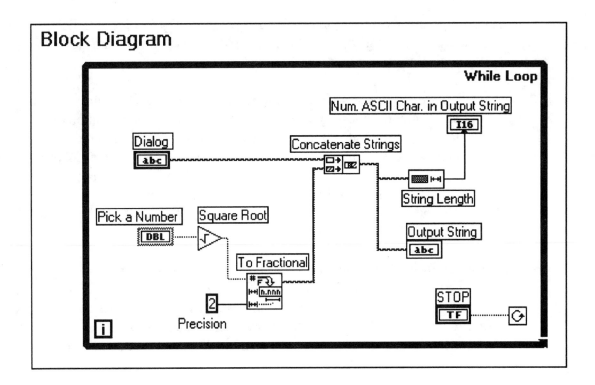

Fig. 7-2 Strings 2.vi of Exercise 2 (continued)

Exercise 3: Using String Functions 3

In this exercise you will build a VI that offers another illustration of the **Concatenate Strings** and **To Fractional** string functions.

Build the VI whose front panel and block diagram are shown in Fig. 7-3.

Front Panel

1.   **String Control/Indicator** objects are in the *String & Table* subpalette of the Controls
       palette. Open two string controls and one string indicator and configure them
       as follows:
       Label: One string control as ***Dialog 1*** and the other string control as ***Dialog 2***, and
              label the string indicator as ***Output String*** using owned labels. The
              String Control and String Indicator are free labels intended for
              your information only.

249

Text: type the text as shown in the front panel of Fig. 7-3 into the Dialog 1 and Dialog 2 string controls using the *labeling tool*. Resize the Output String indicator as shown in Fig. 7-3.

This part is optional but if you wish, you can make the Output String display more or less in the center of the string indicator and be in bold letters. To do that use the space bar on the keyboard to make nine spaces before the word *Random* and couple of spaces after the word *Number* in the Dialog 1 string control. Similarly, make two spaces before and two spaces after the word *is* in the Dialog 2 string control. Then choose *Dialog Font* from the *Text Settings* menu in the Control Bar or enter *Ctrl+3* from the keyboard.

Array is in the *Array & Cluster* subpalette of the Controls palette. Open one empty array shell. Pop up inside the shell and choose *String Indicator* from the *String & Table* subpalette of the Controls palette. Drop the string indicator inside the array shell. Resize the string indicator inside the array shell to a smaller size, as shown in the front panel of Fig. 7-3. Also resize the array shell so that you can see at least ten elements.

Label this String Array as ***Random Number Array*** using the *Labeling Tool* and an owned label. The *String Array* shown in the front panel of Fig. 7-3 is a free label intended for your information only.

Block Diagram

2. **While Loop** is in the *Structures* subpalette of the Functions palette. Open one While Loop and resize it as necessary.

Concatenate Strings is in the *String* subpalette of the Functions palette. Open one Concatenate Strings function.

To Fractional is in the *Additional String to Number* subpalette of the *String* subpalette of the Functions palette. Open two *To Fractional* string functions. As shown in the front panel of Fig. 7-3, in both of these functions, a value of **0** is wired to the precision input, causing the output string equivalent of the *number* input to have no decimal places.

Wait Until Next ms Multiple is in the *Time & Dialog* subpalette of the Functions palette. In this VI it creates a time delay of 1 second between iterations, as determined by the value of the numeric constant wired to the input of this function. To change the delay time, enter another value into this numeric constant.

Random Number, Increment, Multiply and the **Numeric Constant** functions are in the *Numeric* subpalette of the Functions palette. Open five *Numeric Constants* and one of each of the remaining functions.

Carriage Return 🔁 is in the *String* subpalette of the Functions palette. It causes the first line to be skipped in the output of the Concatenate Strings function. The Dialog 1 text will thus be placed on the second line.

3. *Wire* all objects as shown in the Block Diagram of Fig. 7-3.

4. As this VI begins execution, the output of the *Concatenate Strings* function is displayed on the *Output String* string indicator. The five inputs to the Concatenate Strings are responsible for forming its output string. *Carriage Return*, the first input, causes the first line to be skipped. *Dialog 1* string control outputs "Random Number" text in the second line. The spacing of this text was discussed in part 1 of this exercise. The third input is the value of i, the iteration terminal, which is first converted to a string by the *To Fractional* function. The fourth input is the text *is* from the Dialog 2 string control. The fifth input is a random number from 0 to 9, which is converted to a string by the *To Fractional* function.

The For Loop executes 10 iterations with a 1 second time delay between iterations. After each iteration the Output String indicator displays *Random Number* followed by the *value of i*, followed by *is,* followed by the *value of the random number*, as shown in the front panel of Fig. 7-3.

Run the VI. Experiment with different parameter values.

Save this VI as **Strings 3.vi** in Workbook.LLB and close it.

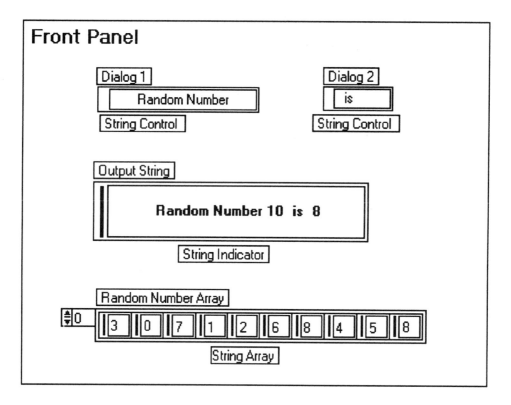

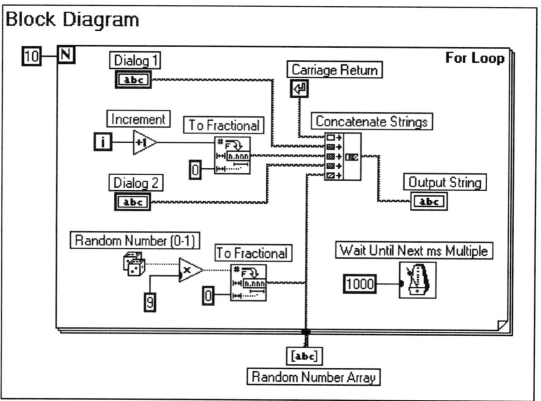

Fig. 7-3 Strings 3.vi of Exercise 3

Exercise 4: Using String Functions 4

In this exercise you will build a VI that illustrates the use of the **Pick Line & Append, Index & Append, Select & Append** string functions as well as some of the functions that we have already used in the previous exercises, such as *Concatenate Strings* and *To Fractional*.

Build the VI whose front panel and block diagram are shown in Fig. 7-4.

Front Panel

1.   **String Control/Indicator** objects are in the *String & Table* subpalette of the Controls palette. Open one string control and one string indicator and configure them as follows:

   Label: the string control as **Test Dialog** and the string indicator as **Output String** using owned labels. The *String Control and String Indicator* are free labels that are intended for your information only.

   Vertical Pointer Slide is in the *Numeric* subpalette of the Controls palette. Open one *Vertical Pointer Slide* and configure it as follows (see Fig. 7-4):

   Pop up on the slide (vertical portion) and choose **Text Labels** from the popup menu.

   Erase **min** inside the digital control window, click with the labeling tool inside the digital control window, and type **Motor Speed**. The digital control window should be resized so that you can see the entire text being typed. After you type *Motor Speed* and press enter, it will appear as the option at the bottom of the slide.

   Pop up inside the digital control window and choose **Add Item After** from the popup menu. The pointer will move up to the next position along the slide. Click with the labeling tool inside the digital control window and type **Load Voltage**. After clicking on the **enter** button, the Load Voltage will appear as the second option from the bottom.

   This step is optional. Resize the Vertical Pointer Slide to a larger size. Pop up on the vertical part of the slide and choose **Fill Options**.

   Select **Fill to Minimum** option from the palette.

   Using the operating tool 🖑, click on the increment/decrement arrow buttons on the left side of the digital control until you see *max*. Erase **max** and type **Impedance** using the *Labeling Tool* and click on the *Enter* button.

   Pop up inside the digital control window next to the slide and choose **Add Item Before** from the popup menu. Click with the labeling tool inside the digital control window and type **Load Voltage**. Click on the *Enter* button.

This step is optional. Pop up on the vertical portion of the slide and choose *Show>Text Display* from the popup menu. This will remove the digital control.

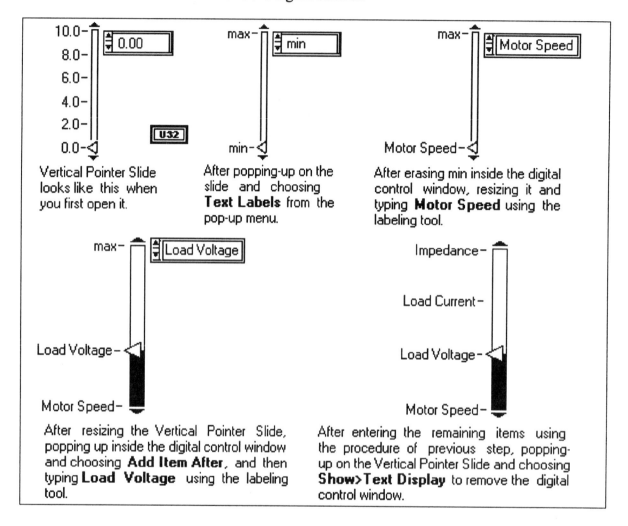

Fig. 7-4   Steps in Configuring the Vertical Pointer Slide

Vertical Toggle Switch is in the *Boolean* subpalette of the Controls palette. Open one Vertical Toggle Switch and configure it as follows:
Resize: as desired.
Mechanical Action: **Switch When Pressed**
Labels: **AC/DC Set** using the labeling tool and an owned label. **DC** and **AC** on the side of the switch are free labels.

Vertical Switch is in the *Boolean* subpalette of the Controls palette. Open one Vertical
     Switch and configure it as follows:
     Label: STOP using an owned label.
     Mechanical Action: **Latch When Pressed**.
     Setting: Using the *Operating Tool,* set the switch to *true* (up). Pop up on the
     switch and **choose *Data Operations>Make Current Value Default***.

Block Diagram

2.   **While Loop** and the **Case Structure** are in the *Structures* subpalette of the Functions
     palette. Open one While Loop and one Case structure and resize them as
     necessary.

The **Pick Line & Append** string function is in the *String* subpalette of the Functions

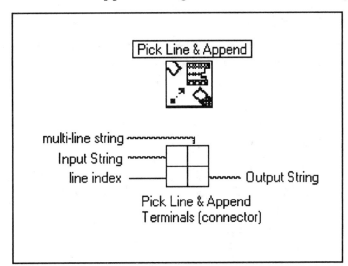

palette. Open one Pick
Line & Append string
function. The icon for this
function and its connector
with four terminals is
shown in this illustration.

The value of the *line index*
determines which line of
the *multi-line string* is
appended to the *input
string*. The input string and
the appended line will
appear in the output string.

Next, open a **String Constant**, which you will find in the *String* subpalette of the

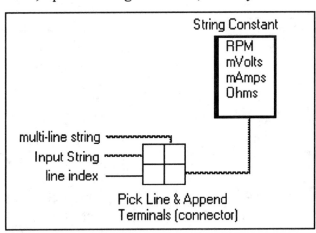

Functions palette, enlarge it,
click with the *Labeling Tool*
inside the string constant, and
begin typing.

As shown in this illustration,
type **RPM** on the first line,
and press *Enter* key on the
keyboard. Then type **mVolts**
on the second line, and so on.
Each line must be terminated
by pressing the *Enter* key.

Wire the string constant to the *Output String* terminal on the connector, as shown here.

Select & Append string function is in the *String* subpalette of the Functions palette. Open one *Select & Append* string function. The icon for this function and its connector with five terminals is shown in this illustration.

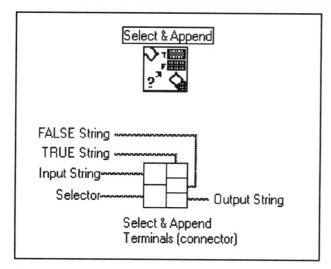

The **Selector** input must be a Boolean object. If the Selector input is *true*, then the string wired to the *true* String terminal will be appended to the *Input String*. If the Selector input is *false*, then the string wired to the *false* String terminal will be appended to the Input String.

Thus, the *Output String* includes the Input String and either the *false* or the *true* string appended to it.

Open two **String Constants**. Type inside one of them *AC* and inside the other *DC*.

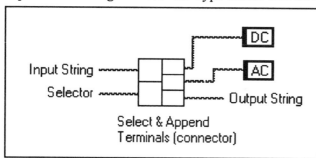

Wire the *DC* string constant to the *true* String terminal and the *AC* string constant to the *false* String terminal, as shown in this illustration.

The **Index & Append** string function is in the *String* subpalette of the Functions palette.

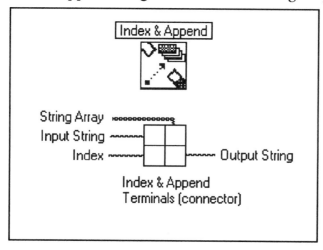

Open one *Select & Append* string function. The icon for this function and its connector with five terminals is shown in this illustration.

The value of the integer *Index* input determines which element is picked from the *String Array* input and appended to the *Input String*. The *Output Array* contains the combined string.

Next, create a String Array for the Index and Append string function. Open the **Array Constant** empty shell. Array Constant is in the *Array* subpalette of the Functions palette. Then open the **String Constant**, which is in the *String*

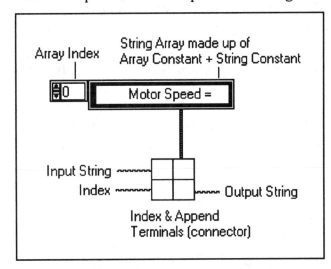

subpalette of the Functions palette. Drop the String Constant inside the empty Array Constant shell.

Resize (enlarge) the string constant inside the array shell, click with the labeling tool inside the array constant, and begin typing.

As shown in this illustration, first insert about 9 or 10 spaces using the space bar on the keyboard and then type *Motor Speed =*. Click with the *Operating Tool* on the Array Index increment or decrement arrow button to advance the String Array to element 1 and type *Load Voltage =* . In element 2 type *Load Current* and finally in element 3 type *Impedance =* .

Wire the String Array that you just created to the *String Array* input terminal on the Index & Append connector, as shown in this illustration.

Concatenate Strings is in the *String* subpalette of the Functions palette. Open two Concatenate Strings functions. Resize them so that one of them has *three inputs* and the other *four inputs*.

To Fractional is in the *Additional String to Number* subpalette of the *String* subpalette of the Functions palette. Open one *To Fractional* string function.

Carriage Return character is in the *String* subpalette of the Functions palette. Open four Carriage return characters. They will be used as inputs to Concatenate Strings.

Random Number generator, **Multiply** function, and **Numeric Constant** are in the *Numeric* subpalette of the Functions palette. Open one **Random Number** generator, one *multiply function*, and three *numeric constants*. Two numeric constants have a value of *1000*, and the one wired to the *Precision* input of the *To Fractional* function has a value of *1*.

Wait Until Next ms Multiple is in the *Time & Dialog* sub-palette of the Functions palette. In this VI it creates a time delay of 1 second between iterations, as determined by the value of the numeric constant wired to the input of this function. To change the delay time, enter another value into this numeric constant.

3.   **Wire** all objects as shown in the block diagram of Fig. 7-5. Notice that *Case 0* contains the *Output String* (front panel string indicator) terminal and *Numeric Cases 1, 2 and 3* contain the *Local Variable associated with the Output String*. For more information on creating a local variable, refer to Exercise 3 in Chapter 5 under the Numeric Case 1 section.

Remember that the Case structure is Boolean by default, but once you wire the *Test Function* terminal to the Case selector [?] terminal, the Case structure changes to Numeric Case. To advance to Case 1, click on the arrow button in the case window that is at the top of the case structure. To advance to Numeric Case 2 or 3, pop up inside the case window and choose *Add Case After* from the popup menu.

4.   When you run this VI, the While Loop allows you to interact with the front panel controls and observe immediate results.

Use the *Operating Tool* 🖑 to change the front panel settings. You can even change the text while the VI is running by clicking with the operating tool inside the string control, typing new text or deleting old text, and then clicking on the *Enter* button.

As soon as this VI begins execution, the Output String indicator will display **This Test is now in progress...** followed by the Test Function name and its value, which changes once every second, followed by the units and the AC or DC qualifying parameter.

The *Vertical Pointer Slide* is configured with four settings. When the slide is set to *Motor Speed*, its terminal in the block diagram has a value of **0**. Its *Load Voltage*, *Load Current*, and *Impedance* settings produce values of 1, 2 and 3, respectively, for its terminal in the block diagram. Notice that the *Test Function* terminal in the block diagram is wired to the *Index* input of the *Index & Append* and *Pick Line & Append* string functions, and also to the *Selector* terminal of the Numeric Case structure. Consequently if you were to set the Test Function to *Load Voltage*, the Index & Append function picks the *Load Loltage =* , the second line in the String Array constant, and appends it to the output of the Concatenate Strings function. So far this will create the text **System Test is now in progress...** followed by **Load Voltage =** text.

What happens next is the formation of a random number between 0 and 1000. This random number is converted to a string by the *To Fractional* function and applied to the *String Input* terminal of the *Pick Line & Append* function, whose index input is still 1 (assuming that Test Function is set to Load Voltage). The index of 1 causes the Pick Line & Append function to pick the second line, *mVolts*, from the string constant and append it to the Input String. As a result, the Output String of the Pick Line & Append function will contain **System Test is now in progress...** on one line and **Load Voltage** = followed by a numeric value and **mVolts** on the line below. All this is displayed by the *Output String* string indicator on the front panel.

The string created thus far is applied next to the *Select & Append* function, whose Selector terminal gets a *true* or a *false* input from the *AC/DC Set* terminal (front panel toggle switch). If set to *true*(up position), *DC* will be appended to the incoming string.

The resulting string is finally applied to the *Output String* local variable in Numeric Case 1. The Numeric Case 1 will be executed because the Test Function being set to Load Voltage this time has a value of 1.

We use Numeric Case structure in this VI with four cases, and each case has the same object, the Output String terminal. It may seem puzzling at first why one would want to do that. However, there is a minor tactical problem. Motor Speed, for instance, must have RPM as its units, but the *Pick & Append* function will also append *AC* or *DC*, depending on the setting of the *AC/DC Set*, the front panel Boolean control. The same is true of *Impedance* whose Ohm units will also be appended *AC* or *DC*. This does not make sense.

The Numeric Case solves this dilemma. The strings associated with Motor Speed and Impedance selections will be applied to Numeric Cases 0 and 3, to be displayed on the Output String indicator before AC or DC is appended. The Load Voltage and Load Current strings will be appended AC or DC and then applied to Numeric Cases 1 or 2, to be displayed on the Output String indicator. The numeric value of the Test Function terminal makes the decision about which one of four cases is to be executed.

Run this VI assuming that the Test Dialog string control contains the appropriate text. Experiment by changing the control settings or changing text.

Save this VI as **Strings 4.vi** in Workbook.LLB and close it.

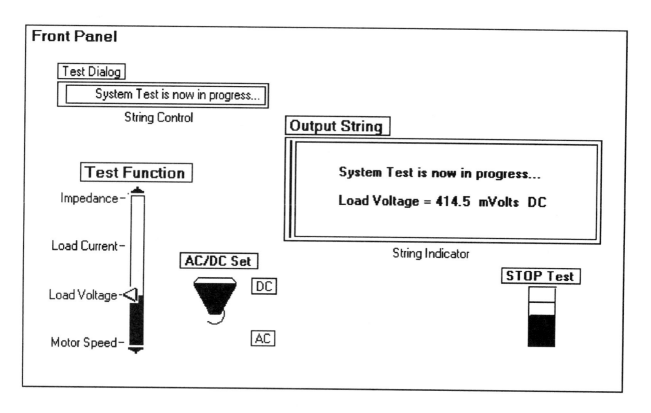

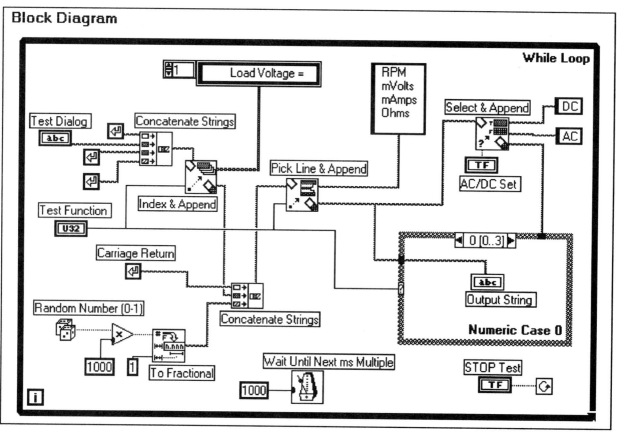

Fig. 7-5 Strings 4.vi of Exercise 4

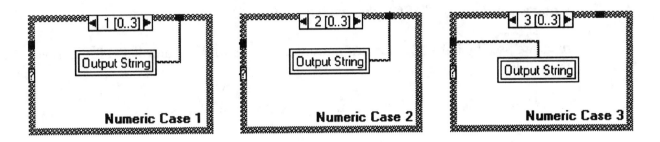

Fig. 7-5 Strings 4.vi of Exercise 4 (continued)

Summary

1. A string is a collection of ASCII characters.

2. Strings are used by LabVIEW for text messages and instrument control and for storing data to disk.

3. A string indicator is used to display a string generated by the block diagram

4. A string control is used to pass string data to the block diagram.

5. A string constant is an object used in the block diagram. It stores a string that seldom has to be changed.

6. The Function palette includes a String subpalette. There, one can find a variety of functions that operate on and manipulate strings.

7. A string array is an array of string indicators, string controls, or string constants.

Chapter 8

Files

In this chapter you will learn how to:
Save data to a file using file functions
Read data from a file using file functions
Save data to a spreadsheet using utility VIs
Read data from a spreadsheet using utility VIs
Use tools that you learned before

The text as well as data that your VI generates can be saved to a file on the disk. In LabVIEW special procedures must be followed to write text or data to a file on the disk or to retrieve information from the disk.

Writing to a New File

A file that does not exist and cannot be found in any directory is a *New File*. The procedure for saving data to a New File is illustrated in Fig. 8-1. The first object that you create contains a complete **path** information. The path tells LabVIEW the directory and the name of the file where the data is to be saved.

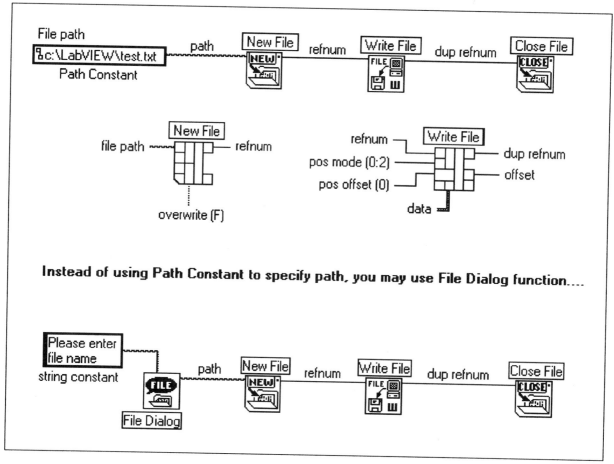

Fig. 8-1 Block Diagram for Writing to a New File

File Path is created in one of two ways: using the *Path Constant* 🚩Path , which can be found in the *File Constants* subpalette of the *File I/O* subpalette of the Functions palette, or using *File Dialog* function shown in Fig. 8-1.

File Dialog function is easy to use. Type a message such as *Please Enter the Name of Function to Create* or something like that inside a string constant and wire the string constant to the *Prompt* input on the File Dialog connector. The function will work even if you didn't wire the prompt.

When the File Dialog function executes, it gives you access to directories and offers you the opportunity to type the name of the new function. Once the path has been created by the File Dialog function, it will be available as output at its *path* terminal.

The File Dialog file/directory selection has the following restrictions that can be wired to the *Select Mode* terminal:

    0   Select existing files
    1   Select a new file
    2   Select an existing or new file
    3   Select an existing directory
    4   Select a new directory
    5   Select an existing or new directory

If the Select Mode terminal is unwired, it defaults to **2**, thus allowing you to select either an existing file or a new file.

As shown in Fig. 8-1, the path just created is applied to the *New File* function. The New File

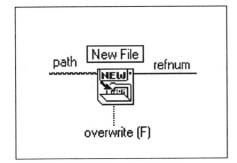

function creates the file specified in the input path and opens this file for writing or for reading. In this section we are concerned with writing data to the file.

The *Overwrite* input whose default value is *false*, shown in this illustration, offers the user the ability to overwrite *(true)* or not to overwrite *(false)* the file specified by the path. If, for example, the file specified by the path already exists and you set the Overwrite input to *true*, then the New File function will erase the contents of the file, thus making it a new file. The New File function also outputs a *refnum* that provides the reference number to other functions about the opened file.

 The *Write File* function is the next block in line in Fig. 8-1. It operates on the file specified by the input refnum. Basically, it takes the data in string format that is applied to the *data* terminal and writes that data to the file specified by the input refnum.

    Pos mode and **pos offset** together specify where the write operation begins:

> *pos mode = 0* and the value of *pos offset* specify how many characters to skip from the beginning of the file before writing new data to the file. For example, if you set pos offset = 4 and pos mode = 0, the write operation will begin after the first four characters in the file.

> *pos mode = 1* and the value of *pos offset* specify how many characters to skip after the end of the file before writing new data to the file.

> *pos mode = 2* and the value of *pos offset* specify where to begin the write operation relative to the current position of the file mark. It is possible to set the file mark at points in the file other than at the beginning or the end of the file.

*If pos offset is not wired, pos mode defaults to **0**. If pos offset is wired, pos mode defaults to **2** and the offset is measured relative to the current file mark.*

What this means for the simple file I/O operations that we will consider in this chapter is that if you want to:

> ***Overwrite*** *or replace the old file data with new data, then don't wire anything to pos mode and pos offset inputs. You will get the same effect as if you wired **0** to both inputs.*

> ***Append*** *the new data to the end of the file, then wire a **1** to the pos mode input and **0** or nothing to the pos offset input.*

The **Offset** output terminal on the Write File connector (shown in Fig. 8-1) specifies the number of bytes or ASCII characters to the end of the file.

Dup refnum is the duplication refnum assigned to the current open file for other file functions to use.

Close File function is the last block in line illustrated in Fig. 8-1. It closes the file specified by the dup refnum. When you open a file, you must remember to close it at the end. This is your responsibility because LabVIEW will not do it by default. High-level languages such as C, also have this type of requirement.

Writing to an Existing File

If you compare Figures 8-1 and 8-2, they appear almost the same. The only difference is that the *Open File* function shown in Fig. 8-2 replaces the New File function of Fig. 8-1.

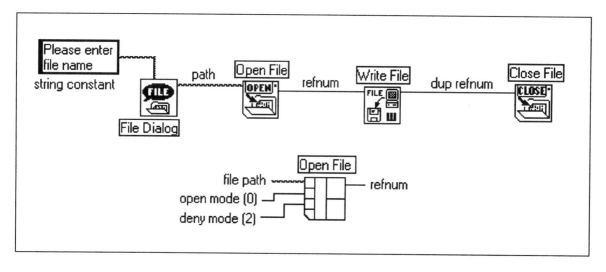

Fig. 8-2 Block Diagram for Writing to an Existing File

266

The **Open File** function requires the complete path of the file to be opened as its input and generates a *dup refnum* for other functions to use. It has the following restrictions on opening a file that you can wire to the *open mode* terminal:

0 Read and write

1 Read only

2 Write only

3 Write only (truncate first)

If this terminal is not wired, it defaults to **0**, allowing the file to be opened for both read and write operations.

It also has the following *Deny mode* restrictions:

0 Deny Read or Write

1 Permit Read, Deny Write

2 Permit Read and Write

If not wired, the *deny mode* defaults to **2**.

Reading from a File

Any file that has been saved on the disk can also be opened and its contents retrieved or read. As shown in Fig. 8-3, you still have to specify the path of the file that you wish to open, open the file, and when you are done reading, close the file.

File Path specifies the location of the file that you want to open. The *Path Constant* or *File Dialog* function can be used to accomplish this, as discussed in the preceding section.

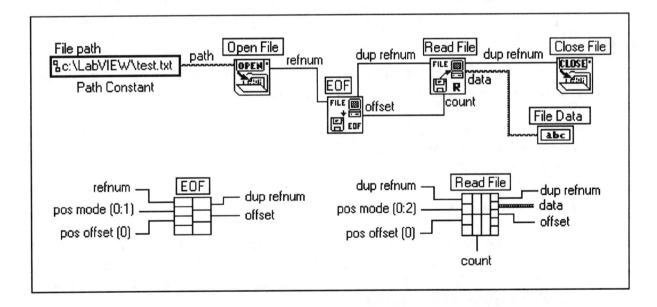

Fig. 8-3 Block Diagram for Reading from a File

267

The *Open File* function opens the file specified by the path string applied to its input and generates a refnum to be used by other file functions that will also operate on the opened file. You might have noticed in examining Fig. 8-2 that, whether you write to or read from a file, the same Open File function is used.

The **EOF** function sets and returns the *EOF, the end of file mark*, for the file that has been opened and specified by the input refnum. Refer to the terminal configuration on the connector of the EOF function, shown in Fig. 8-3.

Pos mode and **pos offset** together specify where the EOF is to be placed:

pos mode = 0 sets the EOF mark at the beginning of file plus the value of *pos offset*. For example, if pos offset = 15, the EOF mark will be set at the sixteenth ASCII character, counting from the beginning of the file.

pos mode = 1 sets the EOF mark to the end of the file plus the value of *pos offset*. Suppose that the length of the file is 1000 ASCII characters and pos offset = 5. These settings (also pos mode = 1) will place the EOF mark at the 1006th character position in the file, counting from the beginning of the file.

pos mode = 2 sets the EOF mark at the current location of the file mark plus the value of the *pos offset*.

If pos offset is left unwired, it defaults to 0 and pos mode defaults to 1. If you wire a value to the pos offset terminal, pos mode defaults to 0 and the placement of the EOF mark is determined by the pos offset value relative to the beginning of the file.

Offset output specifies the number of bytes or ASCII characters to the end of the file, counting from the beginning of the file.

The **Read File** function reads data from the file that has been opened and specified by the dup refnum. Refer to the connector and the terminal configuration of the Read File function as shown in Fig. 8-3.

Pos mode and **pos offset** together specify where the read operation begins:

pos mode = 0 and the value of *pos offset* specify how many characters to skip from the beginning of the file before reading data from the file. For example, if you set pos offset = 4 and pos mode = 0, the read operation will begin after the first four characters in the file.

pos mode = 1 and the value of *pos offset* specify how many characters to skip after the end of the file before reading new data to the file.

pos mode = 2 and the value of *pos offset* specify where to begin the read operation relative to the current position of the file mark. It is possible to set the file mark at points in the file other than at the beginning or the end of the file.

If *pos offset* is not wired, *pos mode* defaults to **0**. If *pos offset* is wired, *pos mode* defaults to **2** and the offset is measured relative to the current file mark.

The ***Data*** output terminal provides the contents of the file read in a string format.

Offset is the output in bytes that indicates the length of the file from the beginning to the current file mark.

Count input specifies the number of bytes or ASCII characters to read.

Exercise 1: Files 1 (Simple Write and Read)

In this exercise you will build a VI that illustrates how a file can be saved on the disk and read from the disk. The VI is designed so that you can instantly see what has been saved on the disk. All of the file functions discussed above are used by this VI.

Build the VI whose front panel and block diagram are shown in Fig. 8-4

Front Panel

1. **String Control/Indicator** objects are in the *String & Table* subpalette of the Controls palette. Open one string control and one string indicator and configure them as follows:

    Label: String control as ***Text to File*** and string indicator as ***Text from File***

    Text: Using the *Labeling tool* type ***Text line number*** in *File String* control. Resize the string indicator as shown in Fig. 8-4.

    Digital Control/Indicator objects are in the *Numeric* subpalette of the Controls palette. Open three digital controls and one digital indicator and configure them as follows:

    Label: the three digital controls as ***Number to file, Pos offset*** and ***Pos mode***, the digital indicator as ***Count***.

    Representation: *I16* for the three digital controls and the digital indicator.

Block Diagram

2. **Sequence Structure** is in the *Structures* subpalette of the Functions palette. Open one Sequence Structure and resize it to fill all objects, as shown in Fig. 8-4.

Sequence Frame 0

Path Constant `↳Path` is in the *File Constants* subpalette of the *File I/O* subpalette of the Function palette. Open one Path Constant and type the complete path to the file where text will be saved. As shown in Fig. 8-4, a suggested path for the file test.txt is A:\test.txt. In your computer this path may be different.

Concatenate Strings and **End of Line** are in the *String* subpalette of the Functions palette and **To Fractional** is in the *Additional String to Number Functions* subpalette of the *String* subpalette. Open one each of the above functions.

Write File and **Close File** functions are in the *File I/O* subpalette of the Functions palette and the **Open File** function is in the *Advanced File Functions* subpalette of the *File I/O* subpalette. Open one each of the above functions.

Sequence Frame 1

Sequence Frame 1 contains objects used by sequence Frame 0. You will also need the **EOF** function, which can be found in the *Advanced File Functions* subpalette of the *File I/O* of the Functions palette.

3. *Wire* all objects in the Sequence Frames 0 and 1, as shown in Fig. 8-4.

4. In this VI, test.txt file is created and one line of text is written to the file. Then the file is opened, and the contents of the file are read and displayed on a string indicator.

    In sequence frame 0, the text supplied by the *Text to file* string control is combined with the number from the *Number to file* from the digital control in the *Concatenate Strings* function, and the resulting output is applied to the data input of the *Write File* function. The last input to the Concatenate Strings function, the *End of Line* control character, terminates the text line and starts the new line. Since the Concatenate Strings function accepts only strings at its input, the numeric value from the *Number to file* terminal must first be converted to string format before being applied.

    The *pos offset* and *pos mode* front panel digital controls allow you to experiment with the effect that they have on the *Write File* function.

    As always the file must first be opened by the *Open File* function, which requires the complete function path at its input. You can use the *File Dialog* function, *path control* or the *path constant* to generate the path. In this exercise the path constant has been used. And as always you are required to close the file after the write operation is completed. This is done by the Close File function.

    Note that in this exercise it is presumed that the file *Test.txt* already exists. If it doesn't, then you can create it either manually or:

by replacing the *Open File* in sequence frame 0 by the *New File* function. As shown in this illustration, wire the Boolean constant [T|F] to the *Overwrite* terminal of the New File function. You will find that this constant is FALSE by default. Click with the operating tool to change the state of this constant to TRUE. After you run the VI once, the New File function will create the file specified in the path constant for you.

In Sequence Frame 1 the Open File function opens the file that you have written to in frame 0, reads the contents of the file, and displays the file contents on the *Text from file* string indicator. The *EOF* function is used here to produce the *offset* value, which is the length of the file in bytes. This offset value is displayed on the Count digital indicator and it is also wired to the *Count* input terminal of the *Read File* function, thus instructing the Read File function on the number of bytes to read. As usual the file is closed by the *Close File* function after the read operation is complete.

Run this VI by first entering the **Text line number** into the *Text to file* string control and **1** into the *Number to file* digital control. Make sure that the path constant in frames 0 and 1 has the proper path. Also set *pos mode* and *pos offset* to **0**. Run the VI several times, each time advancing the *Number to file* count by 1. Observe what you probably expected: the file is overwritten each time.

Now set the pos mode = **1**, leaving pos offset at **0** and repeat the above procedure. Notice that this time the new information is appended to the end of the file.

Save this VI as **Files 1.vi** in Workbook.LLB and close it.

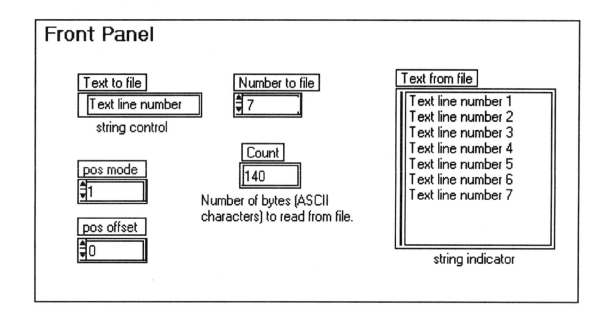

Block Diagram

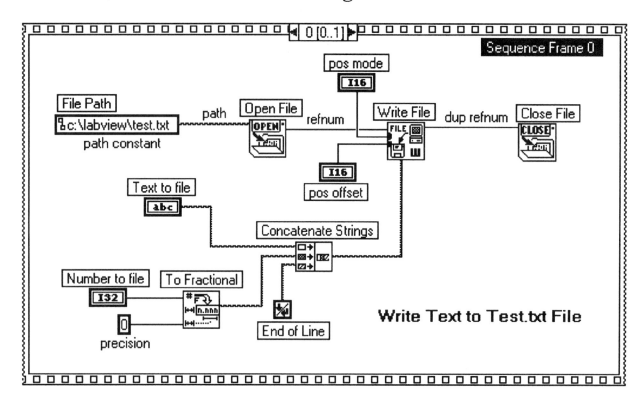

Fig. 8-4   Files 1.vi of Exercise 1

272

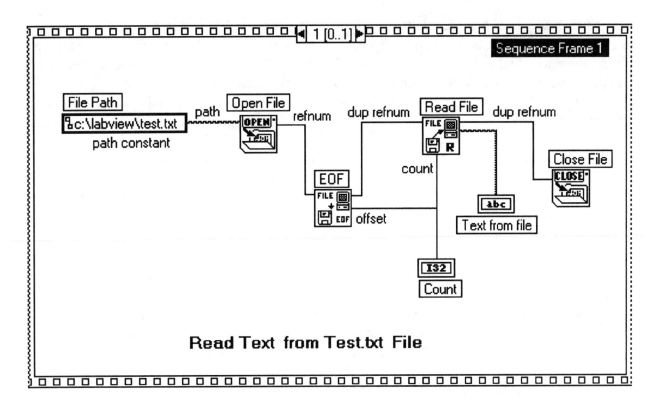

Fig. 8-4   Files 1.vi of Exercise 1 (continued)

Exercise 2: Files 2 (Collect, Store and Retrieve Data)

In this VI we will involve more of the library resources in collecting an array of data points, storing them to a file, and retrieving this data. The data collected will be, for illustration purposes, that of a sine and cosine waves. The process of data generation will be done in slow motion so that you will be able to view each line of data written to the file on the string indicator and also on the waveform chart.

The VI that you are to build is shown in Fig. 8-5. The Block Diagram consists of four *Sequence* frames. Sequence frame 0 includes *Numeric Cases* 0, 1 and 2 and *Sequence* frame 1 also includes three frames of Numeric Case structure. Notice that the additional Numeric Case frames are shown immediately below the Sequence frame in Fig. 8-5. Following is the detailed, step-by-step procedure for building this VI.

Front Panel

1. **Waveform Chart** is in the *Graph* subpalette of the Controls palette. Open one Waveform Chart, resize it as necessary, and configure it as follows:
   Labels: **Data to file chart** is an owned label and **Angle (degrees)** is a free label
   Auto Scale X and *Y*: disable
   Y scale: max = 1 and min = −1.
   X scale: max = 72 and min = 0.
   Palette: disable
   Legend: resize for two plots, and using the *Labeling Tool*, delete Plots 0 and 1 and replace them with **sine** and **cosine**, as shown in Fig. 8-5. Pop up on the inside Legend *sine* window and choose the color you wish for the sine plot. Choose another color for the *cosine* plot by popping up inside the Legend cosine window. Instead of color, you may use a different *point style* for the plots, as shown in the front panel of Fig. 8-5.

   String Indicator is in the *String & Table* subpalette of the Controls palette. Open two string indicators and label them using an owned label as **Data line to file**. Label the other string indicator with an owned label as **Data from file**. Resize it and add the *Scrollbar* by popping up inside the string indicator and then choosing **Show>Scrollbar** from the popup menu.

   Digital Control/Indicator objects are in the *Numeric* subpalette of the Controls palette. Open one digital control and one digital indicator and configure them as follows:
   Label: digital control as **Num data pts.** and digital indicator as **File length (bytes)**
   Representation: **I16**

   File Path Control is in the *Path & Refnum* subpalette of the Controls palette. Open one File Path Control and, using the *Labeling Tool*, type the complete path of the file. A suggested path is shown in the front panel of Fig. 8-5. Label the file path control as **File Path** using an owned label.

274

Vertical Pointer Slide is in the *Numeric* subpalette of the Controls palette. Open one Vertical Pointer Slide and label it as shown in Fig. 8-5. For more information on configuring the vertical pointer slide, see Fig. 7-4 of Chapter 7. Label the slide using an owned label as *File Status*.

Block Diagram

2.   **Sequence Structure** is in the *Structures* subpalette of the Functions palette. Open one Sequence structure and resize it as necessary. You will notice that as you open the sequence frame, there is no frame window at the top to identify this frame as frame 0. Don't worry about that right now. This unmarked frame is Frame 0. This situation will be corrected when you get to the next frame.

Sequence Frame 0

Open Case Structure inside the Sequence Frame 0 and resize it. You will find Case Structure in the *Structures* subpalette in the Functions palette.

Wire the **File Status** terminal to the *Selector* terminal **[?]** of the Case and observe the Boolean Case change to Numeric Case. You will next build three Numeric Case frames inside the Sequence frame 0 as follows:

Numeric Case 0

Open one **Open File** function. It is in the *Advanced File Functions* subpalette of the *File I/O* subpalette of the Functions palette.

Wire all objects as shown in Sequence Frame 0 of Fig. 8-5.

Numeric Case 1

Switch to Numeric Case 1 by clicking on the arrow button in the Case window.

Open one **Open File** function and one **EOF** function, which you will find in the *Advanced File Functions* subpalette of the *File I/O* subpalette of the Functions palette inside Numeric Case 1.

Wire all objects as shown in Numeric Case 1 of Fig. 8-5.

Numeric Case 2

Switch to Numeric Case 2 by clicking inside, Case window and choosing *Add Case After* from the pop up menu.

Open one **New File** function, which you will find in the *Advanced File Functions* subpalette of the *File I/O* subpalette of the Functions palette. *Wire all objects* as shown in Numeric Case 2 of Fig. 8-5. Notice that the Boolean constant set to *true* is wired to the *overwrite* input terminal of the New File function. You will find the Boolean constant in the *Boolean* subpalette of the Functions palette. Use the operating tool to change its state from *false* to *true*.

Sequence Frame 1

Switch to Sequence Frame 1 by popping up on the frame border and choosing *Add Frame After*. Notice that the frame window appears and identifies this frame as Frame 1, with Frame 0 behind it.

For Loop is in the *Structures* subpalette of the Functions palette. Open one For Loop inside Sequence Frame 1, resize it, and *wire* the *Num. data pts.* terminal to the Loop counter terminal *N*, as shown in Sequence Frame 1 of Fig. 8-5.

All of the following objects are to be placed inside the For Loop:
Sine and **Cosine** functions are in the *Trigonometric* subpalette of the *Numeric* subpalette of the Functions palette. Open one of each.

Concatenate Strings is in the *String* subpalette of the Functions palette. Open one Concatenate Strings function and resize it to accommodate eight inputs.

To Fractional is in the *Additional String to Number* subpalette of the *String* subpalette of the Functions palette. Open three *To Fractional* string functions. As shown in Fig. 8-5 a numeric constant **2** is wired to the *precision* input of two of these functions and **0** to the third. Recall that the precision input decides on the number of decimal places that the numerical value will have in the output.

Wait Until Next ms Multiple is in the *Time & Dialog* subpalette of the Functions palette. In this VI it creates a time delay of 0.5 second between iterations, as determined by the value of the numeric constant wired to the input of this function. To change the delay time, enter another value into this numeric constant.

Tab and **End of Line** control characters are in the *String* subpalette of the Functions palette. Open one of each.

The **Bundle** structure is in the *Cluster* subpalette of the Functions palette. Open one Bundle structure. In this VI the Bundle combines the sine and cosine waves for display on the *Data to file chart*.

Multiply, Divide and **Numeric Constant** are in the *Numeric* subpalette of the Functions palette. Open two multiply functions, one divide function, and five numeric constants.

Open one **Pi** 🔲 constant, which is in the *Additional Numeric Constants* subpalette of *Numeric* subpalette of the Functions palette.

Wire all objects inside the For Loop as shown Sequence Frame 1 of Fig. 8-5. This does not include the Numeric Case, which you will build after wiring. Follow the suggested object layout shown in Fig. 8-5, leaving room for the case structure in the lower righthand corner of the For Loop.

Open **Case Structure** inside the For Loop, resize it, and ***wire*** the *File Status* local variable to the selector terminal [?] of the case structure. For more information on how to create a local variable, see Exercise 3 of Chapter 6 under the Numeric Case 1 section.

Numeric Case 0

Open the **Write File** function, which you will find in the *File I/O* subpalette of the Functions palette.
***Wire*:**

> **0** and **1** numeric constants to the *pos offset* and *pos mode* input terminals of the Write File function, respectively.

> Concatenate Strings output to the *data* input terminal of the Write File function.

> *Refnum* from sequence local input to the *refnum* input terminal of the Write File function. Notice that the tunnel , a black rectangle, is formed when you wire through the wall of the For Loop and the Numeric Case 0.

Numeric Case 1

Switch to Numeric Case 1 by clicking on the arrow button in the Case window. *Open* the **Write File** function, which you will find in the *File I/O* subpalette of the Functions palette.
Wire:

> from the tunnel (data) to the *data* input terminal of the Write File function.

> from the tunnel (refnum) to the *refnum* input terminal of the File Write function.

Numeric Case 2

Switch to Numeric Case 2 by clicking inside the Case window and choosing ***Add Case After*** from the popup menu.
Open the **Write File** function, which you will find in the *File I/O* subpalette of the Functions palette.
Wire:

> from the tunnel (data) to the *data* input terminal of the Write File function.

> from the tunnel (refnum) to the *refnum* input terminal of the Write File function.

Sequence Frame 2

Switch to Sequence Frame 2 by popping up anywhere on the frame border and choosing *Add Frame After* from the popup menu.

Open one **Close File** function, which is in the *File I/O* subpalette of the Functions palette. *Wire* the *sequence local* (refnum) to the *refnum* input terminal of the Close File function.

Sequence Frame 3

Switch to Sequence Frame 3 by popping up anywhere on the frame border and choosing *Add Frame After* from the popup menu.

Create the **File Path** local variable. For more information on how to create a local variable, refer to Exercise 3 in Chapter 6 under the Numeric Case 1 section.

Open **File** and **EOF** functions are in the *Advanced File Functions* subpalette of the *File I/O* subpalette of the Functions palette. Open one of each.

Read File and **Close File** functions are in the *File I/O* subpalette of Functions palette. Open one of each.

Wire all objects as shown in Sequence Frame 3 of Fig. 8-5.

3. The sequence structure used in this VI ensures that various operations are executed in the proper order.

In Frame 0 the Vertical Pointer Slide specifies the Numeric case number to be executed. The local variable of the Vertical pointer slide appears also in Sequence Frame 1 and also controls the Numeric case in that frame. The three Numeric Cases in Sequence frames 0 and 1 decide whether an existing file will be opened or a new file will be created. If a New File is created, the new data will be written from the beginning of the file. But if an existing file is opened, then the user is given an option to overwrite or append new data. The Vertical Pointer Slide is used to select these options.

In Sequence Frame 0 the sine and cosine data points are collected in a column format. The value of sine and cosine is calculated in 5 degree increments. The first column includes the value of the angle in degrees and the second and third columns, contain the sine and cosine values. Two tabs between columns separate the columns, and the End of Line control character terminates the line of data and starts a new line. With each iteration of the For Loop one line of data is stored in the file, and displayed on the *Data line to file* string indicator and as two points on the *Data to file chart*. The *Num. data pts.* digital control specifies the number of data lines. The *Wait Until the Next ms Multiple* provides the time delay between loop iterations, thus slowing down the operation so that you can follow it. The time delay is set to 0.5 seconds in this VI. You can change that to another value. Upon the completion of the write operation, the file is closed in Sequence Frame 2.

In Sequence Frame 3 the file containing the data that was written in the preceding frames is now opened for read operation. The data extracted from the file is displayed on the *Data from file* string control and the number of ASCII characters in the file is displayed on the File Length digital indicator. Notice that the file length information is provided by the *offset* output terminal of the EOF function. It is displayed and also applied to the *count* input, thus specifying the number of bytes starting at the beginning of the file that the *Read File* function should read.

In short the four sequence frames specify the complete file path, open the file or create a new file, write to the file, and then read the contents of the file. As you view the execution of this VI, you will see the data lines being stored and displayed on the chart in slow motion. At the end of execution you will see on the string indicator the actual content of the file that was opened.

In the Front Panel, enter 73 into the *Num. data pts.* digital control, the complete path of the file where data will be saved. With the *Operating tool* set the File Status (vertical pointer slide) to *Overwrite*.

Run the VI. Experiment with different settings of the Front Panel Controls. Check the contents of the file where data was stored. You can use any word processor to open the text file. Microsoft Window's *Write*, for example, can be used for this purpose.

Save this VI as **Files 2.vi** in Workbook.LLB and close it.

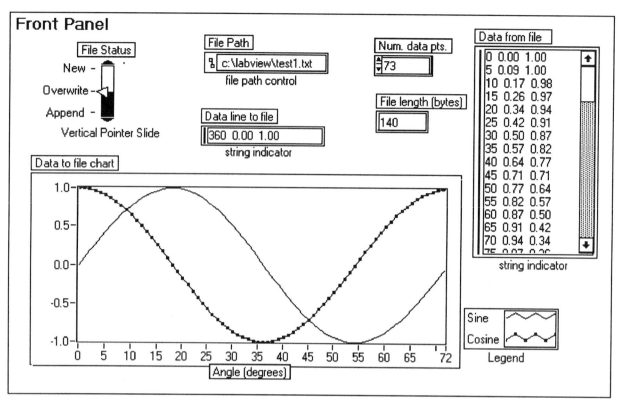

Block Diagram

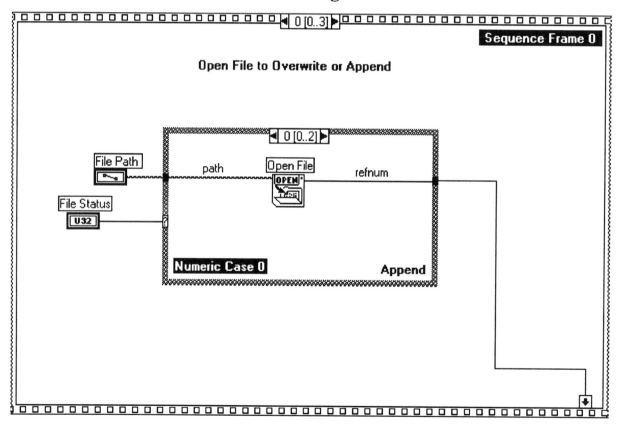

Fig. 8-5 Files 2.vi of Exercise 2

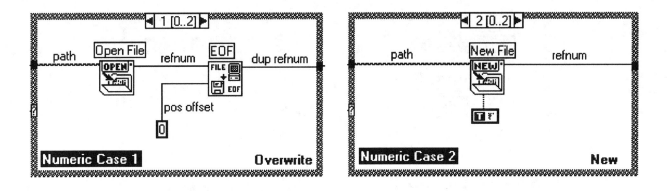

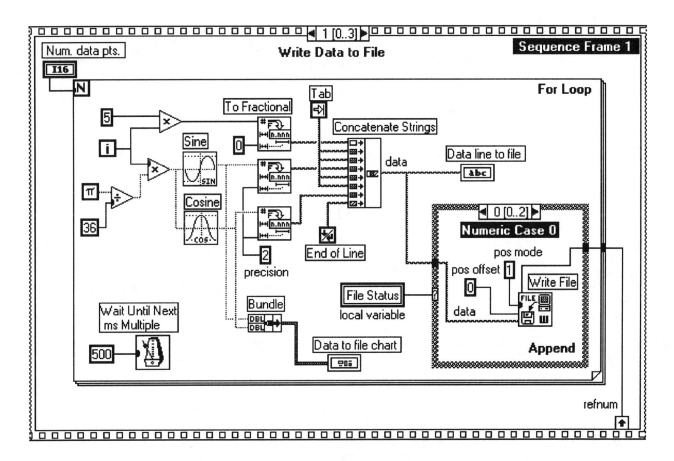

Fig. 8-5 Files 2.vi of Exercise 2 (continued)

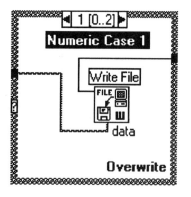

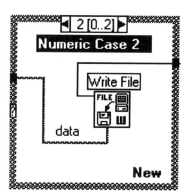

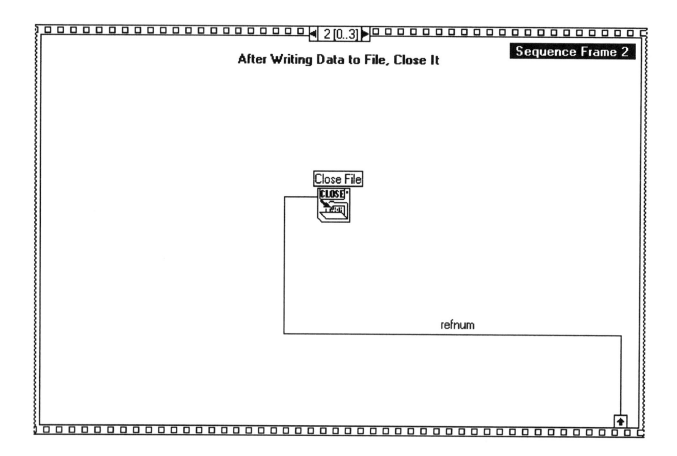

Fig. 8-5 Files 2.vi of Exercise 2 (continued)

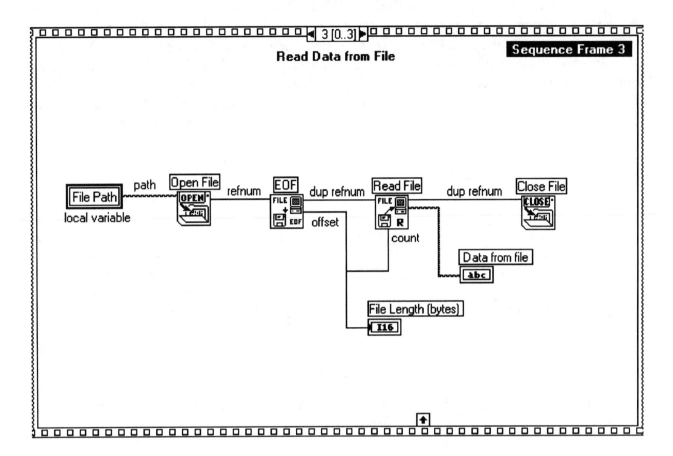

Fig. 8-5 Files 2.vi of Exercise 2 (continued)

Utility File I/O VIs

In the previous exercises the procedure of saving data to a file or reading data from a file required the user to configure array file I/O functions such as Open File or New File, Read or Write File, and Close File. LabVIEW also has utility VIs that include all of those individual steps. Also the input data is in the form of an array of single precision numbers and does not have to be converted to the string format by the user. This illustration shows the icon and the connector of the *Write To Spreadsheet File.vi.*

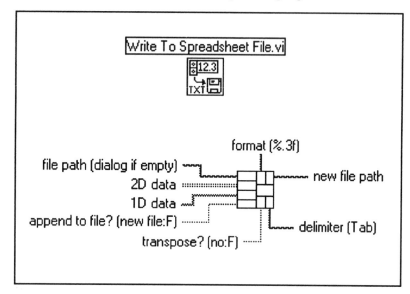

File path input is the complete path to the file. If this input is not wired, then the VI will open a dialog box, giving you access to directories and allowing you to choose the file.

2D and **1D** inputs are the array data that are to be saved in the selected file.

Append to file? Boolean input can be used to append or overwrite the file. It is *false* by default. If you wire a *true*, the new data will be appended to the file.

Transpose? Boolean input is used to transpose the array input data (switch rows and columns) before saving it. It is *false* by default.

Delimiter string input is *Tab* by default. The data that you save using this VI is in the spreadsheet format. This means that the VI inserts a *tab* between the columns and an *end of line* control character at the end of the data line. You can override this default setting by wiring another character such as a comma in string format.

Format string input specifies the format to be used by this VI on the input data. It is *%.3f* by default. The **%** begins the format specification and is a required control character. Following the period (.) is the precision string specifying the number of decimal places. The conversion character **f** specifies how to convert the input number. The default specifier **f** converts the input number *to a floating point number with fractional format.* You can override this default format specification by wiring another format string. The number before the period, for instance, may be used to specify the field width, and f can be replaced by a **d**, which converts the input data to *decimal integers.* Refer to the LabVIEW Function Manual for more information.

The *Read From Spreadsheet File.vi* icon and the connector is shown in Fig. 8-6. This VI will open the file specified in the file path input string and output the file data as an array. After the *read* operation is complete, the VI will close the file. If the file path input is left unwired, then the VI will open the dialog box, allowing you to choose the file. The inputs and outputs for this VI are described below.

File Path is the complete path of the file to be read. If the path is not wired, the VI will open the file dialog box from which you can select the file.

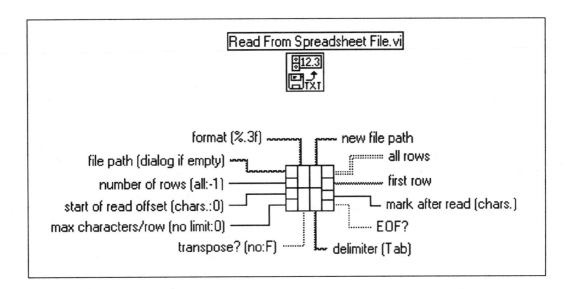

Fig. 8-6 Icon and Connector of the Read From Spreadsheet File.vi

The *Number of Rows* numeric input specifies the maximum number of rows to be read by the VI. If the Number of Rows < 0, the VI will read the entire file. The default value is −1. A row is defined as a character string ending in a line control character such as carriage return, line feed, carriage return followed by a line feed, or a string that has the maximum line length as specified by the *Max Characters/row* input.

Start of Read Offset is a numeric input specifying the number of characters or bytes from the beginning of the file where reading is to begin. The default value of the offset is 0.

Max Characters/Row is the numeric input specifying the maximum number of characters that the VI is to read. The default value is 0, which means that there is no limit on the number of characters to be read by the VI.

Transpose? Boolean input specifies whether to transpose the data after converting it from a string format. The default value is *false*.

285

Mark After Read is the numeric output of the number of characters or bytes read from the file.

EOF? Boolean output indicates whether the read operation extended beyond the end of the file.

Delimiter string input is used to format columns in spreadsheets. Although the default delimiter is *tab*, you can use other delimiters.

Format input string specifies the conversion of characters to numbers. The default format is *%.3f*.

All Rows is a two-dimensional array data output. This is the data read from the file.

First Row is the first row is a one-dimensional array of the *All Rows* output data.

As shown in this illustration, there are other Utility File Function VIs. The ***Write Characters To File.vi*** opens a file and writes the input *character string* to the file and then closes the file.

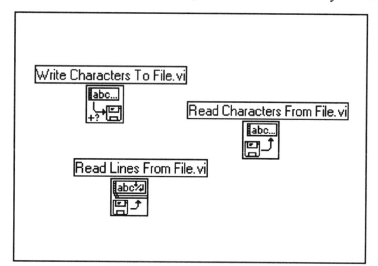

Similarly the ***Read Characters From File.vi*** opens the file, reads the characters at the specified position in the file, outputs the character string, and closes the file.

The ***Read Lines From File.vi*** reads the specified line of characters, outputs it as a line string, and then closes the file.

Exercise 3: Files 3 (Using the Utility File I/O VIs)

This exercise illustrates the use of the Utility File I/O VIs. The VI that you will build collects data from three different sources and saves it to a spreadsheet, then reads that data from a file and displays it on the X-Y graph and on the digital array indicator. As the VI runs, you will be able to see immediately the data that was saved to the file.

Build the VI according to the following guidelines. The front panel and the block diagram are shown in Fig. 8-7.

Front Panel

1. **X-Y Graph** is in the *Graph* subpalette of the Controls palette. Open one X-Y Graph, resize it as necessary, and configure it as follows:
   Labels: **Data from file graph** is an owned label.
   Auto Scale X and *Y*: leave enabled (default)
   Palette: remove from screen.

   Digital Control/Indicator objects are in the *Numeric* subpalette of the Controls palette. Open two digital controls and one digital indicator and configure them as follows:
   Label: the two digital controls as **K** and **Num. Cycles**, the digital indicator as **Num bytes from file**. All are owned labels.
   Representation: **I16** for the two digital controls and the digital indicator.

   File Path Control is in the *Path & Refnum* subpalette of the Controls palette. Open one File Path Control and, using the *Labeling Tool*, type the complete path of the file. A suggested path is shown in the front panel of Fig. 8-7. Label the file path control as **File Path** using an owned label.

   Vertical Pointer Slide is in *Numeric* subpalette of the Controls palette. Open one Vertical Pointer Slide and label it as shown in Fig. 8-7. For more information on configuring the vertical pointer slide, see Fig. 7-4 of Chapter 7. Label the slide, using an owned label as, **Select Plot**.

   Array is in the *Array & Cluster* subpalette of the Controls palette. Open one empty array shell and configure it as follows:
   Dimension: Two. Pop up inside the array index window and choose **Add Dimension** from the popup menu.
   Create Digital Array Indicator: Pop up inside the empty array shell, navigate to the Numeric subpalette, choose Digital Indicator, and drop the digital indicator inside the array shell.
   Resize: Optional. You can leave the array with one digital indicator and operate the arrow index buttons to view a particular element, or you can resize the array to display many elements, as shown in the front panel of Fig. 8-7.

287

Block Diagram

2. **Sequence Structure** is in the *Structures* subpalette of the Functions palette. Open one Sequence structure and resize it as necessary. You will notice that as you open the sequence frame, there is no frame window at the top to identify this frame as frame 0. Don't worry about that right now. This unmarked frame is frame 0. This situation will be corrected when you get to the next frame.

<u>Sequence Frame 0</u> *(Save Data From File)*

For Loop is in the *Structures* subpalette of the Functions palette. Open one For Loop, resize it and *wire objects inside the For Loop as follows*:

Formula Node is in the *Structures* subpalette of the Functions palette. Open one Formula Node and type inside the Formula Node :
x = (2*K/N)*(i −N/2);
Pop up on the border of the Formula Node and create **N** and **K** inputs, and **i** and **x** outputs.

The *Numeric subpalette* of the Functions palette has all of the remaining objects that you need inside the For Loop as follows:
Multiply function: you need three.
Divide Function: you need one.
Random Number function
Sine and **Sinc** functions are in the *Trigonometric* subpalette of the Numeric subpalette.
To Word Integer function is in the *Conversion* subpalette of the Numeric subpalette of the Functions palette.
$\boxed{2\pi}$ is in the *Additional Numeric Constants* subpalette of the Numeric subpalette of the Functions palette.
Numeric Constant: you need three: **50, 100** and **100**. Notice that the 100 numeric constant is wired from outside the For Loop to the loop counter *N* and *N* input of the Formula Node.
$\boxed{i}$ is the loop iteration terminal. It was inside the loop when you opened it.
Wire all objects inside the For Loop as shown in Sequence Frame 0 of Fig. 8-7.

Build Array is in the *Array* subpalette of the Functions palette. Open one Build Array structure and resize it to accommodate six inputs as shown in Sequence Frame 0 of Fig. 8-7.

Transpose 2D Array is in the *Array* subpalette of the Functions palette. Open one Transpose 2D Array function.

Write To Spreadsheet File.vi is in the *File I/O* subpalette of the Functions palette. Open one write to spreadsheet VI.

Wire all objects inside Sequence Frame 0 as shown in Fig. 8-7.

Sequence Frame 1 *(Read Data from File)*
Switch to Sequence Frame 1 by popping up on the frame border and choosing *Add Frame After*. Notice that the frame window appears and identifies this frame as Frame 1, with Frame 0 behind it.

> **Case Structure** is in the *Structures* subpalette of the Functions palette. Open one Case Structure inside Sequence Frame 1 as shown in Fig. 8-7, resize it, and *wire Select Plot* terminal the selector terminal **[?]** of the Case Structure.

Numeric Case 0
You will need the following objects inside Numeric Case 0:
> **Index Array** is in the *Array* subpalette of the Functions palette. Open two
> Index Array functions, and resize them by dragging the lower corner
> > down to accommodate two index inputs. Disable the upper index
> > input by popping up on the index and choosing *Disable Indexing*.
> > The black rectangle will change to white as shown here
> **Bundle** is in the *Cluster* subpalette of the Functions palette
> $\boxed{\pi}$ is in the *Additional Numeric Constants* subpalette of the *Numeric* sub-
> > palette of the Functions palette.
> **Numeric Constant** is in the *Numeric* subpalette of the Functions palette.
> > You will need three numeric constants: **3, 4** and **180**.
> **Multiply** and **Divide** functions are in the *Numeric* subpalette of the
> > Functions palette. You will need one of each.
> *Wire* all objects inside Numeric Case 0, as shown in Fig. 8-7.

Numeric Case 1
Switch to Numeric Case 1.
Wire all objects inside Numeric Case 1 as shown in Fig. 8-7. All objects in this
> Numeric Case were covered in Numeric Case 0 above. *Data from file
> graph* is a *local variable*. Refer to Exercise 3 in Chapter 6 under the
> Numeric Case 1 section for more information on local variables.

Numeric Case 2
Switch to Numeric Case 2 by popping up inside the Case window at the top of the
> case and choosing *Add Case After*.
Wire all objects inside Numeric Case 2 as shown in Fig. 8-7. All objects in this
> Numeric Case were covered in Numeric Case 0 above. *Data from file
> graph* is a *local variable*. Refer to Exercise 3 in Chapter 6 under the
> Numeric Case 1 section for more information on local variables.

Read From Spreadsheet File.vi is in the *File I/O* subpalette of the Functions palette.

Wire all objects inside Sequence Frame 1 and outside the Numeric Case structure, as shown in Fig. 8-7. Note that *File Path* is a local variable. Refer to Exercise 3 in Chapter 6 under the Numeric Case 1 section for more information on local variables.

3. In this VI the function of Sequence Frame 0 is to collect data from three different sources and save this data in the spreadsheet format to the text file as specified by the path control. 100 data points (0 to 99) of the Sinc function are collected as an array at the border of the For Loop. Also 100 points for the sinewave and 100 points for the random number generator have been collected at the border of the For Loop. The x, i and angle arrays are formed at the border of the For Loop as well. These arrays are completed when the For Loop executes 100 times.

The six arrays are combined in the Bundle structure and transposed by the Transpose 2D Array function before being applied to the Write To Spreadsheet File.vi utility. Transposing of the arrays is necessary because they are formed by the For Loop horizontally. Transposing switches rows and columns so that the x array will be in the first column, the i array in the second column, the Sinc array in the third column, and so on.

The purpose of Sequence Frame 1 is to extract the data array of interest from the spreadsheet and display it on the X-Y graph. The Read From Spreadsheet File.vi utility opens the file specified by the path control, reads the data, and outputs it as a two-dimensional array. This two-dimensional array is applied to the Numeric Case structure.

The Select Plot Vertical Slide decides which Numeric Case will be executed. If you set the vertical pointer slide with the operating tool to the Sinewave position, its corresponding terminal in Sequence Frame 1 has a value of 0 that is applied to the selector terminal [?] of the Numeric Case, thus forcing Numeric Case 0 to be executed.

Inside Numeric Case 0 the two Index Array functions slice away columns 3 and 4 from the incoming two-dimensional array. Column 3 is the 100 points of the sinewave and column 4 is the corresponding 100 points of the angle, or the argument of the sinewave.

In this segment 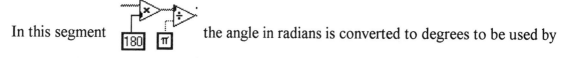 the angle in radians is converted to degrees to be used by the X-Y graph for the X-axis. The x-array and the y-array are combined in the Bundle structure and then applied to the X-Y graph.

290

In a similar fashion, choosing the Sinc function on the Vertical Pointer Slide will force Numeric Case 1 to be executed, and the Random Number setting will cause Numeric Case 2 to be executed.

The setting of the **K** value on the front panel determines the range of the X-axis. Notice that the setting of 20 in the front panel of Fig. 8-7 results in X-axis range −20 to +20. K is used only for the Sinc function display.

The *Num. Cycles* digital control setting specifies the number of cycles of the sinewave to be collected and displayed. This control applies only to the sinewave data.

The six columns of data are also displayed on the *Data from file array* Digital Array Indicator. The total number of bytes or characters read from the file is displayed on the *Num. bytes from file* digital indicator.

Run this VI. Be sure to enter first the file path in the path control and the values of K and the Num. Cycles.

Save this VI as **Files 3.vi** in Workbook.LLB and close it.

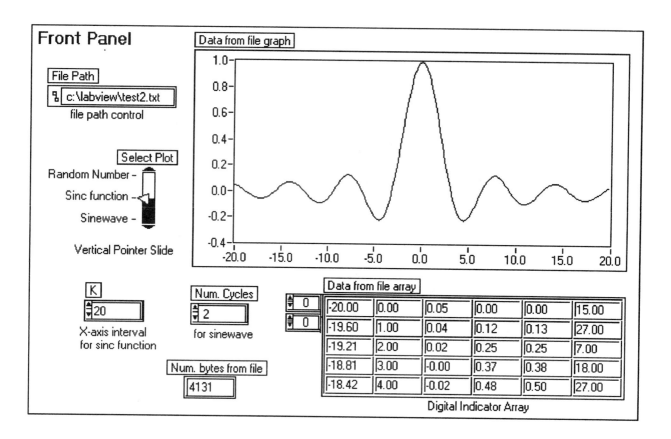

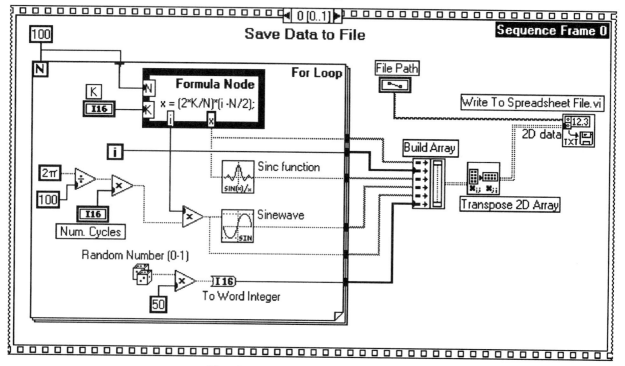

Fig. 8-7   Files 3.vi of Exercise 3

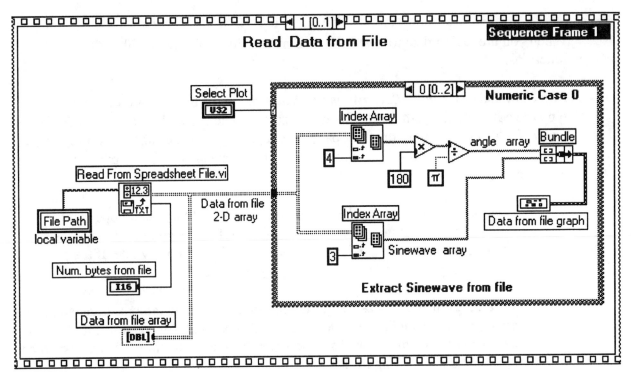

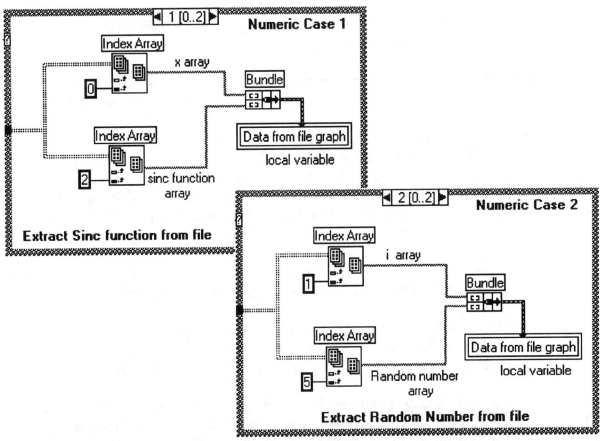

Fig. 8-7 Files 3.vi of Exercise 3 (continued)

293

Summary

1. When you are saving data to a *new file*, you must wire the following File I/O functions:

    File Path can be a *File Path Constant* that you open in the block diagram and where you type the complete file path for the file where data is to be saved, or it can be a *File Path Control* which you open in the front panel. If you don't like either of these options, you can use the *File Dialog* function, which allows you to specify the file by giving you access to directories.

    New File function creates the file specified by the path input and opens it for writing new data. It generates the *refnum*, the reference number that uniquely identifies the file, to be used by functions that follow the New File. If the path input is not wired, it uses its default setting, the File Dialog.

    Write File function writes data to the file specified by the refnum. It generates the *dup refnum*, the duplication reference number that uniquely identifies the opened file, to be used by functions that follow the Write File function. The data written to the file must be in string format.

    Close File function closes the file specified by the dup refnum input. It is your responsibility to close each file that you open.

2. The procedure for saving data to an *existing file* is the same as that used for saving data to a new file, except that the **Open File** function is used in place of the New File function.

3. To extract data from a file you must wire the following File I/O functions:
    File Path can be a *File Path Constant* that you open in the block diagram and where you type the complete file path for the file where data is to be saved, or it can be a *File Path Control* that you open in the front panel. If you don't like either of these options, you can use the *File Dialog* function, which allows you to specify the file by giving you access to directories.

    Open File opens the file specified by the path input. It generates a refnum output to be used by other functions that follow the Open File Function.

    The **Read File** function reads from the file specified by the refnum input a number of bytes or characters as specified by the *count* input and outputs them at the *data* output terminal. The data read from the file will be in string format.

    The **EOF** function returns the End of File mark for the file specified by the refnum input. *Pos mode* and *pos offset* together specify where the EOF mark is placed. The EOF reverts to its default setting, placing the EOF mark at the end of the file if pos mode and pos offset are left unwired.

This will force the EOF function to produce at its *offset* output the file length in bytes (a count of bytes from the beginning of the file to the EOF mark at the end of the file), making it convenient to wire the *offset output* of the EOF function to the *count input* of the Read File function and thus specifying that the entire file is to be read.

The *Close File* function closes the file specified by the dup refnum input. It is your responsibility to close each file that you open.

4. Utility File VIs relieve you of the responsibility of wiring the opening, closing and read/write functions. They do all that and don't require that you present the data for writing in string format. They also save your data to a spreadsheet file that other spreadsheet applications can read.

> *Write To Spreadsheet File.vi* accepts the input data as a one-dimensional or two-dimensional array and saves it to the file specified by the *file path* input in the form of a spreadsheet. It places *tab* characters between the columns and the *end of line* control character constant at the end of each line. You may choose to *transpose* the data or to *append* the data to the end of the file by wiring the appropriate Boolean inputs.

> *Read From Spreadsheet File.vi* reads data from the file specified *file path* input and outputs the data as a two-dimensional array of single precision numbers, including all rows or the *first row* of the two-dimensional array. If the file path is not wired, the utility will open the dialog box for you to choose the file.

> *Write Characters To File.vi* writes the character string to the file specified by the file path input.

> *Read Characters From File.vi* reads the characters at the specified position in the file and outputs the character string.

> *Read Lines From File.vi* reads the specified line of characters from the file and outputs it as a character string.

All Utility File I/O VIs first open the file, perform the read or write operation, and then close the file.

Chapter 9

Data Acquisition

In this chapter you will learn about:
Basic data acquisition theory
Data acquisition components
Data acquisition VIs
Immediate single point data input acquisition
Waveform input data acquisition

Basics of Data Acquisition

What Is Data Acquisition?

Data acquisition is the process that allows you to bring inside the computer from the outside world information representing a physical variable. The physical variable may be temperature, pressure, relative humidity, speed of a motor, a chemical process variable, and many others. Since electronic components can recognize only voltage or current and are unable to recognize directly such physical quantities as temperature or pressure, we need a transducer.

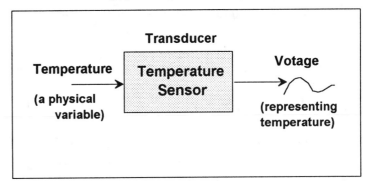

The transducer converts a physical variable into voltage or current. As shown in this illustration, a temperature sensor converts temperature into a voltage analog signal that represents temperature. The analog signal is then applied to the data acquisition board, where it is converted into a digital signal. This brings us to an important question. What components do you need to perform data acquisition?

Data Acquisition Components

LabVIEW Software... First, you need a software environment in which you can operate. Of course, we are using LabVIEW as the environment inside which we will be acquiring data.

DAQ Board... plugs into your PC's expansion slot. It serves as the interface between the real world and the computer, allowing data to enter or leave the computer.

DAQ board contains many components that are necessary for data acquisition. A typical board has 16 analog input data channels that are multiplexed and applied to the instrumentation amplifier. The A/D converter digitizes the analog data. The onboard FIFO (**F**irst **I**n **F**irst **O**ut memory) provides a temporary storage of data in buffered data acquisition applications.

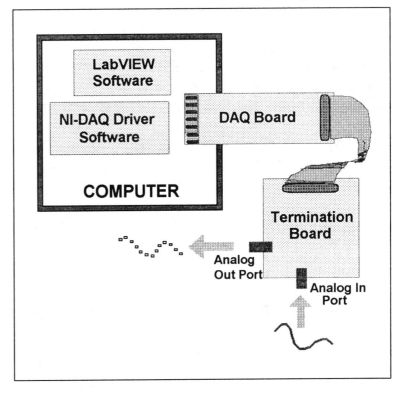

There are also two D/A converters that convert digital data to analog form and pass it to the analog output ports for use by external devices.

There are also digital I/O ports that allow for exchange of digital data between the computer and external devices.

The onboard counter/timer chips provide an opportunity for the user to interact with the hardware. In many applications such as motion control, software overhead is too excessive, resulting in software being unable to keep up with a control application. In that case the use of timed waveforms can be quite effective in speeding up the application.

National Instruments (NI) offers several DAQ boards that vary in speed and resolution.

NI-DAQ Driver Software... is a high-level software for the plug-in DAQ boards. NI-DAQ takes care of all low-level hardware and system programming, providing transparent DMA (direct memory access) and interrupt services. It has routines for analog and digital I/O, counter/timer, calibration, and configuration. It also provides support for RTSI (Real-Time System Interface Bus developed by National Instruments for DAQ board products), where multiple DAQ boards are synchronized in a data acquisition process.

Termination Board... plugs in the DAQ board via a ribbon cable and provides you with access to various pins and signals that are on the DAQ board and are not otherwise easily accessible because the board is inside the computer. A typical termination board has a provision for wiring passive components to the analog input channels to provide signal conditioning such as filtering. A general purpose breadboard area allows you to construct additional circuits.

Finally you must configure the DAQ board. This makes LabVIEW aware that indeed you have a data acquisition board plugged into the computer ready for use. To configure the DAQ board, you must run the WDAQCONF utility, which you will find in the LabVIEW group window inside Windows Program manager. Among other things, the WDAQCONF utility assigns the *device number* to your board. You may have more than one board plugged in and each board has its own device number. If you have only one board then its device number will be 1. When you build data acquisition VIs later in this chapter, you will be asked to provide the device number.

How Is Data Acquired?

The process of data acquisition begins with sampling the input waveform, as shown in this illustration. The sample and hold (S/H) circuit breaks down the continuous input analog waveform into discrete samples. Each sample corresponds to the instantaneous value of the analog input voltage during the sampling pulse. The analog to digital converter (A/D) produces a 12 bit word for each sample.

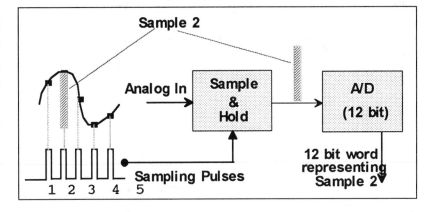

Notice that once it is sampled, the input waveform loses its continuity, represented by a group of digitized samples. If this waveform has to be restored, the best we can do is to represent it by those black dots, the sampling points, that you see in this illustration, and anything between the dots has been lost forever. This is the price that one has to pay in digitizing the waveform.

The *Sampling Rate* specifies the frequency at which the analog waveform is to be sampled. According to Nyquist, your sampling frequency must be at least twice the highest frequency component in the waveform being sampled. If you are sampling a sinewave whose frequency is 25 kHz, for example, your minimum sampling frequency should be 50 kHz.

Nyquist's sampling theorem sets the theoretical minimum sampling rate. However, in practical applications the actual sampling rate is higher.

Although the actual sampling rate can be set by the user in a particular application, the maximum sampling rate is set by the design of the board. Actually the maximum sampling rate depends on the A/D converter settling time specification. A/D experiences a transient response after each conversion, and the next conversion cannot be done until the transients subside to an acceptable level, as determined by the settling time.

For example, the MIO-16E-10 is a multipurpose I/O data acquisition board with 16 analog inputs and a settling time of 10 μsec. The inverse of the 10 μsec. settling time determines the maximum sampling rate of 100 kHz. According to Nyquist, the highest theoretical frequency that can be sampled using this board is 50 kHz which, as mentioned earlier, might be too restrictive, and a lower value should be used.

Resolution and Accuracy

Resolution is another important data acquisition parameter. It is the number of bits that the A/D converter uses to represent an analog signal. It also represents the smallest analog input that the A/D is capable of detecting. Resolution is determined as follows:

$$\text{Resolution} = (\text{Voltage Range})/(\text{Gain} \cdot 2^N)$$

where:

> *Voltage Range*, also known as the full scale voltage (FS), refers to the minimum and maximum voltage levels that the A/D can digitize. It is typically 0 to 10 V or −10 to 10 V.
>
> *Gain* is the gain of the instrumentation amplifier that precedes the A/D converter.
>
> N = number of bits.

If, for example, you are using a board with 12 bits of resolution and a voltage range of 0 to 10 V, the worst case resolution is

$$\frac{10}{2^{12}} = 2.44 \text{ mV}$$

This means that any analog input change smaller than 2.44 mV cannot be detected by the A/D converter. Thus inputs of 1 mV and 1.5 mV will be assigned the same 12 bit code at the A/D converter's output. Or if the analog input changes from 5.000 V to 5.001 V or to 4.999 V, the A/D digital output will remain unchanged and the code at the output of the A/D will remain at the 5.000 V level.

Notice that with a 12 bit A/D, a 10 V input range is divided into 4096 (2^{12}) small voltage ranges, each range 2.44 mV wide and each having a unique 12 bit code assigned to it. The higher the number of bits, the finer will be the voltage intervals into which the input range is divided and the better will be the approximation by the samples of the waveform being digitized. A board with a 16 bit resolution will divide a 10 volt input range into 2^{16} or 65,536 intervals, each interval being equal to 0.15 mV.

Fig. 9-1 illustrates the A/D conversion of a triangular waveform. In this example we are using a 3 bit A/D converter and 8 volt FS voltage. With three bits, there are only 8 binary codes, but between 0 and 8 V there are infinitely many analog input possibilities. This is the only reason that we are forced to quantize by partitioning the 8V FS range into 8 discrete ranges of 1 V each.

This makes our resolution and consequently the quantization uncertainty equal to 1 V. As shown in the illustration of Fig. 9-1, any analog input voltage is represented by the same code over the 1 volt interval known as the *code width*. For example, analog inputs of 2.5 V to 3.5 V produce the same code of 011.

In this idealized illustration, each code width is exactly 1 V and code transitions occur at regular interval of 0.5 V, 1.5 V, 2.5 V, 3.5 V, etc. The conversion of an analog input to a code can be specified as a nominal value ± tolerance. For example, 3 V ± 0.5 V will produce the output code of 011. Since the value of LSB (the least significant bit) is 1 V ($8/2^3$), this conversion can also be specified as 3 V ± 0.5 LSB. Thus any conversion can be specified as the analog input corresponding to the middle of the code width and a tolerance of ± 0.5 LSB.

In practice, the code width varies from one interval to the next, the *differential linearity* specification places limits on the width of the code. If the manufacturer specifies the differential linearity of ±0.5 LSB, the width of the code can be anywhere between 0.5 LSB and 1.5 LSB (1 ± 0.5 LSB). Excessive differential non-linearity can lead to missed codes.

The errors that can distort the ideal picture of the A/D conversion shown in Fig. 9-1 include the *offset error, gain error, linearity error* and the *differential non-linearity,* which is responsible for the variation in code width and a possibility of missed codes.

The *accuracy* of the A/D converter is often specified in terms of *linearity errors: differential and integral.* The ideal converter has a conversion response as shown in Fig. 9-1, where points at the top of each transition, if connected, fall on a straight line. Any deviation from this straight line represents linearity errors of a real A/D converter. In an ideal converter, the difference between the midpoint of any code width and the midpoint of the adjacent code width is exactly 1 LSB. In a real converter this difference can vary, resulting in a deviation from the straight line.

The manufacturer specifies this type of an error as the difference between the ideal midpoint of a code width and the actual measured midpoint of the code width, and expresses these deviations as a % of the FS voltage, or in parts per million (ppm) of the FS voltage. (Remember that % represents parts per hundred, and ppm represents parts per million, so that 0.01 percent is the same as 100 ppm).

The *differential linearity error* is concerned with the variation in the code width, and the *integral linearity error* is concerned with the overall shape of the conversion curve.

Single-Ended or Differential Analog Inputs
This is the option that the user has in wiring the analog input. If the analog input is referenced to one common ground and is above 1 V in amplitude, and its leads are less than 15 ft. from the board, it should be wired as a single-ended input, otherwise it should be wired as a differential input. A differential input uses two analog input pins on the DAQ board, with one input used as a ground. A board with 16 analog inputs can accommodate 16 single-ended inputs, or 8 differential inputs.

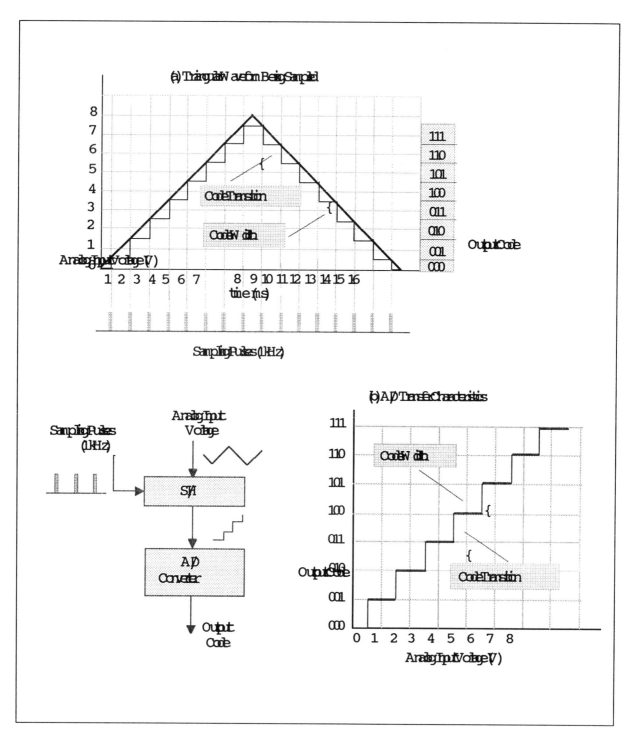

**Fig. 9-1 A/D Converter Characteristics: (a) Sampling a Triangular Waveform,
(b) A/D Transfer Characteristics**

Data Acquisition VIs

LabVIEW provides for you a variety of VIs to satisfy your data acquisition needs. As shown in Fig. 9-2, they are part of the *Data Acquisition* subpalette of the Functions palette. Each of the icon options in the Data Acquisition subpalette has its own subpalette. As shown in Fig. 9-2, when you click on the *Analog Input* icon inside the Data Acquisition subpalette, the Analog Input subpalette opens with various analog input VIs.

The Data Acquisition subpalette also includes *Analog Output, Digital I/O, Counter,* and other subpalettes.

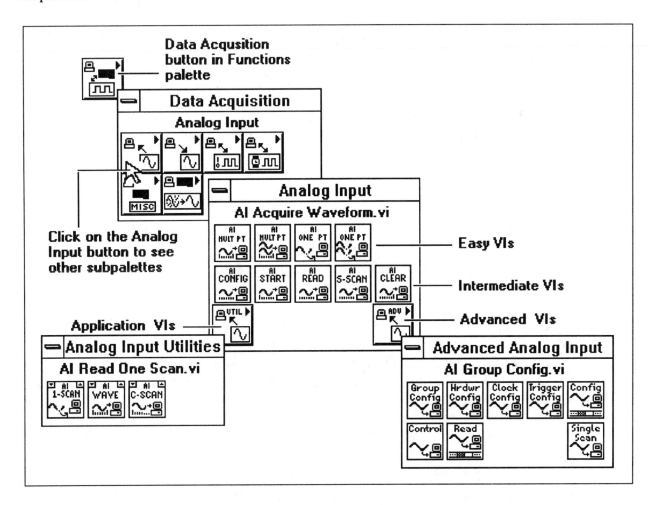

Fig. 9-2 Data Acquisition VIs. This illustration shows Analog Input VIs.

There are three categories of data acquisition VIs:

Easy VIs perform most common I/O operations. They are easy and simple to use because the complexity of configuring and setting up the data acquisition VI is designed into the Easy VI. They usually include the Intermediate VIs, which in turn are made up of advanced VIs. The Easy VIs, however, lack flexibility and power. *AI Sample Channel.vi and AI Acquire Waveform.vi* are examples of Easy VIs.

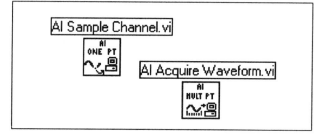

Intermediate VIs are made up of Advanced VIs. They have more power and flexibility. Examples of Intermediate VIs include the AI Read.vi, AI Single Scan.vi, shown in this illustration, and others. The three VIs in the Input Utility Analog Input subpalette, shown in Fig. 9-2, are also Intermediate Vis and are examples of special purpose applications that offer solutions to common analog input problems.

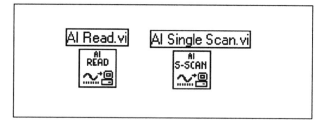

Advanced VIs are the fundamental building blocks for all data acquisition VIs. They have maximum power and flexibility and are not more difficult to learn than the intermediate VIs. Although you get more power and flexibility using Advanced VIs, you may also find that your block diagram will have a lot more blocks and various other objects.

Consider an AI *Sample Channel.vi,* which is an Easy VI. This VI will occupy only one block in your block diagram if you used it. But if you decided to accomplish the same thing with Intermediate and Advanced VIs, then instead of one block, you will have 8 blocks: 5 Advanced VIs, two intermediate VIs and the General Error Handler.vi from the Time & Dialog palette. See the hierarchy diagram of Fig. 9-3.

Of course, you will have the opportunity to provide your own parameter values rather than accepting the default values programmed into the Easy VI. This is where the power and the flexibility come in when you use the Advanced and the Intermediate VIs. In any case, there is more work in using the Advanced VI, and your block diagram may be a lot more cluttered. But you will have the opportunity to fine-tune various parameters and thus optimize the performance of your VI.

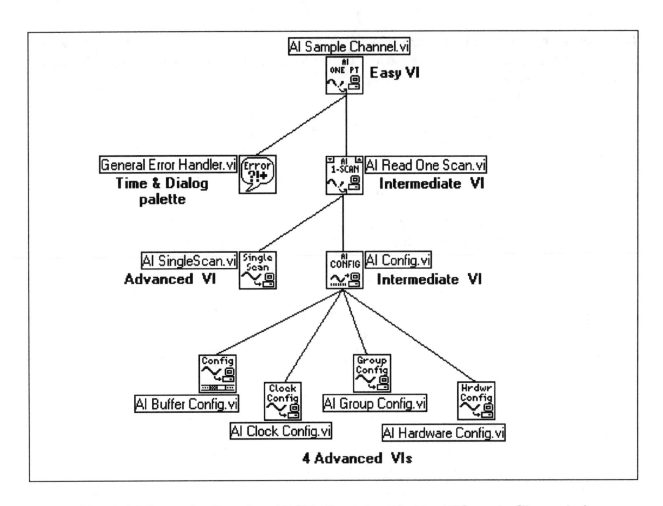

Fig. 9-3 Hierarchy Showing All VIs Contained in the AI Sample Channel.vi

Data Acquisition Programming Options

As mentioned earlier, the Intermediate and the Advanced data acquisition VIs give you greater flexibility in programming. If you decide to use the Intermediate or the Advanced Vis, you should be aware of several programming options. You should also be familiar with some terminology that will be used in this section.

A Scan is one acquisition or one reading from each analog or digital input channel used in a data acquisition process.

An Update is one write to each of the analog output channels. Typically, a DAQ board has two analog output channels or ports. Each of these ports is driven by a D/A converter. Remember that data coming from the computer is in digital form and must be converted to analog form before being applied to the analog output port. The digital output data is applied to the digital ports.

The **Scan Rate** is the speed in scans/sec with which all channels participating in a data acquisition process are being acquired. If your data acquisition process uses 8 analog input channels (0 through 7) and a scan rate of 1000 scans/sec, then

$$8 \, \frac{channel}{scan} * 1000 \, \frac{scan}{sec} = 80,000 \, \frac{channel}{sec}$$

and

$$80,000 \, \frac{channel}{sec} * 1 \, \frac{sample}{channe} = 80,000 \, \frac{sample}{sec}$$

As you increase the number of channels to be scanned and the scan rate, you may find that your board is unable to provide the sampling rate that you need. For example, the MIO-16E-10 DAQ board, as mentioned before, has a maximum sampling rate of 100 ksamples/sec.

Analog Input Data Acquisition Options

In this section we will consider two types of data acquisition options. As you will see, these options offer a single point immediate or hardware timed and buffered types of data acquisition:

Single Point Input (Immediate or Hardware Timed)
Waveform Input

Immediate Single Point Input

In this type of application only one point is acquired at a time. You can use an Easy VI or an Intermediate VI in this type of data acquisition application. As shown in this illustration, if you run AI Read One Scan.vi, only one data point will be acquired from each analog input channel. However, if you place this VI in a loop, you can acquire many data points.

In this illustration 500 data points are acquired and timed every 200 msec. The timing here is accomplished through the use of software time delay. This is not *hardware timing,* which is faster and more accurate.

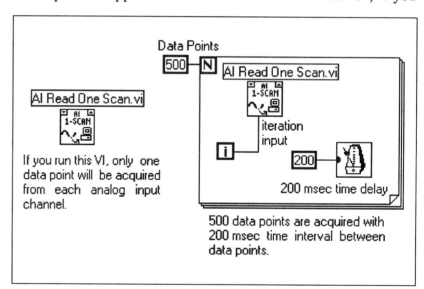

If you run this VI, only one data point will be acquired from each analog input channel.

500 data points are acquired with 200 msec time interval between data points.

AI Sample Channel.vi, the Easy VI, could have been used in the above illustration. But as you can see from the hierarchy diagram in Fig. 9-3, the *AI Read One Scan.vi*, an Intermediate VI, is included in the AI Sample Channel.vi. By using the AI Read One Scan.vi directly, we can save on some of the software overhead and thus speed up our data acquisition process. Notice that the iteration terminal **i** of the For Loop is wired to the iteration input of the AI Read One Scan.vi.

This speeds up the operation because the VI will be initialized only on the first iteration and only data will be acquired on all subsequent iterations. If you use a While Loop instead of the For Loop, you will have a continuous data acquisition process.

Hardware Timed Single Point Input

Hardware timed single point input is faster and more precise than the Immediate Single Point data acquisition option described in the preceding section.

Hardware timing enables the *scan clock*, which times precisely the acquisition of data. The scan clock is on a DAQ board and its scan rate is selected by the user. Each scan of data, consisting of one data point from every channel, is placed in FIFO (first-in-first-out temporary memory storage). AI Single Scan.vi removes data from FIFO one scan at a time.

As you can see from this illustration, you need several additional VIs to configure hardware timed data acquisition.

AI Config.vi configures the hardware for an analog input operation.

AI Start.vi sets, among other things, the scan rate.

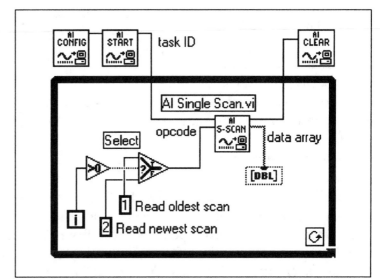

AI Single Scan.vi reads and returns one scan of data from FIFO if the acquisition is non-buffered, or from the acquisition buffer if data acquisition is buffered. Notice how the iteration terminal **i** of the While Loop is used to control the S-Scan.vi; only on the first iteration (**i=0**) does the Select function apply *opcode 2* to the AI Single Scan.vi, causing it to retrieve the newest scan (from FIFO if the acquisition is non-buffered). On all subsequent iterations the Select.vi applies opcode 1, forcing AI Single Scan.vi to retrieve the oldest scan from the buffer.

AI Clear.vi clears the data acquisition task ID, thus releasing all resources that have been committed to this particular data acquisition.

Waveform Input

Waveform input data acquisition is a **buffered** and a **hardware timed** process. It is timed because the hardware clock is activated to guide each data acquisition point quickly and accurately. It is buffered because the data acquired during the scanning process is stored in the memory buffer and later retrieved by the VI.

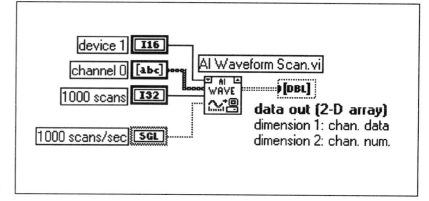

AI Waveform Scan.vi, shown in this illustration, is an Intermediate Application VI that can do a waveform input type of data acquisition.

As shown in this illustration, you specify the number of scans to acquire as well as the scan rate. Recall that one scan means one data point from each channel in the list of channels. That means that we can specify other channels in addition to channel 0 if desired. For example, by entering 0:3 in the string array control in the Front Panel, you will specify four channels to be scanned: channels 0 through channel 3.

As specified in the illustration, this VI will acquire 1000 data points from channel 0 in 1 second because it is scanning at 1000 scans or channels per second. The output is a two-dimensional array where each row is one complete scan from all channels. This means that each column will include data for a particular channel. In the above illustration, column 0 will include 1000 points of data for channel 0. You can compare this one scan of data to one trace on an oscilloscope screen.

AI Acquire Waveform.vi is an Easy VI that can also do a waveform input type of data acquisition. Actually the AI Waveform Scan.vi shown in the above illustration is included inside the AI Acquire Waveform.vi. As mentioned earlier, Easy VIs are made up of the Intermediate and the Advanced VIs. They possess simplicity and lack flexibility. This VI is no exception.

Notice in the hierarchy diagram of Fig. 9-4 how many other VIs are included in an Easy VI such as the AI Acquire Waveform.vi. It uses an application VI, which in turn uses some Intermediate VIs. The Intermediate VIs use a number of Advanced VIs. The Advanced VIs are responsible for the hardware configuration, scan clock setting, and many other chores that are transparent to the user.

To view the VI hierarchy and all the VIs that make up a particular VI, double click on the VI icon and choose *Project>Show VI Hierarchy*.

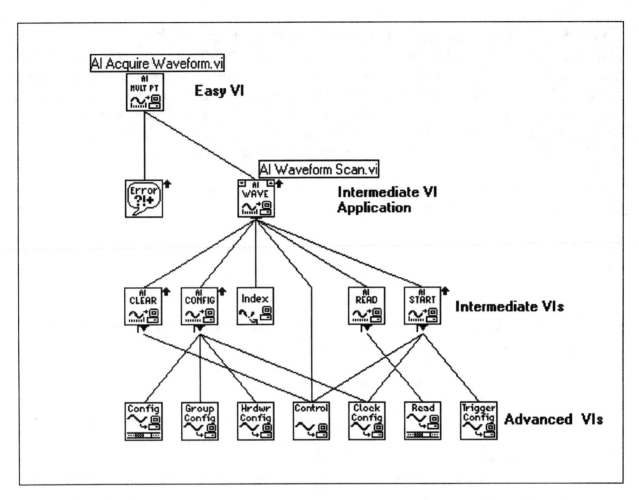

Fig. 9-4 Hierarchy Diagram for the AI Acquire Waveform.vi, an Easy VI

Exercise 1: Temperature Data Acquisition (Easy VI)

In this exercise you will build a temperature data acquisition VI using AI Sample Channel.vi. This is an Easy VI. As indicated before, because Easy VIs are made up of the Intermediate and the Advanced VIs, all the intricacies and the complexities of the data acquisition are made transparent to other user. This Easy VI may not have the flexibility or the power for some data acquisitions because the default configuration inside the VI may not be at its optimum setting. As far as our simple applications in this exercise are concerned, this VI is acceptable.

Hardware Requirements: DAQ board, DAQ extension board, temperature sensor (usually provided on the DAQ extension board)

Build this VI in accordance with the description of the front panel and the block diagram as follows:

Front Panel

1.   **Waveform Chart** is in the *Graph* subpalette of the Controls palette. Open one Waveform Chart and configure it as follows (see Fig. 9-5):

   Scale:

   Vertical: **65** (min) and **85** (max)

   Horizontal: **0** (min) and **200** (max)

   Pop up on the waveform chart and choose *X Scale>Formatting...*, then choose [1.0– / 0.5– / 0.0–] from the *Scale Style* palette.

   Legend:

   Delete **0**, the default waveform name, and type *Temp Data*, as shown here.

   Labels:

   [Temp Data ⌐⌐⌐]

   Owned: *Temperature Chart*

   Free: *Data Points* and *Temperature °F*

   AutoScale X and *AutoScale Y:* Disable.

   Thermometer is in the *Numeric* subpalette of the Controls palette. Open one thermometer and label it as shown in Fig. 9-5.

Block Diagram

2.   **For Loop** is in the *Structures* subpalette of the Functions palette. Open one For Loop and resize it as necessary.

You will be opening next inside the For Loop the data acquisition VI, AI Sample Channel.vi. Here is some information about its terminals and wiring requirements. This VI can be found in the Analog Input palette shown in Fig. 9-2 and in the illustration on the following page.

The following inputs must be wired:

Device input refers to the DAQ board number. If you have only one board, then this value will be *1*. If you have more than one board plugged in, then each will be assigned a value during the configuration when you run the WDAQCONF utility.

310

Channel input refers to the *Analog Input* channel that you will be using for acquiring data. This is a *string* input.

The high and low limit inputs need not be wired; their default values are +10 V and −10 V. These values specify the largest and the smallest input values applied to the data acquisition channel. LabVIEW uses these values to compute the gain for the programmable instrumentation amplifier whose output is used by the A/D converter.

Sample is the output terminal. It is wired to the indicator object to display the data point. The sample output, as mentioned earlier, *is only one data point*.

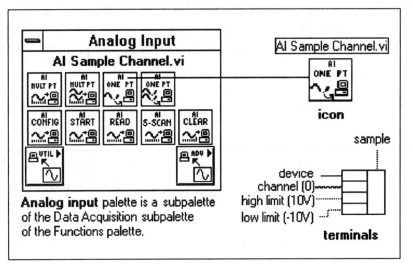

Analog input palette is a subpalette of the Data Acquisition subpalette of the Functions palette.

Open the following objects inside the For Loop:

AI Sample Channel.vi is in the *Analog Input* subpalette of the *Data Acquisition* subpalette of the Functions palette. Open one such VI.

Numeric Constant and the *Multiply* functions are in the *Numeric* subpalette of the Functions palette. Open four numeric constants and one multiply function. Enter the appropriate values as shown in Fig. 9-5.

String Constant is in the *String* subpalette of the Functions palette. Open one string constant and type **0** into it. It is used for the channel input.

Wait Until Next ms Multiple function is in the *Time & Dialog* subpalette of the Functions palette. Open one such function.

Wire all objects inside the Block Diagram as shown in Fig. 9-5.

3. The *DAQ board* and the appropriate *extension board* should have been installed at this time and configured by running the *WDAQCONF configuration utility*.

Find out where the temperature sensor chip is located on the extension board. In some boards including Lab PC⁺, this chip is hard wired next to AI Channel 0 and you have to move a jumper in order to connect the chip to channel 0. If the chip on your board is connected to an analog input channel other than **0**, then

> *make sure that you change the 0 value stored in the channel string constant in the block diagram to the new value.*

Also check the board number. Its value was assigned when you ran WDAQCONF. If it is *not 1*, then go back to the block diagram and change the value stored by the Device numeric constant.

4. This exercise illustrates the ***Immediate Single Point Input*** type of data acquisition where AI Sample Channel.vi acquires one data point from channel 0 on device 1 (DAQ board number) and returns the voltage associated with that data point (sample output).

The temperature sensing chip outputs approximately 25 mV at room temperature. This value is scaled (multiplication by 300 as shown in the Block Diagram) to bring it approximately into the °F range. Notice that this is only a rough calibration.

This temperature data point is next applied to the *Thermometer* indicator and also to the *Temperature Chart*. If you didn't have the For Loop, then that's all you would get, just that one point.

But the For Loop is set up to acquire 200 points with a 200 msec time delay between points provided by the *Wait Until Next ms Multiple* function. With each iteration of the loop, an additional data point is acquired.

If a *While Loop* with an ON/OFF switch was used instead of the For Loop, then the data acquisition would continue indefinitely. To stop it, you would have to click on the ON/OFF switch.

Also the time required to complete this data acquisition is 40 seconds (200 point times 0.2 seconds). To change this time, change the number of data points to be acquired or the time delay, or both.

Run this VI. As the VI is running, touch the temperature sensor chip with your fingers and note the temperature data variation on the Temperature Chart.

Save this VI as **DAQ1.vi** in the Workbook.LLB and close it.

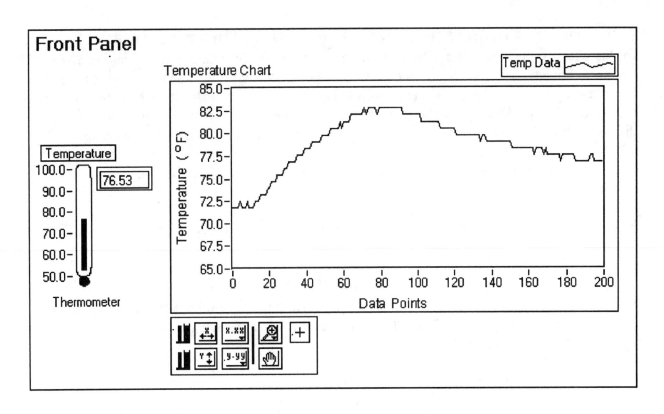

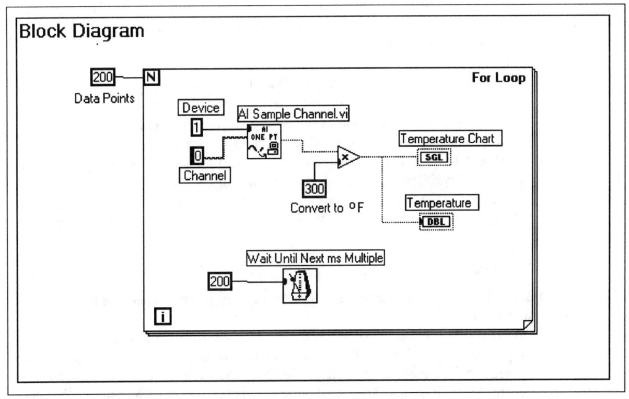

Fig. 9-5 Front Panel and Block Diagram for VI in Exercise 1

Exercise 2: Temperature Data Acquisition (Intermediate VI)

In this exercise you will build a VI that will acquire temperature data, except this time you will use an intermediate VI, AI Read One scan.vi. This VI scans all the channels wired to the DAQ board analog inputs and returns one scan of data, one measurement from each channel as a one-dimensional array. Although in this exercise we accomplish the same type of data acquisition, the difference is in the way we process the data because now the data is in the form of an array.

Hardware Requirements: DAQ board, DAQ extension board, temperature sensor (usually provided on the DAQ extension board)

You will build this VI in accordance with the front panel and the block diagram shown in Fig. 9-6 as follows.

Front Panel

1. **Waveform Chart** and **Waveform Graph** are in the *Graph* subpalette of the Controls palette. Open one Waveform Chart and one Waveform Graph and configure them as follows (see Fig. 9-6):

    Scale:

          Vertical: **70** (min) and **90** (max)

          Horizontal: **0** (min) and **200** (max)

                   Popup on the waveform chart and choose *X Scale>Formatting...*, then choose ▢ from the *Scale Style* palette.

    Legend: disable (optional)

    Labels:

          Owned: *Temperature Chart* (Waveform Chart)

                 Temperature Graph (Waveform Graph)

          Free: *Data Points* and *Temperature °F* (chart and graph)

    AutoScale X and *AutoScale Y:* Disable (chart and graph)

    Array is in the *Array & Cluster* subpalette of the Controls palette. Open one empty array shell *and label it* with an owned label as *Channel.*

    String Control is in the *String & Table* subpalette of the Controls palette. Open one string control and *drop it* inside the array shell that you opened in the preceding step.

Block Diagram

2. **For Loop** is in the *Structures* subpalette of the Functions palette. Open one For Loop and resize it as necessary.

    Index Array is in the *Array* subpalette of the Functions palette. Open two Index Array functions. You will use one of these inside the For Loop and the other outside the For Loop. The Index Array outside the For Loop will process a two-dimensional array, so it will need an additional dimension index. To add dimension, either drag the lower corner of the icon or pop up in the index (black rectangle) and choose *Add Dimension* from the popup menu. The icon should look like this:

rectangle and choosing *Disable Index*ing. After you are done, the icon will appear as shown here:

Numeric Constant and the **Multiply** function are in the *Numeric* subpalette of the Functions palette. Open five numeric constants and one multiply function. Enter the appropriate values into the numeric constants, as shown in Fig. 9-6.

Wait Until Next ms Multiple function is in the *Time & Dialog* subpalette of the Functions palette. Open one such function.

AI Read One Scan.vi is in the *Analog Input Utilities* subpalette of the *Analog Input* subpalette of the *Data Acquisition* subpalette of the Functions palette. *Open one AI Read One Scan.vi.*

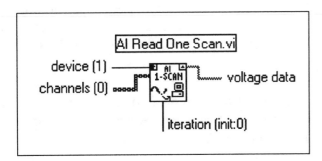

As you can see from this illustration, you need to wire only three terminals: *Device* input is a numeric constant representing the DAQ board number. *Channels* input is a string control array that was created in the front panel. *Voltage data* output is a one-dimensional array representing one scan of data. Although in this exercise we are wiring only one analog input channel, in general many input channels are possible.

Iteration input speeds up the data acquisition if you place AI Read One Scan.vi inside a loop to take more than one measurement. If you wire the *iteration input* of this VI to the loop iteration terminal **i**, this VI will take care of all necessary configurations such as hardware configurations on the first (**i** = **0**) iteration of the loop. Then on all subsequent iterations it will only take measurements from the designated channels. This saves on a considerable amount of software overhead. In this exercise we use this VI inside the For Loop where you will wire the iteration terminal i of the For Loop to the iteration input of this VI.

Wire all objects in the block diagram as shown in Fig. 9-6.

3. The DAQ board must be activated and the temperature sensing chip connected to the appropriate analog input channel. See section 3 of Exercise 1.

4. This exercise also illustrates the ***Immediate Single Point Input*** type of data acquisition, but in contrast to Exercise 1, the AI Read One Scan.vi returns a one-dimensional array of measurement from each wired analog input channel, referred to as one scan. In this exercise, only channel 0 is wired, so each scan contains only one measurement. Nevertheless it is still an array.

The For Loop acquires 200 scans or 200 temperature measurements from channel 0. Each measurement is scaled to convert it to approximate degrees Fahrenheit. The Wait Until Next ms Multiple function provides a100 ms delay between data points for a total acqui-

315

sition time of 20 seconds. If you used a While Loop with an ON/OFF switch instead of the For Loop, the data acquisition would continue indefinitely until you click on the switch to stop it.

In this exercise the Index array functions are used to extract a subset of the array. Inside the For Loop the Index Array function extracts the zero-th element of each scan and displays it on the Waveform Chart.

Each scan (after scaling) is also applied to the border of the For Loop where a two-dimensional array containing 200 scans is created. When the For Loop completes its execution, this two-dimensional array is applied to the Index Array, which extracts the zero-th column (the data for channel 0). Recall that each row of the array represents one scan and each column represents the data for one channel. The resulting one-dimensional array (zero-th column) is then applied for display on the Waveform Graph (Temperature Graph).

As the VI is running, you will be able to see the acquired data point by point on the Waveform Chart (Temperature Chart). Only after the VI completes execution will you see the entire temperature curve being displayed on the Waveform Graph (Temperature Graph).

You may use the cursor on the Temperature Graph to ready precisely a specific point on the curve. Notice in the front panel of Fig. 9-6 that the cursor position as shown reads 84.96 °F for data point number 50. Since the time delay inside the For Loop is 100 ms, the data point 50 will occur 5 seconds after the data acquisition begins. In this exercise the X-scale can represent time in seconds by dividing each data point by 10.

Enter 0 in the channel string array control on the front panel.

Run this VI. As the VI is running, touch the temperature sensor chip with your fingers and note the temperature data variation on the Temperature Chart.

Save this VI as **DAQ2.vi** in the Workbook.LLB and close it.

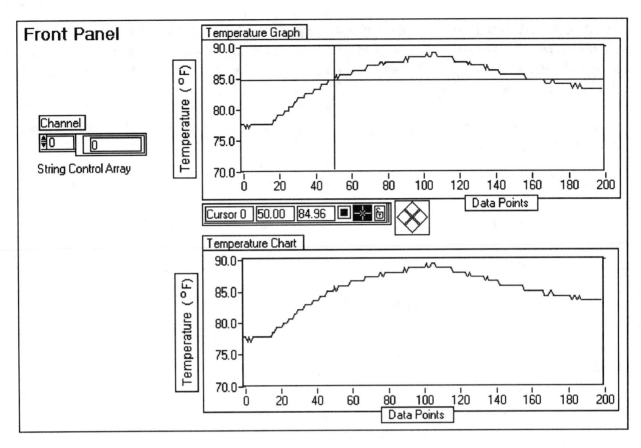

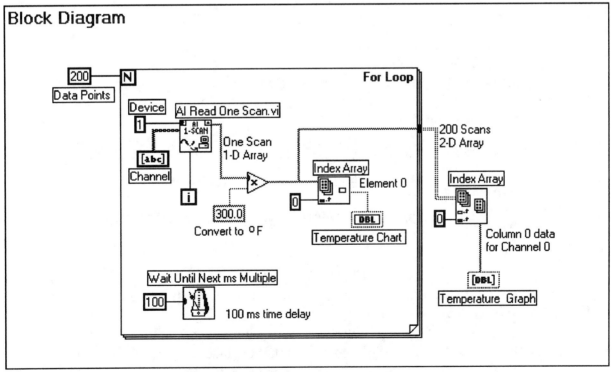

Fig. 9-6 The Front Panel and Block Diagram for Exercise 2

317

Exercise 3: Data Acquisition and Storage to Spreadsheet

In this exercise you will build a VI that acquires two channels of data and then stores the data to a spreadsheet. This is an example of an *Immediate Single Point Input* type of data acquisition using the Intermediate VI, AI Read One Scan.

Hardware Requirements: DAQ board, DAQ extension board, waveform generator (sine wave and square wave)

Construct the VI whose front panel and block diagram are shown in Fig. 9-7, as follows.

Front Panel

1. **Waveform Graph** is in the *Graph* subpalette of the Controls palette. Open two Waveform Graphs and configure them as follows (see Fig. 9-7):

    > *Scale:*
    > > ***Sine Wave Graph***
    > > Vertical: **−5** (min) and **+5** (max)
    > > Horizontal: **0** (min) and **100** (max)
    > > ***Square Wave Graph***
    > > Vertical: **0** (min) and **+5** (max)
    > > Horizontal: **0** (min) and **100** (max)

    > *Legend:* disable (optional)
    > *Labels:* Owned:
    > > ***Sine Wave Graph***
    > > ***Square Wave Graph***
    > > Free: (both graphs)
    > > ***Data Points*** and ***Volts***

    > *AutoScale X* and *AutoScale Y:* Disable (both graphs)
    > **Array** is in the *Array & Cluster* subpalette of the Controls palette. Open two empty array shells and configure them as follows:

    > *Channel:*
    > > ***String Control*** is in the *String & Table* subpalette of the Controls palette. Open one string control and ***drop it*** inside the array shell. ***Label*** this array as ***Channel*** using an owned label.

    > *Data Array:*
    > > ***Digital Indicator*** is in the *Numeric* subpalette of the Controls palette.

Block Diagram

2. **For Loop** is in the *Structures* subpalette of the Functions palette. Open one For Loop and resize it as necessary.

    Index Array is in the *Array* subpalette of the Functions palette. Open two Index Array functions. Add dimension and disable the row index as you have done in Exercise 2. The Array Index should look like this:

318

AI Read One Scan. vi 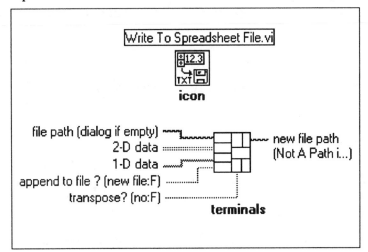 is in the *Analog Input Utilities* subpalette of the *Analog Input* subpalette of the *Data Acquisition* subpalette of the Functions palette. Open one such VI. See Exercise 2 for a terminal description for this VI.

Numeric Constant is in the *Numeric* subpalette of the Functions palette. Open four numeric constants and one multiply function. Enter the appropriate values into the numeric constants, as shown in Fig. 9-7.

Write To Spreadsheet File.vi is in the *File I/O* subpalette of the Functions palette. Open one such VI. As shown in this illustration, this VI accepts at its input either a one-dimensional or a two-dimensional array and stores it to a spreadsheet file separating columns of data by tabs.

In this exercise we will apply a two-dimensional array of data as the input to this VI. This is the only input that you have to wire. The default settings for all other inputs will do just fine.

You could, however, change some of the default settings.

For instance, the **append to file** input default setting is *false*. If you wire a *true* Boolean constant (from the Boolean subpalette of the Functions palette) to this input, then every time you save new data, it will be appended at the end of the old data. The *false* input (default) erases the old data. The **transpose** input switches the rows and columns of the two-dimensional input array. The default setting is *false* (no transpose), but if you wanted the input data to be transposed, then you would have to wire a *true* (Boolean constant) to this input.

Wire all objects inside the Block Diagram as shown in Fig. 9-7.

3. The DAQ board must be activated. If Ch.0 on your DAQ board can accommodate an external input or the temperature sensing chip by means of a jumper, as is the case with the Lab PC⁺ board, make sure that Ch.0 is connected to the external source.

4. Connect a square wave generator to channel 0 and a sinusoidal source to channel 1. Adjust the amplitudes of both sources to about 4 Vpk and set the frequency to 10 Hz.

5. In this exercise two measurements are taken from channels 0 and 1 on each scan and stored into a two-dimensional array. As the For Loop iterates from 0 to 99, a two-dimensional array of 100 rows and 2 columns is formed at the border of the For Loop.

Notice that channels are scanned from highest to lowest. So if you enter 1,0 into channels string control array in the Front Panel, the AI Read One Scan.vi will take a measurement from channel 1 first and then from channel 0. This means that the first column in the two-dimensional array (column 0) will include 100 points of data from channel 1 and the second column will contain 100 points of data from channel 0.

After the loop completes execution, the two-dimensional array is applied to two Index Array functions, Write To Spreadsheet File.vi and to the Data Array.

The two Index Array functions extract the Sine Wave and the Square Wave data to be displayed on the Waveform Graphs. Notice that the numeric constant 0 extracts the 0 column (Sine Wave data) and the numeric constant 1 extracts column 1 (Square Wave data) from the two-dimensional array.

The *Array Data* displays the two-dimensional array. You can operate the two indexes with the operating tool to see the value of an element or resize the array as shown in Fig. 9-7 to see several elements.

6.   **Run** this VI after entering **1,0** into the *Channel* string control array.
     Note: As soon as you run the VI, the Write to Spreadsheet File.vi opens the dialog, letting you specify the name of the spreadsheet file where you want to save the data.

0.020	4.031
1.631	4.033
3.047	4.033
4.058	4.033
4.539	4.036
4.165	0.063
3.267	0.066
1.895	0.066
0.354	0.066
-1.204	0.066
-2.588	0.066
-3.599	0.063
-4.094	0.066

Enter *Test_Run.txt* or some other name of your choice. Notice the **.txt** extension, specifying this file as a text file.

After running the VI, you can view your file using any text editor. In this illustration a portion of the two columns of data was viewed using the *Write* text editor, which is in the Accessories group in Windows. Any other text editor or word processor can also be used.

Open the *cursor* in both waveform graphs by popping up on the graph and choosing *Show>Cursor* from the popup menu. You may also choose the shape and color of the cursor by popping up on the cursor with the operating tool. Refer to Chapter 6 for more information on cursors.

The cursor helps you to read precisely points on the curve. Notice in Fig. 9-7 that the cursor is set to data point 33 and reads the value of 1.85 V for the sine wave and the other cursor reads the value of 4.03 V for the square wave. The Data Array also shows these values. **Save** this VI as **DAQ3.vi** in Workbook.LLB and close it.

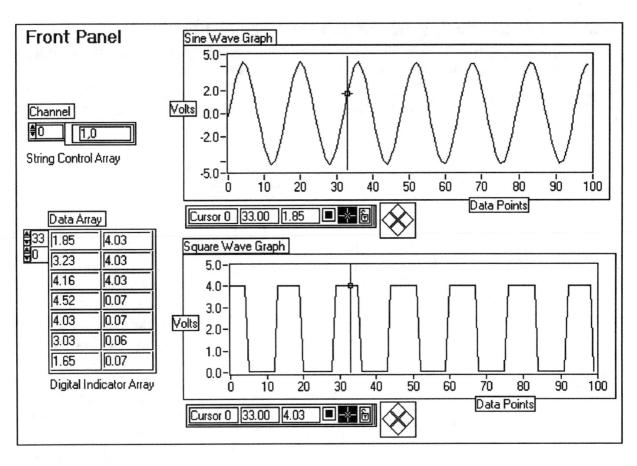

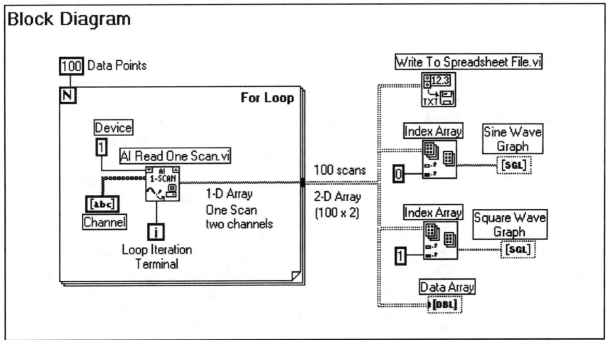

Fig. 9-7 The Front Panel and Block Diagram for Exercise 3

Exercise 4: Retrieving Data from the Spreadsheet

In this exercise you will build a VI that opens the spreadsheet file, retrieves the data, and displays the data on waveform graphs. We will use the data that you saved in Exercise 3.

Build the front panel and the block diagram shown in Fig. 9-8 as follows.

Front Panel

1. The front panel for this exercise is very similar to that of the preceding exercise. Copy the front panel from Exercise 3 and leave out the *String Control Array* and the *Digital Indicator Array.*

Block Diagram

2. **Read From Spreadsheet File.vi** is in the *File I/O* subpalette of the Functions palette. Open one such VI. Shown in this illustration are the icon and some of the terminals.

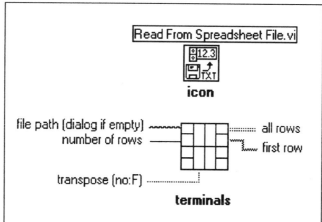

The *file path* input can be left unwired. The default is the dialog box. During execution this VI will give you access to directories and files, allowing you to open the data text file.

Number of rows is a numeric input that specifies the number of rows to be read from the file.

All rows output is the two-dimensional array of data that has been retrieved from the text file specified by you and is now available for processing.

Index Array is in the *Array* subpalette of the Functions palette. Open two Index Array functions. Add dimension and disable row index for each Index Array function, as you have done in the preceding exercise.

Numeric Constant is in the *Numeric* subpalette of the Functions palette. Open three numeric constants and enter the appropriate values into these constants, as shown in Fig. 9-8.

3. *Wire* all objects in the block diagram as shown in Fig. 9-8.
4. *Run* this VI. At the beginning of execution a dialog window will open, giving you access to directories and files. Choose *Test_Run.txt* (or whatever file name you used in the preceding exercise). Observe the retrieved data plotted on the waveform graphs. These are the same two waveforms that you acquired in the preceding exercise.

Save this VI as **DAQ4.vi** in Workbook.LLB and close it.

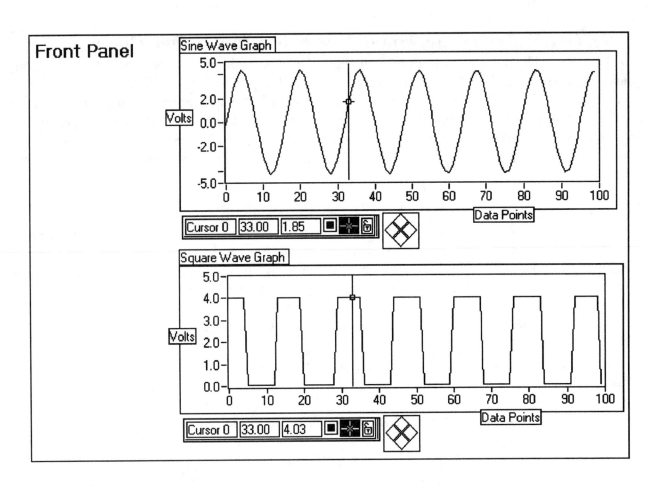

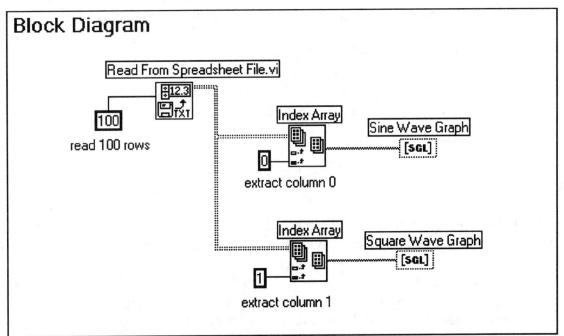

Fig. 9-8 The Front Panel and Block Diagram for Exercise 4

323

Exercise 5: Data Acquisition (Waveform Input: One Channel)

This exercise illustrates a Waveform Input type of data acquisition. This type of data acquisition, as discussed in the Data Acquisition Programming Options section earlier in this chapter, differs considerably from the Immediate Single Point type of acquisition where one data point is measured at a time from one or more channels and returned immediately for display, processing or storage. The previous exercises used the Immediate Single Point type of data acquisition. We were using a loop to acquire many points. If we didn't use the loop, we would get only one data point.

In contrast to the Immediate Single Point type of data acquisition, the Waveform Input type acquires many points and stores this data in a buffer (a temporary memory that in our case will be FIFO, the First In First Out memory). After the acquisition is complete, this data is transferred from the buffer and is returned in the form of an array. In addition, hardware timing is used because you specify sampling rate or the frequency with which measurements are made.

In short the Waveform Input is much faster because it is ***buffered and hardware timed.***

In this exercise we will acquire a specified number of samples at a specified sampling rate and display the data on a waveform graph.

Construct the front panel and block diagram shown in Fig. 9-9 as follows.

Front Panel

1. **Waveform Graph** is in the *Graph* subpalette of the Controls palette. Open one Waveform Graph, resize it as necessary, and configure it as follows (see Fig. 9-9):

    Scale:

    Vertical: *AutoScale Y* enable

    Horizontal: choose *Precision* as **3**

    enter **0.000** (min) and **0.005** (max)

    AutoScale X : disable

    Legend: optional

    Labels:

    Owned: ***Sine Wave Graph***

    Free: ***time (sec)*** and ***Volts***

    Cursor: optional

    Digital Control is in the *Numeric* subpalette of the Controls palette. Open two digital controls. Set their *Representation* to **I16** (pop up on control and choose *Representation>I16* from the popup menu).

    Label one of them as ***Num Samples*** and the other as ***Sampling Rate*** using owned labels. The samples/sec units label is a free label and is optional.

    Vertical Switch is in the *Boolean* subpalette of the Controls palette.

    Label the switch as ***STOP*** using an owned label.

    Mechanical Action: ***Latch When pressed***

    Choose *Data Operations>Make Current Value Default* from the popup menu.

324

Block Diagram

2. **While Loop** is in the *Structure* subpalette of the Functions Palette. Open one While Loop and resize it as necessary.

AI Acquire Waveform.vi is in the *Analog Input* subpalette of the *Data Acquisition* subpalette of the Functions palette. Open one AI Acquire Waveform.vi. As shown in this illustration:

device is a numeric constant representing the DAQ board number.

channel is a string constant representing the channel number.

number of samples is a numeric constant representing the number of data points to be acquired.

sample rate is the frequency in samples/sec with which measurements or data points are taken from the specified channel.

waveform is a one-dimensional array of data points returned from the buffer.

actual sample period is the time between samples. We will use this value to set the time interval between data points along the horizontal scale of the waveform graph.

Bundle is in the *Cluster* subpalette of the Functions palette. Open one Bundle function and resize it to three inputs.

Numeric Constant is in the *Numeric* subpalette of the Functions palette. Open three numeric constants, label one as *device* with an owned label and enter the value **1** (DAQ board number). Enter the appropriate values into the remaining constants, as shown in Fig. 9-9.

String Constant is in the *String* subpalette of the Functions palette. Open one string constant, label it as *channel* with an owned label, and enter the value **0** (analog input channel number used for data acquisition).

Wait Until Next ms Multiple is in the *Time & Dialog* subpalette of the Functions palette. Open one *Wait Until Next ms Multiple* timer function.

3. *Wire* all objects in the Block Diagram as shown in Fig. 9-9.

4. At this time the DAQ board should be connected and configured, and the extension board should be connected to the DAQ board. Apply to channel 0 a sinusoidal input 4 Vpk and 1 kHz frequency. Enter **500** into the *Num Samples,* and **15000** into the *Sampling Rate* digital controls on the Front Panel.

5. In this exercise 500 measurements are acquired from channel 0 into a buffer at a sampling rate of 15000 samples/sec. The AI Acquire Waveform.vi returns this data as a one-dimensional array and displays it on the waveform graph, which we called Sine Wave Graph.

The fact that this is a much faster type of data acquisition is evident from the frequency of the sine wave that we are sampling here. Recall that in the previous VIs using the immediate single point input, we used 10 Hz for the sine wave frequency.

Run this VI. Notice that the use of the While Loop provides an interactive data acquisition environment. Each block of 500 samples of data is returned by the AI Acquire Waveform.vi and displayed on the Sine Wave graph. This occurs each second with the time delay provided by the Wait Until Next ms Multiple timer function. This operation resembles the oscilloscope, where the traces occur at regular intervals.

As the VI is running you can experiment by changing the amplitude and frequency of the sine wave as well as the number of samples and the sampling rate.

To stop this VI click on the STOP switch.

Save this VI as **DAQ5.vi** in Workbook.LLB and close it.

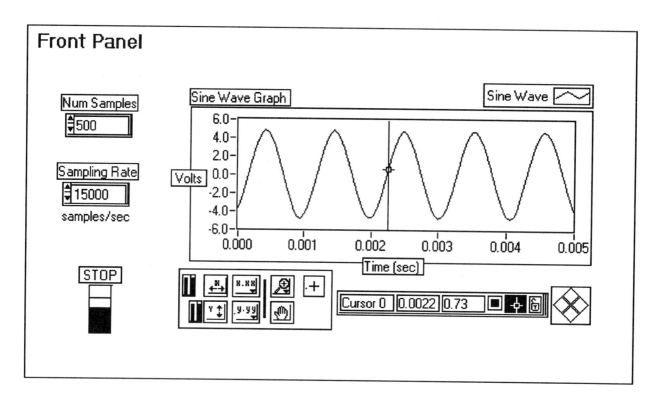

Fig. 9-9   The Front Panel and Block Diagram for Exercise 5

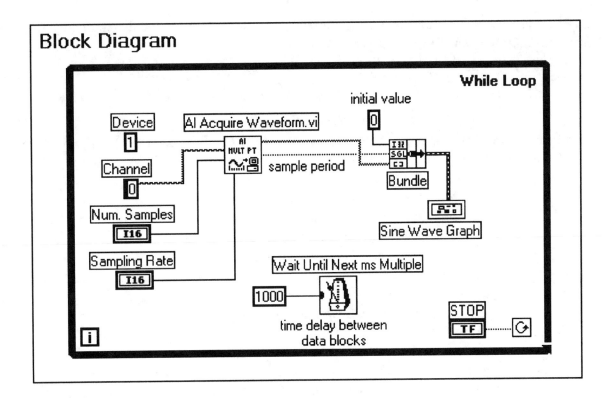

Block Diagram

While Loop

Device

AI Acquire Waveform.vi

initial value

Channel

sample period

Bundle

Num. Samples

Sine Wave Graph

Sampling Rate

Wait Until Next ms Multiple

1000

time delay between
data blocks

STOP

Fig. 9-9   The Front Panel and the Block Diagram for Exercise 5 (continued)

Exercise 6: Data Acquisition (Waveform Input: Multichannel)

As was the purpose of the preceding exercise, this exercise also illustrates the Waveform Input type of data acquisition, except this time we will acquire data from multiple channels.

In the preceding exercise AI Acquire Waveform.vi was used to acquire data from one channel. Notice the names of the inputs: *Num Samples* (number of measurements from a single channel) and *Sampling Rate*.

In this exercise AI Acquire Waveforms.vi is used to acquire data from multiple channels. The 's' at the end implies more than one channel; otherwise there is a great deal of similarity between the two VIs. They both use buffering and hardware timing. The main difference lies in the number of channels being sampled.

In this exercise we have to acquire data from more than one channel, and thus we have to deal with the idea of scanning channels. Remember that one scan means one measurement from each channel in the group. Notice the wording used in the block diagram in Fig. 9-10. Instead of number of samples, we use *samples/ch,* and instead of sampling rate, we use *scanning rate*.

In this exercise we will acquire a specified number of samples at a specified sampling rate and display the data on a waveform graph.

Construct the front panel and block diagram shown in Fig. 9-10, as follows.

Front Panel

1. **Waveform Graph** is in the *Graph* subpalette of the Controls palette. Open two Waveform Graphs, resize them as necessary, and configure them as follows (see Fig. 9-10):

   > *Scale:* (both graphs)
   > Vertical: *AutoScale Y* enable
   > Horizontal: choose *Precision* as **3**
   > enter **0.000** (min) and **0.005** (max)
   > *AutoScale X* : disable

   Legend: optional
   Labels: (both graphs)
   > Owned: *Sine Wave Graph* and *Square Wave Graph*
   > Free: *time (sec)* and *Volts*

   Cursor: optional

   Digital Control is in the *Numeric* subpalette of the Controls palette. Open two digital controls. Set their *Representation* to *I16* (pop up on control and choose *Representation>I16* from the popup menu).

   Label one of them as *Num Samples/ch* and the other as *Scanning Rate* using owned labels. The scans/sec units label is a free label and is optional.

   Vertical Switch is in the *Boolean* subpalette of the Controls palette.
   Label the switch as *STOP* using an owned label.
   Mechanical Action: *Latch When pressed*
   Choose *Data Operations>Make Current Value Default* from the popup menu.

Block Diagram

2. **Index Array** is in the *Array* subpalette of the Functions palette. Open two Index Array functions. Add dimension and disable the row index as you have done in Exercise 2.

   While Loop is in the *Structure* subpalette of the Functions palette. Open one While Loop and resize it as necessary.

   Wait Until Next ms Multiple is in the *Time & Dialog* subpalette of the Functions palette. Open one Wait Until Next ms Multiple timer function.

   Bundle is in the *Cluster* subpalette of the Function palette. Open two Bundle functions and resize them to include three inputs.

   Numeric Constant is in the *Numeric* subpalette of the Functions palette. Open six numeric constants, label one as *device* with an owned label, and enter the value **1** (DAQ board number). Enter appropriate values into the other numeric constants, as shown in Fig. 9-10.

String Constant is the *String* subpalette of the Functions palette. Open one string constant, label it as *channels* with an owned label, and enter **1,0** (analog input channels being scanned).

AI Acquire Waveforms.vi is in the *Analog Input* subpalette of the *Data Acquisition* subpalette of the Functions palette. Open one AI Acquire Waveforms.vi. As shown in this illustration:

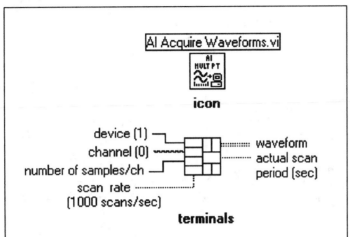

device is a numeric constant representing the DAQ board number.

channel is a string constant representing the channel number.

number of samples/ch is a numeric constant representing the number of data points to be acquired from each channel.

scan rate is the frequency of scanning channels in scans/sec. On each scan one measurement is taken from each channel.

waveform is a two-dimensional array of data points being returned from the buffer. Each row of the array includes data from one scan. Hence, each column row includes data for one channel.

actual sample period is the time between scans. We will use this value to set the time interval between data points along the horizontal scale of the waveform graph.

3. *Wire* all objects in the block diagram as shown in Fig. 9-10.

4. At this time the DAQ board should be connected and configured, and the extension board should be connected to the DAQ board. Apply to channel 1 a sinusoidal input 4 Vpk and 1 kHz frequency and apply a 4 Vpk square wave of the same frequency to channel 0. Set Samples/ch digital control to 500 and the Scan Rate digital control to 15,000.

5. In this exercise 500 measurements are acquired from each of the two channels at a scan rate of 15000 scan/sec. The data is stored in the buffer until acquisition is complete. Then AI Acquire Waveforms.vi returns the data as a two-dimensional array.

    The two index array functions extract column 0 data and column 1 data and display this data on the two waveform graphs.

Run this VI. As in the previous exercise, the While Loop provides an interactive data acquisition environment. 500 data points are taken from each channel and displayed as a trace on the two waveform graphs. This process is repeated every second as a result of the 1 second time delay provided by the *Wait Until Next ms Multiple* timing function. Experiment with different amplitudes, frequencies, number of samples/ch, and scanning rates as well as with different waveforms.

Save this VI as **DAQ6.vi** in Workbook.LLB and close it.

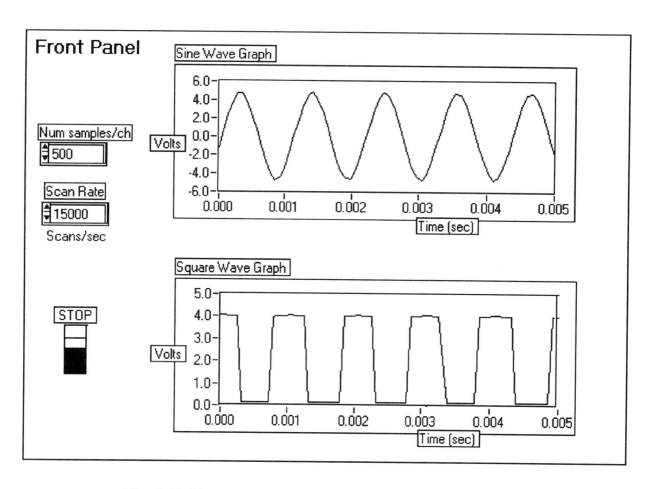

Fig. 9-10 The Front Panel and Block Diagram for Exercise 6

Block Diagram

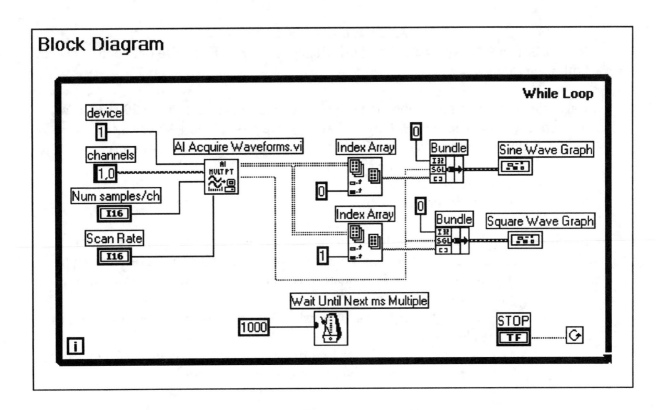

Fig. 9-10 The Front Panel and Block Diagram for Exercise 6 (continued)

Additional Exercises

1. Repeat Exercise 6, except instead of using two waveform charts, use only one to display both waveforms.

2. Using the immediate single point input type of data acquisition, acquire 200 points of temperature data. Using the following format, store this data to a spreadsheet:

    Column 0: sequential row ID (1 for first row, 2 for second row, etc.)
    Column 1: data point time (for a row)
    Column 2: temperature data point

    Separate the columns using two tabs.

3. In this data acquisition exercise the front panel must give user the following options:
    a. Acquire one channel sinewave data and display it on a waveform graph.
    b. Acquire two channels of square wave and sine wave data. Display data on two waveform graphs.
    c. Acquire two channels of square wave and sine wave data and store data to a spreadsheet.
    d. Acquire one channel of temperature data and determine *min* and *max* values for the data and display the data on a waveform graph.

    Use the waveform input type of data acquisition similar to that used in Exercise 5 or 6 to obtain 500 data points per channel with a scanning rate of 15,000. Frequencies and amplitudes are to be chosen by you.

Summary

1. Data acquisition is a process by which analog information is converted to digital form and passed inside the computer for storage, display or processing.

2. To conduct data acquisition you need a software environment that supports this activity. LabVIEW is such an environment. You also need a data acquisition board with many features to support the data acquisition process and a software driver for the DAQ board to coordinate various data acquisition activities. And last but not least, you need a termination board that plugs into the DAQ board providing for you access to various points on the board.

3. The process of data acquisition begins with sampling the analog waveform and then converting it to the digital form using an A/D converter. The D/A converter that is also on the DAQ board does just the reverse: it converts digital data to analog form to be passed to devices outside the computer.

    Sampling rate limit is an important parameter that represents the speed capability of the DAQ board. According to Nyquist, the sampling frequency must be at least twice as large as the maximum frequency component of the analog waveform being sampled. Hence, the highest frequency that a board with a 100 ksample/sec maximum sampling frequency limit can handle is 50 kHz.

Resolution is another important data acquisition parameter. It is the number of bits that the A/D converter uses to represent an analog signal. It also represents the smallest analog input that the A/D is capable of detecting.

4. The Data Acquisition VIs that simplify the task of data acquisition are found in the Data Acquisition subpalette of the Functions palette. They fall into one of three categories: Easy, Intermediate or Advanced VIs.

    The Easy VIs are simple to use but lack the power and configuration flexibility. Sometimes the default configuration settings are not suitable for your VI's optimum performance. That is why the Intermediate VIs are much better.

5. A *scan* is one measurement from each analog input channel participating in the data acquisition process.

    An *update* is one output to each of the analog output channels.

    Scan Rate is the speed in scans/sec at which data channels participating in the data acquisition process are acquired. The sampling rate is directly proportional to the scan rate and the number of channels being scanned.

6. The *Immediate Single Point Input* type of data acquisition acquires one point at a time. The measurement is returned immediately by the VI. AI Read One Point.vi or AI Sample Channel.vi are examples of VIs that can do this type of data acquisition.

    One such VI can be placed in a loop to acquire more than one measurement.

7. Hardware timed single point input is faster and more precise than the Immediate Single Point data acquisition option. Hardware timing enables the *scan clock*, which times precisely the acquisition of data.

8. *Waveform Input* data acquisition is a *buffered* and a *hardware timed* process. It is timed because the hardware clock is activated to guide each data acquisition point quickly and accurately. It is buffered because the data acquired during the scanning process is stored in the memory buffer, such as FIFO, and later retrieved by the VI.

Appendix A

LabVIEW Environment
(LabVIEW Version 3)

In this appendix you will learn about:
Control bar options
Pull-down menu options
Editing techniques
Wiring
VI library
VI documentation

LabVIEW Program Development Environment

LabVIEW is launched by clicking on the LabVIEW icon from the Program Manager, LabVIEW Group window. What comes up next is the program development environment consisting of two windows: the *front panel* and the *block diagram*. It is here that a virtual instrument program is developed using the graphical programming language; no code is ever written. The front panel contains a variety of controls and indicators such as numerical controls and indicators, graphs, knobs, dials switches, etc. The block diagram, on the other hand, contains various functions and subVIs wired together to perform the desired task, be it measurement, simulation or control. The front panel provides the means of passing control and information such as numerical data to the dblock diagram. Any numerical data that the block diagram generates and must be displayed is passed to the front panel.

Consider next a typical virtual instrument (VI) as shown in Fig. A-2. This VI adds three floating point numbers A, B, C and outputs their sum. It also divides A by C and outputs the integer quotient (IQ) and the remainder (R). It is not important at this time to understand what this VI does but rather to become familiar with the VI configuration and its components.

As stated earlier, each VI must have a block diagram and a front panel. At the top of the block diagram and the front panel there are three bars. The top bar includes the name of the VI currently in the window (only if this VI was saved; otherwise it given a default name of Untitled). The middle bar contains various pull-down menus and the bottom bar includes the command icons.

There are two modes in which LabVIEW can operate: *Run* mode and *Edit* mode. Fig. A-1 shows the command bar when it is in the Run mode.

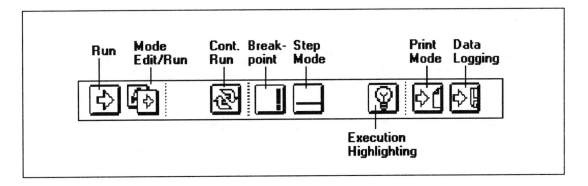

Fig. A-1 Command Bar in Run Mode

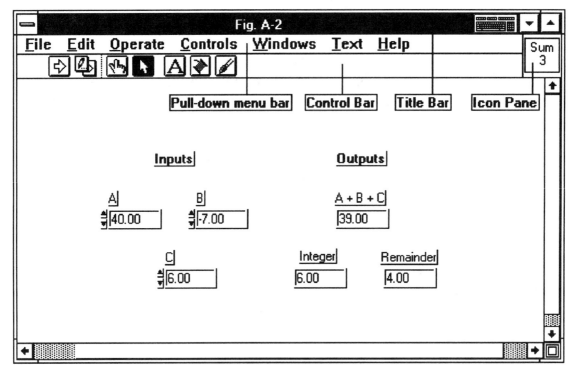

Front Panel

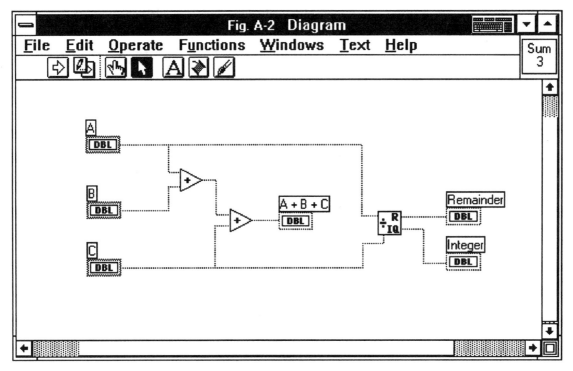

Block Diagram

Fig. A-2 A Typical VI

Run Mode

When LabVIEW is placed in the Run mode by clicking (with the left mouse button), the control bar takes the form shown in Fig. A-1. The control bar icons have specific functions that are discussed next. The reader is also referred to Fig. A-3, which shows these icons in their disabled (off) and enabled states.

Run By clicking on this icon, the user issues a command to execute the VI that is active (appears in the front panel and block diagram). If the VI runs, then the arrow changes to that shown in Fig. A-3 and a *STOP* icon appears between the Mode and Continuous Run icons. If it does not, the run arrow becomes broken. A broken arrow is an indication that this vi cannot be compiled due to errors. The execution may be terminated by clicking on the *STOP* icon. The *STOP* icon offers a convenient way of stopping the VI when it runs into an endless loop problem and there is no other way to stop it. From a practical standpoint it is better to include some sort of a mechanism that stops the VI naturally. We will see examples of that later.

Continuous Run By clicking on this icon, the active vi will be executed endlessly. To stop the execution, click on the Continuous Run icon again (it toggles). The Continuous Run execution may also be terminated by clicking on the *STOP* icon.

Breakpoint By clicking on this icon, a breakpoint in the active vi is set. Clicking on the same icon will disable the breakpoint.

Step Mode By clicking on this icon, which looks like a horizontal line in its off state, the Step mode option is enabled and the icon changes to one with three pulses. If you click next on the Run icon, an additional icon with a single pulse appears next to the icon with three pulses, as shown in Fig. A-3. The single pulse icon may then be used to single-step through the active VI, a procedure that, as we shall see later, is extremely useful in troubleshooting a vi.

Execution Highlighting After clicking on this icon, the icon changes to a yellow color bulb and the Execution Highlighting is thus enabled. In this mode of operation the user can observe data flow from node to node. If the Step Mode is enabled as well, the flow halts at each node on a step-by-step basis. This is another very helpful troubleshooting tool.

Print Mode It is enabled by clicking on this icon. After VI completes execution, the front panel will be printed.

Datalogging Clicking on this icon enables Cataloging. Once vi is running, the user is prompted to enter the file name where data is to be stored (the *.txt* file extension must be used). Note the change in the Cataloging icon after the data generated by the VI during execution is logged into the user specified file. (See Fig. A-3.)

Command Icon	Status/Comment (after clicking on command icon)
Run Icon	⇨ VI is running. Broken run button means that VI has errors. It cannot be compiled or executed. Stop button appears between Edit/Run and Continuous Run buttons only when VI is running.
Continuous Run Disabled	**Continuous Run Enabled**
Breakpoint Disabled	**Breakpoint Enabled**
Step Mode Disabled	**After clicking on Step Mode icon** **After clicking on Step Mode and Run icons.**
Execution Highlighting Disabled	**Execution Highlighting Enabled**
Print Mode Disabled	**Print Mode Enabled**
Datalogging Disabled	**Datalogging Enabled** **Data stored to file at end of run.**

Fig. A-3 LabVIEW in Run Mode. Shown are various command bar icons in their disabled and enabled states.

Edit Mode

The Edit Mode, enabled by clicking on the Mode icon in Fig. A-4, offers several useful tools in creating a new VI or in making changes in the existing VI. The command bar changes to a new configuration of icons representing the editing tools as shown in Fig. A-4.

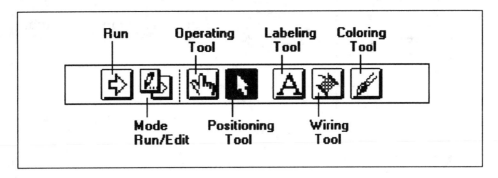

Fig. A-4 Command Bar in Edit Mode

The reader is referred to Fig. A-5 where editing tool icons are shown in their disabled and enabled states. Also shown is the shape of the mouse cursor, which as can be seen, assumes in most cases the shape of the enabled tool icon. To enable a tool, you must click (with the left mouse button) on the tool icon. The function of each of these editing tools is described briefly next.

Operating Tool   The shape of the operating tool of a right hand with extended index finger. This symbol is very appropriate to represent the operating tool. This tool is used to change numeric values of panel controls and indicators. Note the change in the shape of the tool when it is over numeric text.

Positioning Tool   As its name implies, this tool, in the shape of an arrow, is used to position, select or enlarge objects in both the panel and diagram windows. Note the slight change in the shape of the arrow as the cursor moves from the window to the upper portion above the window. Also the cursor assumes the corner shape when it is over a corner of the object in either window. When the cursor assumes the corner shape, it may then be used to change the size of the object in either window.

Wiring Tool The shape of this tool, a spool of wire, is also appropriate for its purpose. It is used predominantly in the block diagram to wire or connect objects.

Labeling Tool   This tool whose shape is shown in Fig. A-5 is used to create free labels or to edit text in the existing labels in either window. Note the change in the shape of the tool as it passes over text.

Coloring Tool   This tool, in the shape of a paint brush, is used to color objects in either the front panel or the block diagram. Note the overlapping rectangles (representing the current foreground and background colors) that appear to the right of the coloring tool as soon as it is enabled.

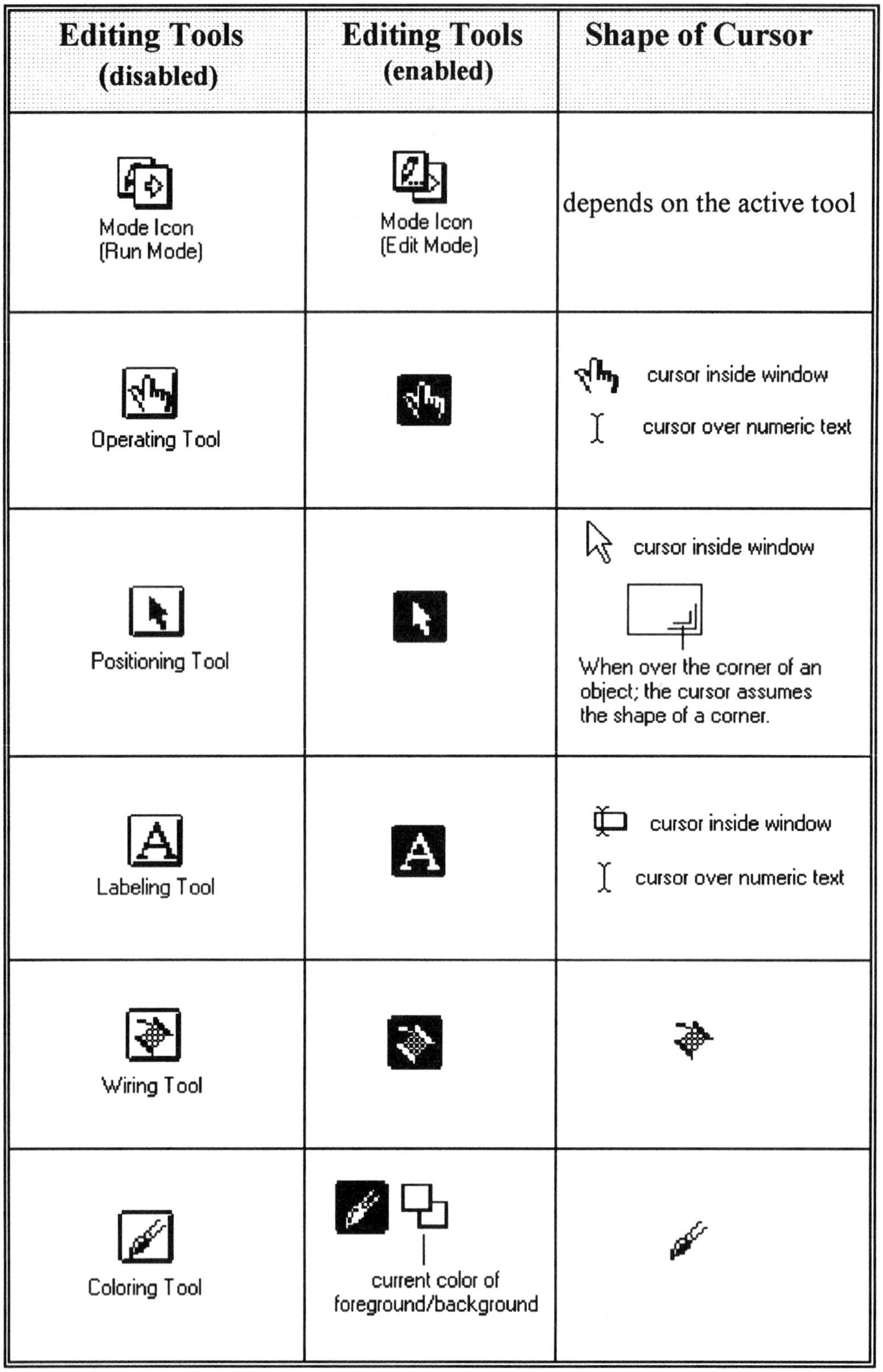

Editing Tools (disabled)	Editing Tools (enabled)	Shape of Cursor
Mode Icon (Run Mode)	Mode Icon (Edit Mode)	depends on the active tool
Operating Tool		cursor inside window cursor over numeric text
Positioning Tool		cursor inside window When over the corner of an object; the cursor assumes the shape of a corner.
Labeling Tool		cursor inside window cursor over numeric text
Wiring Tool		
Coloring Tool	current color of foreground/background	

Fig. A-5 Editing Tools When LabVIEW is in Edit Mode

Icon Pane

The active VI (the VI that is currently in the window) can be used as a *subVI* in anotherVI. This means that this VI can be represented by an icon with a connector in anotherVI. The Icon Pane is located in the upper right hand corner of the window. For example, the VI in Fig. A-2 can be used as a subVI because it has an icon (with connector) whose name is Sum 3. More will be said later on how to create an icon with a connector for a VI.

Pull-Down Menus

The pull-down menu bar is shown in Fig. A-2 and its enlarged version is shown in Fig. A-6. While some of the menus and their options are common to most of the word processors and other software written for windows, others are specific to the LabVIEW programming environment. The pull-down menus provide a host of valuable and useful tools in the course of a vi development. Many of the menu options are seldom if ever used, which is why the pull-down menu description that follows is limited to some of the more frequently used items. As the reader becomes familiar with the LabVIEW environment, he will probably prefer the use of the shortcut keys. They offer speedy execution of many tasks.

| File   Edit   Operate   Functions   Windows   Text   Help |

Fig. A-6 Pull-Down Menu Control Bar in Panel Window

File Menu

The File menu offers the use of the following important features:

> *Open and close a vi file*
> *Save to disk a vi file*
> *Print a vi file*

There are other options in the File menu but the three listed above are the most important and most frequently used in the course of vi development. Following is a brief description of selected File menu options (see Fig. A-7):

New	Opens an empty front panel and block diagram for new VI development.
Open...	Opens an existing VI file (user is presented with a directory from which to choose the desired file).
Close	The active VI is closed and removed from the window.
Save	Saves unconditionally the active VI.
Save As...	Saves the active VI file under a name provided by the user.
Print Documentation...	Prints the active vi in a format selected by the user.
Print Window...	Prints the active window (front panel or block diagram).
Data Logging	Saves data accumulated by the VI immediately after its execution to a log file. Accomplishes the same goal as the Datalogging icon. (See Fig. A-3.)

Fig. A-7 The File Pull-Down Menu

Get Info...	Allows the user to enter the active VI description.
Edit VI Library...	Allows the user to hide or delete a VI file from VI library.

Note the underlined letters in the pull-down menu bar as well as within the pull-down menu. These allow you to use the keyboard to navigate through the menus. For instance, the File menu is brought up by depressing the *Alt+F* keys (F is underlined in File). After releasing the *Alt+F* keys, depress next the S key if you wish to save the active VI file to disk.

The *shortcut keys* for some of the options within the menu are shown on the righthand side of the menu. For example, to perform the same Save operation using the shortcut keys, depress *Ctrl+S*. Shortcut keys offer a fast way to get things done and are generally faster than using the mouse.

Edit Menu

The Edit menu, shown in Fig. A-8, provides editing tools for making changes in the existing vi or for developing a new VI. Some of the important features of this menu include:

> *Moving selected part of window to Clipboard*
> *Removing bad wires in diagram window*
> *Repositioning objects inside window to suit desired symmetry*

A brief description of frequently used options in the Edit menu follows:

Cut	Selected region is deleted from the window and moved to Clipboard.
Copy	Selected region is moved to Clipboard (not deleted).
Paste	Contents last stored in Clipboard are moved to the active window.

```
 Edit  Operate  Functions  Win
 Cut                    Ctrl+X
    Copy                Ctrl+C
    Paste               Ctrl+V
    Clear

    Remove Bad Wires    Ctrl+B



    Alignment              ▶
    Align               Ctrl+A
    Distribution           ▶
    Distribute          Ctrl+D

    Move Forward        Ctrl+K
    Move Backward       Ctrl+J
    Move To Front    Ctrl+Shift+K
    Move To Back     Ctrl+Shift+J

    Preferences...
    User Name...
```

Fig. A-8 The Edit Pull-Down Menu

Clear   Acts like the *delete* key on the keyboard, because it deletes the selected region of the active window.

Remove Bad Wires   Removes any bad connections from the block diagram. Because this option is used often, the use of the shortcut key *Ctrl+B* saves time.

Operate Menu

The Operate menu, shown in Fig. A-9, offers the user tools to run and stop the active VI. It is probably one of the least frequently used menus because the options within this menu are available elsewhere. For example, the *Run* option provides the same action as the arrow run icon in the Control Bar, and the shortcut key *Ctrl+R* also provides the same action. The same is true for the *Change to Run Mode* option, which does the same task the *Mode* icon in the Control Bar. (See Figs. A-3 and A-5.)

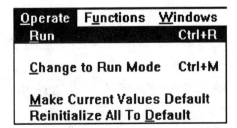
```
 Operate  Functions  Windows
 Run                     Ctrl+R

    Change to Run Mode   Ctrl+M

    Make Current Values Default
    Reinitialize All To Default
```

Fig. A-9 The Operate Pull-Down Menu

Controls Menu

The Controls menu, as shown in Fig. A-10, contains the essential building blocks used in developing aVI. Although it can be invoked by clicking (with the left mouse button) on the *Controls* option in the pull-down menu bar shown in Fig. A-10a, it can also be brought to the Panel window by *popping up* (with the right mouse button) anywhere inside the front panel area (Fig. A-10b). The popping up feature of LabVIEW offers convenience and speed in accomplishing a desired task, such as opening the Controls menu.

The reader may observe that the Control Bar options are the same in the front panel and block diagram with one exception: *the front panel has the Controls option and block diagram has the Functions option*. The reason for this difference goes back to remarks made earlier regarding the architecture of LabVIEW. It has to do with the function or the purpose of the front panel and the purpose of the block diagram. The front panel of a practical instrument and also the front panel of a VI includes controls, indicators, and graphs that provide a means for displaying data generated by the instrument. Inside a practical instrument there is usually a circuit board with many interconnected IC chips and other components that perform various arithmetic, logical and other tasks. The data thus generated within the instrument is applied to the front panel for display. In LabVIEW the Functions menu provides the various functions that can be wired together to accomplish the required operation or measurement.

As can be seen in Fig. A-10, the Controls menu provides Numeric and Boolean controls and indicators as well as strings, arrays, clusters and graphs.

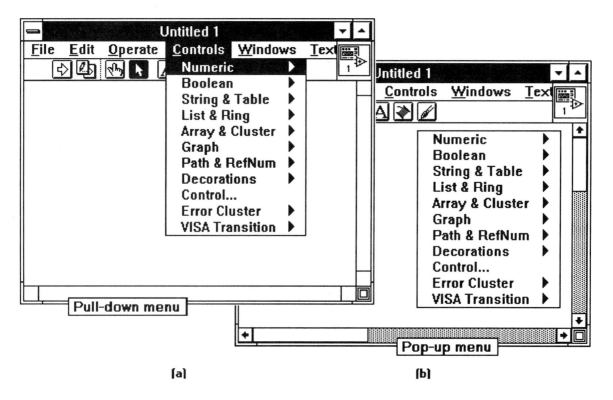

Fig. A-10 Controls Menu: (a) Controls Pull-Down Menu, (b) Controls Popup Menu

Windows Menu

The Windows menu, shown in Fig. A-11, gives the user access to the clipboard to view any saved information as well as the ability to switch to the block diagram from the front panel or to switch to front panel from the block diagram. The shortcut key **Ctrl+F** does this task much faster. This menu also offers the user a listing of all opened VIs as well as the active VI. The currently active VI is designated by a checkmark. As shown in Fig. A-11, the block diagram of Untitled 8 is active.

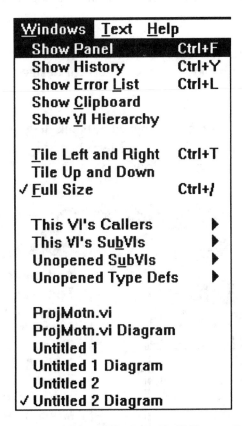

Fig. A-11 The Window Pull-Down Menu

Text Menu

The Text menu, shown in Fig. A-12, allows the user to control various aspects of any text typed inside the active window. This includes the type of font, its size and its color. The style option offers choices such as bold, plain, underline, etc.

Fig. A-12 The Text Pull-Down Menu

Fig. A-13 shows the Pull-Down Menu bar available in the Diagram Window. It is the same as the menu bar shown in Fig. A-6 for the front panel, with one exception. The front panel menu bar includes the Controls menu, while the block diagram has the Functions menu.

<u>F</u>ile   <u>E</u>dit   <u>O</u>perate   F<u>u</u>nctions   <u>W</u>indows   <u>T</u>ext   <u>H</u>elp

Fig. A-13 Pull-Down Menu Control Bar in the Block Diagram

Thus the Controls menu in front panel provides the building blocks for the construction of the instrument panel, while the Functions menu provides objects for designing instrument's function in in the block diagram.

The Functions menu shown in Fig. A-14 may be opened in block diagram either by clicking (with the left mouse button) on the Functions option in the Menu bar or by popping up (with the right mouse button) anywhere inside the Diagram Window.

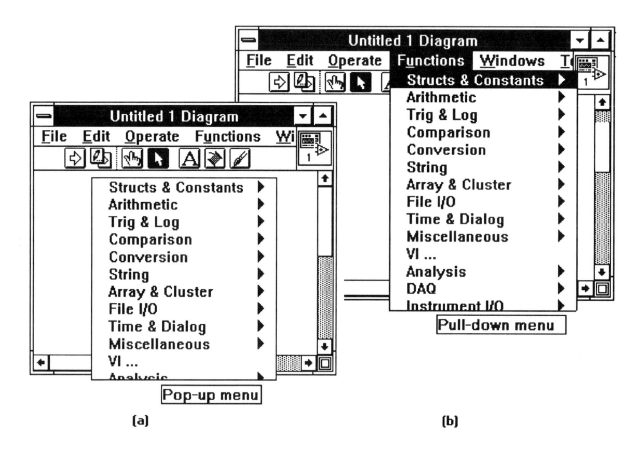

(a)   (b)

Fig. A-14 Functions Menu: (a) Functions Pull-Down Menu, (b) Functions Popup Menu

EDITING

The task of editing arises in the process of building a VI or making changes to an existing VI. Such tasks as *selecting, moving, deleting, resizing, copying, labeling,* and *arranging* objects inside either window, as well as several other tasks, are essential to a speedy and successful completion of a final product. The reader must therefore become familiar with these techniques. The editing exercises that follow provide an opportunity for the user to practice.

The user should be familiar with the following terms that will be used throughout:

click on an object Depress the *left* mouse button when the mouse cursor is over the object

popping-up Depress *right* mouse button when the mouse cursor is over an object. Popping up may also be done in an empty area of a window when the Controls or the Functions menu has to be opened in the window.

dragging an object Click and, while holding down the left mouse button, move the mouse in any direction. The object will move on the screen as the mouse is moved.

In the series of exercises that follow, we will demonstrate various techniques associated with editing.

Each exercise is started in an empty front panel and block diagram. Usually when LabVIEW is just launched, the empty front panel and block diagram become immediately available. But if other VI files have been opened before, then there may be no empty windows. In that case choose *File>New*, and an empty panel window will appear.

When making changes to an existing VI or building a new VI, *always* place LabVIEW in *Edit* mode by clicking on the *Mode* icon in the Control bar (see Fig. A-5). Also click on the Positioning Tool in the Control bar. It is probably the most often used editing tool. Fig. A-5 shows the Positioning Tool and its cursor shapes.

Exercise 1: Getting Objects from the Menu to LabVIEW Window

The following procedure can be used regardless of the type of object in question. Suppose that we need a *Waveform Chart* in the front panel. To accomplish this:

1. Click on the Positioning Tool in the Control bar. (The Positioning Tool is shown in Fig. A-5.)
2. Choose **Controls>Graph>Waveform Chart** - first click on *Controls* and after double clicking on *Graph* (inside the Controls pull-down menu), a submenu appears with various graph choices. Click on the *Waveform Chart* (see Fig. A-15). This type of operation can be done faster by popping up anywhere inside the front panel and then dragging the mouse. This means that you depress and *hold down* the right mouse button. Drag the mouse cursor through various choices down to the *Graph* option. You will notice that when you pause on the *Graph* option, a submenu with various graph choices appears on the side. While still holding down the right mouse button, move the mouse cursor over the submenu graph choices. Whenever the cursor is over a graph option, the name of that graph appears at the bottom of the menu. *As soon as you release the right mouse button, the menu will disappear and the last choice will be opened in the front panel.* Practice this operation with other objects. Moving objects from menus to the front panel or the block diagram is a task that is done frequently.

Once an object is inside the window, other editing tasks can be done on that or any other object inside the window.

Exercise2: Selecting and Deleting Objects

In order to perform an editing task on an object, you have to let the system know which object you want to work on. This is done by *selecting* the object. Let's try this on a Square LED. First, get the LED from the Controls menu:

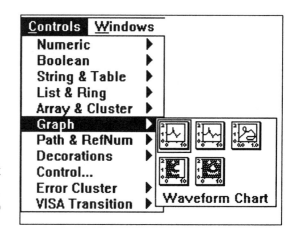

Fig. A-15 Choosing Controls>Graph>Waveform Chart

1. Click on the Positioning Tool.
2. Choose *Controls>Boolean>Square LED* as shown in Fig. A-16

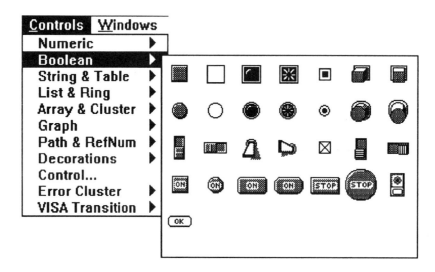

Fig. A-16   Choosing Controls>Boolean>Square LED

Once the Square LED is opened in the front panel, it can be selected:

To Select: (single object)	Click on the object. The mouse cursor should be close to the center of the object. If a *corner symbol* appears, reposition the mouse cursor because the corner symbol is associated with resizing and not with selecting. Once selected *a dashed outline* appears around the object.
To Select: (multiple objects)	Position the mouse cursor anywhere in the window. *Press and hold down* the left mouse button. The shape of the *arrow* mouse cursor will change to a cross. As you move (drag) the cursor, a dashed rectangle is formed. When the left mouse button is released, the rectangle will disappear and all objects that were inside the rectangle will be selected. Note that all selected objects have a *dashed outline*. This procedure may also be used to select a single object.

348

To Deselect: Click outside the dashed outline. The dashed line will disappear and the object is thus deselected.

To Delete: First, *select* the object to be deleted. Then press the *delete* key on the keyboard. The object will disappear.

3. Practice selecting, deselecting and finally deleting the Square LED.

Note: LabVIEW Editor **does not** have the **Undo** command; it takes too much memory. So anything that you delete cannot be retrieved. There is one exception to that: the graphics editor used for subVI icon design has an Undo option, which will be covered later.

Exercise 3: Moving, Duplicating, and Resizing Objects

When designing or modifying VIs, it is often necessary to change the size of objects or their position inside the window. Let's try this on a Square LED. It was deleted last, so let's bring it back..

1. Click on the Positioning Tool in the Controls bar.
2. Choose *Controls>Boolean>Square LED*. Once the LED appears in the front panel, it may be edited.

To Move an Object - Select the desired object. Then drag the object. This means that as you click on the object, you must hold down the left mouse button. As you move the mouse, the object follows the motion of the cursor. Once again, when clicking make sure that the corner symbol does not appear.

To Duplicate an Object - Select the desired object. While pressing the *Ctrl* key on the keyboard, drag or move the object in any direction following the rules for moving. When you release the left mouse button, you will see a copy of the object.

To Resize an Object - Position the tip of the mouse cursor over a *corner* of the object. The cursor *arrow shape* changes to the *corner shape* (see Fig. A-5 for descriptions of Positioning Tool cursor shapes). While *holding down* the left mouse button, move the cursor in an outward direction. You will notice the object increasing in size. When the left mouse button is released, the object will assume the enlarged size.

The moving and resizing rules above apply to all objects in the front panel or the block diagram.

3. Practice these rules on the Square LED presently in the front panel or on other objects you bring into the front panel.

Exercise 4: Labeling

Labeling of objects is necessary for descriptive or identification purposes. For example, if there are two digital controls in the front panel, their counterparts (as we will learn later) are in the block diagram. Unless they are labeled, one cannot tell them apart in the front panel or in the block diagram. This creates a problem because they probably have different functions. There are two types of labels: the *owned labels* and the *free labels*.

Creating an Owned Label

Click on the Positioning Tool (see Fig. A-5). Pop up on the object and select *Show>Label*. This means: place the mouse cursor over the object, depress the right mouse button *and hold it down*, then drag the mouse in choosing *Show>Label*. The selection of the *owned* label is shown in Fig. A-17. As soon as you release the left mouse button, a gray rectangle will appear over the object. Immediately start typing the object's name. When finished typing, click on the *Enter* icon next to the *Run* arrow in the control bar. Note that the owned label appears in the front panel and in the block diagram.

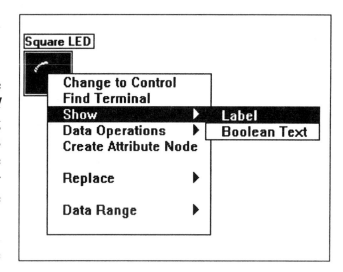

Fig. A-17 Creating a Free Label by Popping Up on the Object and Choosing Show>Label

Creating a Free Label

Click on the Labeling Tool in the Control bar (see Fig. A-5). Position the Labeling Tool cursor near the object and click (with the left mouse button). A gray rectangle will appear. Begin typing. After you are finished typing, click on the *Enter* icon next to the *Run* arrow in the Control bar. The *free label* will appear next to the object in the position selected by you earlier.

Note:

The user should understand the ***important difference between the owned label and the free label.*** After the owned label is typed, it appears over the object in the front panel and it also appears over the corresponding object in the block diagram; the system is aware that the owned label represents a particular object. The free label, on the other hand, has more meaning to the user because it provides a special functional description of the object, such as ON or OFF labels next to the switch, or coordinate axis labels such as *Output Voltage (Vdc)* along the ordinate and *Time (msec.)* along the abcissa. The free label typed in the front panel will not appear in the block diagram, and vice versa.

1. At this time open the Square LED, or another object in the front panel using
    Controls>Boolean>LED.
2. Open other objects of your choice in the front panel using the procedure of step 1.

3. Open objects from another option of the Controls menu in the front panel. For example, by choosing **Controls>Numeric>Digital Indicator** you will get a *Digital Indicator* from the *Numeric* option of the Controls pull-down menu.

4. Label the objects you selected with *owned labels* and others with *free labels*. Some objects should have both labels.

5. Select an object that has only an *owned* label. Move or reposition this object. Note that the owned label moves with the object.

6. This time, select only the label of the object in step 5. Try to move the label alone. Note that the label can be moved without the object. This means that the object's label may be moved to a more convenient position.

7. Select an object that has both labels: owned and free. Try to move the object. Notice that the owned label moves with the object but the free label does not.

8. Suppose that you would like to reposition or move
   - (a) an object together with the free label or
   - (b) several objects at the same time.

   To accomplish this, follow the procedure outlined in Exercise 2 for selecting multiple objects. Try this now. Select several objects or an object with a free label and try to move the selected group of objects to a different location in the window. After you selected a group of objects, a dashed outline will appear around the selected group. Place the mouse cursor on any of the selected objects and drag that object (don't forget to hold down the left mouse button as you drag the object). Notice that as you drag one of the selected objects, the rest of the selected objects move along with it.

Exercise 5: Coloring

The coloring option provides the user with the ability to color objects, giving them a distinctive appearance. This is not necessarily done for cosmetic reasons, although if you have a color printer, coloring will add an attractive feature to the front panel or the block diagram. But even if the printed copy is not of great concern, the appearance of the program on the screen, its readability, and the ability to follow data flow is enhanced when the objects are colored. It will not have that overall gray appearance where all objects seem to merge into the gray background. Also special emphasis may be given to some objects by coloring them.

To activate the coloring option:

1. Click on the *Coloring Tool* in the Control bar. Notice that the overlapping rectangles representing the currently active background and foreground colors appear and that the cursor changes its shape from the arrow to the paintbrush.

2. Position the paintbrush cursor over the object to be colored. Press and *hold down* the right mouse button. A palette of colors appears above the object, as shown in Fig. A-18.

3. Continue to hold down the right mouse button and move the cursor over the color choices in the color palette. Notice that as the cursor is over a particular color, the object to be colored assumes that color. As soon as you release the right mouse button, the object will assume the last color choice.

4. Note the letter **T** that appears on the left side of the color palette. Choosing *T* instead of a color will make the object to be colored **Transparent**. This feature may be used to make the box around the label invisible.

5. The *Foreground* and *Background* rectangles indicate the currently active colors of the foreground and the background. In choosing colors, you may select the foreground or the background, or both. The active rectangle (foreground/background) is indicated by a thick outline. The **Tab** key on the keyboard toggles between the foreground and the background options. The **Tab+A** selects both the foreground and the background.

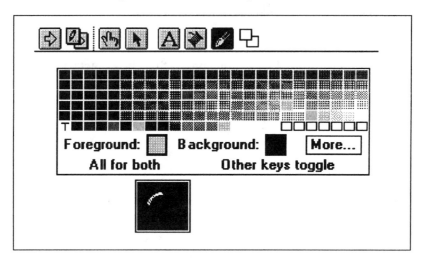

Fig. A-18 Color Palette for Coloring Objects

6. While you are in the Color Palette, position the over the rectangle labeled ***More....*** A window labeled *More Colors* will appear as shown in Fig. A-19. It allows you to custom mix the colors. The numbers in the *Red, Green, Blue* rectangles indicate relative mounts of the red, green and blue components in the final mixture. You may enter your own values to arrive at the desired hue. The color values shown in Fig. A-19 represent a green-blue combination, the same color that was used on the Square LED shown in Fig. A-18.

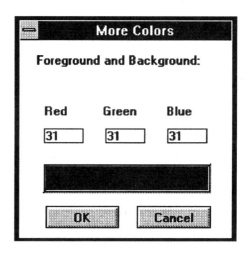

Fig. A-19 More Colors Submenu for Mixing Custom Colors

Exercise 6: Editing Text

Editing text in LabVIEW is a frequent task. Such operations as entering text into a label or identifying special features of your VI using free labels involve the use of the text editor. To activate the text editor:

1. Make sure that you are in the *Edit* mode by clicking on the *Mode* icon in the Control Bar.

2. Click on the **Text** option in the pull-down menu bar. The menu that appears is shown in Fig. A-12. The **Apply Font** option offers a standard set of fonts frequently used in a VI construction. These are shown in Fig. A-20. Notice the **Ctrl+1, 2, 3 or 4** shortcut keys for quick selection of these fonts from the keyboard.

3. If the user needs other fonts, the **Font** option offers a larger selection of fonts that are system dependent. The *Size* option offers a choice of sizes for the selected font, and the *Style* option offers font characteristics such as *Plain, Bold, Underline*, etc. A bold font often used in labeling is provided by the *Dialog Font* option; it has a shortcut key, *Ctrl+3* (see Fig. A-20).

4. In editing text it is often necessary to delete a portion or an entire segment of text. This can be done in one of several ways:

    4.1 First, highlight the text to be deleted using the *Labeling Tool*. This is done by clicking on the text (with the left mouse button) and then, while holding down the mouse button, drag the cursor across the text to be selected. When you release the mouse button, the selected text will appear white on a dark background. Press next the *Delete* key on the keyboard, thus deleting the selected text.

    4.2 The text may also be deleted one character at a time by clicking on the right side of the text to be deleted and then using the *Backspace* key on the keyboard to delete.

    4.3 The numerical text may also be deleted using the **Operating Tool** and following either procedure 4.1 or 4.2.

5. *Let's try practicing the text editor on a Waveform Chart.*
   Open the Waveform Chart in the front panel by choosing
   Controls>Graph>Waveform Chart.

6. Resize the chart so that it takes up more than half of the front panel. Don't forget to click first on the *Positioning Tool*.

7. Change the ordinate scale as follows:

    7.1 Change the maximum value to 80. Follow the procedure in 4.1 or 4.2 by first deleting the current maximum value. Then type 80.

    7.2 Change the minimum value to 20 by first deleting the current minimum value and then typing 20

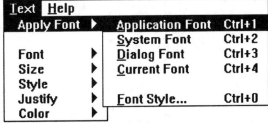

Fig.A-20 Text Pull-Down Menu and Apply Fonts Submenu

8. Change the maximum value along the abcissa to 200. Follow the procedure used in step 7.

9. Let's give this chart a name. Choose **Show>Label**. This is done by popping up on the Waveform Chart (with the right mouse button) and, while *holding down* the right mouse button, navigating down to *Show* (in the menu that pops up) and then to the right to *Label*. After releasing the right mouse button, menus disappear and a gray rectangle appears over the

chart. Type **Temperature Chart**.

> *Note:* Whenever an object is brought to the front panel or the block diagram, a gray rectangle appears over the object. You can at this time type the name of the object as long as you do it right away because as soon as you click on something else, the gray rectangle will disappear. The only way then to label the object is to pop up on it and use *Show>Label*, as was done in step 9.

10. Additional descriptive features may be added to the chart by using free labels. Choose the Labeling Tool and somewhere close to the ordinate type **Deg. F**, and along the abcissa type **Time (msec)**.

11. Suppose that we want to change all text on the chart to bold type. To do this, first select the chart by clicking on it (with the left mouse button). Note that a dashed outline encloses the chart. Then either choose *Text>Style>Bold* from the text pull-down menu or enter *Ctrl+3* from the keyboard. What happened? The chart name (owned label) as well as the numerical values were changed to bold type, but the free labels remained unchanged because we selected the Waveform Chart alone. But actually there are three objects in the front panel: the Waveform Chart and the two free labels. The *owned label,* as was mentioned before, belongs to the object that in this case is the waveform chart, and the *free labels* are separate objects.

To remedy this problem, select all three objects simultaneously using the procedure for multiple object selection from Exercise 2, and then enter *Ctrl+3* from the keyboard. The final front panel configuration for this exercise is shown in Fig. A-21.

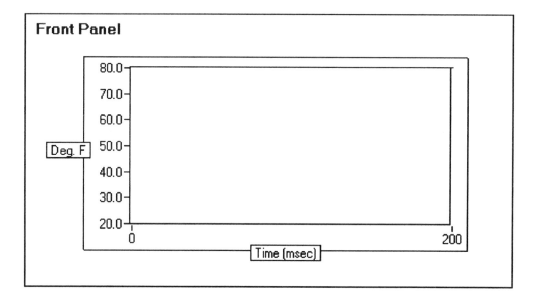

Fig. A-21 Front Panel for Exercise 6

354

Exercise 7: Aligning and Distributing Objects

The Alignment and Distribution options can be used to position objects inside the front panel or the block diagram. Objects can be arranged with a desired order or symmetry. These options are in the Edit pull-down menu.

To see how these options work, let's try an experiment.

1.   Open a *Digital Control* in the front panel by popping up inside the front panel and then selecting *Numeric>Digital Control* from the menu. The other way is to select *Controls>Numeric>Digital Control* from the Controls menu. This is shown in Fig. A-22.

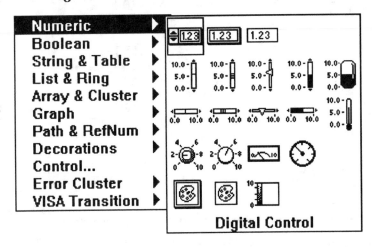

Fig. A-22 Choosing a Digital Control From the Controls Menu

2.   Once the Digital Control is in the front panel, make two copies of this control. Use the procedure in Exercise 3 for *duplicating objects*. You should now have three Digital Control objects in the front panel. Move them around so that they are positioned vertically. Do not pay attention to the spacing between them. This is shown in Fig. A-23 on the left side of the front panel. Also label them with *owned labels*, so that the top digital control is **A**, the middle one is **B**, and the bottom digital control is **C**.

3.   Next, select the three Digital Controls using the procedure described in Exercise 2 for selecting multiple objects. Each of the selected objects will be enclosed by a dashed border.

4.   Select from the *Edit* menu *Alignment>Left Edges*, as shown in Fig. A-24a. To do this, click (with the left mouse button) on *Edit* menu, double click on the *Alignment* option, and finally click on the *Left Edges* in the Alignment submenu. Note that the Alignment submenu has five other choices that can be used in the alignment of objects:

                    Horizontal Centers
                    Right Edges
                    Top Edges
                    Vertical Centers
                    Bottom Edges

355

Hold down the left mouse button and move through the various choices. Note that the name of each choice appears at the bottom of the submenu. As soon as you release the mouse button, the last choice will be selected. Note that the three objects have been aligned along the left edges. In the next step we will make the vertical spacing between them equal.

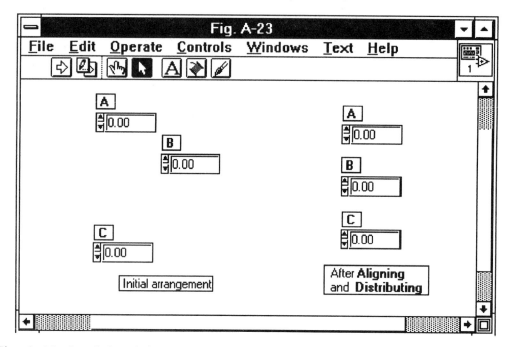

Fig. A-23 Applying Alignment and Distribution to Objects in the Front Panel

5. Select ***Distribution>Top Edges*** from the ***Edit*** menu. The procedure is very similar to the alignment selection in the preceding step (see Fig. A-24b).

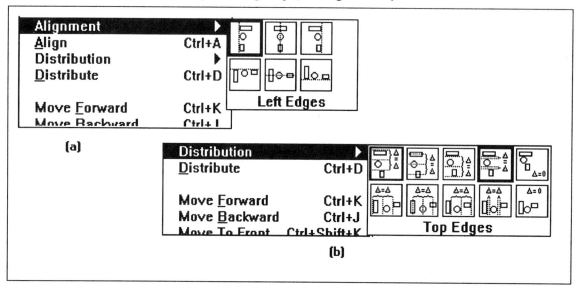

**Fig. A-24 Selecting: (a) Alignment>Left Edges, (b) Distribution>Top Edges
from the Edit Menu**

Note that in the Distribution submenu there are nine other choices for distributing or simply spacing objects in either the front panel or the block diagram. At this time experiment using different sets of objects and other options in the Alignment and Distribution submenus.

Exercise 8: Wiring

Thus far we have focused our attention on how to edit using various editing tools from the pull-down menus. Although all of the work was done in the front panel, the same editing techniques apply equally well to the objects in the block diagram. As was mentioned before, every VI must have a front panel and a block diagram.

Wiring is the first task used only in the block diagram. As we already know, the objects in the front panel represent a collection of *Controls* and *Indicators*. Controls allow us to pass data to the program in the block diagram, and the program, on the other hand, passes data or results back to the *Indicators*.

Each object in the front panel must have its counterpart, a *Terminal*, in the block diagram. It is very important to label each object in the front panel with an *owned label*. This is necessary because several objects of the same type, such as digital controls or digital indicators, in the front panel will have exactly the same symbolic representation in the block diagram. Unless they are labeled with an owned label (not a free label) in the front panel, they cannot be distinguished in the block diagram. When an object is labeled with an owned label in the front panel, the same label will appear in the block diagram.

Wiring of objects in the block diagram is associated with *Data Flow* in the program. A wire connected from the output of one object to the input of another graphically represents the path that the data takes. More will be said about the data flow and other functional aspects of a VI, but now our major concern is how to wire objects inside the block diagram.

1. Let's begin our wiring exercise opening in the front panel two Digital Controls and two Digital Indicators.
    Select *Controls>Numeric>Digital Control* for accessing a digital control and *Controls>Numeric>Digital Indicator* for the digital indicator. Once you have a digital control and a digital indicator in the front panel , you may duplicate them to get two more.
2. Label the digital controls with owned labels, one as **A** and the other as **B.**
    Label the digital indicators with owned labels, one as **AB** and the other as **A+B.**
3. Switch to the block diagram by using the shortcut keys *Ctrl+F*.
4. Once in the block diagram , get the *Add* and the *Multiply* functions from the Arithmetic menu. To accomplish this, choose
    Functions>Arithmetic>Add and *Functions>Arithmetic>Multiply*
    Fig. A-25 shows how to choose the Add function. You can get the Functions pull-down menu either by clicking on the *Functions* in the Control Bar or by popping up anywhere in the block diagram.

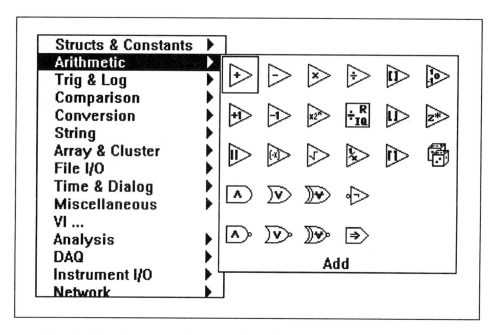

Fig. A-25   Choosing the Add function from the Arithmetic Menu

5.   Arrange objects by moving them so that they appear more or less as shown in Fig. A-26.

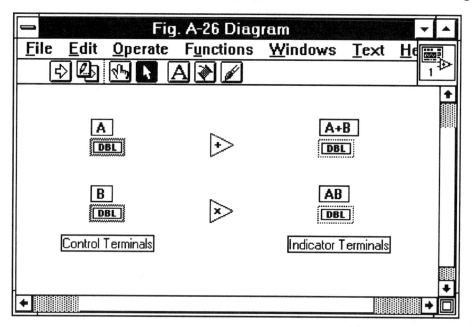

Fig. A-26   Block Diagram with Objects to Be Wired

6. In Fig. A-26 we now have two functions. The **Add** with (+) inside the icon will accept two inputs and produce a sum at the output. The **Multiply** with a (x) inside the icon will accept two inputs and produce the product at its output. The *Digital Control* terminals **A** and **B** provide the numerical inputs from the front panel. The outputs from the **Add** and the **Multiply** functions are applied to the *Digital Indicator* terminals labeled **A+B** and **AB.** The *Digital Indicators* on the front panel will display the **SUM** and the **Product**.

As mentioned earlier, the wiring symbolically represents the data flow. In this case the Digital Control terminals A and B must be wired to the inputs of the Add and the Multiply functions, and the outputs from the Add and the Multiply functions must be wired to their respective *Digital Indicator* terminals.

To simplify the wiring process, any function icon can be changed to another form that reveals the inputs that need to be wired. To accomplish this, click (with the right mouse button) on the function icon and choose **Show Terminals** from the menu that appears. This is shown in Fig. A-27a. When you release the mouse button, the icon changes to the terminal representation shown in Fig. A-27b. Notice the two inputs and the output are clearly indicated. This option toggles, so if you want to go back to the icon, click on the terminal and choose **Show Icon**.

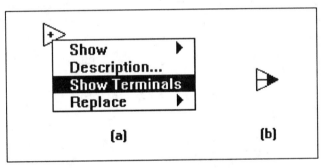

Fig. A-27 (a) Choosing Show Terminals Option to Convert an Icon to Terminal Representation, (b) Terminal Representation of Icon

7. We are now ready to begin wiring. Click on the Wiring Tool in the Control Bar. Notice the change in the cursor shape. It looks like a spool of wire with an extended piece of wire, as shown in Fig. A-5. Position the cursor (tip of the wire) over Digital Indicator A and observe that it begins to blink. Click and hold down the right mouse button. Then drag the mouse to one of the inputs on the Add function terminal, making sure that the extended wire of the cursor is over the input. Notice again that once you are over the input, it begins to blink. Click the right mouse button only once and observe the orange wire in place between Digital Control A and one input of the Add function.

If the wiring was successful, a solid wire will be in place. However, if you got a BAD wire, it will appear as a dashed line as shown in Fig. A-28. Delete the bad wire by entering the **Ctrl+B** shortcut key from the keyboard or choosing **Remove Bad Wires** from the Edit menu and repeating the wiring process in step 7.

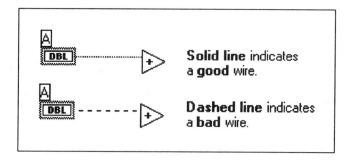

**Fig. A-28   Solid Wire Shows Correct Wiring. BAD Wire
Appears As a Dashed Line**

8.   Repeat the wiring process described in step 7 and wire Digital Control B to one of the inputs of the Multiply function.

9.   A **Wire Junction** may be created, as shown in Fig. A-29. A Wire Junction is useful when the data source, such as a Digital Control A, or B, for that matter, has to be wired to more than one terminal input. To create a wire junction click (with the left mouse button) with the wiring tool on the wire where the junction is to be created and drag the cursor to the input of the terminal. As the input area of the terminal begins to blink, click with the left mouse button. Observe a solid wire that extends from the junction to the input of the terminal.

Use this procedure to wire Digital Control A to the other input of the Multiply function.

10. Repeat the procedure described in step 9 by creating a junction and wiring Digital Control B to the remaining input of the Add function.

11. Complete the wiring by connecting the output of the Add function to the **A+B** Digital Indicator and the output of the Multiply function to the **AB** Digital Indicator. Your completed block diagram should look like that shown in Fig. A-30.

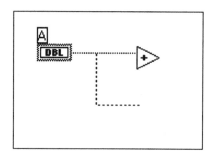

Fig. A-29 A Wire Junction

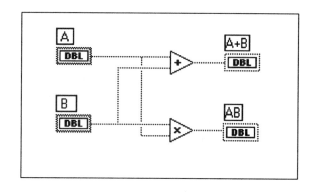

Fig. A-30 Completed Block Diagram

360

More Wiring Tips....

12. You can *Delete* one or more wire segments by first selecting them. To select a wire segment, use the arrow cursor of the *Positioning Tool* (click on the Positioning Tool icon in the Control Bar). Place the tip of the Positioning Tool cursor over the wire segment to be selected and click with the left mouse button:

A *single* click will select one segment.

A *double* click will select also the adjoining segment.

A *triple* click will select all segments joined by junctions.

This is shown in Fig. A-31. To delete a selected segment enter *Delete* from the keyboard.

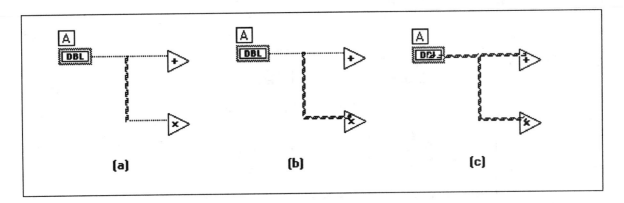

Fig. A-31 Selecting Wire Segments

13. Sometimes the configuration that you are wiring forces you to change *Wiring Direction*. Changing the wiring direction can be done in one of two ways:

A. Use the *Space* bar on the keyboard during wiring.
   When not wiring, the Space bar causes toggling between the Operating Tool and the Wiring Tool.

B. After you started the wiring path and before you get to the end (terminal), *click and hold down* the left mouse button. This will freeze the wiring segment that you made thus far. Change the direction at this point and continue with the wiring.

14. Check the wiring. If there are no broken wires, then you have completed your first VI. You can actually run it. Switch to the front panel (*Ctrl+F*) and activate the *Operating Tool* by clicking on the Operating Tool (hand with extended finger) in the Control Bar. Use the Operating Tool to enter values into Digital Controls A and B. To increment or decrement values, click on the Up or Down arrows located on the left side of the Digital Control with the extended finger of the Operating Tool cursor. The other way to enter values is to place the Operating Tool cursor over the Digital Control's window. Note the change in the shape of the cursor. Now enter the desired value from the keyboard.

For example, enter 5 into Digital Control A and 75 into Digital Control B and run the VI by clicking on the **Run** button in the Control Bar. The VI will execute once and display the sum and the product on the Digital Indicators corresponding to the A and B values that you entered. This is shown in Fig. A-32.

This VI will be used in the next appendix.

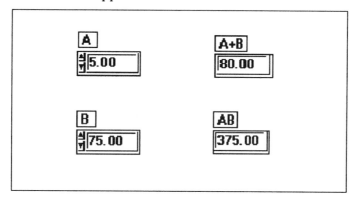

Fig. A-32 Front Panel After VI Is Executed

Exercise 9: Saving the VI to the Library File

All VIs that you build and would like to keep can be saved in some directory, as is common practice. In LabVIEW, however, you have another option. Your VI can be saved in a VI Library. The Library is not a directory, but rather it is a file that can contain many VI files. There are several advantages associated with a VI Library. Any VI stored in a Library can have a name that is up to 31 characters long instead of the usual 8 characters. To save disk space, all VIs are compressed when you save them and decompressed when you load them. Portability becomes simpler too because all the VIs are in the same file.

The VI Library must have a name 8 characters or less and a **.LLB** extension. A VI file may have a name 31 characters or less, as mentioned earlier, with a **.vi** extension.

Let's experiment and save the VI that you just finished wiring.

1.   Choose **Save As** from the **File** menu.
2.` From the File Dialog box that comes up, choose **NEW**.
3.   The next dialog box that comes up allows you to choose the Directory or the VI Library and the name. Enter the name such as **My_VIs**, as shown in Fig. A-33, and click on **VI Library**.

You don't have to provide the extension .LLB. After you click on VI Library, the system will add the proper extension.

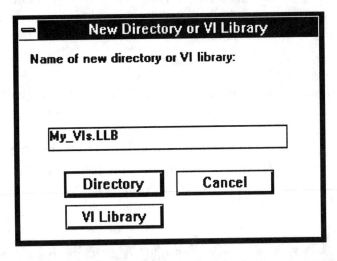

Fig. A-33 Creating a VI Library Called My_VIs.LLB

4. The next dialog box that appears is called File Dialog. Note that the name of the VI Library that was just created appears at the top. Now you have to enter the name for the VI file that you want to save in the VI Library. Choose a name such as *Add_Multiply.vi* and click on the **OK** button. The Dialog box will disappear and your VI file is saved. The path for your file is *LabVIEW>MyVIs.LLB>Add_Multiply.vi*.

5. To view the file that was just saved, choose *Open* from the *File* menu and then open *My_VIs.LLB* library, as shown in Fig. A-34. Finally double click on the *Add_Multiply.vi*.

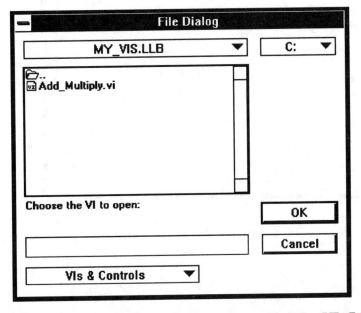

Fig. A-34 Add_Multiply.vi File Is Stored in My_VIs Library

Exercise 10: VI Description

A VI that you build should be documented. Although this is not essential, it is often helpful, especially if the VI was constructed quite some time ago and you have forgotten its objectives. Obviously if the VI is simple, documentation is not necessary. Let's go through the procedure on how to document a VI.

1. Open the VI that will be documented. Take, for instance, the one that you just finished wiring, the Add_Multiply.vi. If it is already open, then proceed to the next step.
2. Choose *Get Info* from the *File* menu.
3. The dialog box that opens is called VI Information. It allows you to type text under *Description*, thus providing VI documentation. An example describing the Add_Multiply.vi is shown in Fig. A-35. Type the VI description and choose OK. Note the path for this VI below the VI name.

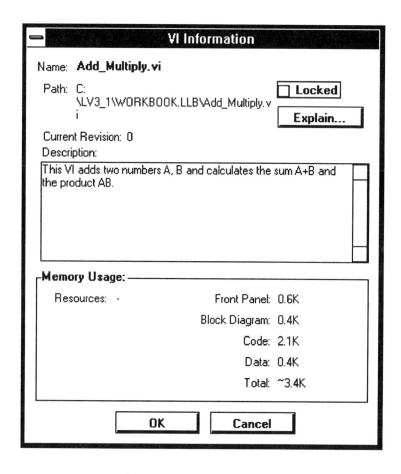

Fig. A-35 Creating VI Documentation

364

Appendix B

Creating and
Troubleshooting a VI
(LabVIEW Version 3)

In this appendix you will learn :

How to create a VI.

How to create an icon and a connector for a VI.

How to use a VI as a subVI.

Data types and data representation.

Format and precision.

How to troubleshoot a VI.

The previous appendix was almost entirely devoted to the description of the LabVIEW Environment. You have learned about the Control Bar options and the various options inside the pull-down menus, among other things. Because wiring is an essential task in building any VI, it was discussed in great detail. Wiring is a skill that you gain with practice. You also learned that a VI Library is a file that contains many other VI files.

The kind of detail that was used in Appendix A in describing the editing, wiring and other tasks will not be used in this appendix or the next. You will be asked to build the given VI and perhaps given not too much more. So Appendix A becomes a valuable resource for you, and you may have to turn to Appendix A when you have forgotten how to do a specific task.

Appendix A represents a foundation upon which you will build your knowledge of LabVIEW. We will begin almost immediately using your newly acquired skills in building VIs. Don't be discouraged if these early VIs seem too simplistic; they are designed to illustrate specific concepts. The VI complexity will come in time.

Exercise 1: Viewing a VI

Before building your own VI, you will open, run and inspect a demonstration VI. You will find out in time the power and versatility of LabVIEW. Simulation is one of many things that can be done in LabVIEW, and this is exactly what our demonstration VI will do. Its name is ProjMotn.vi and, as you might have guessed from its name, it simulates projectile motion.

We know from physics that when a projectile is aimed at a given angle and given an initial velocity, its path through space will follow a parabolic path before descending back to earth. This is an idealistic model where drag forces due to friction are neglected. The range is the distance along the ground between the starting point and the point where the projectile returns to ground, and the altitude is the maximum vertical distance of the parabolic path.

The path for this VI is C:\LabVIEW\Workbook.LLB\ProjMotn.vi. Actually Workbook.LLB is the VI Library where you will save all the VIs that you will build later, and Workbook.LLB is in the LabVIEW directory.

You are not expected to understand the design of this VI, although you can peek at the block diagram by using Ctrl+F. The purpose of this exercise is to operate a typical VI, observe its response and observe the various objects in the front panel.

So, go to Workbook.LLB and open the ProjMotn.vi. The front panel shown in Fig. B-1 opens as soon as you open the ProjMotn.vi.

Note that the front panel contains controls and indicators. There are Digital Controls for inputting the angle and the initial velocity, and there are Digital Indicators for displaying the altitude, range, and the time of flight. There is also the X-Y graph for displaying the parabolic projectile path.

Run the VI by clicking on the *Run* button.

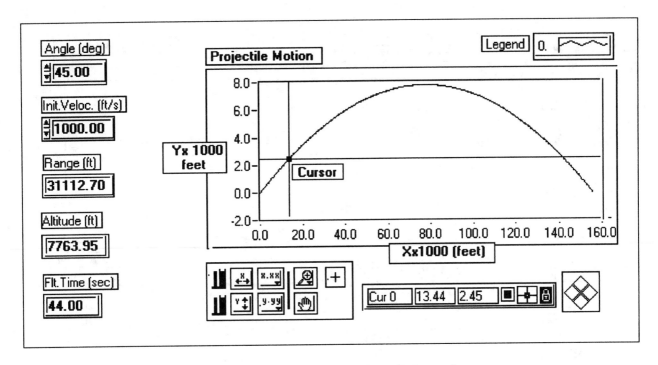

Fig. B-1 Front Panel of ProjMotn.vi

As soon as you click on the Run button, you will note that another VI's front panel, called the Pop_Up.vi and containing another graph, appears.

This is an example of what can be done when you run out of space in the original front panel. Notice that in the original front panel, the X-Y graph displays a plot of the projectile's vertical position (along the Y-axis) versus its position along the ground (along the X-axis). But suppose we also wanted to see how the projectile's vertical distance and its position along the ground vary with time. Well, the popup graph does just that. When you are finished observing the popup graph, click on the **Done** button. The popup graph will disappear, and you are back to the front panel of the ProjMotn.vi.

Enter different values for the angle and the initial velocity, and run the VI again. Note the different results for range, altitude and time of flight.

Note the **Cursor Display** bar below the X-Y graph, as shown in Fig. B-2. The cursor display shows the exact value of the cursor coordinates. You can move the cursor along the parabolic curve by using the diamond shaped cursor control on the right side of the cursor display bar. To do that, use the *Operating Tool*.

367

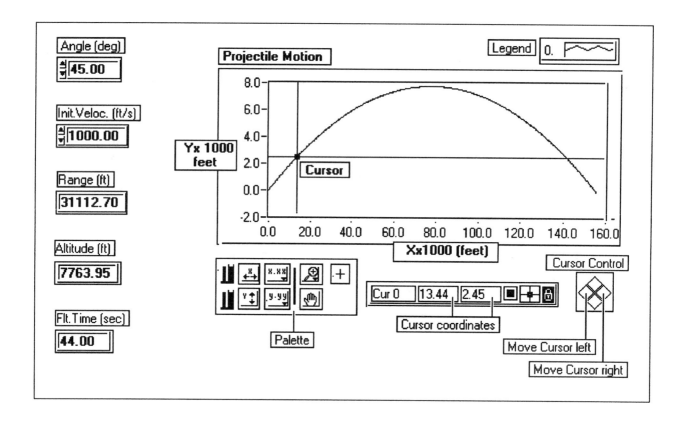

Fig. B-2 Cursor Display Shows the Exact Coordinates of the Cursor. The Cursor Can Be Moved Along the Curve by Using the Positioning Tool on the Cursor Control.

Once you are finished with this VI, close it by choosing **Close** from the File menu or using the shortcut keys **Ctrl+W**. Do not save any changes that you might have made.

Exercise 2: Creating a VI

Although you have already built a VI in the wiring exercise of the last appendix, the situation is slightly different here. The VI that you have to build has been configured. You are given its completed front panel and block diagram windows, and now it is your job to build this VI.

The VI that you have to build, *Sum_4.vi*, is shown in Fig. B-3. This VI can add four numbers and output the sum. We will later create an icon and a connector for this VI. Since the conventional Add function can add only two numbers, this VI will be a handy icon to have in future applications.

The front panel includes three Digital Controls and one Digital Indicator, and the block diagram uses the Add functions. You will find:
Digital Control and Indicator in the ***Controls>Numeric*** menu.
Add function in the ***Functions>Numeric*** menu.
So without further delay, switch to the ***Edit Mode*** and build the VI shown in Fig. B-3.

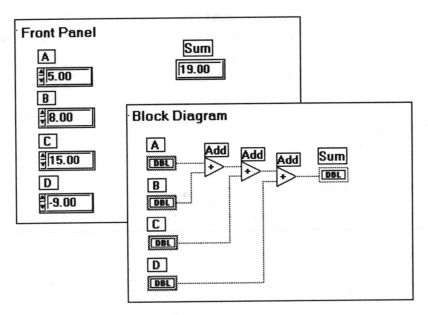

Fig. B-3 The Front Panel and Block Diagram of Exercise 2

The completed VI should now be ready to be executed. Check the **Run** button in the Control Bar. If the Run button is broken (a broken Run button is shown in Fig. A-3 of Appendix A), your VI cannot be executed as it stands because it has errors. This is similar to syntax errors in a high-level language (such as C language) program. The errors must be corrected before your VI can be executed. Consult the Troubleshooting section later in this appendix and correct all errors.

Run your VI by clicking on the Run button. Input different values into the Digital Controls and check the Digital Indicator to see if the Sum is correct.

Provide the *VI Description*. See Exercise 10 of Appendix A.

You will be saving your VIs in the VI Library **Workbook.LLB**.
If you have not done so already, create the VI Library **Workbook.LLB**. See Exercise 9 of Appendix A.
Save Sum_4.vi in WorkBook.LLB.

Exercise 3: Creating an Icon and a Connector for a VI

All VIs that you build are hierarchical in character. This means that any VI, regardless of how large it is, may be used as a *subVI* in another VI. This capability of LabVIEW permits a modular construction of a complex VI. A complex VI may include one or more subVIs, each with an icon and a connector. Each subVI is designed to perform a specific function. The modularization of a large VI makes it is easier to troubleshoot and if changes need to be made in a subVI, they can be better handled without affecting the rest of the VI. Any VI can be converted into a subVI. All it needs is an *Icon* and a *Connector*. It is the purpose of this exercise to show you how to create an Icon and a Connector for a VI, and we will use the Sum_4.vi that you just finished building as an example.

369

1. First open the Sum_4.vi. Remember, it is in the WorkBook.LLB VI Library.
2. Open the front panel. Click on the Icon Pane with the right mouse button (hold down the mouse button). The Icon Pane is shown in Fig. B-2.
   Choose **Edit Icon**, as shown in Fig. B-4.

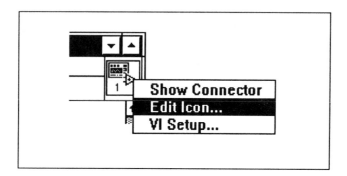

Fig. B-4 Choosing Edit Icon from the Icon Pane Menu

3. You are now in the Icon Editor. The Icon Editor window is shown in Fig. B-5. The Icon Editor Work Area is where you draw the symbol for your icon. Your drawing is also shown in the small rectangle labeled *B&W* icon that you will design. Although most of the time the graphics are done in black and white, you can click on the color rectangle and design your icon in color.

The Icon Editing Tools palette is shown to the left of the work area. At this time you must familiarize yourself with the function of each editing tool. A brief description of most of the tools is given in Fig. B-6.

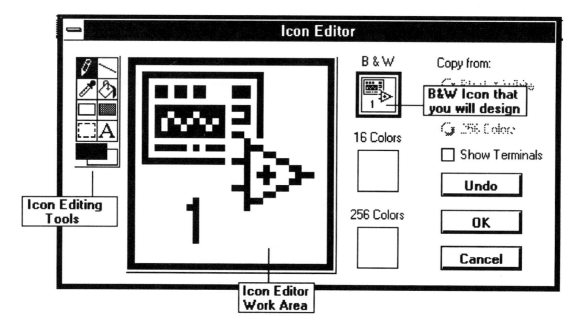

Fig. B-5 Icon Editor Window

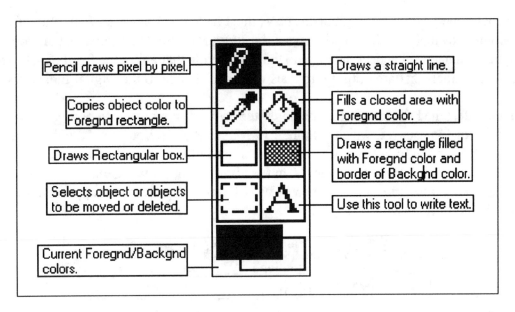

Fig. B-6 Icon Editing Tools Palette

4. Having gained some familiarity with the icon editing tools, you are now ready to design the symbolic representation for the VI that the icon represents. The symbolic representation can be anything that gives the user an idea of what the icon does, and it has nothing to do with the way the VI works. Fig. B-7 shows an idea of how Sum_4.vi may be represented. Click on *OK* when the icon is completed. Note that icon editor has an *Undo* option. This is the only place in LabVIEW where the Undo option is included.

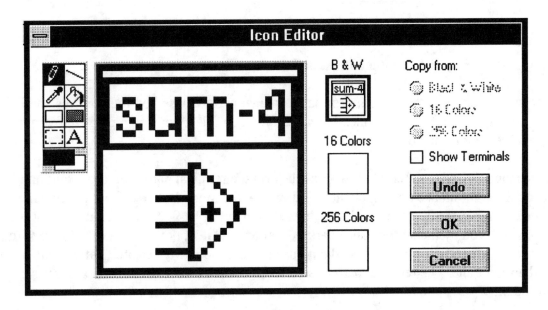

Fig. B-7   Icon Symbol for Sum_4.vi

5. As mentioned earlier any legitimate subVI must have two things: an *Icon* and a *Connector*. A connector that you design will have a *Terminal Pattern*. The terminals that you select as input terminals will accept data from Digital Controls that are in the front panel, while those terminals that are output terminals will provide data to the Digital Indicators.

Having designed the icon in the previous step, you are now ready to configure the Connector for your VI, which is Sum_4.vi. Make sure that you are in the front panel. Then click on the Icon Pane with the right mouse button (as you did in step 2), hold down the mouse button and select from the popup menu, *Show Connector*. Once you release the mouse button the connector with a terminal pattern will appear in the Icon Pane as shown in Fig. B-8.

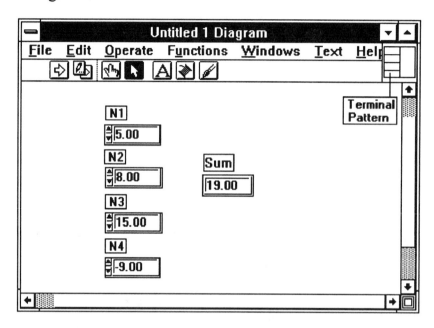

Fig. B-8 Connector with Terminal Pattern in Icon Pane

The system chooses the most appropriate terminal pattern based on the controls and indicators that appear in the front panel. However, you can select your own pattern if you don't like the one picked for you.

To change the existing terminal pattern, click on the terminal pattern in the Icon Pane (click the right mouse button and hold it down) and choose *Patterns* from the popup menu. The terminal pattern options will appear as shown in Fig. B-9. Note the pattern that was picked for you by the system has a dark border around it. If now you drag the cursor to a pattern of your choice and release the mouse button, the newly selected pattern will appear in the Icon Pane. The terminal pattern selected for you by the system is fine, so let's stay with that.

6. Next, we must assign controls and indicators in the front panel to the various terminals in the terminal pattern. This is probably the only time that you will use the Wiring Tool in the Panel Window. As you probably know by now, the Wiring Tool is used

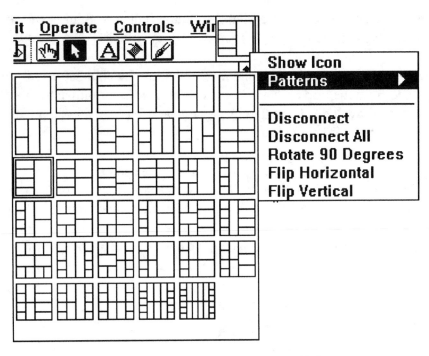

Fig. B-9 Connector Terminal Patterns Palette

predominantly in the block diagram. To assign a control or indicator to a terminal, use the four-step procedure as described in Fig. B-10, which shows assignment of the bottom terminal on the left side of the connector to Digital Control Number 4. Repeat this procedure and assign the other three Dgital Controls to the remaining three terminals on the

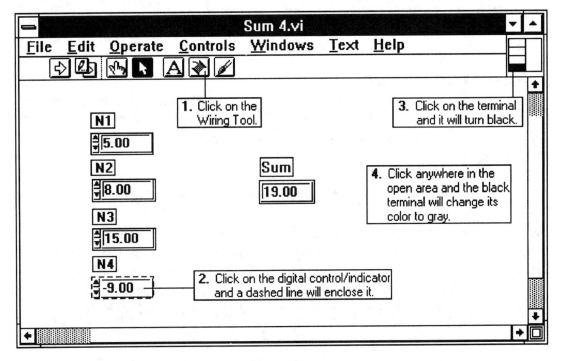

Fig. B-10 Assigning Controls and Indicators to the Connector Terminals

left side of the connector. Also assign the Digital Indicator Sum to the large terminal on the right side of the connector.

To Delete a particular terminal assignment, click on the connector (with the right mouse button) and from the pop up menu choose *Disconnect*, as shown in Fig. B-11. Choosing *Disconnect All* will delete all terminals, or clear all terminal assignments (the terminals will change to white after being cleared).

The other options in the connector popup menu are used only to change connector orientation. For example *Rotate 90 Degrees,* does just that: it rotates the connector 90 degrees clockwise. The remaining two options rotate the connector 180 degrees.

After completing the connector, **Save** all changes by using *Ctrl+S* or choosing Save from the File menu.

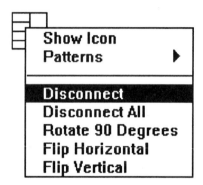

Fig. B-11 Options in the Connector Popup Menu

Exercise 4: Using a SubVI
The purpose of this exercise is to demonstrate how a subVI can be used in another VI. As mentioned earlier, *a subVI must have an Icon and a Connector* if it is to be used in another VI. In Exercise 3, we created an Icon and a Connector for Sum_4.vi. In this exercise we will use Sum_4.vi as a subVI.

1. To begin this exercise, open new front panel and block diagram by choosing *New* from the File menu.
2. Switch to the front panel, open four Digital Controls, and label them with owned labels as A, B, C, D. Also open one Digital Indicator and label it as A+B+C+D. Except for the labels, the resulting Panel Diagram will be the same as that shown in Fig. B-3.
3. Switch to the block diagram (use Ctrl+F) and pop up anywhere in the open area. Choose from the popup menu (in the Functions menu) *VI...*, as shown in Fig. B-12.

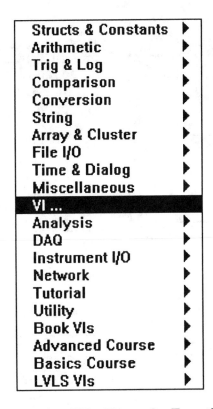

Structs & Constants	▶
Arithmetic	▶
Trig & Log	▶
Comparison	▶
Conversion	▶
String	▶
Array & Cluster	▶
File I/O	▶
Time & Dialog	▶
Miscellaneous	▶
VI ...	
Analysis	▶
DAQ	▶
Instrument I/O	▶
Network	▶
Tutorial	▶
Utility	▶
Book VIs	▶
Advanced Course	▶
Basics Course	▶
LVLS VIs	▶

Fig. B-12 Choosing VI... From the Functions Menu

This gives you access to directories and VI files. Choose Sum_4.vi from Workbook.LLB. Remember that Workbook.LLB is in the LabVIEW directory. Note that the familiar icon we created in Exercise 3 appears in the block diagram, as shown in Fig. B-13a. This is the VI for which we designed an icon and a connector in Exercise 3.

4. The subVI's owned label can be shown by popping up on the icon and selecting *Show>Label*, as illustrated in Fig. B-13b. This feature toggles, so to hide the label, select again Show>Label.

5. Also the subVI icon can be switched to show its connector with the terminals. To do that, pop up on the subVI icon and select from the popup menu, *Show Terminals*, as shown in Fig. B-13c. This feature toggles, allowing you to return to the icon by selecting again *Show Terminals* from the popup menu. The connector with terminals makes it easier to wire an object to a particular terminal.

6. The *Help Window* is one of the most useful features of LabVIEW. It provides the functional description for an object in the window and shows its connector with terminals and terminal names. To see the Help Window for a desired object, enter *Ctrl+H* from the keyboard and click on the object. Fig. B-14 shows how this works for our Sum_4.vi. Note that the brief VI description at the bottom of the Help Window was stored in Exercise 2 when this VI was created.

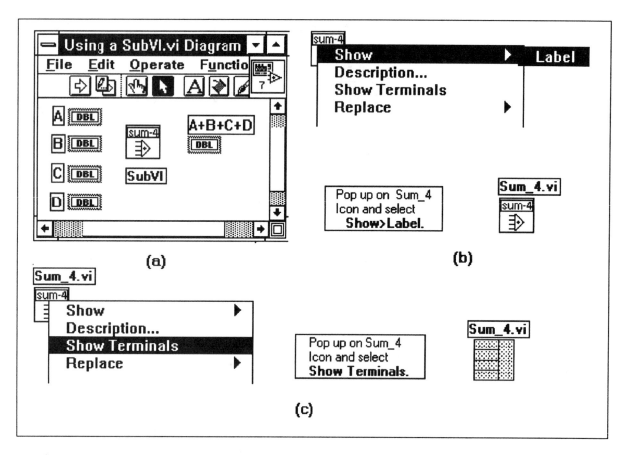

Fig. B-13 Using a SubVI: (a) Block Diagram, (b) Showing the SubVI Icon's Label,
(c) Showing the SubVI's Connector with Terminals

In addition to providing helpful descriptive information about the subVI as well as other objects in the window, the Help Window is also very useful in wiring objects. Often it is necessary to wire an object in the window to the correct terminal. Suppose, for example,

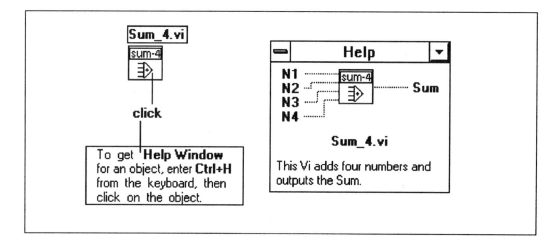

Fig. B-14 Help Window for Sum_4 SubVI.

that the Digital Control named C must be wired to Terminal N3 on Sum_4 SubVI. To accomplish this, first change the subVI to show the connector with terminals. Then start wiring. As you place the tip of the wiring tool over the Digital Control C, it begins to blink. Drag the wiring cursor to any terminal on the subVI and note that the corresponding terminal in the Help Window also blinks. Move the wiring cursor over the terminals of the subVI and watch the Help Window. When the N3 terminal in the Help Window begins to blink, you found the correct terminal on the subVI. This is shown in Fig. B-15.

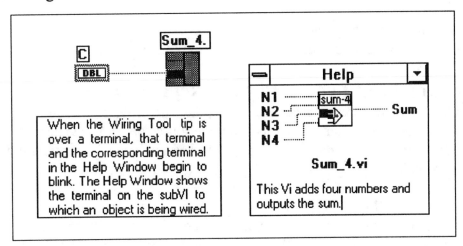

Fig. B-15   Using the Help Window in the Wiring Operation

Complete wiring digital controls A, B, C, D and the digital indicator A+B+C+D to the Sum_4 subVI. As described above, use Help the Window to help you in the wiring process. The completed front panel and block diagram are shown in Fig. B-16.

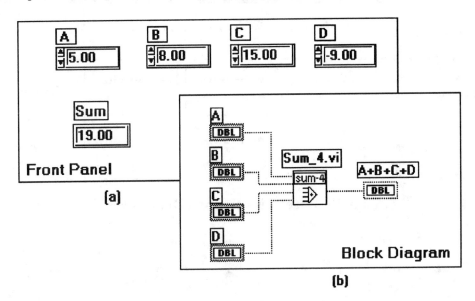

Fig. B-16   Using Sum_4.vi As a SubVI: (a) Front Panel, (b) Block Diagram

7. Once again, note the advantage of the subVI icon. Although this particular subVI doesn't contain a great deal of graphical code, in general a subVI can include a large and complex configuration. This icon helps to keep the block diagram neater and less cluttered. Also, it is easier to troubleshoot the configuration and make changes in individual subVIs without affecting too much the rest of the diagram.

If the Run icon in the Control bar is broken, the VI cannot be executed. Consult the troubleshooting section later in this appendix.

Run this VI using different values.
Save this VI as **Using a SubVI.vi** in the WorkBook.LLB.

Understanding Data Types and Data Representation

When two objects are interconnected by a wire, the wire provides the path for the data. The flow of data is in one direction only, from the source object to the destination object. Because there are different data types, LabVIEW has a unique wire representation for each data type.

As shown in Fig. B-17, blue color wires are assigned to integer numbers, while orange color wires represent floating point numbers. Green and purple wires represent Boolean and string data, respectively. Also the thickness of the wire differentiates between the scalar quantities, and one-dimensional and two-dimensional arrays.

	Scalar	**Array (1D)**	**Array (2D)**	**Color**
Number				Integer: **Blue** Float: **Orange**
Boolean				Green
String				Purple

Fig. B-17 Wires Representing Data Types

378

Data Representation applies to the attribute or the quality of a number. A number can be any one of the following:

1. Floating Point Number (having decimal places)
2. Integer (no decimal places)
3. Unsigned Integer (no decimal places, and must be positive)
4. Complex (has real and imaginary components)

What is even more important is that any one of the above options can occupy more or less memory, and that depends on how we represent numbers.

As was mentioned earlier, wires represent data flow, and the color and thickness of the wire identifies the type of data. This is very convenient because if we see a thin blue wire in the block diagram, we know that it must carry integer data.

Wires don't produce data, they only transport data, and that data must originate at the source to which one end of the wire is connected. If the source of data is a digital control, as was the case in the Sum_4.vi that you built, then that digital control can be configured in several ways. Other sources of data may be a dial, a knob, or a vertical slide.

To configure a digital control, pop up on the digital control and choose from the popup menu *Representation*. This will open a submenu with various data representation options, as shown in Fig. B-18.

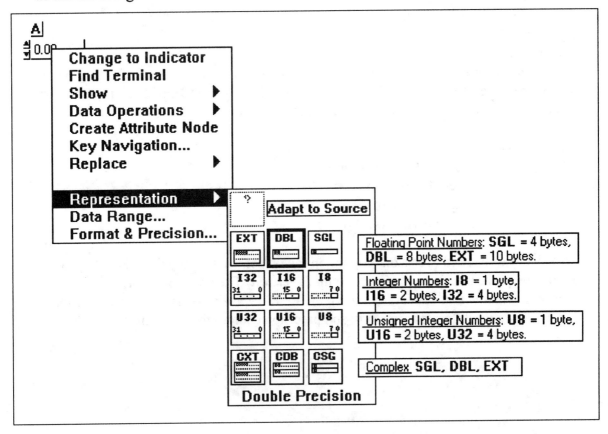

Fig. B-18 Choosing Data Representation for a Digital Control

Note that the floating point numbers can be **SGL, DBL** or **EXT**. Double is a default assignment to all floating numbers used in LabVIEW. If you choose not to change that default assignment, a digital control that you bring to the Panel Window will have the DBL representation. This means that each number that you enter into that digital control will occupy 8 bytes (one byte is 8 bits) of memory space. It also means that you can use any number between 10^{-308} and 10^{308} with 7 digits of precision (up to 7 decimal places).

On the other hand, an **SGL** representation uses only 4 bytes in memory, allowing you to use numbers between 10^{-38} and 10^{38}, also with 7 digits of precision.

Similarly **I8** occupies only 1 byte in memory, allowing you to use integer values between -128 and $+127$. **U8** (unsigned), on the other hand, also occupies 1 byte in memory and allows you to use values from 0 to 255. Note that between -128 and 127 there are the same number of integer values as between 0 and 255. That's why both I8 and U8 occupy 1 byte of memory. **I16**, on the other hand, needs 2 bytes of memory, allowing you to use integer values between $-32,768$ and $+32,767$. **U16** also uses 2 bytes of memory, offering a range of 0 to 65,535.

Thus the data representation that one chooses can have a great effect on memory consumption. This may not be a consideration if the VI does not process a great deal of data. However, if the VI application is data intensive with large files, choosing the appropriate data representation would be an important consideration.

Format and Precision

Precision means the number of decimal places that you would like your floating point number to have. You can have 7 or less decimal places with DBL or SGL representations and up to 15 decimal places with the EXT representation.

Format gives you a choice of:
1. Floating Point Notation
2. Scientific Notation
3. Engineering Notation
4. Relative Time (sec)

To Select Format and Precision, pop up on the object, such as the digital control, and choose from the popup menu *Format and Precision*. Then from the Format and Precision window that appears as shown in Fig. B-19, make an appropriate selection. Fig. B-20 shows different formatting and precision choices for the number 123.4567.

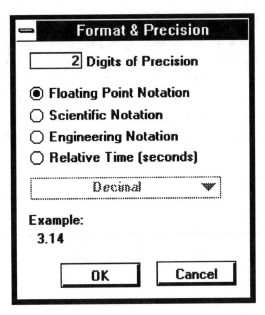

Fig. B-19 Format and Precision Window

Format	Precision	Digital Display
Floating Point	4	123.4567
Floating Point	2	123.46
Scientific	4	1.2346E+2
Scientific	2	1.23E+2
Engineering	4	123.4567E+0
Engineering	2	123.46E+0
Relative Time (seconds)	4	2:03.4567
Relative Time (seconds)	2	2:03.46

Fig. B-20 Format and Precision Example

Exercise 5: Troubleshooting a VI

In LabVIEW execution of a VI is dictated by the flow of data. A typical block diagram includes many objects, including control terminals, indicator terminals, function nodes, subVI nodes and others. All objects are interconnected by wires, which provide the paths for data. Any node will execute only if all the data is present at its input terminals. After the node executes, it provides data at its output terminal, which becomes the source of data for the next node. Consider the Sum_4.vi block diagram shown in Fig. B-21.

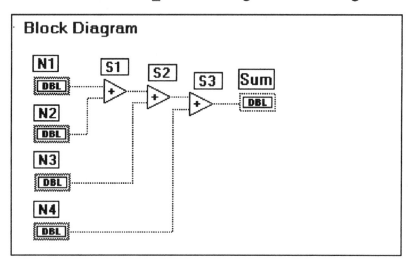

Fig. B-21 Block Diagram for the Data Flow Example

Digital Control terminals N1, N2, N3 and N4 are the sources of data. When execution begins, N1 and N2 apply data to Add function S1, N3 applies data to S2, and N4 applies data to S3 at the same time. Nodes S2 and S3 cannot execute because they don't have all the data at their input terminals. However, S1 can execute because both of its input terminals have data. As soon as S1 executes, the data at its output terminal is passed to the input of S2. Now S2 executes because it has data at both of its input terminals. After S2 executes, it passes its data to S3, which executes last. This process continues until all nodes have executed.

In high-level programming there are generally two types of errors: syntax errors and run-time errors. Syntax errors occur because some programming rules have been broken. Syntax errors must be corrected before a program can be executed. Run-time errors, however, can be very frustrating. For example, if you wrote in your program $z = x/y$ and it should have been $z = x*y$, the computer will execute the division because there are no syntax errors, resulting in wrong results after the execution. It is up to you at that point to find the errors. There is always the chance that you will overlook them, no matter how many times you go over the code.

One troubleshooting technique that is extremely effective is *Single Stepping* through the program. LabVIEW offers this technique, which involves executing one node at a time. After each execution, numerical values will be shown at the input and output terminals. This technique allows you to see VI execution in slow motion. After each node executes, a value produced by that node will be shown. You have to decide at this time whether that value is correct. As the execution proceeds from node to node, an inspection of node output values will allow you to catch any run-time errors that the VI may have.

We shall next try the Single Stepping technique on the Sum_4.vi.

1. Open the Sum_4.vi (it is in Workbook.LLB) and switch to block diagram.
2. *Single Step* through the VI by following the procedure described in Fig. B-22.

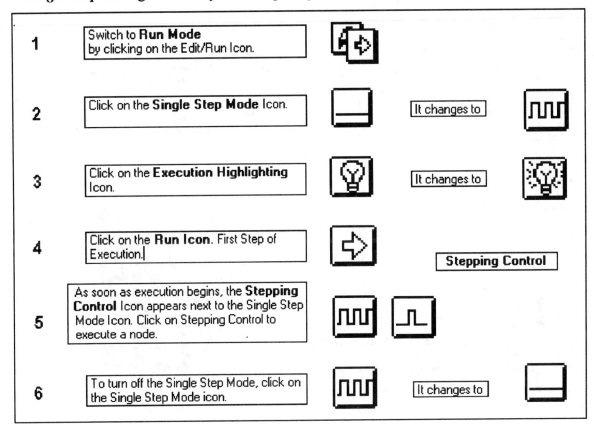

Fig. B-22   Procedure for Single Stepping Through a VI

3. Each time you click on the Stepping control, bubbles representing data flow move along the wires from the source to the input terminal of a node. Fig. B-23 shows the configuration after you click on the Stepping Control once. The middle Add function is flashing, and that means this node will be executed immediately after you click on the Stepping Control Icon. Note that bubbles appear at both of its input terminals, which means that data is available at both of its input terminals.

In order for any node to be executed, data must be present at all of its input terminals.

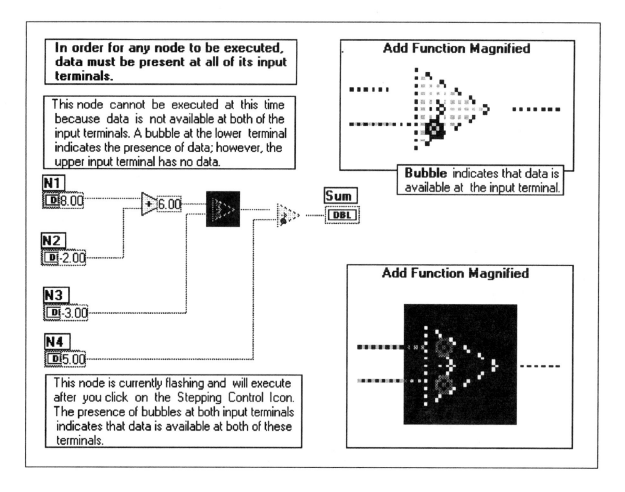

Fig. B-23 Sum_4.vi Configuration After the First Add Function Was Executed

4. Complete single stepping throught the VI. Note the values at the node outputs after each step.

5. *Probe Display* allows you to view data on any wire. This is a very helpful tool, especially when you are stepping through your VI. To enable the probe, you must be in the *Run Mode*. Click on the *Edit/Run* mode icon in the Control Bar (see Fig. A-5) if you are now in Edit mode. Then position the cursor over any wire, click and hold down the right mouse button. From the popup menu, choose *Probe*. This is shown in Fig. B-24.

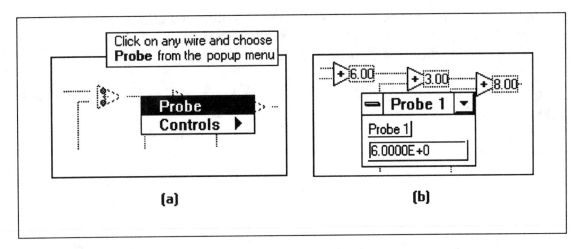

Fig. B-24 (a) Choosing a Probe Display, (b) Probe Display

The Probe display can be moved anywhere within the VI. For example, by moving Probe displays to the front panel, you can simultaneously view data on the indicators and the Probe displays as you are stepping through the VI or running it continuously. Whereas a digital indicator can display only the numerical data, a probe will display whatever data happens to be on that wire.

The probe is therefore a convenient tool that can be activated on any wire. This is especially important when you are troubleshooting a VI. Activating a probe on the wires that don't have any indicators allows you to view the data and make decisions on the quality of the data. Watching your VI execute on a node-by-node basis and viewing the data produced by each node will allow you to detect errors. The probe is a temporary tool that is deleted as soon as you close the window.

Enable one or more probes and single step through the Sum_4.vi again.
To turn off the single stepping, click on the Single Step Mode icon (see Fig. B-22).

6. The VI may also be executed in a ***Continuous Run*** mode using all the features of the Single Step mode: the flowing bubbles representing data flow and the display of node output values after node execution. The VI will continue to execute node by node endlessly until you stop it by clicking on the ***Stop*** button.

    To enable the Continuous Run execution, first disable the Single Step Mode by clicking on the Single Step Mode icon, enable the ***Execution Highlighting***, and then click on the ***Continuous Run*** mode icon.
    Run the Sum_4.vi in the Continuous Run Mode.

A broken **Run** icon (its shape is shown in Fig. A-3) means that the VI cannot be executed because it has syntax errors. Syntax errors result from violation of programming rules during VI construction and must be corrected before running the VI.

You can view the errors by clicking on the broken Run icon. The errors can then be located and corrected.

7. Let's see how this works. Suppose an error is inserted into our Sum_4.vi. One type of error is a missing wire. Select and delete the wire between the Digital Control N4 and the input of the first Add function. As soon as the wire is deleted, the Run icon becomes **broken**.

    Click on the broken icon. You will see an **Error List** window showing the error statement and a brief description of the error in the lower part of the window.

    When you double click on the error (or single click on the error and then click on **Find)**, the block diagram opens with the problem node enclosed by dashed lines. At this time correct the error by replacing the wire. This procedure is shown in Fig. B-25.

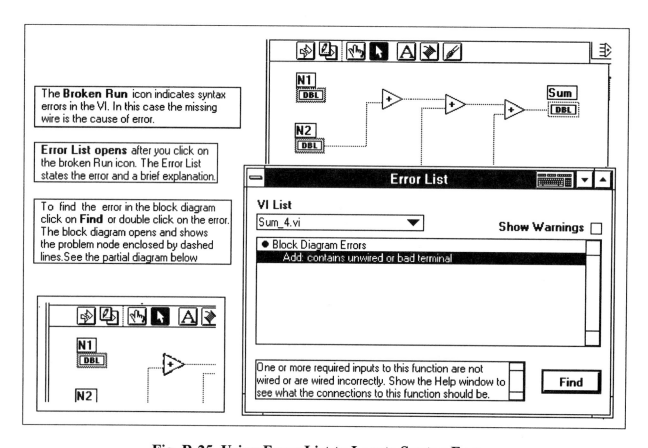

Fig. B-25 Using Error List to Locate Syntax Errors

386

Appendix C

Structures

(LabVIEW Version 3)

In this appendix you will learn about:
While loop
For loop
Case structure
Sequence structure
Formula node

Introduction

It has been said that the entire C programming language can be broken down into three *Control Structures* and any C program can be written in terms of these structures. These structures are:

Repetition Structure
Selection Structure
Sequence Structure

LabVIEW also has these structures. It has two repetition structures: the *While Loop*, which is equivalent to Do/While in C language, and the *For Loop*. The *Case* structure in LabVIEW, which can do single or multiple selections, is an example of a Selection Structure. The Sequence Structure occurs naturally in C language because all instructions are executed in sequential order, and it is given special attention in LabVIEW. As you may remember from the last appendix, the execution order in LabVIEW is based on data flow; a node can execute only if data is available at all input terminals. Therefore, LabVIEW has a special node called the *Sequence* structure that is intended for special sequence operations. LabVIEW also includes the *Formula Node* for mathematical operations.

Repetition Structures

The While Loop

Consider the concept of the repetition structure shown in Fig. C-1. The program instructions are executed once before the condition is tested. If the result of the test is *true*, the program instructions will be executed again. If it is *false*, the next statement following the loop will be executed in C language, and in LabVIEW the loop terminates.

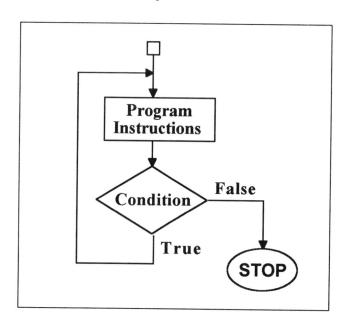

Fig. C-1 The Do/While Repetition Structure

388

This type of repetitive execution of a group of program instructions is called the *Do/While* structure in C language, and in LabVIEW it is known as the *While Loop*.

To Open the While Loop ....

You must be in the *block diagram* and in *Edit* mode. Either click on the Functions pull-down menu or pop up (with the right mouse button) anywhere in the open area. From the popup menu choose *Structs & Constants* and then select the *While Loop* from the submenu that appears on the side, as shown in Fig. C-2.

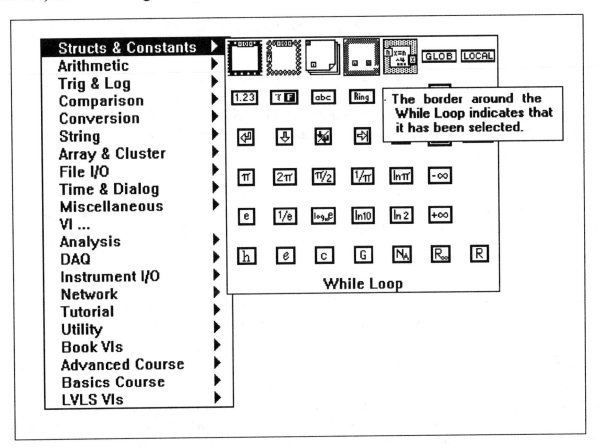

Fig. C-2 Selecting the While Loop

When you select the While Loop and bring it into the block diagram, it will have the appearance shown in Fig. C-3. Generally the size of the While Loop that you open is too small and you will need to resize it.

To Resize the While Loop, place the cursor on any corner of the While Loop. The cursor assumes the shape of the *corner* (see the cursor shape in Fig. A-5). Drag the cursor in an outward direction to resize the While Loop.

To Move the While Loop, place the cursor on the border of the While Loop and then drag the loop to the new position in the window. Hold down the Ctrl key if you want to make a copy of the While Loop. Refer to Exercise 3 in Chapter 2 for the duplicating procedure.

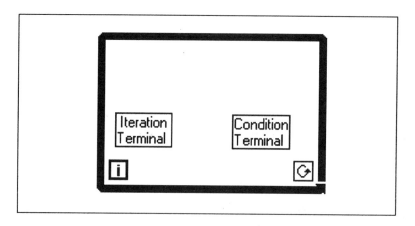

Fig. C-3 The While Loop

As shown in Fig. C-3, the While Loop has two permanent objects inside. The **Iteration Terminal** counts the number of times that the loop has executed. The Iteration terminal outputs an integer value and starts the count from **0**.

The other object inside the While Loop is the **Condition Terminal**. Unlike the Iteration terminal, which outputs a value, the Condition Terminal expects a *Boolean input*. This terminal decides whether the condition in Figs. C-1 and C-3 is true or false. If *true*, the objects inside the loop will be executed one more time. If *false*, execution is terminated.

*It should be noted that LabVIEW's While Loop behaves exactly the same way as the Do/While repetition structure in C language because **all objects will execute once before the condition is tested.** This means that even if the condition is false, the loop will execute once.*

Example 1

An example of the While Loop is shown in Fig. C-4. The *Equal?* function, which can be found in the *Comparison* submenu of the *Functions* menu, compares the two inputs and outputs a *true* if they are equal. Otherwise it outputs a *false*. The inputs to the *Equal?* function are the iteration variable **i** and a integer constant **100**. The output of the *Equal?* function is complemented and then applied to the *Condition Terminal*.

As this VI is executed, the iteration counter i begins its count at i = 0. The Equal? function compares 0 with 100 and outputs a *false* which becomes *true* after complementation. The Condition terminal receives a *true* and, after the iteration counter is incremented, the objects within the loop are executed again. This must be repeated 100 times (0 to 99) and only when i assumes the value of 100 will the Condition Terminal receive a *false*, causing the loop to terminate.

Note also the delay that has been inserted causes a 100 ms delay between iterations. The *Wait Until Next ms Multiple* can be found in the *Time & Dialog* submenu of the Functions pull-down menu. This example illustrates the repetition character of the While Loop, which causes the

Sum_4 subVI to be executed repetitively 100 times. Anything else placed inside the loop will also be executed 100 times.

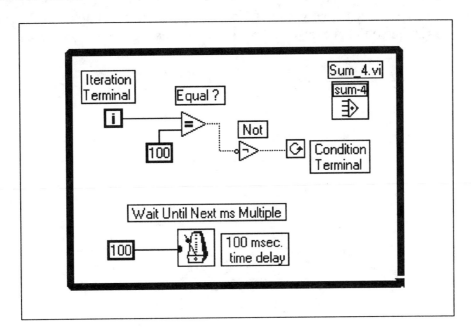

Fig. C-4   While Loop Example

The For Loop

Another instance of the repetition control structure is the For Loop. As in the case of the While Loop, the For Loop can execute repetitively a group of instructions. The While Loop checks the state of the condition with each iteration. As long as the condition is *true*, it continues the repetitive execution of the instructions. It stops execution as soon as the condition becomes false.

The For Loop, on the other hand, executes a group of instructions a fixed number of times. Accordingly, it initializes a counter to N=0, as shown in Fig. C-5, checks the counter against a user supplied value, **C**, and then executes a group of instructions inside the For Loop. The counter is then incremented and the procedure repeats. As soon as the value of the counter is equal to C, the loop stops.

Fig. C-6 shows the LabVIEW version of the For Loop. The iteration terminal has the same meaning it had in the While Loop. It is an output terminal initialized to i=0 and is incremented with each iteration. The N terminal, representing the number of times that the For Loop is to be executed, is an input terminal. The user must provide an integer value for N.

The For Loop can be resized and moved around the window following the procedure described for the For Loop.

Example 2

An example of the For Loop is shown in Fig. C-7. In this example the Sum_4 subVI is executed 100 times with a 100 ms time delay between iterations. Compare this example with that shown in Fig. C-4. In both cases the subVI is executed 100 times, but the algorithm used in each case was very different.

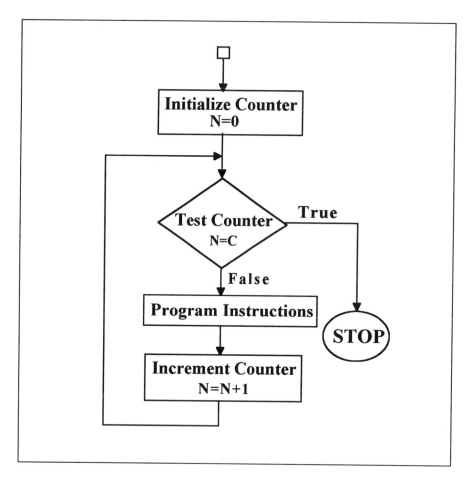

Fig. C-5 The For Loop Repetition Control Structure

The While Loop checks the Boolean condition after each iteration. This condition is generated in Fig. C-4 using a comparator. But suppose that a Boolean switch such as the toggle switch was used. Then Sum_4 subVI would continue to execute an indefinite number of times until you push the switch to stop the While Loop.

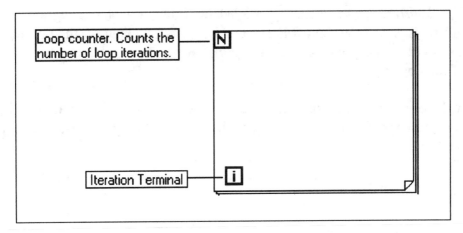

Fig. C-6 The For Loop in LabVIEW

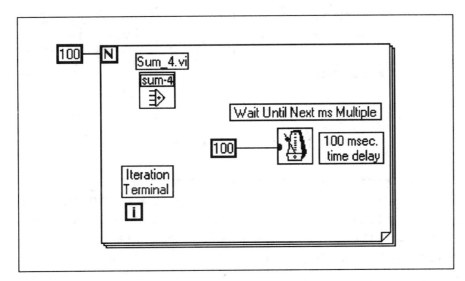

Fig. C-7 The For Loop Example

The For Loop, on the other hand, executes a fixed number of times as determined by the value of N provided by the user. In this case once the For Loop begins execution, the user is not allowed to intervene and change the value of N. The loop will execute N times, and only when it stops can you change the N value.

Which loop to use depends on the application. If your application is such that you have no idea how many times the loop will execute, then use the While Loop. If, on the other hand, you know exactly how many times the loop must execute, then use the For Loop.

The Shift Register

A shift register is a device that can store data that has occurred in the past. This concept is similar to a shift register moving or shifting binary data from one stage to the next in a digital circuit. But in a digital circuit the shifted data is restricted to the binary type only. In the LabVIEW shift register, the data may be of any type, including strings, floating point, and so on. The shift register in LabVIEW may be implemented in a For Loop or a While Loop.

393

To Create a Shift Register, open a For Loop or a While Loop in the block diagram. As shown in Fig. C-8, the shift register is implemented in the For Loop. By clicking on the border of the For Loop and choosing from the popup menu *Add Shift Register*, you create two terminals on opposite sides of the For Loop.

The right terminal stores the current data at the end of each iteration. This data is shifted to the left terminal and is present there at the beginning of the next iteration. One iteration means that all instructions inside the loop have been executed.

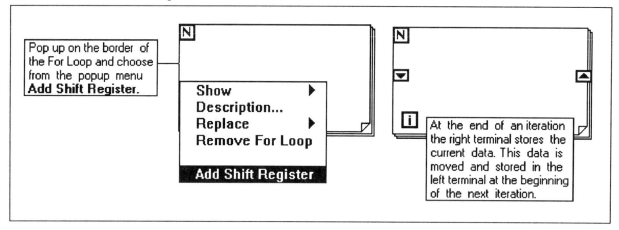

Fig. C-8 Creating a Shift Register

A single terminal on the left side of the loop is capable of storing only one value from the previous iteration. If you want to store values from two iterations ago, you need two terminals on the left side of the loop and three terminals to accommodate values from the three previous iterations. You can have as many terminals as room on the left side of the loop allows. The more of the past history that you want to store, the more terminals you will need. Fig. C-9 shows how to add additional terminals.

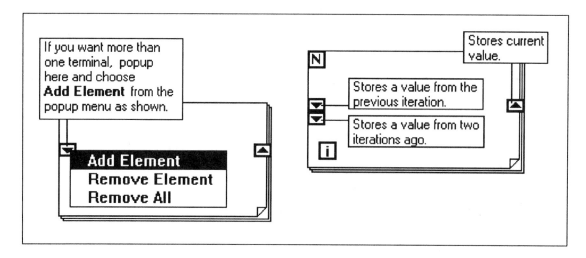

Fig. C-9   Adding More Terminals to the Shift Register

Example 3

The operation of the shift register is illustrated in Fig. C-10. Here the For Loop is configured as a shift register. The value of N, the number of times the loop is to repeat, is set to 5 and the iteration counter i is wired to the right terminal of the shift register. There are four shift register terminals on the left side of the For Loop. They are wired to the digital indicators A, B, C and D. Since N=5, the loop will execute 5 times, i=0, to i=4. With each iteration of the loop, the successive values of i will be stored in terminals A, B, C, D.

The shift register that you create should be initialized. To initialize a shift register, a value to be stored before the first iteration of the loop must be wired to each of the left terminals. Actually the shift register will still work if it is not initialized.

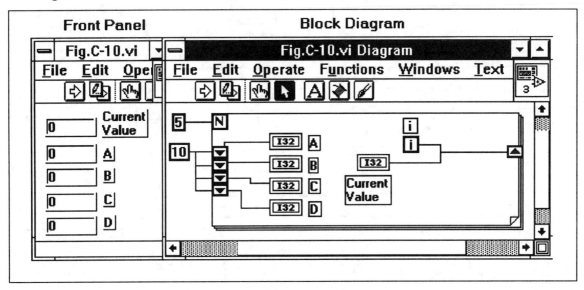

Fig. C-10 Shift Register Example

If not initialized, the shift register will use the default values as the initial values. The default values depend on the data type. In the case of an integer constant, the default value is 0.

Suppose that you executed the shift register and later ran it again. The values stored in the shift register after the first run will then be used as initial values for the second run. This may lead to unpredictable and also incorrect results. This is why you must always initialize your shift register.

The shift register shown in Fig. C-10 was executed in single step mode, and the results are shown in Fig. C-11. At the end of the first iteration, i=0, **0** is the current value of I to be stored in the right terminal of the shift register and the initial value of 10 is shifted into the four left terminals. Note that with each iteration, **0** is shifted in succession through each of the left terminals. On the fifth iteration (four iterations ago) it is stored in terminal D. The value of **1**, which occurred three iterations ago is stored in terminal C; **2**, which occurred two iterations ago, is stored in terminal B; and the value **3**, which occurred last iteration (one iteration ago), is stored in terminal A. As mentioned earlier, the shift register may also be implemented in a While Loop by following the procedure described for the For Loop.

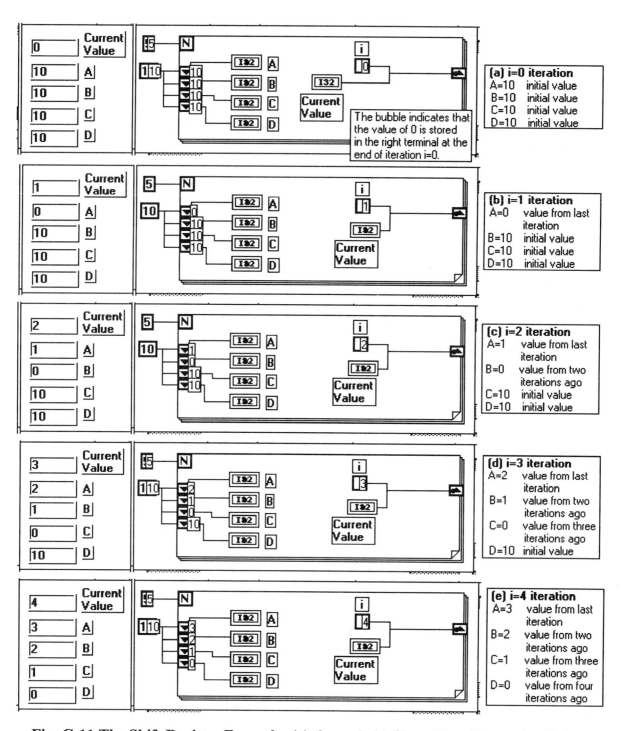

Fig. C-11 The Shift Register Example: (a) through (e) Show How Successive Values of i Are Shifted into Terminals A, B, C and D with Each Iteration of the Shift Register

Selection Structures

The If/Else Selection Structure

The double selection structure in a high-level programming language such as C has the configuration shown in Fig. C-12. This is the If/Else selection structure. The condition is first tested and if the result is *true*, all program statements included in *task 1*, are executed. If the result of the test is *false*, all program statements included in *task 2* are executed.

The If/Else selection structure offers the programmer a branching option. The outcome of the condition test determines which of the two program segments is to be done next.

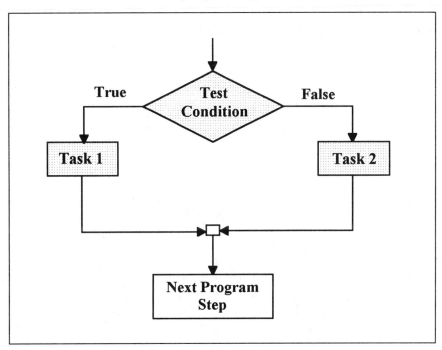

Fig. C-12   The If/Else Selection Structure

The Nested If/Else Selection Structure

The If/Else structures may also be *nested*. This means that one If/Else structure is inside the other. The flowchart shown in Fig. C-13 illustrates the nested If/Else structure, and the table in Fig. C-14 lists the tasks to be selected on the basis of the condition tests.

As you can see either from the table or from the flowchart, task 1 will be executed if both conditions 1 and 2 test as true. If, on the other hand, both conditions 1 and 3 test as false, then task 3 will be executed.

The single If/Else statement shown in Fig. C-12 offers a choice of two tasks to be executed. Notice that by nesting If/Else statements, a greater range of tasks is possible. By nesting the two If/Else statements shown in Fig. C-13, we made available a choice of four tasks. Eight tasks are possible by nesting three If/Else structures, and so on.

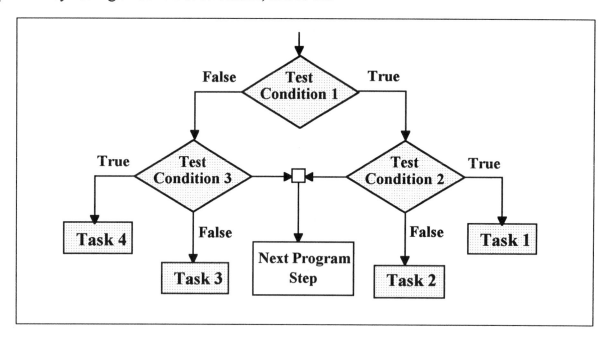

Fig. C-13 Two Nested If/Else Selection Structures

Task	Condition 1	Condition 2	Condition 3
Task 1	True	True	
Task 2	True	False	
Task 3	False		False
Task 4	False		True

Fig. C-14   Task Selection Based on the State of Conditions

398

The Case Structure in LabVIEW

In the previous section we considered If/Else as well as the nested If/Else selection structures through the perspective of a high-level programming language such as the C language. LabVIEW also has this structure and it is called the *Case Structure*.

To Open the Case Structure...

You must be in the *Diagram Window* and in *Edit* mode. Click either on the Functions pull-down menu or pop up (with the right mouse button) anywhere in the open area. From the popup menu choose *Structs & Constants*, and then select the *Case* from the submenu shown in Fig. C-15.

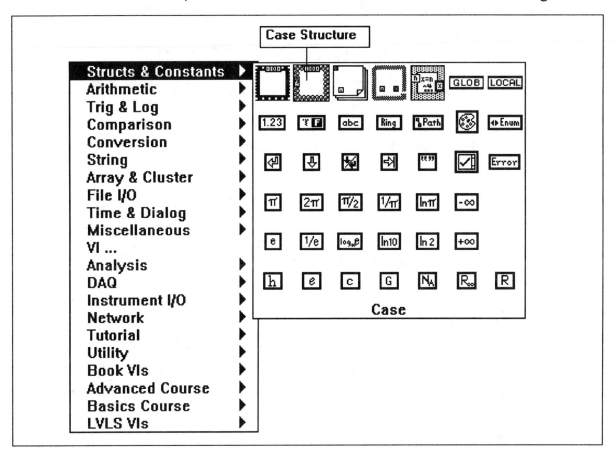

Fig. C-15 Selecting the Case Structure

After the Case structure is opened, it appears as shown in Fig. C-16. As shown in the illustration, the Case structure consists of two diagrams. They are stacked one on top of the other. It is not possible to pull them apart as shown in the illustration. To reveal the other diagram you must click on the black rectangle on the side of the True/False label.

To Resize the Case structure, place the cursor on any corner and drag it in an outward direction.
To Move the Case structure, place the point of the cursor on the border of the Case structure and drag it to the new position. If you also hold down the Ctrl key on the keyboard, you can make a copy of the Case structure.

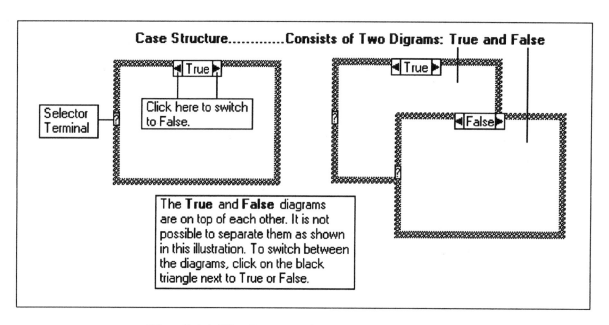

Fig. C-16 The Boolean Case Structure in LabVIEW

You may have noticed that the Case structure in Fig. C-16 has a *Selector Terminal*. For the Boolean Case structure, the input to the *Selector Terminal* must be a *true* or a *false*. For a *true* input, all code in the True Diagram of the Case structure will be executed. Conversely, for the *false* input, all code in the False Diagram will be executed.

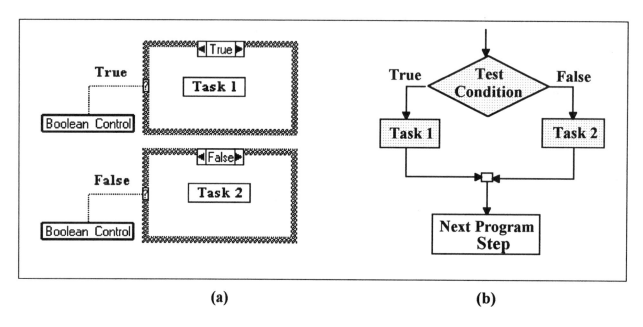

(a)   (b)

Fig. C-17 (a) A True or False Input to the Selector Terminal Determines Which Case Window Will Be executed, (b) If/Else Selection Structure from Fig. C-12.

The If/Else selection structure used in a high-level programming language such as C was discussed earlier and illustrated in Fig. C-12 by a flowchart. For comparison, the same flowchart is placed next to LabVIEW's Case structure, as illustrated in Fig. C-17. In comparing the two, you will observe that they accomplish exactly the same thing. In LabVIEW the test condition is implemented in a Boolean control such as a switch, which is tested for a *true* or a *false*. The result of the test determines which of the two Case diagrams will be executed.

Example 4
A simple illustration of the Boolean Case structure is shown in Fig. C-18.

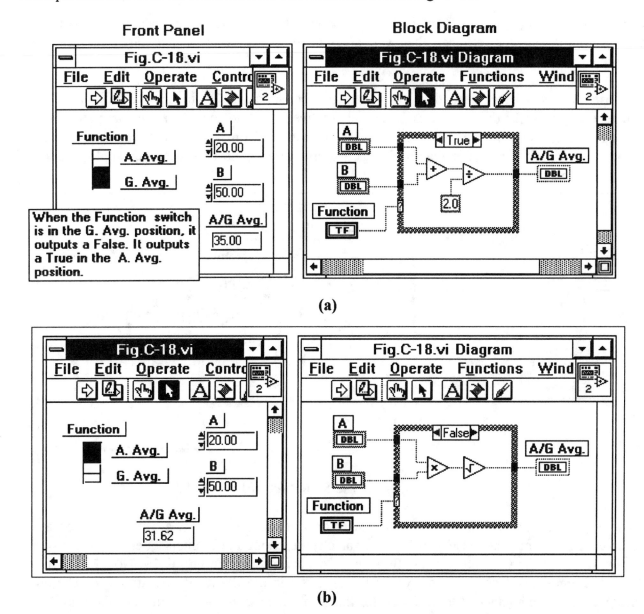

Fig. C-18 Boolean Case Structure Example: (a) The Function Switch in the A. Avg. position causes the True diagram of the Case structure to be executed. (b) In the G. Avg. position, the False diagram is executed.

In Fig. C-18a the Function switch is set to A. Avg. In this position the output of the switch is *true*. The *true* applied to the selector terminal of the Case structure in the block diagram will cause the True diagram to be executed. Notice that in the True diagram, A and B are added and divided by 2, producing the arithmetic average (A. Avg). Similarly when the Function switch is set to G. Avg. a *true* is applied to the selector terminal. As you can see in Fig. C-18b block diagram, the square root is taken of the product AB, thus producing the geometric average (G. Avg). In both cases the output is applied to the digital indicator called A/G Avg. This illustrates **Conditional Branching**; the condition *true* or *false* determines which one of two tasks will be executed.

Conditional branching need not be limited to a choice of two tasks. When a Boolean control is applied to the selector terminal, then you are limited to only one of two tasks that can be performed as described earlier.

Suppose that you have more than two tasks to choose from. Obviously the Boolean Case structure is unsatisfactory in this case. The alternative is to use the **Numeric Case structure**. Actually it is the same as the Boolean Case structure, and it is opened as illustrated in Fig. C-15. What makes it different from the Boolean Case structure is the type of input applied to the *Selector* terminal.

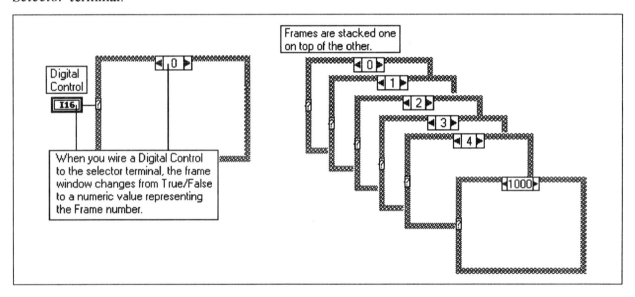

Fig. C-19   Numeric Case Structure in LabVIEW

As soon as you wire a digital control to the selector terminal, the window at the top of the Case frame changes from True/False to a numeric value representing the Frame sequence number (the default status of the Case structure is Boolean). This is illustrated in Fig. C-19. Notice also that the case frames are stacked one on top of the other, as in the Boolean Case structure. The big difference is in the number of frames: two for the Boolean Case and literally tens of thousands, if you need that many, for the Numeric Case structure.

In order to wire a digital control to the selector terminal of the case structure, you must recall several procedural matters discussed in Appendix B. First, you must open a digital control in the front panel. The default data type for the digital control is floating point, meaning that it has decimal places, and you need an integer data type for frame sequence numbers. To change the data type representation of the digital control, refer to Fig. B-18 in Appendix B.

Objects other than the digital control may also be wired to the selector terminal of the Case structure. Text Ring, for instance, might have more meaning from an application standpoint. And there are others as well. More will be said about these later.

The Case structure has a popup menu that offers several useful tools for modifying a Case frame. As shown in Fig. C-20, you can open the popup menu by clicking (with the right mouse button) in the numeric window at the top of the frame. From the menu you can choose such tools as *Add Case After, Add Case Before. Make This Case* option, for example, allows you to choose any of the active Case frames, as shown in Fig. C-20.

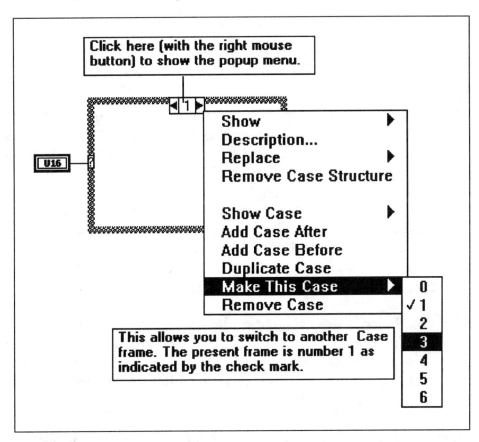

Fig. C-20 The Popup Menus of the Numeric Case Structure

Some of the other options allow you to duplicate and delete a frame. As a matter of convenience there is a quick way to switch to the next frame or to the previous frame. As shown in Fig. C-21b, click with the left mouse button to either side of the frame number. If you have more than two Case frames and you wish to advance to another frame that is neither the next nor the previous one, then click on the numeric window with the left mouse button and choose the desired frame from the popup numeric menu, as shown in Fig.4-21a.

403

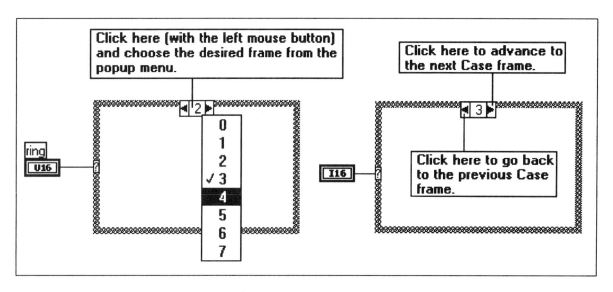

Fig. C-21   Switching to Another Case Frame

Example 5

A simple application example using the Numeric Case structure is shown in Fig. C-22. The control object labeled as **Function** in the front panel is a **Text Ring** that can be found in the *Controls>List&Ring* menu. Recall that the Digital Control with almost the same appearance as the Text Ring accepts only numerical values. The Text Ring, on the other hand, accepts text type items. Use the *Labeling* tool to write words into the Text Ring.

The Text Ring is a control type object capable of outputting numerical values. Note that in the block diagram its terminal is designated as U16. As explained in Fig. B-18 of Appendix B, U16 is a data type whose range of positive integers extends from 0 to 65,535. This means that we can enter that many words or items into the Text Ring.

In this example the Text Ring contains only four entries: Add, Subtract, Arithmetic Average and Geometric Average. These entries obviously have specific meaning pertaining to the four tasks that this VI can do. Use the *Operating* tool to select a specific task from the Task Ring by clicking on the increment and decrement arrow controls located immediately to the left of the Text Ring window.

When the *Add* function is selected, the Text Ring outputs a **0**, which is applied to the Case structure in the Diagram window (note the Digital Display window immediately to the right of the Text Ring window). The **0** input to the Case structure causes the **0** frame to be executed after you click on the Run button. The result of this operation is applied to the Answer indicator and is displayed in the front panel. This is shown in Fig. C-22a.

Fig. C-22b shows the front panel and block diagram after the Subtract function is executed, and Figures C-22c and d show the status of the front panel and block diagram after the Arithmetic and Geometric averages have been executed, respectively. Observe the code in the respective Case structure diagrams and the displayed answers using the A and B values as shown.

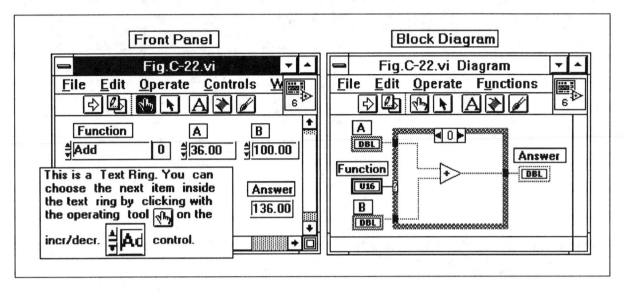

(a)

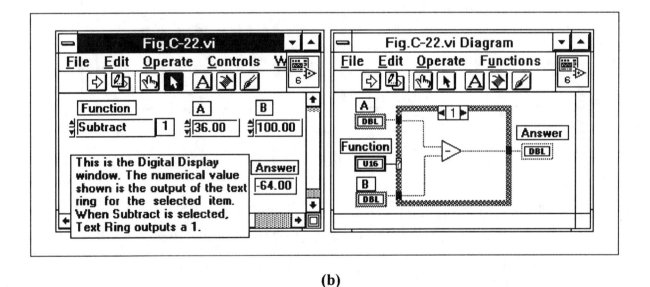

(b)

Fig. C-22   Front Panel and Block Diagram for Example 5 After Executing:
(a) Add,   (b) Subtract,   (c) Arith. Avg.,   (d) Geom. Avg.

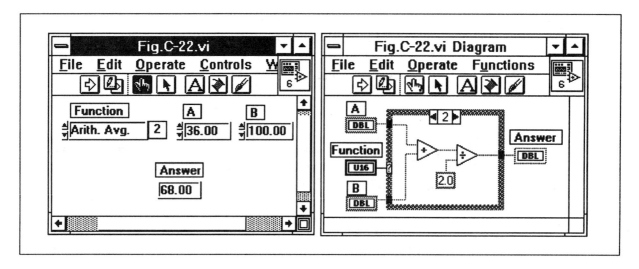

(c)

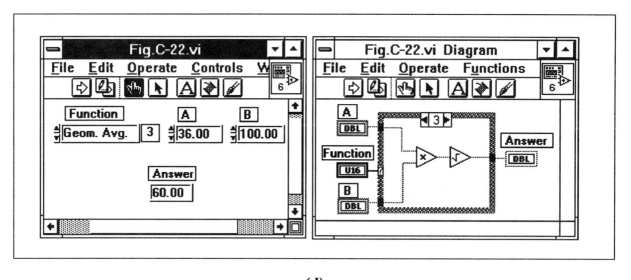

(d)

Fig. C-22   Front Panel and Block Diagram for Example 5 After Executing:
(a) Add,   (b) Subtract,   (c) Arith. Avg., (d) Geom. Avg. (continued)

Sequence Structure

Thus far, we spoke of programming tools that provide branching and repetitive execution of a group of instructions. In this regard the Sequence structure is different. In high-level languages the sequence or the order of program instructions occurs quite naturally; the order of instruction execution is the same as the order in which the instructions are written. Therefore in the high order language, there is no concern about such matters.

LabVIEW, however, differs considerably from the traditional high-level languages. First, it is a graphical type and not a syntax based language where one must be familiar with codes and rules of syntax in order to write a program. You forget to include a semicolon in C language and the program won't run. In this respect LabVIEW is much more user friendly, because it allows you to wire objects together as you build your program. There are still some rules that you must be familiar with in LabVIEW but they are not as overwhelming as they are in the traditional languages.

There is yet another fundamental difference between the LabVIEW structure and that of the traditional languages. It has to do with the way the program instructions are executed. As mentioned above, in traditional languages the program instructions are executed in the order in which they were written. In LabVIEW, however, the program execution is based on data flow. As illustrated in Fig. B-23 of Appendix B, a node in the block diagram will not execute until data is present at all of its input terminals. This is true for all nodes: their execution is based on the availability of data at all of their input terminals. To illustrate a possible dilemma, consider the VI block diagram shown in Fig. C-23.

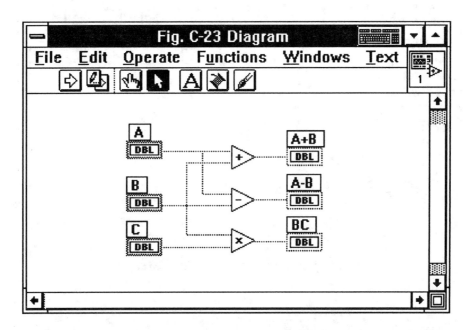

**Fig. C-23 It is not possible to predict in this figure the order
in which the three operations will be executed.**

If this VI were executed, what would be your guess about the order in which the three operations would be executed? If you're not sure, then you are on the right track because nobody can predict the exact order of execution. But suppose that it was absolutely imperative that multiplication took place first, then the addition, and that subtraction was done last.

Here is where the Sequence structure can save the day. But first let's dispense with all the formalities on how to open it, how to use it, and so on.

To Open the Sequence Structure....

You must be in the block diagram and in Edit mode. Pop up (or click on the Functions pull-down menu) anywhere in the open area of the diagram. From the popup menu choose **Structs & Constants** and then select the **Sequence Structure** as shown in Fig. C-24.

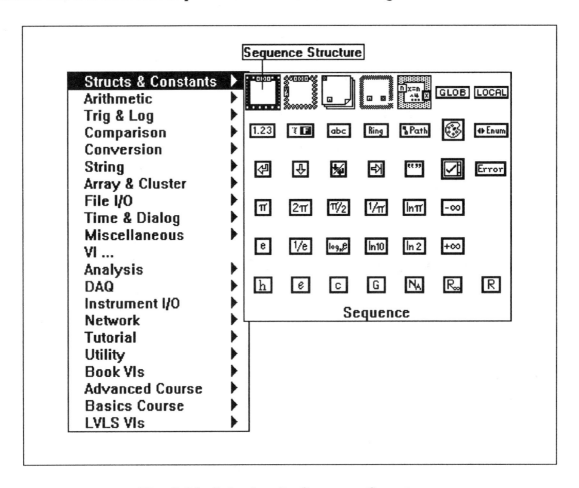

Fig. C-24   Selecting the Sequence Structure

The opened Sequence structure is shown in Fig. C-25. For **_Resizing_** and **_Moving_** the Sequence structure inside the block diagram , refer to previous sections because the procedure is exactly the same.

As did the Case structure, the Sequence structure consists of many frames stacked one on top of the other, with the top frame, being the first frame, identified as frame number **0**. To navigate between frames see Figs. C-20 and C-21. As you have probably noticed already, the Case and Sequence structures are exactly the same in this regard.

Observe the shape and design of the Sequence structure; it resembles a strip of movie film, because of the sprocket holes. One can visualize the movie strip moving inside the projector and thus projecting and showing to the observer a succession or a sequence of pictures to make up one integrated motion. The movie strip symbol is thus very appropriate in representing the Sequence Structure.

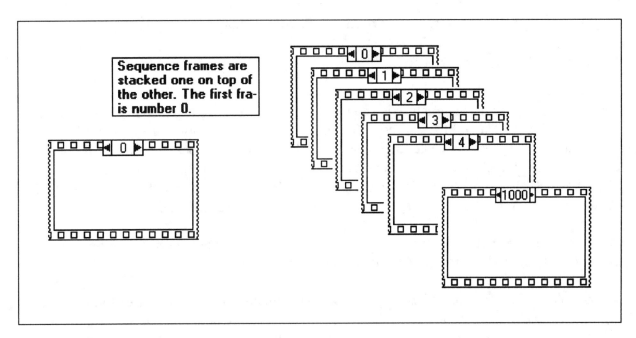

Fig. C-25 The Sequence Structure in LabVIEW

Sequence Local provides a means of passing data between the frames of the Sequence Structure. As shown in Fig. C-26, you can create a Sequence local by clicking (with the right mouse button) on the border of the Sequence structure and then by choosing **_Add Sequence Local_**. Sequence Local can be used to pass data to the frames that follow the frame in which the Sequence Local was created, but not to the preceding frames.

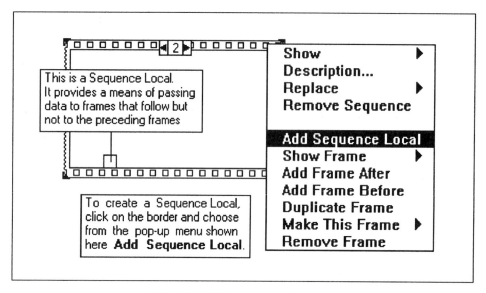

Fig. C-26 Creating a Sequence Local

Example 6

An example of the Sequence structure is shown in Fig. 4-27. The front panel and block diagram are shown in Figs. C-27a and C-27b, respectively. Let's examine the block diagram window. The Sequence structure inside the While loop consists of three frames, frames 0, 1, and 2. Remember that you can't see all the frames at the same time because they are stacked. To see the next frame you have to click on the increment/decrement control at the top of the frame. For convenience the other two frames, Frame 1 and Frame 2, are shown in Figs. C-27c and C-27d.

Because the Sequence structure is inside the While loop, the three frames will be executed repeatedly until you click on the *Quit* switch in the front panel.

This example uses two new functions: **Tick Count** and **Wait**. Both are found in the *Functions>Time & Dialog* popup menu. Tick Count and Wait are counters that begin their count in milliseconds as soon as you open Microsoft Windows. If you boot up on Windows directly then they essentially begin their count on power-up. Although they count time, their count can be used only as a reference time and it cannot be converted to the absolute time that your watch indicates. The resolution of these counters is also system dependent.

We begin in Frame 0 where the Wait counter is used. Notice that 1000 ms (see the front panel) applied to the Wait function serves as a time delay. The Wait counter will wait or delay its output by the numerical value that you apply. Notice in front panel that value was set to 1000 (the units are automatically in ms, so if you enter 10000, that means 10 seconds.). The Wait counter output is converted to seconds (by dividing by 1000), and applied to the digital indicator *Wait Time* and to the Sequence Local to be used in other frames that follow. The shaded Sequence Local shown at the bottom of Frame 0 means that it is not available in this frame because it was formed in Frame 1. Remember that a sequence local is not available in frames that precede the frame in which it was formed.

410

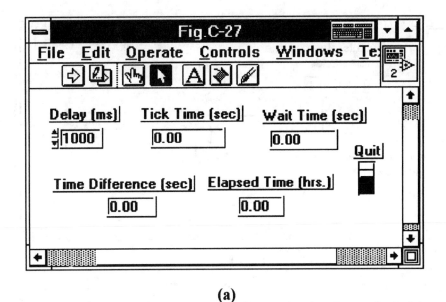

(a)

(b)

Fig. C-27 Example 6: (a) Front Panel, (b) Block Diagram and Frame 0 of the Sequence Structure, (c) Frame 1, (d) Frame 2

411

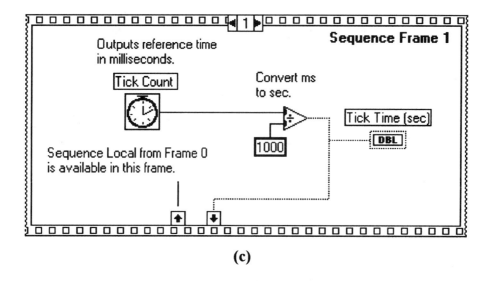

(c)

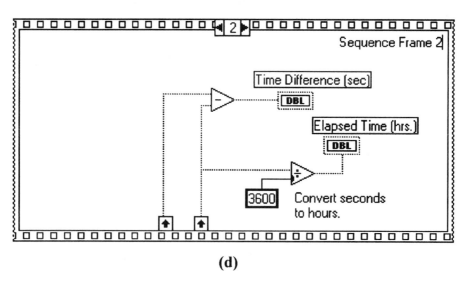

(d)

Fig. C-27 Example 6: (a) Front Panel, (b) Block Diagram and Frame 0 of the Sequence Structure, (c) Frame 1, (d) Frame 2 (continued)

Frame 1 uses the Tick counter in exactly the same way. The Tick counter has no input, and it outputs only the reference time in milliseconds. In a similar fashion, its output is converted to seconds, and then applied to the *Tick Time* digital indicator (see front panel) and also to Sequence Local.

In Frame 2 the Tick time is subtracted from the Wait and the difference is displayed in the *Time Difference* digital indicator. Also the Tick time is converted to hours (by dividing by 3600) and displayed on the *Elapsed Time* digital indicator.

The numerical results of running this VI can be seen in the Panel window. The Time Difference is 0, meaning that, despite the fact that the Wait counter is forced to stop for 1 second on each iteration, it still keeps in step with the Tick counter, which counts continuously. The Elapsed time of slightly more than two hours indicates the amount of time that the computer has been ON since power-up to the time when this VI was executed.

As mentioned earlier, the Sequence structure is a handy tool when you have a number of tasks that must be executed in a specific order. The counters used in this VI can be used quite effectively in measuring the time difference between events. Generally speaking, you may run into trouble trying to measure time differences on the order of 1 millisecond because you may be limited by system resolution. Depending on the type of application, software overheads may also play an important role in these type of measurements.

Formula Node

Formula node is not a structure in the traditional sense of the word but rather a rectangular configuration. Any formulas included inside the Formula node will be executed. There is a limited amount of syntax that can be used inside the Formula node. Nevertheless it is an option available for the user. The same equation can often be duplicated by wiring function blocks.

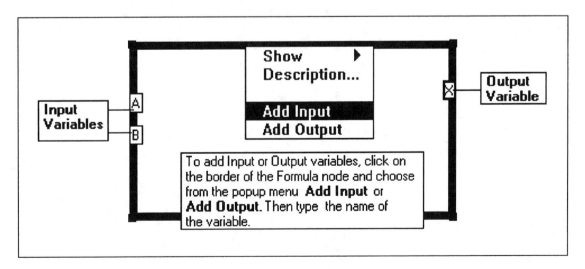

Fig. C-28   Formula Node

413

The Formula node rectangle is shown in Fig. C-28. It can be resized and moved about the diagram in the usual way. In order to pass data to the Formula node, you must create input variable terminals, and you need output variable terminals in order to pass data from the Formula node.

To Create Input or Output terminals, click on the border of the Formula node and choose ***Add Input*** or ***Add Output*** from the popup menu. Type immediately the name of the input or the output terminal. To delete a terminal, pop up on the terminal and choose ***Remove***.

The syntax that can be used inside the Formula node is shown in Fig. C-29. Note its similarity to that of C language.

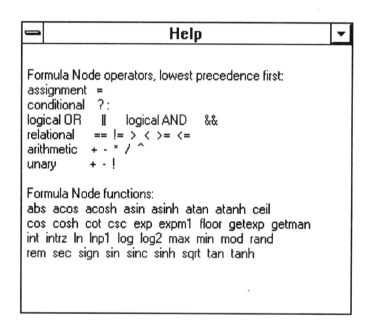

Fig. C-29 Syntax Allowable in Formula Node

Example 7

Fig. C-30 illustrates the use of the Formula node in solving the quadratic equation. The inputs A, B and C are selected by the user from the digital controls in the front panel, and the two roots RT1 and RT2 are displayed on the digital indicators also in the front panel. This is a simple example without a provision for generating complex conjugate roots. This aspect will be considered in a later exercise.

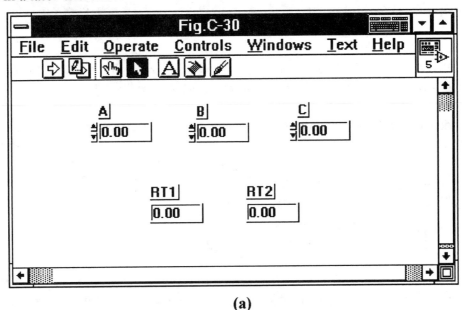

(a)

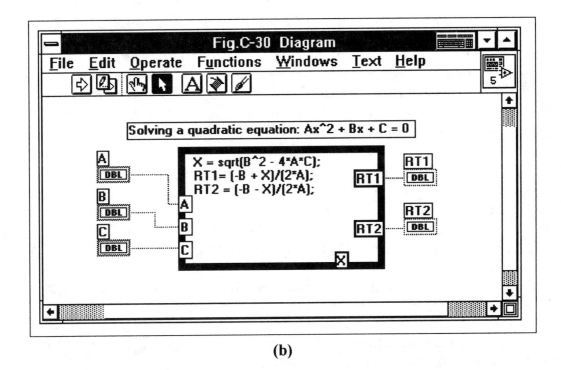

(b)

Fig. C-30 Front Panel and Block Diagram for Example 6

Exercise 1

In this exercise you will build a VI and investigate the operation of the While Loop and the Numeric Case Structure.

The front panel and block diagram are shown in Fig. C-31. The Case structure in this VI consists of four frames. Even though frames 1, 2 and 3 are shown separately, they are in reality stacked one on top of the other, as you recall. To access any frame above zero, refer to the illustration in Fig. C-21.

Note: Inside the front panel or block diagram, all comments of a descriptive nature that are not part of the VI are inside quotation marks. This applies to all future exercises.

Here are some more helpful tips on where to find things that you need for this VI.

Front Panel

Text Ring ... Controls>List & Ring (in LabVIEW v.3.1)
Controls>Numeric (in LabVIEW v.3.01)
Digital Control, Indicator... Controls>Numeric
Boolean Control... Controls>Boolean. Choose *Vertical Switch*.

Using the *Labeling* tool, type your first text entry into the Text Ring window. You may need to resize the Text Ring if your text doesn't fit. To enter the second text item as well as all other items, use the *Positioning* tool to pop up on the Text Ring and choose from the popup menu **Add Item After**. In the same menu **Add Item Before** allows you to insert a text entry between two existing items, and **Remove Item** allows you to delete a text entry.

Use the Operating Tool to select an item in the Text Ring or to change a value in the Digital Control by clicking on the increment/decrement control. You can also use either the Positioning tool or the Labeling tool to change (by typing) the numerical value in the Digital control window.

Block Diagram

Case Structure, While Loop... Functions>Structs & Constants popup menu.

Build this VI according to the front panel and block diagram shown in Fig. C-31. If the Run button is not broken, then you are ready to run this VI. If the Run arrow is broken, you must troubleshoot and repair the VI. Refer to the troubleshooting techniques described in Appendix B.

Set the STOP switch to the ON position with the *Operating Tool*. Enter A and B values and Run the VI. Experiment with different numerical values.

Create an Icon and a Connector for this VI so that later you can use it as a subVI. Consult Appendix B on how to create an Icon and a Connector.

Save this VI as **Calc.vi** in Workbook.LLB.

416

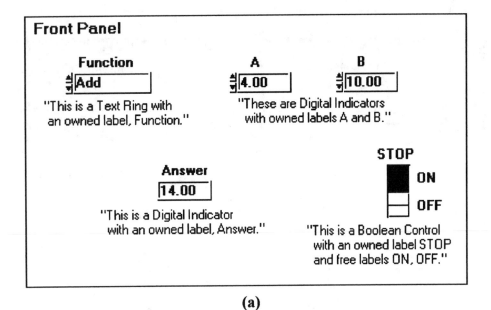

(a)

(b)

**Fig. C-31 Exercise 1: (a) Front Panel, (b) Block Diagram,
(c) Frames 1, 2 and 3 of the Case Structure**

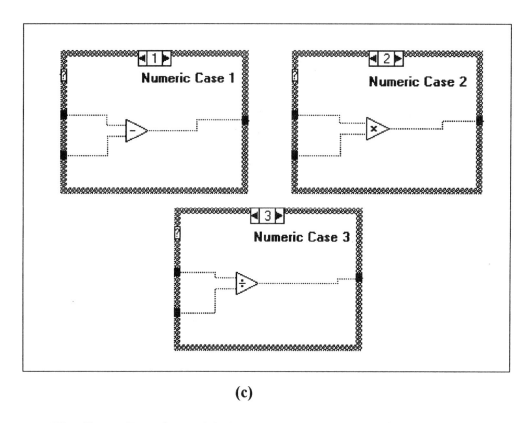

**Fig. C-31 Exercise 1: (a) Front Panel, (b) Block Diagram,
(c) Frames 1, 2 and 3 of the Case Structure (continued)**

Let's experiment next with some of the operational characteristics of the While Loop. Switch to the block diagram and move the Answer digital indicator outside the While loop. Rewire the indicator if necessary and make sure that the Run button is not broken.

Run the VI with different values for A and B. Change these values as the VI is running and watch the Answer indicator. Stop the VI and then run it again. Record your observations.

Next, restore the VI to its original configuration by moving the Answer digital indicator inside the While loop. This time, move the digital controls A and B outside the While loop.

Run the VI again and try changing the values of A and B as the VI is running. Stop the VI and run it again. Record your observations.

Explain what happened in both cases. What role does the While loop play in this VI? Would this VI operate without the While loop? If so, what would be the difference in its performance?

Restore the VI to its original configuration and *save* it as *Calc.vi* in Workbook.LLB. It should have been saved when you created the Icon and Connector for this VI. Close this VI.

Exercise 2: Quadratic Equation

In this exercise you will build a VI that finds the roots of a quadratic equation. In Example 7 we considered only real roots, but in this exercise the roots can be real as well as complex conjugates. You will explore in this exercise the use of the While loop, the Boolean Case structure and the Formula node.

The front panel and block diagram are shown in Fig. C-32. The Boolean Case structure has two diagrams, which, as you recall, are stacked on top of each other. The True case is shown in Fig. C-32b and the False case, in Fig. C-32c.

Helpful tips on where to find objects follow:

Front Panel
Digital Controls and Indicators... Controls>Numeric.
Boolean Control... Controls>Boolean. Choose Vertical Switch.

Block Diagram
While Loop, Case Structure, Formula Node... Functions>Structs & Constants.
Less than 0?.... Functions>Comparison.
Digital Constant... Functions>Structs & Constants.

The Vertical Switch may be configured so that you don't have to click on it each time you want to run the VI. First, position the switch to ON with the *Operating Tool*. Then pop up on the switch (with the right mouse button) and choose *Data Operations>Make Current Value Default*. Pop up on the switch again and from the *Mechanical Action* submenu choose *Latch When Pressed*.

The first Formula node in the block diagram calculates $B^2 - 4*C$. B and C are input values set by the user in the front panel and $X = B^2 - 4*C$ is the output value. The comparison function <0 checks for the sign of X. If X is negative, it applies a True to the selection terminal ? of the Case structure, forcing the code inside the True diagram to be executed. The second Formula Node inside the True diagram takes the **X**, **B** inputs and calculates the real and the imaginary components of the roots. These are outputted and displayed on the digital indicators.

But if X is positive, the comparator <0 applies a False to the Case structure and the False diagram shown in Fig. C-32c is executed. The third Formula node accepts **B**, **X** inputs, calculates the real components of the roots, and outputs them to be displayed on the digital indicators. Note that a **0** (digital constant) is passed from the Case structure to be displayed on the imaginary digital indicators *Im1* and *Im2*. In this case the roots are real, so the imaginary components must be **0**.

There is another aspect of the Case structure that must be stressed here. Whenever you pass values inside the Case structure or pass values from the Case structure to an outside object, the values must pass through a *Tunnel*. Note the black rectangles on the borders of the Case structure. These are tunnels.

419

If you create a tunnel in a True diagram of the Case structure, for example, and then don't make any use of this tunnel in the False diagram, that tunnel rectangle will turn *white* and will eventually be a syntax error (broken Run button). *The tunnel that is created in one diagram must be used by all diagrams of the Case structure.* This is true for the Boolean as well as for the Numeric Case structures. This is one of the reasons why a **0** constant is applied to the tunnels in Fig. C-32c. If one or more of the tunnel rectangles are white after you finished building the VI, the Run button will be broken and your VI won't run.

Build this VI according to the front panel and block diagram shown in Fig. C-32. Remember that the Run button must not be broken after you finish. If it is, try *Ctrl+B,* and if that doesn't work, see what the errors are by first clicking on the broken Run button and then double clicking on the error. Also refer to the troubleshooting section in Appendix B.

Create an Icon and a Connector for this VI so that later you can use it as a subVI. Call it **Quad.vi** and save it in Workbook.LLB.

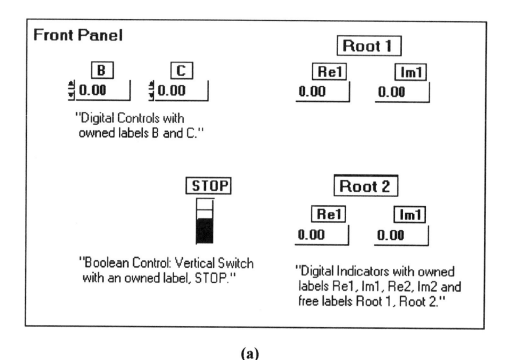

(a)

**Fig. C-32 Exercise 2: (a) Front Panel, (b) Block Diagram,
(c) False Diagram of the Case Structure**

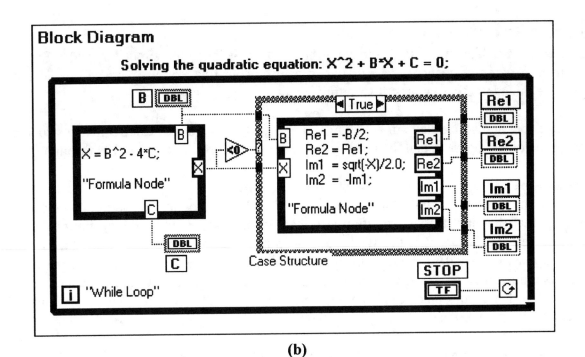

(b)

Boolean Case

(c)

**Fig. C-32 Exercise 2: (a) Front Panel, (b) Block Diagram,
(c) False Diagram of the Case Structure (continued)**

Run the VI using different values from the front panel. Close the VI.

Exercise 3: Lottery

This exercise combines the use of the While loop, the For loop, Shift register, and a Sequence structure in a game of chance, a simulation of a lottery. In this exercise you will explore on a larger scale the interactive aspects of structures and functions.

The front panel and block diagram are shown in Fig. C-33. Frame 0 of the Sequence structure is shown in the block diagram, and the remaining 5 frames are shown in Figs. C-33c through g.

While Loop reads A, B, C, D at the beginning of operation.

The operation of this VI begins with the execution of the While loop in the Diagram window. Remember that the input to the *Condition terminal*, which is provided by the output of the NOR gate, must be *true* (binary 1) if the While loop is to run. As soon as the input to the Condition terminal is *false* (binary 0), the While Loop stops. In order for the NOR gate to output a True, both of its inputs must be False. One of the inputs comes from the STOP switch, which is set to ON, and the other input comes from the Sequence structure. We will presently discuss how this very important control signal is generated by the Sequence structure.

As the While loop begins to run, it first accepts the A, B, C, D inputs (these are your lottery numbers that you picked in the front panel. Because these numbers come from outside, the While loop reads them only once at the beginning of the operation. If you want to input a new set of numbers, you must first stop the execution with the Stop switch.

Frame 0 generates 4 random numbers, N1 to N4.

Next, Sequence frame 0 is executed. This frame generates four random numbers. To do that, a For Loop shift register is used with its N set to 5. Inside the For loop is a random number generator that outputs random numbers between 0 and 1. When these values are multiplied by the *Max Num*, a front panel control that is set to 35 (reduce this number if you want to improve your odds) in this case, we get numbers between 0 and 35 at the output of the multiply function. These numbers, however, have a decimal place, and we know that lottery numbers must be integers. So, by running these numbers through the *Round to the Nearest* function, we get integers that are applied to the shift register. With N set to 5, the For loop executes 5 times, thus storing four random numbers, N1 to N4, in the shift register. When the For loop stops, these numbers are applied to Sequence locals and are thus available in all frames after frame 0.

Frame 1 compares A with N1 to N4.

The *Equal?* function is used here to compare A with all of the random numbers. The Equal? function output is *true* or *false*, depending on whether its two inputs are equal or not. The outputs from the four Equal? functions are applied to OR gates. If the final OR gate output is *true*, that means that one of the four random numbers is equal to A. Conversely, if the final OR gate output is *false*, none of the random numbers is equal to A. The last OR gate output is applied to the Sequence local to be used later in Frame 5.

Frames 2, 3, 4 compare B, C, D with random numbers.

Frames 2, 3, and 4 are identical to Frame 1. The only difference is that in Frame 2 we are comparing B with the random numbers, in Frame 3 C is being compared, and in Frame 4 we are comparing D. In all cases the last OR gate output is applied to the Sequence local to be used in Frame 5.

Frame 5 decides if the 4 random numbers match the numbers you picked.
The OR gate outputs from Frames 1 through 4 are all ANDed in Frame 5. This means that they all must be *true* in order for the output of the last AND gate to be *true*. And if it is *true*, then the four random numbers match the numbers that you picked (A, B, C, D) and you won. The output of the last AND gate is applied to the tunnel instead of the Sequence local because it is passed outside the Sequence structure. Recall that the Sequence locals are used to pass data between frames only. Thus the output of the last AND gate in Frame 5 is applied to the NOR gate shown in the block diagram.

As mentioned earlier, as long as the two inputs to the NOR gate are False (Boolean 0), its output *true* is applied to the Condition terminal, forcing the While loop to execute repeatedly all the frames of the Sequence structure.

But when there is a match between the numbers you picked and the four random numbers, the True output from the last AND gate in Frame 5 is applied to the NOR gate in Fig. C-33b. The resulting False output from the NOR is applied to the Condition terminal, forcing the While loop to stop.

The output from the iteration terminal **i** is applied to the digital indicator *Num of Tries* to display the number of times you had to play *Get-4* before you won.

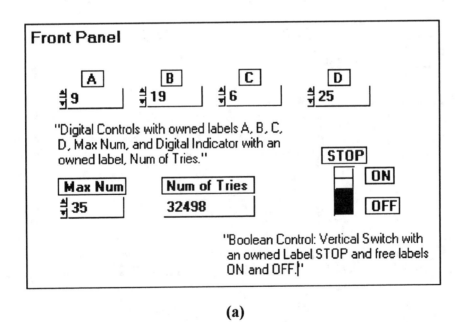

(a)

Fig. C-33 Exercise 3 (Get-4): (a) Front Panel, (b) Block Diagram. Compare the four random numbers: (c) with A , (d) with B, (e) with C , (f) with D. (g) Do the random numbers match A, B, C, D?

423

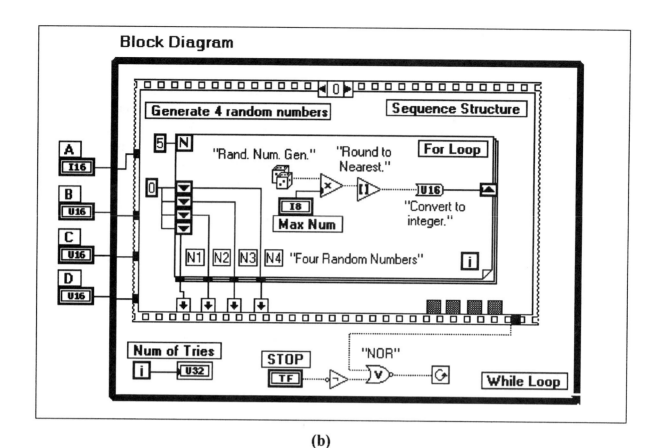

(b)

(c)

Fig. C-33 Exercise 3 (Get-4): (a) Front Panel, (b) Block Diagram. Compare the four random numbers: (c) with A , (d) with B, (e) with C , (f) with D. (g) Do the random numbers match A, B, C, D? (continued)

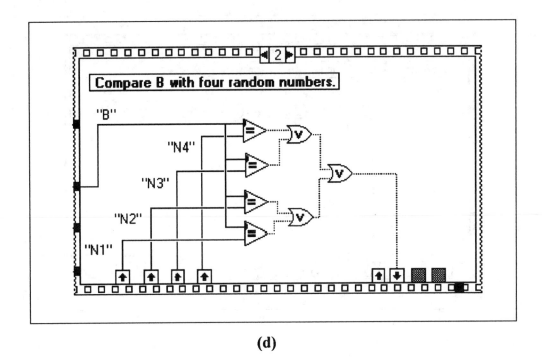

(d)

(e)

Fig. C-33 Exercise 3 (Get-4): (a) Front Panel, (b) Block Diagram. Compare the four random numbers: (c) with A, (d) with B, (e) with C, (f) with D. (g) Do the random numbers match A, B, C, D? (continued)

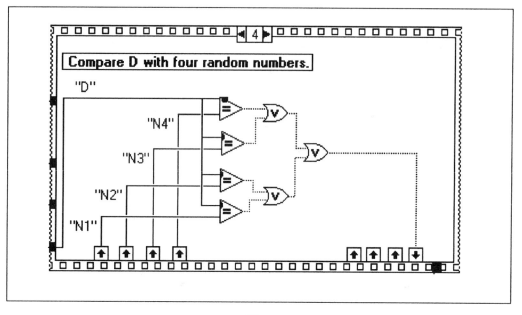

(f)

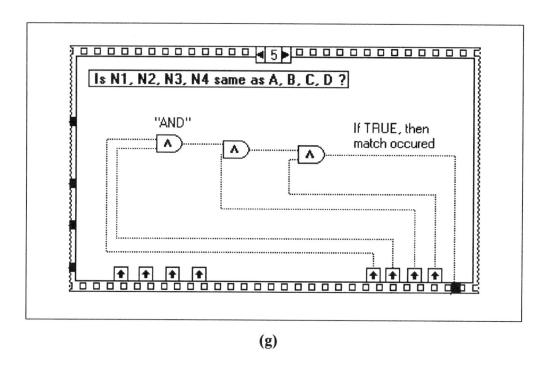

(g)

Fig. C-33 Exercise 3 (Get-4): (a) Front Panel, (b) Block Diagram. Compare the four random numbers: (c) with A , (d) with B, (e) with C , (f) with D. (g) Do the random numbers match A, B, C, D? (continued)

426

INDEX